KT-454-076

CAMBRIDGE COMPANIONS TO LITERATURE

The Cambridge Companion to Greek Tragedy
edited by P. E. Easterling

The Cambridge Companion to Virgil
edited by Charles Martindale

The Cambridge Companion to Old English Literature
edited by Malcolm Godden and Michael Lapidge

The Cambridge Companion to Dante
edited by Rachel Jacoff

The Cambridge Chaucer Companion
edited by Piero Boitani and Jill Mann

The Cambridge Companion to Medieval English Theatre
edited by Richard Beadle

The Cambridge Companion to Renaissance Humanism
edited by Jill Kraye

The Cambridge Companion to English Renaissance Drama
edited by A. R. Braunmuller and Michael Hattaway

The Cambridge Companion to Shakespeare Studies
edited by Stanley Wells

The Cambridge Companion to Shakespeare on Film
edited by Russell Jackson

The Cambridge Companion to Ben Jonson
edited by Richard Harp and Stanley Stewart

The Cambridge Companion to English Poetry, Donne to Marvell
edited by Thomas N. Corns

The Cambridge Companion to Milton
edited by Dennis Danielson

The Cambridge Companion to English Restoration Theatre
edited by Deborah C. Payne Fisk

The Cambridge Companion to English Literature, 1500–1609
edited by Arthur F. Kinney

The Cambridge Companion to English Literature, 1650–1740
edited by Steven N. Zwicker

The Cambridge Companion to British Romanticism
edited by Stuart Curran

The Cambridge Companion to the Eighteenth-Century Novel
edited by John Richetti

The Cambridge Companion to Samuel Johnson
edited by Greg Clingham

The Cambridge Companion to Jane Austen
edited by Edward Copeland and Juliet McMaster

The Cambridge Companion to Victorian Poetry
edited by Joseph Bristow

The Cambridge Companion to the Victorian Novel
edited by Deirdre David

The Cambridge Companion to Oscar Wilde
edited by Peter Raby

The Cambridge Companion to Thomas Hardy
edited by Dale Kramer

The Cambridge Companion to George Bernard Shaw
edited by Christopher Innes

The Cambridge Companion to Joseph Conrad
edited by J. H. Stape

The Cambridge Companion to James Joyce
edited by Derek Attridge

The Cambridge Companion to T. S. Eliot
edited by A. David Moody

The Cambridge Companion to Ezra Pound
edited by Ira Nadel

The Cambridge Companion to Modernism
edited by Michael Levenson

The Cambridge Companion to Virginia Woolf
edited by Sue Roe and Susan Sellers

The Cambridge Companion to Henry David Thoreau
edited by Joel Myerson

The Cambridge Companion to Walt Whitman
edited by Ezra Greenspan

The Cambridge Companion to Mark Twain
edited by Forrest G. Robinson

The Cambridge Companion to American Realism and Naturalism
edited by Donald Pizer

The Cambridge Companion to Edith Wharton
edited by Millicent Bell

The Cambridge Companion to Ernest Hemingway
edited by Scott Donaldson

The Cambridge Companion to William Faulkner
edited by Philip M. Weinstein

The Cambridge Companion to Eugene O'Neill
edited by Michael Manheim

The Cambridge Companion to Tennessee Williams
edited by Matthew C. Roudané

The Cambridge Companion to Arthur Miller
edited by Christopher Bigsby

The Cambridge Companion to American Women Playwrights
edited by Brenda Murphy

The Cambridge Companion to Modern British Women Playwrights
edited by Elaine Aston and Janelle Reinelt

The Cambridge Companion to the French Novel: from 1800 to the Present
edited by Timothy Unwin

The Cambridge Companion to the Classic Russian Novel
edited by Malcolm V. Jones and Robin Feuer Miller

The Cambridge Companion to Chekhov
edited by Vera Gottlieb and Paul Allain

The Cambridge Companion to Ibsen
edited by James McFarlane

The Cambridge Companion to Brecht
edited by Peter Thomason and Glendyr Sacks

The Cambridge Companion to Beckett
edited by John Pilling

The Cambridge Companion to John Keats
edited by Susan J. Wolfson

The Cambridge Companion to George Eliot
edited by George Levine

The Cambridge Companion to Shakespeare
edited by Margreta de Grazia and Stanley Wells

CAMBRIDGE COMPANIONS TO CULTURE

The Cambridge Companion to Modern German Culture
edited by Eva Kolinsky and Wilfried van der Will

The Cambridge Companion to Modern Russian Culture
edited by Nicholas Rzhevsky

The Cambridge Companion to Modern Spanish Culture
edited by David T. Gies

THE CAMBRIDGE COMPANION TO

GEORGE ELIOT

EDITED BY
GEORGE LEVINE
Center for the Critical Analysis of Contemporary Culture
Rutgers University

1783075
LIBRARY
ACC. No. 36021893
DEPT. OWL
CLASS No.
UNIVERSITY OF CHESTER

CAMBRIDGE
UNIVERSITY PRESS

PUBLISHED BY THE PRESS SYNDICATE OF THE UNIVERSITY OF CAMBRIDGE
The Pitt Building, Trumpington Street, Cambridge, United Kingdom

CAMBRIDGE UNIVERSITY PRESS
The Edinburgh Building, Cambridge CB2 2RU, UK
40 West 20th Street, New York, NY 10011–4211, USA
10 Stamford Road, Oakleigh, VIC 3166, Australia
Ruiz de Alarcón 13, 28014 Madrid, Spain
Dock House, The Waterfront, Cape Town 8001, South Africa

http://www.cambridge.org

© Cambridge University Press 2001

This book is in copyright. Subject to statutory exception
and to the provisions of relevant collective licensing agreements,
no reproduction of any part may take place without
the written permission of Cambridge University Press.

First published 2001

Printed in the United Kingdom at the University Press, Cambridge

Typeface Adobe Sabon 10/13pt *System* QuarkXpress® [SE]

A catalogue record for this book is available from the British Library

Library of Congress Cataloguing in Publication data

The Cambridge companion to Georg Eliot / edited by George Levine.
p. cm. – (Cambridge companions to literature)
ISBN 0 521 66267 2 (hardback) – ISBN 0 521 66473 X (paperback)
1. Eliot, George, 1819–1880 – criticism and interpretation. 2. Women and literature – England – History – nineteenth century. 3. Didactic fiction, English – History and criticism. I. Levine, George Lewis. II. Series.
PR4688.C26 2001
823′.8–dc21 00–064235

ISBN 0 521 66267 2 hardback
ISBN 0 521 66473 X paperback

CONTENTS

NOTES ON CONTRIBUTORS

TANYA AGATHOCLEOUS is a graduate student in Literatures in English at Rutgers University. She has written a biography of George Orwell for the young adult division of Oxford University Press, and is now writing her dissertation on cosmopolitan visions of the Victorian city.

SUZY ANGER is Assistant Professor of English at the University of Maryland, Baltimore County. She has published articles on Carlyle and George Eliot, is editor of a forthcoming collection of essays on the Victorians, and is currently completing a book on Victorian hermeneutics.

KATHLEEN BLAKE, Professor of English, University of Washington, is author of *Play, Games, and Sport: The Literary Works of Lewis Carroll* (1974) and *Love and the Woman Question in Victorian Literature: The Art of Self-Postponement* (1983), and is editor of *Approaches to Teaching George Eliot's "Middlemarch"* (1990). She has published many essays on a wide range of Victorian literature, and is currently working on a book on Victorian literature and political economy.

ROSEMARIE BODENHEIMER is Professor of English at Boston College. She is the author of *The Politics of Story in Victorian Social Fiction* (1988) and *The Real Life of Mary Ann Evans: George Eliot, Her Letters and Fiction* (1994). She is currently working on Dickens and autobiography.

KATE FLINT is Professor of English, Rutgers University. She is author of *The Woman Reader, 1837–1914* (1993) and *The Victorians and the Visual Imagination* (2000), and has written numerous articles on Victorian and twentieth-century literature, painting, and cultural history. Her current research is on the place of the Americas in the Victorian and Edwardian cultural imagination.

DONALD GRAY is Emeritus Professor of English at Indiana University, Bloomington. He has written essays on Victorian poetry, fiction, and publishing history, has edited schoolroom editions of *Alice in Wonderland* and *Pride and Prejudice*, and an anthology of Victorian poetry. He has served as editor of *Victorian Studies*.

NANCY HENRY is Assistant Professor of English at the State University of New York at Binghamton. She has edited George Eliot's *Impressions of Theophrastus Such* (1994) and the Everyman edition of Elizabeth Gaskell's *Sylvia's Lovers* (1997). She has published several articles on George Eliot and is currently working on a book on George Eliot and the British Empire, and the Everyman edition of Gaskell's *Ruth*.

GEORGE LEVINE, Kenneth Burke Professor of English, Rutgers University, is author of several books, including *The Realistic Imagination* (1981), *Darwin and the Novelists*, (1988), and *An Annotated Bibliography of George Eliot* (1988). He has published extensively on George Eliot, on Darwin, and on the relations between science and literature. He has completed a new book on the relation of epistemology to narrative, particularly in nineteenth-century fiction.

JOSEPHINE MCDONAGH is Reader in Romantic and Victorian Culture at Birkbeck College, University of London. She is the author of *De Quincey's Disciplines* (1994) and *George Eliot* (1997), and is currently writing about child murder and British culture.

DIANA POSTLETHWAITE is Professor of English at St. Olaf College in Northfield, Minnesota. She is the author of *Making it Whole: A Victorian Circle and the Shape of Their World* (1984), a study of George Eliot and her intellectual circle, focusing on positivism, phrenology, mesmerism, evolutionary biology, and psychology. She has published articles on nineteenth-century literature, and reviews fiction regularly for the *New York Times Book Review* and numerous other venues.

BARRY QUALLS, Professor of English, Rutgers University, is the author of *The Secular Pilgrims: The Novel as Book of Life* (1982), and of articles and reviews on nineteenth-century English literature and on the Bible and its literary impact. He is the Dean of Humanities in the Faculty of Arts and Sciences at Rutgers University, New Brunswick.

ALEXANDER WELSH, Emily Sanford Professor of English at Yale University, has written extensively on nineteenth-century literature and culture, with books on Scott, Dickens, and Freud as well as George Eliot. His *George Eliot and Blackmail* (1985) affords a comprehensive study of the later novels.

ACKNOWLEDGMENTS

This volume owes a great deal to my editors at Cambridge University Press, Linda Bree and Josie Dixon, both of whom have offered valuable suggestions at crucial stages of the book's development. I owe a long-standing debt to Michael Wolff, who taught me, in my early days with *Victorian Studies*, much of what I know about George Eliot, and who continues to teach me in discussions up to the present day. Tanya Agathocleous, who has done important work on the chronology and the bibliography of this volume, has been a constant help in the detailed work of putting the book together. Her editorial skills are matched by her scholarship and her literary insight. I am grateful too to the Bogliasco Foundation and the Liguria Study Center in Bogliasco, Italy, where I was given the time to edit all of the essays and to think about George Eliot while my love of Italy and of the Italian language was intensified.

TEXTS AND ABBREVIATIONS

Since "George Eliot" was a pseudonym, this volume adopts the traditional style of never referring to her with a separable surname, "Eliot," but always as "George Eliot." Because, however, she was "a woman of many names," as Rosemarie Bodenheimer describes her in this volume, the contributors to this volume will occasionally refer to her, when appropriate, as Mary Anne Evans, Mary Ann Evans, Marian Evans, Marian Evans Lewes, or Mary Anne Cross. For a convenient summary of the way George Eliot used these various names, see chapter 2, below.

All references to George Eliot's novels and stories, except where specifically indicated otherwise, will be to the Oxford World Classics editions. The novels will be abbreviated in the following way:

AB	*Adam Bede*
DD	*Daniel Deronda*
FH	*Felix Holt*
JR	"Janet's Repentance"
M	*Middlemarch*
MF	*The Mill on the Floss*
R	*Romola*
SCL	*Scenes of Clerical Life*
SM	*Silas Marner*

Other writings of George Eliot will be noted as follows:

GEL	*The George Eliot Letters*, 9 vols., ed. Gordon S. Haight (New Haven: Yale University Press, 1954–78)
ITS	*Impressions of Theophrastus Such*, ed. Nancy Henry (Iowa City: University of Iowa Press, 1994)
Journals	*The Journals of George Eliot*, ed. Margaret Harris and Judith Johnston (Cambridge: Cambridge University Press, 1996)

Pinney	*Essays of George Eliot*, ed. Thomas Pinney (New York: Columbia University Press, 1963)
SEPW	*George Eliot: Selected Essays, Poems, and Other Writings*, ed. A. S. Byatt and Nicholas Warren (Harmondsworth: Penguin, 1990)

Unless otherwise noted, all reviews of George Eliot's works will be cited from:

CH	*George Eliot: The Critical Heritage*, ed. David Carroll (London: Routledge & Kegan Paul, 1971)

Annotations in the text take the following form: volume or book:chapter: page. Thus, a citation from *The Mill on the Floss* might read (MF, IV:6:354). This would mean that the quotation can be found in book 4, chapter 6, page 354. Most citations will have only two numbers, chapter and page. Where a single number appears, it refers to a page number unless otherwise indicated.

References within chapters are all keyed to the bibliography of works cited at the end of the book. Some of the works cited will also be listed in the section on further reading, which is arranged according to chronological periods of criticism of George Eliot.

CHRONOLOGY

1819 Born in South Farm, Warwickshire, on November 22 to Robert Evans, a land agent, and Christiana Pearson (Evans's second wife). Baptized Mary Anne Evans at the parish church of Chilvers Coton, she is the couple's third child, joining Isaac (born 1816) and Christiana (called "Chrissey," born 1814).

1820 The family moves to Griff House – a farmhouse near the Coventry Road. Here Robert Evans continues work for the landowner, Francis Newdigate, and Mrs. Evans runs the farm's dairy.

1824 GE joins her sister Chrissey at Miss Lathom's boarding school in Attleborough.

1828 Moves with Chrissey to Mrs. Wallington's school, the Elms, in Nuneaton; she is befriended by Maria Lewis, an Irish governess and evangelical, with whom she corresponds and exchanges religious ideas for the next ten years.

1832–5 Goes to a school in Coventry run by Rebecca and Mary Franklin, daughters of a Baptist minister; she excels at classes and gives piano recitals.

1836 Her mother dies of cancer in February; Robert Evans falls ill as a result and GE (now spelling her name, Mary Ann, without the "e") takes on the role of caring for him and the house.

1837–40 Her sister Chrissey marries Dr. Edward Clarke. Mary Ann studies German and Italian and reads religious and evangelical writings; corresponds frequently about these with Maria Lewis. In January 1840, she publishes, for the first time, in the *Christian Observer* – the piece is a religious poem entitled "As o'er the Fields."

1841 Moves with her father to Foleshill, on the outskirts of Coventry, after her brother Isaac marries and takes over Griff House. Encounters Charles Hennell's *An Inquiry into the Origins of*

Christianity and becomes close friends with his sister, Cara Bray, and her religiously skeptical husband, Charles – philanthropist, author, and leading figure in a Unitarian circle; Mary Ann begins to question her faith.

1842 On January 2, GE refuses to go to church. What she would later call a "Holy War" ensues between her and her father; she lives with Isaac and his wife Sarah at Griff for several weeks and then returns home, and to church, in May – on the condition that her father leave her to her own beliefs; befriends Sara Hennell, Charles's other sister.

1844 Takes over a translation of Strauss's *Leben Jesu* ("The Life of Jesus") from her friend, Rufa Hennell, Charles Hennell's new wife.

1845–46 Meets Harriet Martineau, then writing for a variety of publications, including the *Westminster Review*; inspired by her example, GE begins writing for the *Coventry Herald*, a radical newspaper owned by Charles Bray. In June of 1846 *The Life of Jesus* is published in three volumes.

1848–49 Nurses her ailing father; Robert Evans dies May 31, 1849. GE and the Brays leave for the Continent and then GE stays on in Geneva by herself for several months.

1850 Returns to England and stays with her brother at Griff, then with Chrissey; after attending a soirée at the house of the publisher John Chapman, who had asked her to write a review, she plans to return to London in the new year as one of his lodgers.

1851 Moves to Chapman's residence at 142 Strand and changes her name to Marian Evans. Becomes very close to him, thereby alienating his wife and mistress; to ease tensions, she moves out temporarily and stays with the Brays. On her return, she begins what she and Chapman termed a "professional relationship" as editor of his recent acquisition, the *Westminster Review*.

1852–53 Among many other literary and intellectual figures, she becomes acquainted with Herbert Spencer; although Marian falls in love and the two are inaccurately rumored to be engaged, Spencer rejects her as anything but a friend. Spencer introduces her to George Henry Lewes, novelist, drama critic, student of science, and editor of a radical weekly magazine, the *Leader*; in 1853 GE becomes seriously involved with the married Lewes; Lewes is separated from his wife but is legally prohibited from divorcing her because he had condoned her adultery in the past.

1854–5 GE translates Feuerbach's *Essence of Christianity*, published by Chapman; it is the only book she publishes under the name "Marian Evans." GE and Lewes begin to live together openly, traveling to Weimar, Germany, where Lewes researches a biography of Goethe; at the end of 1854 they move on to Berlin. In March of the next year, the couple return to England, where GE works on a translation of Spinoza's *Ethics*.

1855–56 GE and Lewes, their unmarried relationship now notorious in London circles, live in Richmond and contend with social ostracism; GE writes several articles and reviews for the *Leader* and the *Westminster Review*; Lewes's literary reputation is secured by the publication of *The Life of Goethe*.

1856–57 GE publishes "Silly Novels by Lady Novelists" in the *Westminster Review*; in 1856 she begins work on "Amos Barton," the first of the *Scenes of Clerical Life*. Lewes mediates with the publisher John Blackwood and the first part of the story appears in *Blackwood's Edinburgh Magazine* under the name "George Eliot." The pseudonym protects Marian Evans from the likely consequences of the scandal, and from the condescension with which women writers were usually greeted, and disassociates her fiction from her translations of Strauss and Feuerbach.

1858 All three of the *Scenes of Clerical Life* are published as a two-volume book in January to favorable reviews; GE works on *Adam Bede*; in the spring, she and Lewes travel to Munich and Dresden.

1859 GE and Lewes move to larger quarters at Holly Lodge, south of the Thames. In February, *Adam Bede* is published in three volumes; it sells well (going through eight printings within the year) and receives good reviews: Queen Victoria is one of its fans. GE begins researching *The Mill on the Floss*, but interrupts her work to publish the fantasy tale, "The Lifted Veil," in *Blackwood's*.

1860 George Eliot is forced to reveal her identity. *The Mill on the Floss* is published by Blackwood; GE and Lewes leave for Italy to avoid publicity. They visit Rome, Venice, and Florence, where GE develops an interest in Savonorola as a subject for a new novel (later to become *Romola*). On their return to England, they live in London and take on the supervision of Lewes's sons; GE sets aside *Romola* to work on *Silas Marner*, her third novel set in the Midlands. Publishes in *Cornhill Magazine* a short story, "Brother Jacob."

1861 *Silas Marner* published in the spring; GE and Lewes visit Italy again to continue research on *Romola*.

1862–63 *Romola* serialized in the *Cornhill Magazine*, rival of *Blackwood's*, after unsuccessful negotiations with John Blackwood. In 1863, Lewes and GE buy a house, the Priory, on the edge of Regent's Park. Established, except perhaps for Dickens, as the most successful novelist in England, she gradually wins respectability. Holds weekly Sunday afternoons to which the most distinguished writers and thinkers come regularly.

1864–65 In 1864, Lewes takes on the editorship of the progressive periodical, the *Fortnightly Review*; GE begins work on a dramatic poem, *The Spanish Gypsy*. By March 1865, she has put it aside to work on *Felix Holt, The Radical*.

1866 Relations restored with Blackwood; he publishes *Felix Holt* and asks GE, in response to pending new legislation for electoral reform, to write "An Address to Working Men, by Felix Holt" for *Blackwood's*. GE and Lewes travel to Germany and France, then proceed to Spain, where GE researches *The Spanish Gypsy*.

1868 *The Spanish Gypsy* is published by Blackwood and sells well, despite mixed reviews.

1869 In a spring visit to Italy, GE and Lewes meet the banker John Cross; he later becomes their financial advisor. Back in England, she begins work on *Middlemarch*; Thornton, Lewes's second son, returns from the colonies gravely ill. GE temporarily abandons *Middlemarch* and begins a second long poem, "The Legend of Jubal"; "Thornie" dies a painful death at the Priory a few months after his arrival, of spinal tuberculosis.

1870–72 Begins a story, "Miss Brooke," which she later decides to connect to the story of Lydgate in *Middlemarch*. GE allows the publication of her *Wise, Witty and Tender Sayings* in 1871, suggested and collected by a devoted fan, Alexander Main. Her reputation as novelist and sage is strengthened by this volume and by the eight-month serialization of the hugely successful *Middlemarch* (beginning December 1871).

1874 *The Legend of Jubal and Other Poems* is published; a one-volume edition of *Middlemarch* comes out to very large sales; GE begins work on *Daniel Deronda*.

1875–76 Lewes, at work on what he hopes will be his magnum opus, *Problems of Life and Mind*, is continuously ill from 1875 onwards; he and GE divide their time between London and the countryside, eventually buying a country home, The Heights at Witley in Surrey, at the end of 1876. Following on the publishing success of *Middlemarch*, *Daniel Deronda* is published in eight monthly installments (beginning February 1876).

1878 Lewes dies on November 30, after the progressive worsening of his illness; GE spends her mourning preparing *Problems of Life and Mind* for publication; she also sets up a scholarship at Cambridge in his name.

1879 *Impressions of Theophrastus Such*, a collection of essays by the fictional "Theophrastus," is published; John Blackwood dies. After deep mourning for Lewes, GE accepts John Cross, who would become her financial advisor, as the first friend to be allowed to visit her. Evidence in the letters of increasing affection for Cross, twenty years her junior.

1880 On May 6, GE and Cross marry. They honeymoon in France and Italy; in Venice, Cross leaps from their hotel balcony into the canal in an apparent suicide attempt; after a visit from his brother, the couple travel back to England and the house at Witley. In December they move into a new London home at Cheyne Walk; shortly thereafter GE falls ill suddenly and dies on December 22; she is denied burial in Westminster Abbey and is buried instead next to Lewes at Highgate Cemetery.

greatest of Victorian novels. Looking back, we can now recognize that her art anticipated the modernist experiments of writers like Henry James and the epistemological skepticism of postmodernism. If George Eliot the woman was susceptible to the conventions and comforts of respectability, George Eliot the writer built her art from a refusal of such conventions, in resistance to the very kind of moral complacency and didacticism of which she has often, in the years following her death, been accused.

Certainly, she disguised it, compromised it, resisted it; but George Eliot created her art out of a cluster of rebellions, particularly against reigning social, moral, and aesthetic conventions. In England she was the single most important figure in transforming the novel from a predominantly popular form into the highest form of art – in the tradition that Henry James was to develop. (This, perhaps, for the most recent critics, is a point against her since while for modernism the notion of high art was highly valued, in post-modern culture high art is under suspicion, its "cultural capital" spent, its superiority to popular culture an effect of power and class.) She was a romantic organicist, opposed to revolution, disturbed at any sudden tear in the social fabric, and she dramatized the dangers of political violence often – in *Romola*, *Felix Holt*, and *Middlemarch*, in particular: she was, as she thought of herself, a conservative-reformer. The foundation for this position was sharply articulated in her essay on the anthropologist Wilhelm Heinrich von Riehl: "What has grown up historically can only die out historically, by the gradual operation of necessary laws" (Pinney, p. 287). But she also saw clearly enough to represent with great force the grounds and the temptations to violence. Again, although she would not formally support the feminist cause, she was a model for women's achievement; although she did not portray successful women who resisted the conventions of their culture, she brilliantly and sympathetically traced their defeats. (On these questions, see the chapters in this volume by Kate Flint and Alexander Welsh.) Although from her first stories forward she wrote about the church and clergy with a compassionate knowingness, she built a powerful case against Christianity; and while she constantly celebrated the value of childhood experience, traditional community, and traditional family structures, she almost bitterly portrayed the failures of community and family. Against the judgments of a complacent society, she wrote of the unnoticed heroism of those it defeated.

She could not be buried in Westminster Abbey in the "Poet's Corner" where the great English writers had frequently found their hallowed place, although, as the famous scientific naturalist John Tyndall claimed, she was a "woman whose achievements were without parallel in the previous history of womankind,"[1] and many of the leading intellectuals of the day agreed. But George Eliot had lived out of wedlock with a married man, George

Henry Lewes; she had, as the young Mary Anne Evans, renounced Christianity. She had translated two books central to the rejection of Christianity by the intellectual avant garde: David Friedrich Strauss's *Life of Jesus*, the key book in the Higher Criticism of the Bible, which in its quest for the historical Jesus naturalized Christianity; and Ludwig Feuerbach's *Essence of Christianity*, which argued that Christianity worships what are in fact entirely human ideals. The Deity is a projection; the reality is the human ideal. (For a discussion of these ideas see the chapters by Suzy Anger and Barry Qualls.) Even after an enormously successful career in which she fought to regain the respectability that scandal had cost her, George Eliot, it seemed, deserved no space in Westminster Abbey although Charles Darwin, of all people, was buried there two years after her death. T. H. Huxley, a friend of Lewes and George Eliot, and renowned as a soldier in the wars against the clergy, rejected the idea of burying George Eliot in the Abbey. "One cannot," he wrote, "eat one's cake and have it too. Those who elect to be free in thought and deed must not hanker after the rewards, if they are to be so called, which the world offers to those who put up with its fetters."[2] The degree of George Eliot's sins against society can be measured by the fact that Huxley warmly supported Darwin's interment in the Abbey, although Darwin's name even now remains anathema to fundamentalist Christianity. "But," write Darwin's biographers, "Darwin had not lived openly in sin as Eliot had."[3] Like good Victorians, both Darwin and George Eliot aspired to public respectability and wanted to be buried in the Abbey. It seems as though, in the end, George Eliot was the greater sinner.

We are a long way from the scandals of mid-Victorian Britain. What matter now are the works of those who might have been objects of scandal, though it is worth remembering the degree to which what we value now was contentious then. We care about George Eliot now because of her novels, but it helps to keep in mind that in her moment, she took great risks and worried constantly about them. She has left a legacy that is badly distorted if we look at the novels as "classics," frozen in time, rather than as works created by an imagination that was deeply informed by the nitty gritty of social engagement, of contemporary controversy, of anything but a pure life. The scandals and personal crises were transformed in the novels in ways that have left their mark on the history of English fiction and on many generations of readers. It is worth noting that Marian Evans (the exact shape of whose constantly changing name is traced in Rosemarie Bodenheimer's chapter in this volume) only began writing the fiction that made her famous as George Eliot in 1856, when she was already thirty-seven years old. Surely, a condition of her writing was just that living openly in scandal that, ironically, was also to keep her out of Westminster Abbey. Although Marian Evans was by then well established among the London intellectual avant-garde, her elopement with Lewes had cast her out of respectable society. It was Lewes, nevertheless, who gave her the encouragement and the time to turn to the writing of fiction.

She had long prepared herself for the move. Her dazzling and ironic essay, "Silly Novels by Lady Novelists" (1856), in which, in effect, she separated Marian Evans from run-of-the-mill "lady novelists," laid the ground for the kind of novel she was to write and might serve as a useful introduction to her fiction. A "really cultured woman," she argues, is distinguished from those run-of-the-mill lady novelists, by being

> all the simpler and the less obtrusive for her knowledge; [true culture] has made her see herself and her opinions in something like just proportions; she does not make it a pedestal from which she flatters herself that she commands a complete view of men and things, but makes it a point of observation from which to form a right estimate of herself. She neither spouts poetry nor quotes Cicero on slight provocation; not because she thinks that a sacrifice must be made to the prejudices of men, but because that mode of exhibiting her memory and Latinity does not present itself to her as edifying or graceful. She does not write books to confound philosophers, perhaps because she is able to write books that delight them. In conversation she is the least formidable of women, because she understands you, without wanting to make you aware that you *can't* understand her. (Pinney, p. 316)

Although this was written before Marian Evans had created George Eliot, it clearly creates – or attempts to create – the George Eliot who was to write the novels we now remember. As her career advanced, critics of the later novels, from *Romola* on, might have felt as Henry James did about that book: "it is overladen with learning, it smells of the lamp, it tastes just perceptibly of pedantry." Starting her career, George Eliot worked effectively to be "edifying and graceful," to write novels that "delight" (*CH*, 500).

She invented the name (a good "mouth filling name," she explained) in order to protect her anonymity when she published *Scenes of Clerical Life* in 1856. The essay on silly novelists revealed a strong sensitivity to the kind of condescension frequently shown to women novelists, a condescension that assumed their natural inferiority. "By a peculiar thermometric adjustment," Marian Evans wrote, "when a woman's talent is at zero, journalistic approbation is at the boiling pitch; when she attains mediocrity, it is already at no more than summer heat; and if ever she reaches excellence, critical enthusiasm drops to the freezing point" (322). Marian Evans was not going to be condescended to. The essay snaps with irony and anger, qualities that George Eliot could repress but could not and did not entirely eliminate from her great fictions.

But, of course, there were other reasons for the pseudonym. Her scandalous life and her avant-garde writings would probably have damaged quite seriously the reception of her first novels. So George Eliot was born, characteristically for her, out of a mixture of motives, as a defense of her respectability, out of a desire to become a popular success, out of her refusal to be "a silly novelist," and as an ideal to which Marian Evans aspired and which, one might say, she almost became. Although it is hard not to think of George Eliot as the sage and enormously respectable woman, sympathetically presiding over solemn Sunday afternoons to which distinguished visitors and young idolaters were regularly invited, the George Eliot who wrote the novels we are still reading was an amalgam (and attempted purification) of the multiple facets of a deeply intelligent and troubled woman. She was at one and the same time the avant-garde intellectual, the learned, ironic, witty, and even caustic reviewer, the translator of heavy but intellectually radical German philosophy and history, the young provincial woman who had nursed her father through a long illness and revered the Midlands countryside, the sophisticate who risked scandal and suffered the consequences of her desire, and an enormously learned aspirant toward an ideal of intellectual and moral excellence that threatened throughout her career to cripple her emotionally.

The degree to which this remarkable amalgam, summed up in the name "George Eliot," had prepared herself for her vocation as novelist is evident in the essays she wrote during the years she was closely associated with the *Westminster Review*. The ironies of "Silly Novels by Lady Novelists" are no mere occasion for easy hits against bad novelists; they are part of George Eliot's determination to make art "true." Her essays are often polemical, severe, brilliant attacks on falsification, distortion, sentimentality, pomposity, and their rhetoric is distinctly polemical. But like her novels, they are directed at problems that plagued her own life, turning the private experience into a way to insist on higher standards, both of morality and intellect, that she thought popular audiences were prepared to accept. Her stunning attack on the evangelical preacher, John Cumming, exposes the heartlessness and stupidity of intellectual pretension, the inadequacy of doctrine in relation to the particularities of human life and feeling – a theme that recurs through virtually all of her novels. She has no patience with this man of "moderate intellect," with "a moral standard not higher than the average," who condemns in righteous anger sinners who fail to adhere to the letter of doctrine: "he insists on good works and signs of justifying faith, as labours to be achieved to the glory of God, but he rarely represents them as the spontaneous, necessary product of a soul filled with Divine love" (162). The critique of Cumming here is paralleled and dramatically developed in the rejection of Maggie Tulliver in *The Mill on the Floss* by the community of St. Oggs, after her reluctant elopement with Stephen Guest. Cumming was certainly a "man of maxims," someone whose moral judgments are "not checked and enlightened by a perpetual reference to the special circumstances that mark the individual lot" (*MF*, VII:2:498). The anger of the Cumming essay filters through all of the novels, and the narrator of *Middlemarch* will say, many years later, "There is no general doctrine which is not capable of eating out our morality if unchecked by the deep-seated habit of direct fellow-feeling with individual fellow-men" (*M*, VI:61:506). George Eliot's implicit defense of Marian Evans's scandalous behavior is similarly articulated in the Riehl essay: "The more deeply we penetrate into the knowledge of society in its details, the more thoroughly we shall be convinced that a *universal social policy has no validity except on paper*" (Pinney, p. 289). In the novels that follow the essay (as in her life, in which she was condemned for her relations with Lewes), George Eliot and Marian Evans appeal to authenticity of feeling, to the higher morality "of a love that constrains the soul, of sympathy with that yearning over the lost and erring which made Jesus weep over Jerusalem." Morality and dogma without mercy and love are no morality and only bad religion. Focusing on the tension between private experience and social constraint, these early essays suggest how George Eliot defined her work against the distortions that pass in the culture for truth and justice.

The tension between abstract reason and concrete feelings is one of the core subjects of both Marian Evans the essayist and George Eliot the novelist. She sought always to bring together intellect and feeling. In the days in which she renounced Christianity and thereby offended her father – the "Holy Wars," she called them in a letter – she retreated from the apparently necessary consequences of her intellectual rejection, for what mattered in the end was what she called the "truth of feeling," a truth that allowed her to return to church without believing in its doctrine, for the sake of her love of her father. In the essay on Cumming, she was to talk of the "cooperation of the intellect with the impulses," a cooperation only available to "the highest class of minds" (Pinney, p. 166). "So long," she would argue, "as a belief in propositions is regarded as indispensable to salvation, the pursuit of truth *as such* is not possible, any more than it is possible for a man who is swimming for his life to make meteorological observations on the storm which threatens to overwhelm him" (Pinney, p. 167).

But if, in the essay on Cumming, Marian Evans is severe about the way in which general ideas miss the particularities of feeling, in her essay on Young, she condemns his "*radical insincerity as a poetic artist.*" Here the problem is not a heartless imposition of ideas in moral judgment of living humans, but the determination to produce "a certain effect on his audience" rather than to say "what he feels or what he sees" (Pinney, p. 367). The separation of feeling and intellect takes another shape here, but it too produces falsification. If Cumming lacks compassion and thus misses "truth of feeling," Young falsifies by failing to consult his own perceptions and feelings. The two produce different versions of untruth, and are both, then, unrealistic.

The energizing principle of George Eliot's art was realism. And realism is a mode that depends heavily on reaction against what the writer takes to have been misrepresentation. Thus, even for those "realists" whose politics might have turned out to be "conservative," it is a rebellious mode. It is rarely, and certainly was not for George Eliot, simply accuracy in representation of things as they are, although it is always that, too. (Like the modernist writers who followed her, she has, as I will try to suggest, quite complicated notions about the possibility of such representation.) It is also and necessarily a kind of authenticity, an honest representation of one's own feelings and perceptions; otherwise accuracy of representation would itself be impossible. Thus, she claims, "The fantastic or the boldly imaginative poet may be as sincere as the most realistic: he is true to his own sensibilities or inward vision, and in his wildest flights he never breaks loose from his criterion – the truth of his own mental state" (367). As Lewes put it in a review he wrote two years later, "the antithesis" of Realism is not "Idealism, but Falsism." "Art," he claims, "always aims at the representation of Reality, *i.e.* of Truth."[4]

The resistant element in George Eliot, in her life and her art, is closely linked with her chosen literary method. Realism has always been a contentious program. George Eliot was self-conscious enough about it that in each of her two first fictions, *Scenes of Clerical Life* (in the story, "The Sad Fortunes of the Reverend Amos Barton") and *Adam Bede*, she paused within the narratives to explain and justify that method. Representing the world adequately means representing its very ordinariness, and the moral project of realism is – in resistance to conventional art – to dramatize the value of the ordinary. So, with her first profoundly inadequate protagonist, Amos Barton, George Eliot pauses to show that she is quite aware of his inadequacy: he was, the narrator says, "in no respect an ideal or exceptional character; and perhaps I am doing a bold thing to bespeak your sympathy on behalf of a man who was so very far from remarkable" (*SCL*, 5:36). The strategy of what has been called George Eliot's "moral realism" is deliberately Wordsworthian, to evoke the romantic side of familiar things, but the project is moral as well as aesthetic. To represent the ordinary honestly is to represent what is hidden from those like Cumming or Young – the richness of human feeling, the grandeur of what we take for granted. So, she continues in "Amos Barton," "Depend upon it, you would gain unspeakably if you would learn with me to see some of the poetry and the pathos, the tragedy and the comedy, lying in the experience of a human soul that looks out through dull grey eyes, and that speaks in a voice of quite ordinary tones" (5:37).

George Eliot's most famous justification of her realism comes in chapter 17 of *Adam Bede*. There she develops more fully the arguments sketched in "Amos Barton," but that she had earlier made in the essay on Riehl. The aesthetic and the moral were for George Eliot entirely intertwined: to treat art lightly, to indulge mere triviality, to allow the exaggerations and pretensions of the silly novelists or the poet Young, was to fail not only aesthetically, but morally. And in a now well-known review of Ruskin's *Modern Painters*, volume III, she wrote: "The truth of infinite value that he teaches is *realism* – the doctrine that all truth and beauty are to be attained by a humble and faithful study of nature, and not by substituting vague forms, bred by imagination on the mists of feeling, in place of definite, substantial reality."[5]

Unquestionably, her theoretical arguments for realism and the weight of significance she imposed on the practice in her art give to some of George Eliot's work a quality of high seriousness – perhaps solemnity – that can help account for the way in which modernist artists rejected her. Yet this solemnity was an aspect of a mind that was extraordinarily agile, subtle, learned, and if she was uneasy with popular entertainment (though she took any lapse in her own popularity as evidence of her aesthetic failure), she was equally opposed to moralizing didacticism. Everything depended on getting her art aesthetically right (and that was also to be the overriding project of modernism). "Art," she wrote,

> is the nearest thing to life; it is a mode of amplifying experience and extending our contact with our fellow men beyond the bounds of our personal lot. All the more sacred is the task of the artist when he undertakes to paint the life of the People. It is not so very serious that we should have false ideas about evanescent fashions – about the manners and conversation of beaux and duchesses; but it *is* serious that our sympathy with the perennial joys and struggles, the toil, the tragedy, and the humour in the life of our more heavily-laden fellow-men, should be perverted, and turned towards a false object instead of the true one. (Pinney, p. 271)

This is a kind of manifesto of moral realism. But it is important not to mistake George Eliot's commitment to the moral vocation of art and realism for a disregard of formal concerns. Art works morally only, she would insist, if it is aesthetically effective. As she was to tell her young friend Frederic

Harrison many years later in a much-quoted letter, she would not, in her novels, "lapse from the picture to the diagram"(*GEL*, IV:300).

Among the many objections of twentieth-century writers and critics to the tradition of literary realism – putting aside the epistemological issues and questions about the inevitability of mediation – is that realism is, as it were, just one damned thing after another. It is a pile of facts that add up to nothing but the facts. Virginia Woolf's famous essay, "Mr. Bennett and Mrs. Brown," is perhaps the most delightful as it is the most representative dismissal of the realist activity of merely recording external fact. Speaking of a detailed passage in Arnold Bennett's *Hilda Lessways*, Woolf insists, "One line of insight would have done more than all those lines of description."[6] But George Eliot's realism, while it is indeed attentive to the external details of the world her characters inhabit, is not like Arnold Bennett's. The details reverberate with significance and the images are as much a part of the consciousness of the characters as representations of material reality. The very possibility of meaning is one of the questions George Eliot's novels directly encounter. So the narrator remarks in *Adam Bede*, "if it be true that Nature at certain moments seems charged with a presentiment of the individual lot, must it not also be true that she seems unmindful, unconscious of another?" (*AB*, 27:292). And shortly afterward, Adam's world darkens permanently at the moment he is calmly examining a large, double-trunked beech tree "at a turning in the road" (27:295). The tree, quite literally there and precisely represented, is more importantly the marker of a stage in Adam's consciousness as he becomes aware that Hetty and Arthur Donnithorne are lovers. George Eliot's realism extends from the external world to the world of individual consciousness – like James and the psychological novelists who followed, she threw the action inside; the question of consciousness, of who is perceiving the external fact and under what conditions, becomes for her an indispensable aspect of the realist project.

The intensity and formal complexity of George Eliot's novels, even in the relatively expansive mode of her early works, must be credited in part to her refusal to disentangle representational precision, psychological states, formal coherence, and moral significance. Getting it right was for her no simple matter of recording external fact precisely, but of making herself capable of the most complete possible honesty by opening her mind and feelings to the otherness of things and people – precisely what she did not find in the poet Young. The point is not that she always succeeded, but that for her realism was a vocation. In that famous chapter 17, the narrator of *Adam Bede* tells us that she aspires

> to give no more than a faithful account of men and things as they have mirrored themselves in my mind. The mirror is doubtless defective; the outlines will sometimes be disturbed; the reflection faint or confused; but I feel as much bound to tell you, as precisely as I can, what that reflection is, as if I were in the witness-box narrating my experience on oath. (17:175)

The strenuousness of George Eliot's art is due not only to this commitment to tell the truth (as though in a trial at law) but to the awareness of how very hard it is to do so, to avoid being false. "Signs," says the *Middlemarch* narrator, "are small measurable things, but interpretations are illimitable" (1:3:21). Her novels explore with a subtlety new to the history of English literature the devious ways of the mind, the natural and psychological and social impediments to knowing or speaking the truth. "So," proceeds the narrator, "I am content to tell my simple story, without trying to make things seem better than they were; dreading nothing, indeed, but falsity, which, in spite of one's best efforts, there is reason to dread. Falsehood is so easy, truth so difficult" (27:176). George Eliot was alert not only to the complications of society, but to the subtle difficulties of the medium, language, itself. There is a famous narrative intervention in *The Mill on the Floss* that can suggest something of this alertness: "O Aristotle! If you had the advantage of being 'the freshest modern' instead of the greatest ancient, would you not have mingled your praise of metaphorical speech, as a sign of high intelligence, with a lamentation that intelligence so rarely shows itself in speech without metaphor, – that we can so seldom declare what a thing is, except by saying it is something else?" (II:1:140). Metaphor always threatens to escape the limits of its denotation and is at the heart of language; thus the writer must be, as George Eliot sought to be herself, a kind of scholar like the one described by Walter Pater some years later, a scholar of language and meaning, scrupulous, meticulous, unrelentingly attentive.

The yields of these labors of realism to resist the conventional simplifications of art or personal interest turned out often to be only partially compensatory. There are costs to the realist program, for the "truth" George Eliot insists on is, primarily, the hard truth that the world is not made in our interest, not "mindful" of us. Reality is largely what conventional art would treat as banal and dismiss in the name of heroism or elegance. The sympathy her art is designed to evoke depends on a recognition of our mutual implication in ordinariness and limitation. With satirical contempt, she mocks the injunction that if "The world is not just what we like; do touch it up with a tasteful pencil, and make believe it is not quite such a mixed, entangled affair" (*AB*, 17:176). She for her part is committed to the "faithful representing of commonplace things" (*AB*, 17:178). The direction of her novels and of realism itself is toward accommodation to the ordinary, toward acceptance of limitation. And thus, through the largest part of her fiction-writing career, her novels describe their protagonists' education in renunciation. Their triumphs are precisely in their acceptance of limits, their return to the ordinariness they at times dreamed of transcending. In *Adam Bede*, of course, Arthur Donnithorne's self-indulgently generous fantasies are thwarted by his incapacity to restrain his sexual desire, but Adam himself succeeds only as he curbs his anger, and it is in his strong capacity for self-sacrifice that he earns the happy ending. More painfully and extravagantly, Maggie Tulliver in *The Mill on the Floss*, having failed in the extreme self-denial she had learned from Thomas à Kempis's *The Imitation of Christ*, must learn true resignation after her elopement with Stephen Guest, and can only triumph in the death that follows her attempt to rescue her brother.

The contest between individual desire and moral responsibility is a recurring theme of all her work, and an almost inevitable corollary of the realist's program. In realism, as the "Finale" of *Middlemarch* puts it, "There is no creature whose inward being is so strong that it is not greatly determined by what lies outside it" (682). She had made a similar point in *Felix Holt*: "there is no private life that has not been determined by a wider public life" (1:3:43). The formal and theoretical justification for the multiplot novel derives from this sense that every individual life is shaped by connections with conditions outside it, conditions of which the representative realist character is unaware. There are many moments in the novels when the reader is reminded of the inadequacy of any sense of character and self-divorced from sensitivity to the reality of others. So in *Middlemarch*, the novel turns early on the juxtaposition of Dorothea and Lydgate, and on Lydgate's immediate inattention to her: "nothing could seem much less important" to him "than the turn of Miss Brooke's mind." "But," the narrator interposes, "any one watching keenly the stealthy convergence of human lots, sees a slow preparation of effects from one life on another, which tells like a calculated irony on the indifference or the frozen stare with which we look at our unintroduced neighbour. Destiny stands by sarcastic with our *dramatis personae* folded in her hand" (1:11:78). It is rather easy to see that such a way of understanding relationships must almost inevitably lead *both* to the multiplot novel (seen usually as "loose and baggy" by modernist writers) and the complications of point-of-view narration (virtually indispensable to the development of modernist narration).

But in twentieth-century criticism, this centrally nineteenth-century recognition of the ways in which every individual can only be understood *in relation to* the social complex and the larger movements of history has often evoked very negative responses. Feminist criticism, for example, has long complained that George Eliot never created a heroine like Marian Evans, that is, a woman who resisted the conventions of society and made a creative and original life for herself, even living outside of wedlock with moral confidence in her choice. Such resistance, within George Eliot's determined realist resistance to focusing on the extraordinary, is inevitably thwarted by conditions. Only someone of genuinely heroic stature (one would have to infer, only someone as exceptional as Marian Evans herself) could have sustained and justified such a life.

Thus on feminist grounds and on many others, George Eliot's realist program was more than potentially politically conservative. In certain respects, it might be said to fit well with D. A. Miller's description of the work of the Victorian novel: "to confirm the novel-reader in his identity as "liberal subject . . . who seems to recognize himself most fully only when he forgets or disavows his functional implication in a system of carceral restraints or disciplinary injunctions."[7] What Miller calls "carceral restraints" might be recognized in George Eliot's insistence on self-restraint. The liberty she allows her protagonists is the liberty of the "subject" who chooses his or (most often in George Eliot's novels) her own restraints. The virtue of the realist protagonist, in accommodating to the ways of the world, lies exactly in the power to recognize limits and responsibilities and restrain the subversive and powerful pulls of desire and personal satisfaction. That conservative-reforming impulse in George Eliot is now usually read as rather exclusively conservative, and her own political views at least half confirm this reading. George Eliot wrote a political speech for her fictional radical, Felix Holt, as a direct intervention after the passage of the Second Reform Bill in 1867. Characteristically, for George Eliot, Felix moves away from direct political action: "What I am striving to keep in our minds is the care, the precaution, with which we should go about making things better, so that public order may not be destroyed, so that no fatal shock may be given to this society of ours, this living body in which our lives are bound up" (Pinney, p. 422). Here the sense of intricate interdependence, the sense of our being "bound up" with a past that we can disrupt only by, in effect, destroying ourselves and the living – organic – society of which we are a part, restrains Felix, and George Eliot, from efforts at radical change. This political stance here accounts for much of George Eliot's realist program, and the passage itself – giving the fictional character Felix a role in the nonfictional life of political England in 1868 – suggests why it is the fiction that determines George Eliot's success as a writer. For in the fiction, brilliantly open as it is to unfulfilled possibilities and an almost infinite range of interpretation and action, George Eliot explores the alternatives to her own positions and the enormous difficulty of choosing and acting on the "right" one.

Ironically, then, the rebellious impulse that led George Eliot to the special qualities of her art, its satiric and yet impassioned rejection of the kinds of falsifications we have identified in Cumming, Young, and the silly novelists, had deeply conservative consequences, and even entailed a rejection in her fiction of the risk-taking, scandalous career of Marian Evans. The novels often revisit the crises of Marian Evans. (Nancy Henry explores the ambiguity of George Eliot's political positioning in her chapter in this volume.) The examples are everywhere, in, for example, the ostracism and redemption of a Maggie Tulliver, who almost elopes with an engaged man; the alienation of a misunderstood Silas Marner; the struggles of Romola, undervalued by her father, betrayed by her husband; the stunning self-repression and disillusion of Mrs. Transome, who, in *Felix Holt*, had thought to derive joy from the child she bears from her illicit sexual relation with the lawyer Jermyn. The restraints of past obligations, family tradition, and social responsibility take precedence over ideal aspirations – in effect they *are* the novels' ideal aspirations. (In this volume Josephine McDonagh discusses how the early novels are marked by their retreat to the past, which, McDonagh claims, pushed George Eliot toward a dead end. In the later novels, as Alexander Welsh shows, the pull toward subjection to "blood," or race, has a similar kind of effect even as George Eliot struggles to move beyond the limits of the restraining past of her realist project.) Resolution comes with assimilation to a community, and not with the kind of ostracism Marian Evans suffered for many years until, with the enormous respectability and prestige of George Eliot's novels behind her, she was accepted socially and, finally, entered a legitimate marriage.

The restraints that, in her grim, clear-eyed honesty, George Eliot's realism imposed on her were, in the end, too "carceral." The power of much of her writing is in her representation of the profound failures of the middle-class society whose values she sought to revivify, and most particularly of the costs of self-restraint, the unjust limitation imposed on remarkable characters, usually, but not exclusively, women. Her novels are shot through with images of disenchantment and loss that survive for readers beyond the constraining plots in which the characters are tied. There is Mrs. Transome, standing before a mirror, "going close to it and looking at her face with hard scrutiny, as if it were unrelated to herself. No elderly face can be handsome, looked at in that way; every little detail is startlingly prominent and the effect of the whole is lost. She saw the dried-up complexion, and the deep lines of bitter discontent about the mouth" (*FH*, 1:1:21). There is Dorothea in Rome awakening to the awfulness of her marriage to Casaubon, and at the end there is the desolate, abandoned Gwendolen, "for the first time being dislodged from her supremacy in her own world, and getting a sense that her horizon was but a dipping onward of an existence with which her own was revolving" (69:689). Such moments of disenchantment, as Barbara Hardy describes them, are a condition of the realist project. They mark stages in the lives of her protagonists as they are "forced," as Hardy says, "from the centre to the periphery, from the dream of self which filled the world to a reduced consciousness."[8] The pain often seems in excess of the deserts, even for egoists like Gwendolen and Mrs. Transome, for while the focus in George Eliot is likely to be on individual limits, she can describe with remarkable acuity the cruelties, injustices, and banalities of the world that imposes those limits.

The tormented escapes and returns of the heroine of *Romola* mark a crisis in George Eliot's realism, a crisis that takes the shape of a representative question: "The question where the duty of obedience ends, and the duty of resistance begins, could in no case be an easy one" (55:431). If learning to value the "commonplace," to find the sacred in the ordinary, to recognize the depth and intensity of the bonds that connect us with family and society, is the central work of George Eliot's realism, the novels are nevertheless marked by a struggle to avoid idealizing rebellion. *Silas Marner* begins with the expulsion of the innocent Silas from the religious community he piously loves, as he is subject to an irrational trial and hypocritical accusation. Silas's catalepsy might be taken as a figure for the condition of other more complex and realistic heroines, like Maggie or Dorothea, who suffer for innocence at the hands of a coarse and unperceptive society. The tension between the protagonist's innocence and, usually, idealism, and the coarse brutality of the society that condemns them creates problems with which the novels sometimes struggle indecisively, as when, at the end of *The Mill on the Floss*, the reader is in effect asked to believe in the idyllic nature of Maggie's childhood, which has, however, been unfolded at length as a series of painful misunderstandings amidst a set of families steeped in primitive tribalism.

Romola is the first of George Eliot's novels to face directly, in its form and subject, the crisis of realism. (In this volume, Josephine McDonagh and Alexander Welsh, in discussing this turning point of her career, offer slightly different interpretations of the significance of *Romola* in the development of George Eliot's career.) On her first attempt at resistance, Romola is turned back by her encounter with Savonarola. Even at the end of the novel, Romola can only drift – not run – away, and becoming a kind of savior in another community redeems her. The novel itself becomes, as George Eliot herself recognized, too "ideal," and precisely because it needs to confirm Romola in her rebellion and independence in ways that are largely inimical to George Eliot's programmatic realism. George Eliot's notorious struggle to write *Romola*, which was surely against the grain of her more natural focus on the English Midlands (she interrupted the writing in order to write *Silas*

Marner), certainly had much to do with the way the book fails to accommodate itself to the methods of realism, despite her extraordinary research into the conditions of Renaissance Florence. The book will not settle for the restraints that Savonarola imposes and Romola, for a while, accepts. As Caroline Levine points out in a recent study, by the end of the novel Romola "has radically revised conventional relations between wife and mistress, having adopted her husband's lover as her own partner. Affirming a startling independence, the women run the household together, free from the demands of men."[9] While other critics have noticed this shift, which might be taken to belie the accusation that George Eliot never created an independent woman like herself, it is important also to notice that Romola's independence is precisely in her choice of responsibilities. As in her own life, George Eliot reassimilates her heroine to her accustomed modes of self-repression. That is, while she seems to wrest herself free from the obligations that George Eliot's moral realism would seem to impose, she creates (as Marian Evans had done) new obligations that are, as the novel suggests, yet more authentic and valuable than the merely legal ones she had been forced to flee. *Romola* hovers between the stern realism of the early novels and the formal and moral shifts of *Daniel Deronda*. It is half historical novel, half fable.

One of the marks of George Eliot's realism is that it is never *quite* the carceral and naïvely representational form it has often been taken to be. The tensions in *Romola* suggest one way in which George Eliot understood the limitations of a naïve representationalism and the "carceral" implications of her narratives. Famously, too, as the passage from *Adam Bede* quoted above makes clear, she knew the difficulties of representation. The novels are a struggle, and a struggle that becomes increasingly part of their form. So, in the famous passages in *Middlemarch* in which the narrator interrupts to remind us of the multiplicity of ways in which the experience can be understood, George Eliot's narrator makes it impossible to sustain a single unequivocal understanding of the real. The multiplotted nature of many of her novels enacts in the very form her refusal to allow the artificial dominance of a single perspective. "But why always Dorothea?" in its sudden radical shift of perspective from Dorothea to the unlikeable Casaubon, dramatically represents George Eliot's recognition that no single perspective can encompass reality and that for realism to do its job it must allow for its incompleteness and disallow the possibility that any single person – the narrator included – can authoritatively interpret reality. Her sophisticated gestures toward what in contemporary theory we would call indeterminacy have led some modern critics to see her as anticipating deconstructionist ideas.[10] Yet it is important to recognize that realism itself, insofar as it is more than a mere naïve ritual of representation, requires self-conscious questioning of its own potentialities for falsification. The truest realism, as George Eliot develops it in her own work, is one that truthfully confronts its own limitations.

In her continuing explorations of the possibilities and limits of realism, George Eliot was clearly feeling, as *Romola* itself had already shown, that the restraints of all those relative conditions that shape individual lives were, in the end, too limiting. *Middlemarch*, the novel that might be taken as the fullest achievement of English realism, is formally and substantively informed by the crisis of limits. Its "Finale" seems to anticipate the criticism of the constraining force of its brilliantly complicated narrative. Dorothea, of course, always threatens to become the ideal heroine of the novel, and much of the book is given to the effort to keep this from happening and from thus distorting the multiple perspectives that give the book its form. There is a telling sentence that in effect lays out for us the possibilities that George Eliot's realism allows to her characters: "Many who knew her," the narrator states, "thought it a pity that so substantive and rare a creature should have been absorbed into the life of another, and be only known in a certain circle as a wife and mother. But no one stated exactly what else that was in her power she ought rather to have done" ("Finale":680).

The key phrase here, the mark of the realist project, is "what else that was in her power." *Middlemarch* imagines all characters as enmeshed in a mass of personal and social relations that are in effect determining. Only the strongest people have the slightest chance of breaking from the limits of that determination, but the realist program refuses heroism as it refuses evil. Only in *Daniel Deronda* does George Eliot fully explore the alternatives to this realist way of imagining. On the one hand, in that novel, George Eliot creates the first woman character who attempts, with some success, to break from the limits of what is thought to be in the power of women – the grand opera singer, mother of Daniel, the Princess Halm-Eberstein. There has been considerable attention, particularly from feminists, focused on this remarkable character. For while in the end she is defeated, and, further, condemned by her son for betraying the patriarchal tradition, she speaks with power of her own right to attempt to fulfill her great talents – almost one would think as Marian Evans might have spoken at times of her own career.

While the princess chooses the kind of exceptional life that was not in the power of Dorothea, *Daniel Deronda* violates another aspect of the realist program. For in *Middlemarch* constraints are imposed not by deliberate and active evil but, as in the case of Lydgate, by "the small solicitations of circumstance, which is a commoner history of perdition than any single momentous bargain" (VIII:79:640). In *Daniel Deronda*, however, as she creates her one determinedly professional woman, so she creates her one unequivocally evil man – almost in the tradition of Dickens's sense of natural wickedness – although imagined with brilliant psychological specificity. Grandcourt is the exceptional villain in George Eliot, utterly different from, for example, Bulstrode, or Arthur Donnithorne, or even Tito Melema. His evil is intrinsic, an unredeemed and unredeemable insistence on personal power and command.

But these kinds of characters, in the excess that leads to their rather extravagant fates, do not belong to the kind of realistic program that governs *Middlemarch* and leaves Dorothea with no alternatives to the secondariness of her life with Ladislaw. One of the other major narrative lines in *Middlemarch*, parallel and intersecting with Dorothea's, works out the problem of heroism with Lydgate, whose "spots of commonness" make his failure to transcend the limits of the Middlemarch community inevitable. Dorothea has struggled, but without the resources available to men, and as a consequence the realism of her representation leads to the novel's conclusion – a kind of culmination of the realist vision – disallowing any action that might create large changes but allowing that "the effect of her being on those around her was incalculably diffusive" ("Finale":682).

That, as *Daniel Deronda* makes clear, was not finally enough for George Eliot. As I have been suggesting, *Daniel Deronda*, which is another multiplot novel, might be understood as a test of realism. In one narrative, Gwendolen Harleth undergoes the realist heroine's fate, and in the other the novel breaks into something like a heroic romance, an almost mythic story of a quest for a mother and, yet more mythically, the possibility of starting a new nation. The two narratives, of course, intersect, but they also comment on each other, and it is possible to read the "Jewish" half as an attempt to create a plausible alternative to realism. Throughout the novel, but particularly in the Gwendolen half, George Eliot's portrait of English society is uncharacteristically cynical and bleak; it is a society to which accommodation would seem mere capitulation. Yet Gwendolen Harleth must in the end make the accommodation, move through the "carceral" patterns, and end in resignation. Gwendolen, of course, is no "Saint Theresa of the midland flats," and she must learn from Daniel himself the lessons of resignation that he, in effect, must unlearn in his part of the story. For Daniel begins in self-abnegation, must learn who he is, must act against the banal (and racist) assumptions of his society, and in the end, with whatever qualifications, he goes off to help found a state that will, in effect, reestablish the spiritual purity of the biblical world, while Gwendolen is left to make what she can of the crushing defeat of her egoistic ambitions and the virtual destruction of her sense of herself.

Realism is a leitmotif of George Eliot's fiction-writing career. In her hands it was both a continuation of the acts of (perhaps involuntary) rebellion that marked the life of Marian Evans, and a means back to that lost respectability, that accommodation with a world that had rejected her, which she sought from the time she eloped with Lewes. Her art everywhere participated in the ambivalent directions of realism itself – determined to get at the truth, deeply sensitive to its inaccessibility and the ways in which everyone, the best and the worst, distorts it for personal interest; reformist and deeply critical of the structures of society, conservative about politics and feminism; daringly exploratory – she called her novels "experiments in life" – and resistant to change. Her novels open new directions in English narrative: psychologically, she richly anticipates the Freudian understanding of the power of the irrational to determine human behavior;[11] she, more than any novelist before Henry James, understood and explored the problems of perspective, of "point of view"; for better or worse, and I take it as for the better, she made the novel as a form something more than, or at least in addition to, popular entertainment, and in this respect certainly anticipated (of course again for better or worse) the directions of modernism. She brought to bear on the novel extraordinary learning, from almost the whole range of nineteenth-century knowledge – German philosophy and biblical criticism and history, the new social science of anthropology, physical and particularly biological science, positivism, psychology, philology, and the study of language. The equipment may at times have seemed heavy, but as a consequence of that enormous learning and philosophical acuity she almost never wrote a word that was not interesting, even when there are moments in the novels that seem to cry out for the fuller embodiment she was always, in principle, seeking. Like any great artist, she was constantly at work exploring the limits of her own methods, seeking new and better ways to get it right.

The tangible result is the greatest realist novel in the language, *Middlemarch*, and several other novels that have entered the life of the English-speaking world – *Adam Bede*, *The Mill on the Floss*, *Silas Marner*. To understand and value this work, it is best to attempt to get a sense of the full range of George Eliot's knowledge and thought, and the nature of her complicated and difficult life. The chapters that comprise this volume attempt to lay out the major elements of her thought and art, the shape and the context of her career. While there is of course something a little artificial in dividing her knowledge and thought into compartments – philosophy, science, religion, politics, the woman question – her thought was rich and complicated enough to require such compartmentalization. One needs to know something of her journalism, something of her poetry, something of the way she connected with the politics of Victorian society.

In the end, however, readers will (and should) want to return to the novels themselves. The object of this volume is to help lift George Eliot from the frozen condition of literary monument, to make the resistant richness of her art more clearly visible, and to make her superb intelligence and imagination more accessible to readers who have begun to recognize the power and originality of her art.

NOTES

1 Cited in Gordon Haight, *George Eliot: A Biography* (Oxford and New York: Oxford University Press, 1968), p. 549.
2 Leonard Huxley, ed., *The Life and Letters of T. H. Huxley* (London: Macmillan, 1900), II: 18.
3 Adrian Desmond and James Moore, *Darwin: The Life of a Tormented Evolutionist* (New York: Warner Books, 1991), p. 666.
4 Alice R. Kaminsky, ed., *The Literary Criticism of George Henry Lewes* (Lincoln: University of Nebraska Press, 1964), pp. 87, 89.
5 *Westminster Review* 65 (April 1856), 626. Reprinted in *SEPW*, p. 368.
6 Virginia Woolf, *The Captain's Deathbed* (New York: Harcourt Brace & Janovich, 1950), p. 108.
7 D. A. Miller, *The Novel and the Police* (Berkeley: University of California Press, 1988), p. x.
8 Barbara Hardy, *The Novels of George Eliot* (London: Athlone Press, 1959), p. 198.
9 Caroline Levine, 'The Prophetic Fallacy: Realism, Foreshadowing and Narrative Knowledge in *Romola*," in Caroline Levine and Mark W. Turner, eds., *From Author to Text: Re-reading George Eliot's* Romola (Aldershot: Ashgate, 1998), p. 137.
10 Two of the best-known essays establishing this kind of argument are by J. Hillis Miller: "Narrative and History," *ELH*, 41 (1974): 455–73 and "Optic and Semiotic in *Middlemarch*," in *The Worlds of Victorian Fiction*, ed. J. H. Buckley (Cambridge, Mass.: Harvard University Press, 1975).
11 See Alexander Welsh, *George Eliot and Blackmail* (Cambridge, Mass.: Harvard University Press, 1985), particularly pp. 344–58.

2

ROSEMARIE BODENHEIMER

A woman of many names

"George Eliot" came into existence on 4 February 1857, as the pseudonym offered by 37-year-old fledgling novelist Marian Evans to her new publisher, William Blackwood, to use as "a tub to throw to the whale in case of curious inquiries" (*GEL*, II:292). Of all the pen names adopted by Victorian writers, George Eliot's is the one that has proven the most enduring, the one that did not fade away once the gender and identity of the author became known. Even now, after countless biographies have charted the personal life of the brilliant woman who managed to live always at an oblique angle to Victorian middle-class respectability, "George Eliot" retains its singular power to identify both the person and the writer. Exactly because it is an assumed name, it brings into play the odd quality of a life that could develop its great capacities only under the cover of partly fictional social roles. It is also the only stable name attached to the person who was baptised Mary Anne Evans after her birth on 22 November 1819. Each new stage of her life was accompanied by a change in signature, so that one might tell a version of George Eliot's story by following the series of names she asked her friends to call her. Above all, "George Eliot," laden with all we know about her through her letters, journals, essays, poems, and novels, represents the triumph of a woman's intellectual breadth and ambition through its expression in writing. The works signed with that name were achieved despite a long career of painfully self-conscious inner conflict, which was intensified both by chronic bodily illness and by a domestic life led outside the pale of legal marriage. They were also, of course, achieved because of those conflicts, which animate the complex social positions and the many shifts in narrative perspective that are characteristic of George Eliot's fiction.

Mary Anne Evans was the third and last surviving child of the marriage between Robert Evans, the respected manager of the Newdigate estate in Warwickshire, and Christiana Pearson, who came from a well-established farming family in the region. Her childhood was spent in Griff House, a substantial farmhouse off the Coventry Road. From this location in the rural middle class, she was well placed to absorb the full spectrum of English provincial life: she was initiated early into the farm and dairy work of women, while her father's work brought him into direct working relationships with people of every status, from the squire – the Newdigate family who employed and relied on him – through the local farmers, coal miners, canal workers, clergy, tradespeople, craftsmen, and laborers. The Evans family was not genteel, but it was respectable and ambitious of practical excellence within the terms of a conservative, customary rural society.

The first thirty years of George Eliot's life in this society provided her not only with the material for several of her novels, but also with a class perspective that differs significantly from those of other Victorian novelists. She is less likely to depict the social world as divided into starkly oppositional social classes, or to join the Victorian obsession with stories of social aspiration and social oppression, than she is to create a variegated community in which the story centers on the fates of characters who disturb or violate the norms of belief or behavior in that community. Despite its quite radical changes, her own social trajectory repeatedly landed her in an anomalous social position that was never exactly defined by class. As an overly intense and bookish child in a practical household, as a fervid evangelical adolescent in a conventional Church of England family, as a 22-year-old rejecter of Christian doctrine, as an independent woman editor and journalist in a world of other self-made London intellectuals, religious freethinkers, and social bohemians, and finally as the unmarried domestic partner of George Henry Lewes, George Eliot was always stretching the norms of acceptable female behavior, and bringing social rejection upon herself. What made her George Eliot was the extent to which she suffered under that rejection, and the talent with which she contrived to write herself into a position of social respectability and adulation despite her unconventional circumstances.

It is difficult to be authoritative about the quality of Mary Anne Evans's early childhood. Much of what her biographers have surmised is deeply colored by her most autobiographical novel, *The Mill on the Floss*, written when she was about forty, while the few stories that friends of her later life recalled would have been told to them in a carefully retrospective way. We know little about her mother Christiana Pearson Evans, although it does seem likely that she was devoted to doing things according to customary family standards, and understood little about her daughter's intellect and imagination. We know that Mary Anne had a period of close companionship with her brother Isaac – three years older and temperamentally very different – which was probably ruptured very early, when the children were sent to different schools at the ages of five and eight. The family did the best it could for Mary Anne by its own lights, sending her to good local schools in Nuneaton and Coventry until she was sixteen. The general picture is of a child very attached and attentive to her surroundings, but far too smart and sensitive to be fully comprehensible to any members of her immediate family. Her inner dialogue with books, and sometimes teachers, was the main conduit for her ambitious intelligence; throughout her life she sought friendships in which affection could be combined with the expression and performance of that interior life. The first important one, with her evangelical teacher Maria Lewis, also provided her with the self-denying and rather excessive religious rigor into which she poured the conflicts of her difficult adolescence.

We are in a position to meet the young evangelical through her first surviving letters, written to Maria Lewis and a few others after the death of her mother and the marriage of her sister Chrissey. These events had recalled Mary Anne from school and left her, at sixteen, with the responsibility for running the Griff household for her father and brother. Some time after the death of Christiana Evans, Mary Ann dropped the "e" from "Anne," possibly to signal the rejection of an unnecessarily elegant frill. The letters she wrote during this period (1836–41) reveal the stresses of an immensely ambitious mind constrained on the one hand by a life of farmwife chores and on the other by a self-imposed regime which included humility, self-repression, the rejection of earthly pleasures (including novel-reading and musical performance), and the judgment of all things according to their compatibility with the doctrine of true life in the hereafter. Maria Lewis, now living unhappily in the role of governess, became the primary audience for epistolary performances that betray in every line the sense of personal intellectual power and the desire for admiration and applause which the young letter-writer rejected in theory. This, for example, from a seventeen-year-old who had reason to doubt her own attractiveness and prospects for marriage, in response to the news of an engagement:

> I trust that the expected union may ultimately issue in the spiritual benefit of both parties; for my own part when I hear of the marrying and giving in marriage that is constantly being transacted I can only sigh for those who are multiplying earthly ties which though powerful enough to detach their heart and thoughts from heaven, are so brittle as to be liable to be snapped asunder at every breeze. You will think me a perfect female Diogenes, and I plead guilty to occasional misanthropic thoughts, but not to the indulgence of them; still I must believe that those are happiest who are not fermenting themselves by engaging in projects of earthly bliss, who are considering this life merely a pilgrimage, a scene calling for diligence and watchfulness, not for repose and amusement. (*GEL*, August 1838; 1:6).

By the time she was twenty, she was sending Maria Lewis increasingly authoritative critiques of the church histories, religious philosophies and biographies she was devouring, along with innumerable apologies for her own egotism. Meanwhile the situation at home had become more difficult. Isaac was planning to marry, and Mary Ann was threatened with losing her role as the woman in charge at Griff, and being demoted to the thankless role of unmarried spinster devoted to the care of an aging father. True to a lifelong habit of loyalty to those who were close to her, she did not allow herself to complain about her family in writing, but her personal and intellectual rage and frustration crept out through distanced and generalized metaphors: "If I were truly spiritually-minded I should rather delight in an occasion of proving to myself the genuineness of my religious experience and of exercising a cheerful submission to the will of my Saviour, instead of acting as a bullock unaccustomed to the yoke, murmuring at the slightest opposition to my taste, the slightest mortification of my fleshly mind" (*GEL*, October 30, 1839; 1:30–31). A year later, she was producing images of self-sacrifice that cry out despairingly for liberation and self-development: "We should aim to be like plants in the chamber of sickness, dispensing purifying air even in a region that turns pale all its verdure and cramps its instinctive propensity to expand. Society is a wide nursery of plants where the hundred decompose to nourish the future ten after giving collateral benefits to their contemporaries destined for a fairer garden. An awful thought! one so heavy that if our souls could once sustain its whole weight, or rather if its whole weight were once to drop on them, they would break and burst their tenements" (October 27, 1840; 1:71–72). Her sense that she was destroying herself – "decomposing" – through service in an alien atmosphere had become overwhelming.

It was not long before Mary Ann's own "tenements" did finally break and burst, taking the form of a religious revolution: after a long period of private reading and questioning, she suddenly refused to go to church with her father. The circumstances of this famous episode, the prolonged family strife it engendered, the accommodation reached between father and daughter, and the conclusions reached by Mary Ann Evans, were deeply revealing and deeply formative. The pattern of behavior and response that we can trace in this so-called family "Holy War" was also to characterize George Eliot's conflict-filled moments of decision in later life, and to create the uneasy blend of radical social critique and conservatism that shapes her fiction.

In March 1841 Robert and Mary Ann Evans left Griff and the management of the Newdigate estate to Isaac, and moved five miles down the road to a house in Foleshill, on the outskirts of Coventry. The family decision left Mary Ann as her father's caretaker, but it also offered the opportunity for a wider acquaintance, possibly – the family hoped – even for a marriage partner to emerge from the religious society of Coventry. By this time, however, Mary Ann's vigorous and romantically responsive mind was knocking against the doctrinal dead ends that had checked both her intellectual forays and her sensory pleasures for so many years. Her letters to Maria Lewis, while still adhering to the pious conventions of their correspondence, began to indicate that this voracious and discerning reader was engaged in inquiries she was not talking about openly. At some point during 1841 she read Charles Hennell's *Inquiry Concerning the Origin of Christianity* (1838), a work which investigated the Gospels with the intent of discovering the truth of their accounts of miracles. Hennell concluded that there was insufficient evidence for the supernatural accounts of Jesus' life, rejected the ritual and dogma of Christianity and the hope of an afterlife, but maintained a general belief in God and in a life of good works. In November Mary Ann met and befriended the couple for whom Hennell had written the *Inquiry*: his sister Cara Bray and her husband Charles Bray, a freethinking ribbon manufacturer whose house, Rosehill, was a provincial center for the gathering of radical and liberal intellectuals and reformers. Suddenly she had what she had never experienced before: a place where she could talk with people whose minds could meet her own, and develop her own religious doubts into a new dedication to the untrammeled pursuit of truth. Her friendship with the Brays strengthened rapidly.

The problem lay in how to negotiate between her old loyalties and her new ones. She had concealed her change of opinion from her father and Maria Lewis; then, as if in response to a New Year's resolution, she chose January 2, 1842, when Maria was visiting, to stage her first refusal to attend church. Within a few months she had broken off her outgrown connection with Maria Lewis, but her rebellion against her father's Tory conformity had more lasting consequences. Barely speaking to her, he began to make plans to move elsewhere, whether with or without his daughter, he would not say. For a while she maintained her Holy Warrior's stance; as she wrote to her neighbor Mrs. Pears, "To *fear* the examination of any proposition appears to me an intellectual and moral palsy that will ever hinder the firm grasping of any substance whatever. For my part, I wish to be among the ranks of that glorious crusade that is seeking to set Truth's Holy Sepulchre free from a usurped dominion. We shall then see her resurrection!" (*GEL*, January 28, 1842; 1:125). A month later, she attempted to explain her position to her baffled father in an extraordinary letter which attempts both to stand by her intellectual principle and to declare her ongoing devotion to him: "I could not without vile hypocrisy and a miserable truckling to the smile of the world for the sake of my supposed interests, profess to join in worship which I wholly disapprove. This and *this alone* I will not do even for your sake – anything else however painful I would cheerfully do to give you a moment's joy" (February 28, 1842; 1:129).

Such pronouncements, full of performative and satirical power, break through the self-repressive strictures of her earlier letters with the welcome rush of dams bursting, but they were not to survive their encounter with the pressure of family loyalty and the "intellectual and moral palsy" of provincial opinion. Two further months of domestic coldness ensued, along with a barrage of unsuccessful attempts by friends, family, and clergy to bring the erring daughter back into the fold. Fearing an even more embarrassing break, Isaac Evans and his wife offered Mary Ann a temporary home at Griff so that the family rift could be repaired. After about five weeks of negotiations and remorse, Mary Ann returned to Foleshill. She had acceded to her father's demand that she attend church with him, and he silently conceded her right to her own thoughts. For the next six years she maintained and developed her intellectual life through her association with the Brays and their circle, at the same time as she played to the full her role as devoted spinster daughter to Robert Evans. When he became seriously ill in 1848, she effectively abandoned her mental life and became his full-time nurse for a year, dedicating herself to this thankless task with all the passion of sacrifice that could have been asked of a fully licensed Victorian angel in the sickroom. When Robert Evans died, she was thirty years old, and exhausted by the long action of proving her daughterly devotion.

The Holy War episode can easily be read as a rebellion against the father or at least as a declaration of independence from his views, but it seems more fruitful in this case to consider the full course of the collision between a brilliant, fearless female mind and its social and emotional determinants. Mary Ann Evans's abrupt way of announcing her new opinions in the way which would prove most immediately embarrassing to her father suggests the uncomfortable depth of the gap between her private ruminations and the conventional understanding of her family, as well as her willful desire to test her father's ability to stick with her despite her bold new stance. From that failed experiment she learned about the intractability of received opinion and the power of social conformity in the minds of those closest to her. She recognized that the more flexible mind must bend to the prejudices around it, that an individual's single-minded devotion to "speculative truth" may be dangerous to traditional family or community cohesion by unleashing a round of frightened and irrational behavior (*GEL*, Letter to Sara Hennell, October 9, 1843; 1:162–63). She also learned that she was capable of compromising her social appearance – in this case by going to church – so long as she retained both her family connection and the internal freedom of inquiry that she required. The incident established her intellectual and moral honesty, her understanding that such honesty would be socially misunderstood and punished, and her need to expiate or redeem the consequences of her unconventional intelligence through sacrificial service. When George Eliot began to write novels, all of these factors came into play – in the stories she invented, in the narrative shifts of perspective between acute social satire and distantly tolerant sympathy, and in the way she had to understand her artistic mission as a service promoting individual human goodness.

After Robert Evans's death in 1849, Mary Ann was free to pursue life as an independent woman. Through the Bray–Hennell connection, she had already made a first entry into radical theological circles by the long labor of translating from the German Strauss's *The Life of Jesus, Critically Examined.* Her publisher, John Chapman, ran a household at 142 Strand in London that accepted lodgers and served as a center for liberal intellectuals and freethinkers. After some months of recuperation in Geneva, Mary Ann moved into this household, hoping to work as a reviewer, and marking her new life by shedding the familial "Mary Ann" in favor of the more sophisticated "Marian." When Chapman bought the liberal journal *Westminster Review* in 1851, Marian Evans became its assistant editor. In fact, she ran the journal herself under Chapman's nominal editorship until the end of 1853, the formal anonymity of her role providing her with a working situation in which her intellectual and managerial authority could function freely and successfully. During these years, Marian Evans became a respected figure in the circle of liberal London thinkers, and made the *Westminster Review* a distinguished organ for current literary, social, religious, and scientific thought. It was she, rather than the impulsive and incompetent Chapman, who established the intellectual commitments of the journal, tactfully stroked its well-known contributors, made the shrewd judgments about their merits and defects, and got the issues out on time. She also wrote a number of articles and reviews herself, under the rule of anonymity which was common in the journalism of that time. Officially under cover, her gender was no impediment to the full exercise of her talents.

These years provided her with the social life and the intellectual authority for which she had prepared herself through her largely solitary self-education. But the quest for companionship in love had always been more turbulent for this woman, whose intensity of feeling so often took precedence over the cautious and respectable behavior she had learned from her family. Both the Bray and the Chapman households were radical in their sexual as well as their religious and social politics: Charles Bray kept a mistress and brought his illegitimate daughter home to be raised by his wife and sister-in-law, while Chapman lived in a *ménage a trois* with his wife and his children's governess. Marian Evans moved in this society both as an emotional intimate of the Bray and Hennell women, and as an intellectual equal with the men, but her ardent desire to mix intellectual companionship with love resulted in a number of painful scrapes. At twenty-four she had paid a long visit to Charles Hennell's new father-in-law, Dr. Robert Brabant, a man in his sixties who encouraged an emotional intimacy that quickly raised the suspicions of Brabant's sister-in-law and wife, and resulted in Mary Ann's early departure. When she first moved to 142 Strand, she and John Chapman had had a brief encounter – quite possibly a sexual affair – which enraged Chapman's wife and mistress and sent Marian back to Warwickshire until she and Chapman had negotiated the purely professional terms of their future relationship. A more serious friendship developed during her editorial years with the philosopher-sociologist Herbert Spencer, with whom Marian spent a good deal of time walking, talking, and going to opera and theater. She fell in love – he did not – yet they managed to maintain their friendship.

Marian's extraordinary capacity for emotional honesty comes through again in a letter she wrote to Spencer asking for his companionship if not his love: "I want to know if you can assure me that you will not forsake me, and that you will always be with me as much as you can and share your thoughts and feelings with me. If you become attached to someone else, then I must die, but until then I could gather courage to work and make life valuable, if only I had you near me." She ended the letter with a proud acknowledgment of her unconventionality: "I suppose no woman ever before wrote such a letter as this – but I am not ashamed of it, for I am conscious that in the light of reason and true refinement I am worthy of your respect and tenderness, whatever gross men or vulgar-minded women might think of me" (*GEL*, July 16?, 1852; VIII:56–57). The Holy Warrior had grown up, but she maintained her position that the truth of reason and feeling should prevail against the social standards for acceptable behavior in women.

As it turned out, her life was to become a long testing ground for that position. After she had abandoned her hopes for Herbert Spencer, she began to see more and more of Spencer's good friend George Henry Lewes, an immensely versatile and lively editor and writer who was one of the contributors to the *Westminster Review.* Born into the illegitimate second family of a father who disappeared from the scene after his birth, Lewes had come out of obscurity to make his way in the London literary world through his intelligence, talent, charm, and energetic entrepreneurship. He was an adept at languages, drama and drama criticism, continental literature and philosophy, and science, and had published a number of books and many articles by the time he met Marian Evans in his mid-thirties. At that time he was coediting the journal the *Leader* with his friend Thornton Hunt, and serving as its main literary and drama critic. Fatefully for George Eliot, Thornton Hunt was also cofathering Lewes's family.

George Henry Lewes and his wife Agnew Jervis Lewes had three sons, after which Agnes began an affair with Thornton Hunt that eventually produced four more children. Following his principles of free-thinking and free-living, Lewes had forfeited his legal right to divorce by condoning Agnes's adultery and even registering Hunt's children under his own name. His generosity may have been motivated by his own father's irregularity and defection, but the situation had begun to wear on him by the time he met Marian Evans. Like her, he was ready for a serious partnership, but he could not offer her a legal marriage. In October 1853 Marian moved out of Chapman's house to a place of her own, and began an intimate relationship with Lewes. On July 20, 1854, Marian Evans and George Henry Lewes left England together for an eight-month stay in Weimar and Berlin, where Lewes was researching his biography of Goethe. After they returned, they lived together lovingly and productively until Lewes's death in 1878. "In the light of reason and true refinement," as Marian had put it in her letter to Spencer, they had done the right thing. Throughout their lives, they even continued to support Agnes Lewes and all of her children from the proceeds of their writing. But by the lights of the Evans family, and the opinions of respectable society, Marian Evans was anathema.

For the rest of their lives, the couple had to manage both their personal and professional lives in ways that would allow Marian to develop a public voice in print, but would also protect her from the worst indignities of her position as a "fallen woman." Internally Marian had to find ways to maintain her pride and her sense of moral rightness against the horrified gossip that sometimes reached her ears, against the knowledge that only the bravest women would visit her, and against the sense of betrayal expressed by her Coventry friends, who had been kept in the dark about the true nature of the relationship with Lewes until after the sudden departure for Germany. As in the Holy War, the results of a long-brewing decision were sprung suddenly on the intimates of the old life – the Bray circle in particular – and caused a rift that was only partially repaired. Marian kept her nonlegal marriage a secret from her own family for three years, after which both the relationship and her fiction writing assured her emotional and financial stability. Once she had broached the subject, her brother Isaac answered through his lawyer and cut off family communication altogether.

Marian now signed herself "Marian Evans Lewes" or "Marian Lewes," and insisted that she be referred to as "Mrs. Lewes." It was not only for the sake of landladies; she knew and felt that she was Mrs. Lewes in every way except the technical legal one. When it came to writing, she was protected by the convention of anonymity: during the first years of their life together in England, her writing for the *Westminster Review* and the *Leader* flourished. Energized by the need to make money, by personal happiness, and by the stimulation of discussion with Lewes, she wrote a series of brilliant reviews in which the full force of her learning, her understanding of German and Continental intellectual developments, and her keen moral and literary judgment are displayed in a stunningly powerful prose style. Encouraged by Lewes, she then made her first foray into the fiction writing which she had long cherished as a dream. On November 6, 1856 "The Sad Fortunes of the Reverend Amos Barton," the first of three novellas which were later to be published as *Scenes of Clerical Life*, was submitted by Lewes to the Edinburgh publisher John Blackwood as the work of "a friend who desired my good offices with you" (2:269), and accepted for publication in *Blackwood's Edinburgh Magazine*.

"George Eliot" was the joint creation of Marian Evans, George Henry Lewes, and John Blackwood, who was (with the exception of *Romola)* to remain George Eliot's publisher throughout her career. Lewes took charge of the initial negotiations, teaching Blackwood to think of his new author as a very diffident, retiring man who needed support and encouragement to go on writing, and enjoining on him absolute secrecy about the origin of the stories. Once Marian got in on the correspondence, she realized the necessity for a pseudonym, even though she still feared that her experiments in fiction would turn out to be failures. As she wrote to Blackwood, "For several reasons I am very anxious to retain my incognito for some time to come, and to an author not already famous, anonymity is the highest *prestige*. Besides, if George Eliot turn out to be a dull dog and an ineffective writer – a mere flash in the pan – I, for one, am determined to cut him on the first intimation of that disagreeable fact" (2:309–10). Although Blackwood may well have guessed who his new author was, he ran a conservative family magazine and was just as happy not to know the truth too exactly. The trio maintained the fiction of a male George Eliot as long as possible in their correspondence, and Blackwood's patience and praise were enlisted in Lewes's efforts to keep Marian writing despite her all-too-ready descents into despair and fears of failure.

Success came early and dramatically to the unknown new author. Marian recorded the good news of favorable reviews and letters in her journal, adding a comment which suggests the redemptive role that fiction-writing played in her moral imagination: "At present I value them [favorable comments about *Scenes of Clerical Life*] as grounds for hoping that my writing may succeed and so give value to my life – as indications that I can touch the hearts of my fellow men, and so sprinkle some precious grain as the result of the long years in which I have been inert and suffering." *Adam Bede* came out in 1859 and was an immediate best-seller. "The success has been . . . triumphantly beyond anything that I had dreamed of, " she exulted in April 1859, adding characteristically "Shall I ever write another book as true as 'Adam Bede'? The *weight* of the future presses on me and makes itself felt even more than the deep satisfaction of the past and present" (*Journals*, 300).

Even as she wrote these words in her journal, Marian was experiencing the inevitable backlash of gossip and rumor stimulated by the secret of the pseudonym. It would have been one thing if the literary world had merely suspected that George Eliot was the woman living with Lewes, and if her success had sweetened that difficult social fact, as it did so triumphantly in the long run. What happened in 1859 was far more ludicrous, and far more disturbing, because it struck at her realistic artistic procedures. Both *Scenes* and *Adam Bede* drew deeply from her Warwickshire childhood – too deeply and too directly, in fact, because living people from her old neighborhood recognized their own life stories in these fictions. Somehow – we do not to this day know quite how – the rumor began that George Eliot was a poor, disreputable Nuneaton clergyman named Joseph Liggins, who would have been familiar with the scenes and the characters who populated the new stories. For the sake of retaining the pseudonym, the Leweses tolerated these rumors for some time, until they became unbearable and elicited an indignant but still pseudonymous letter of denial published in *The Times*. Shortly afterwards the Reverend John Gwyther of Yorkshire declared himself to Blackwood as the original of Amos Barton, while other Warwickshire characters continued to insist that George Eliot, whoever he was, had stolen other stories directly from life. Despite Blackwood's desire to maintain the secret as long as possible – he was clearly afraid that sales would drop if people knew that George Eliot was Marian Evans Lewes – the Leweses finally gave up the effort, and allowed the truth to be circulated. These trials were harrowing enough to depress the new author's elation, and to deepen her sensitivity to the uncontrollable reign of gossip and rumor in the literary marketplace. After the Liggins affair, Lewes increased his efforts to protect Marian from any town talk about her books, and showed her only an occasional favorable review. In time, the pain of her position as the subject of talk and misinformation was reworked in her writing: in *Middlemarch*, George Eliot became the greatest depictor of gossip and rumor in the English language.

The Liggins affair was also disturbing because it called into question George Eliot's relationship with the past. In the space of five years, between the ages of thirty and thirty-five, she had effectively cut her ties with the provincial life of Warwickshire, but she negotiated this passage by developing a complex mixture of piety about the sacredness of early affections and deadly accuracy about the stifling limitations of thought in traditional rural societies. Her first three novels – *Scenes of Clerical Life*, *Adam Bede,* and the more directly autobiographical *The Mill on the Floss* – were generated from the capacious and detailed memory that was stimulated by the act of writing retrospective imaginative narrative.[1] She brought the middle- and lower-middle-class society of these provincial towns and farms to life as no writer had ever done before, lavishing sympathetic – if distanced – attention even on the religious beliefs and practices she had so thoroughly rejected in the first flush of her Holy War. She exhorted her readers to sympathize with the ordinariness of her characters, while her narrators engaged in the extraordinary moral generalizations and leaps of ironic imagination that redeemed the narrow minds they described. This relation with the past, infused for George Eliot with an almost religious fervor, depended on the safe distance she had achieved in her London life with G. H. Lewes. It is not surprising that she reacted with horror to actual voices from Warwickshire who claimed that her complex narrative realism was nothing more than a retailing of true-life stories. After *The Mill on the Floss* (1860), a novel which cut closest to the family bone, George Eliot began to search further afield for the settings of her fiction.

The decade of the 1860s brought a new quality of life along with a series of new experiments in writing. In just three years George Eliot had become both famous and financially stable, but if anything her tendencies to anxiety and depression increased during her forties. She set herself a series of writing projects which proved extremely difficult to bring to conclusion: the historical novel *Romola*, which led her into massive researches on fifteenth-century Florence, the long blank-verse poem, *The Spanish Gypsy*, and the social-problem novel, *Felix Holt, the Radical*, which attempted to address issues of working-class politics. Only *Silas Marner*, which came quickly to mind and almost wrote itself during the last months of 1860, is free from the sense of laboriousness which shadows much of the writing of this decade. George Eliot was all too aware of the Casaubon-like tendencies which made her working life so fraught with struggle. As she settled herself to work after a trip to Florence in 1861, she wrote in her journal, "At least there is a possibility that I may make greater efforts against indolency and the despondency that comes from too egoistic a dread of failure." Going on to recall her escape from youthful despair, she could not so easily separate herself from it: "It was that sort of despair that sucked away the sap of half the hours which might have been filled by energetic youthful activity: and the same demon tries to get hold of me again whenever an old work is dismissed and a new one is being meditated" (*Journals*, 90).

The steady pace of reading, writing, walking, correspondence, and receiving visitors that filled the days in the Lewes household was frequently interrupted by illness. Marian suffered from bouts of severe headaches, which destroyed her ability to work, and George Henry Lewes was chronically afflicted with headaches, nausea and other stomach ailments, dizziness and weight loss. Their lives often seemed to be contests between work and collapse, and were punctuated by frequent trips abroad or to the country for the sake of one or the other's health. Being in the country was often almost magically transformative for Marian, who retained her love of rural air and landscape, and her ability to undertake strenuous walks and tours while on holiday. But the perpetual struggle against illness, without the benefits of aspirin or antibiotics, fed into the patterns of anxiety and depression that manifest themselves so clearly in her journals and letters. It is impossible to know the extent to which the illnesses were exacerbated by the necessary repressions on which their lives were built: Marian's proud and sometimes prickly negotiation of her impossible social situation, and Lewes's role as the perpetual optimist who protected her, said only good things about her work, and cheered her through endless moments of despair.

Beginning in 1860, Marian was destined to make her home in London proper, and to take on the familial duties of stepmotherhood. Since 1856 Lewes's three sons had been placed at the Hofwyl School for international students in Switzerland, where they could receive a healthy education and protection from the marital irregularities of their parents. As the beneficiaries of yet another Eliot – Lewes policy of secrecy, they wrote letters home as though their original household were intact. In 1859 Lewes told them the truth during his annual visit, preparing them for the moment when the eldest, Charles Lee Lewes, would finish school and make his home with his father and Marian while he looked for a permanent occupation. For the sake of Charles, the Leweses moved into London – temporarily, they imagined – to give him the benefits of city life. During the decade of the sixties, the fortunes of Charles and his brothers Thornton and Herbert played a significant role in George Eliot's life. She was never, in fact, to move permanently out of London again: in 1863 she and Lewes bought their own house there, the Priory in Regent's Park. More importantly, the pleasures and trials of substitute parenthood entered fully into her psychological experience, and into the fiction she would produce for the rest of her writing life.

Charles Lewes proved to be a model stepson. He was attentive to domestic life, worked steadily at a post office job that he secured with a little help from Anthony Trollope, and shared with Marian the love of music and some talent at the piano. When the Leweses went abroad, he stayed at home and tended to the house and the correspondence. After five years of life as a successful family trio, Charles married and moved out, though he continued to play his role as home secretary for the rest of their lives. The other boys presented far more radical problems. Thornton (named fatefully after Lewes's erstwhile friend and colleague Thornton Hunt) was not so easily socialized; in his case the Leweses resorted to the classic Victorian strategy of sending difficult younger sons to the colonies. Thornie contrived to fail the examination which would have qualified him for the Indian Civil Service, and was finally packed off for the South African frontier colony of Natal, to seek his fortune as he might. Despite his intrepid nature, he failed to sustain an independent life there. Nonetheless, his unpromising younger brother Herbert was sent out to join Thornie in an attempt at upcountry farming for which neither young man had any real preparation. In 1869 Thornie returned home suddenly, suffering painfully from an undiagnosed illness, which turned out to be tuberculosis of the spine. Marian nursed him until he died several months later, in October 1869. Herbert remained in South Africa, tried hopelessly to make a living from cattle, married, and fathered two children before he, too, took ill. He died in Natal, before reaching the age of thirty.

The anxiety and pain caused by these sad stories can only be glimpsed in the Eliot–Lewes letters and journals of the 1860s. For Marian, parental responsibility offered a new source of legitimation in her anomalous situation, and she sometimes offered her parental worries and sacrifices to her correspondents as proof that she was a full participant in the duties of Victorian womanhood. At the same time, she could not help but express her delight when she and Lewes were free to live alone again in their accustomed double solitude, nor could she conceal the depth of her anxiety about the hapless lives of the two younger boys. Early in the 1860s her fiction featured a number of devious young men who steal and squander the resources of parental figures: the Cass brothers in *Silas Marner*, Tito Melema in *Romola*, David Faux in the story "Brother Jacob." After Thornie's death, however, her sympathies turned to the dilemma of vocation in the young man's life, which she explored in *Middlemarch* through the wishful or compensatory stories of Fred Vincy and Will Ladislaw, and again in the story of Daniel Deronda.

The final decade of George Eliot's life was in many ways a triumphant one. She wrote and published her masterpieces *Middlemarch* (1872) and *Daniel Deronda* (1876). The greatness of *Middlemarch* was immediately recognized. As Marian remarked in her first diary entry for 1873: "No former book of mine has been received with more enthusiasm – not even Adam Bede, and I have received many deeply affecting assurances of its influence for good on individual minds. Hardly anything could have happened to me which I could regard as a greater blessing than this growth of my spiritual existence when my bodily existence is decaying" (*Journals*, 142–43). The notion that she now had a "spiritual existence" which she could convey to her readers and admirers became a theme of this period, as did the notion that she was living on the verge of death. This new definition of her relationship with her audiences fed into the gradual development of a virtual George Eliot cult in the last years of her life, aided by the Leweses' energetic efforts to surround her with as many admirers as possible. What had really happened was that George Eliot now had a social existence: she had written her way not only to celebrity but also to respectability.

Both men and women of social standing began to frequent the Lewes's open house for visitors on Sunday afternoons at the Priory, and to invite the pair into society together. Their social calendars included visits to friends at Oxford and Cambridge, and engagements with other famous and soon-to-be-famous writers. For the younger generation in particular, George Eliot was a revered figure of liberal wisdom who promised the kind of sympathetic understanding manifested by the narrators of her books. The couple began to see so many people that they had to escape regularly to obscure country retreats in order to regain the quiet time to write that George Eliot had enjoyed in abundance earlier in her career. With fame and fortune well in place, they finally bought a second country house, the Heights at Witley, at the end of 1876.

With the idea of perpetuating her "spiritual existence" through personal connection as well as readership, George Eliot took special pains to cultivate the friendship and the confidences of her younger admirers, who sometimes became substitutes for the family she did not have. The difficulties of her own turbulent youth made her especially responsive to the conflicts and struggles of others. Moreover, as she wrote to her young friend Emilia Pattison in 1869, "I am conscious of having an unused stock of motherly tenderness, which sometimes overflows, but not without discrimination" (*GEL*, v:52). Among her flock of worshippers were a number of talented men and women who contributed to the George Eliot legacy in their own ways. Oscar Browning, who confided in her when he was dismissed from his teaching post at Eton, later wrote one of the earliest biographies. Emanuel Deutsch, a Jewish scholar and Zionist who died of cancer in his forties, provided material and inspiration for the Jewish focus of *Daniel Deronda*. Elma Stuart, a passionate George Eliot fan who played the role of grown-up daughter in need of maternal advice, ensured her perpetual association with her idol by having herself buried next to George Eliot in Highgate cemetery. Alexander Main, another ardent enthusiast, was for some reason allowed by George Eliot to publish many editions of *Wise, Witty and Tender Sayings of*

George Eliot, in which he extracted favorite bits of wisdom from the novels and presented them entirely out of context for the gratification of a middle-brow marketplace. Edith Simcox, an intellectual and active social reformer in her own right, recorded in her *Diary of a Shirtmaker* the hopeless and passionate love she felt for George Eliot, bestowing on later readers one of the most intense accounts of the writer's last years.[2] Through these and other confidential relationships, George Eliot played out in an arena other than fiction her need to redeem her own life by making its experience tell in the lives of others.

Yet, while she was ready to play the mentor with individual friends, she was unwilling or unable to use her singular experience in the cause of feminist efforts to widen the scope of action for Victorian women in general. Her close friend and feminist activist Barbara Bodichon, as well as other acquaintances, kept her well in touch with the founding of Girton College for women at Cambridge, and with the movement for women's suffrage. But the "Woman Question" raised only discomfort in George Eliot. She was willing to support women's higher education so long as it would afford women an equal opportunity of access to the knowledge on which good judgment might be founded, but she did not like the idea that young women might be moved to political action rather than to individual efforts of goodness and social melioration (IV:425; IV:468; VI:287). In part such positions arose from a fear of doing disservice to her friends' causes by associating them with her irregular womanhood. More profoundly, they recapitulate once more the painful lesson of the Holy War: that strongly held theoretical positions, no matter how enlightened and correct, can cause pain, disruption, and the release of irrational destructive behavior in actual families or communities. In her novels George Eliot elucidated more powerfully than anyone the social attitudes which restrict and stifle talented women, but she would not take the step of turning such knowledge into radical theory or practice.

The final phase of her life uncannily recapitulates the blend of unconventional action and conservative instinct that characterizes George Eliot's experience as a whole. Despite her status as a kind of Victorian icon, she did not leave the public stage without reminding her audiences of the powerful idiosyncratic choices that had shaped her career. On November 30, 1878 George Henry Lewes died of stomach cancer. For some months, Marian isolated herself in deep and inconsolable grief. Seeing almost no one, depending on Charles Lewes as a mediator, she devoted herself to completing and revising Lewes's massive *Problems of Life and Mind*. She was herself ill with the kidney disease which was to cause her own death two years later, but she persevered in this obsession as if she were Dorothea Brooke completing the life work of a Casaubon deserving of love and admiration.

Once she began to see visitors, her young friend John Cross became her most frequent companion. Although his name is occasionally mentioned in her diary and letters, the extent of their intimacy as it grew during the summer of 1879 was not confided to anyone. On May 6, 1880, Marian Evans Lewes married John Walter Cross in a church ceremony, and they escaped to the Continent for their honeymoon. No one knew of the wedding except the Cross family and Charles Lewes; her friends were left to find out through letters mailed after the departure. It was as if Marian was compelled to repeat the pattern established by her elopement with Lewes twenty-five years earlier. Facing misunderstanding, social disapproval, and the fear that she would once again be caught in the act of betraying old loyalties for a new connection, she responded with the same instinct for secrecy and flight.

Although Cross was twenty years younger than the famous writer, the marriage had a certain emotional and practical logic. During the 1870s the whole of the large Cross family, with John's widowed mother Anna Cross at its head, were family friends of the Leweses, who spent some Christmases at the Cross house in Weybridge. John, a banker, handled the substantial Lewes investments, knew a good deal about their affairs and visited frequently. Marian had developed the affectionate habit of calling him "Nephew Johnnie." Anna Cross died just a few days after George Henry Lewes; when John and Marian met again they were both in mourning. Although there has always been a wide field for speculation about the conscious and unconscious motives for marriage on both sides, one thing is clear. After years of excommunication from the Evans clan, Marian wished before her death to be a legal part of a respectable family, including a husband who could serve as the executor of her estate and the trusted overseer of her literary remains. The costs of her decision to live with Lewes may be measured by the need for this alliance. As if on cue, her brother Isaac Evans completed her unfinished business, responding to her marriage announcement by sending her a personal note of congratulation.

Only a few months went by before Isaac Evans came to pay his last respects to his brilliant and troubling sister by attending her funeral. The marriage celebrated in May ended in December with George Eliot's death. In the intervening months she was not the only one of the pair to require nursing: during the honeymoon in Venice John Cross had made a sudden leap from the balcony of their hotel to the canal beneath, and much of the marriage journey had been taken up with his recovery. Whether he suffered from mania, depressive illness, or other explanatory conditions is unknown; in any case Marian's share of anxiety was not destined to be mitigated by her young spouse. Once they had returned in July, the pain and weakness caused by her own illness dominated their lives until the end.

John Cross did not marry again. He carried out his role as the guardian of George Eliot's respectability by publishing in 1885 *George Eliot's Life as Related in Her Letters and Journals*, a three-volume narrative collage in which excerpts from her letters and journals were woven together with connective tissue that he supplied. In his effort to present George Eliot as an impeccable Victorian icon, Cross foregrounded her reverential and pious voices and cut out all the passages which displayed the satirical, witty, irreverent, and sexual being of Marian Evans. By the end of the century, the monumental figure he had created was no longer in fashion, and the literary reputation of George Eliot went temporarily into decline.

The contemporary George Eliot lover may enjoy a concrete experience of the writer's always contested social and legal identities by paying a visit to another monument, the large granite one which marks her gravesite in London's Highgate cemetery. Rising next to the modest stone on the grave of George Henry Lewes, this shiny tower reads:

Here Lies the Body
of
"George Eliot"
Mary Ann Cross
Born 22 November 1819
Died 22 December 1880

NOTES

1 It is interesting to observe this process at work in the journals of George Eliot's trips abroad. She would keep a semi-daily diary, but often wrote up the journey later as a retrospective narrative that was far more detailed and voiced than anything one could expect from the diary entries.

2 Edith J. Simcox, *Autobiography of a Shirtmaker*. ed. Constance M. Fulmer and Margaret E. Barfield (New York and London: Garland Press, 1998).

3

JOSEPHINE MCDONAGH

The early novels

George Eliot began her career as a novelist in a frenzy of activity, producing from the start works of exceptional quality for a novice. After the initial publication in serial form in *Blackwood's Edinburgh Magazine* of the three stories that would make up *Scenes of Clerical Life* in 1857, her first works of fiction were published at the rate of almost one a year: *Scenes of Clerical Life* (1858), *Adam Bede* (1859), *The Mill on the Floss* (1860), *Silas Marner* (1861), *Romola* (published serially in *Cornhill Magazine* from July 1862, and in three volumes by Smith, Elder, in 1863). In addition, she also published her novella, "The Lifted Veil," in *Blackwood's* in 1859, and wrote a second novella, "Brother Jacob," in 1860, although this was not published until 1864. While the rate of production in what we might think of as the second part of this career was certainly intense (six works of fiction and poetry over thirteen years), in comparison with the first it seems almost leisurely. Just five years into the novelist's career, then, the critic Richard Simpson was already in a position to write a retrospective review. In this, Simpson conveys the impact George Eliot's fiction had made on the reading public when it first appeared: "Readers who in 1858 took up the *Scenes of Clerical Life* . . . with the languid expectancy with which the first writings of new novelists are received, were astonished that, instead of an author, they had found a man" (*CH*, 221). The quality that so impressed, according to Simpson, was George Eliot's ability in her fiction to summon the sense of a human encounter. Notwithstanding the jarring reference to George Eliot "the man" in the context of a review that otherwise refers to her in the feminine, Simpson describes the way in which the author rose from the work as a living person: the world "he" created seemed real and believable, apparently unmediated by literary convention, and "his" judgments embued with human sympathy and love. In George Eliot's work, one entered a world so skillfully and lovingly forged that, paradoxically, it appeared natural and uncontrived.

The precocious accomplishment in the early works is partly explained by the fact that George Eliot came to fiction writing at a relatively late age. She began work on "The Sad Fortunes of the Reverend Amos Barton," the first of the *Scenes*, when she was almost thirty-seven, after a long apprenticeship as a translator of philosophical works, a reviewer of almost anything, and an editor for the *Westminster Review*. She was also an avid reader of fiction as well as of poetry, drama, philosophy, theology, and science, and had been all her life. Thus, her first "experiment" in fiction, as she styled it herself, was hardly the work of an inexperienced amateur, unacquainted with the intricacies of literary device. Nevertheless, in a journal entry called "How I Came to Write Fiction," she dramatized her entry into fiction as the opening of a new phase, "a new era in my life," not work for which she had spent years of practice and preparation (*Journals*, 289). However, while George Eliot clearly believed that the beginning of her novelistic career marked a "new era," there is no supporting evidence within her private commentaries to suggest she felt at any stage that she had passed from an "early" to a "late" phase in her own development. Although there is an unusual gap of three years between the publication in book form of *Romola* and her new work, *Felix Holt* (1866), she does not identify this as the beginning of a new phase of writing, or a new project. Indeed, the continuity in her style and her themes and preoccupations – even locations and character types – across the body of her works is so strong that a division into "early" and "late" seems in many ways a false or artificial classification. As many commentators have noticed, her characters resemble each other: Adam Bede is like Felix Holt and Daniel Deronda; Dinah Morris and Romola resemble Dorothea Brooke; as, in a different way, do Hetty Sorel and Bertha in "The Lifted Veil" resemble Rosamond Vincy and Gwendolen Harleth. Similar themes occur across the body of the work, such as, for instance, the conflict of passion and duty, and of free will and determinism, or the problems of egoism and virtues of sympathy. These are often presented in motifs – for example, gambling or blindness – which recur similarly across the body of the work, and in a style that remains thoroughly committed to a realist aesthetic.

Nevertheless, by the 1880s, critics were confidently invoking the categories of the "early" and "late" works. Leslie Stephen encapsulated the tone of much criticism when he wrote in 1881 that "[t]here is no danger of arousing any controversy in saying that the works of her first period . . . have the unmistakable mark of high genius" (*CH*, 468–69) – a genius that was felt to have waned as George Eliot entered her later period. For Stephen, the "early works" encompassed *Scenes of Clerical Life*, *Adam Bede*, *The Mill on the Floss*, and *Silas Marner*. Other critics have included *Romola* in the category, as well as "The Lifted Veil," although in many ways this idiosyncratic tale holds more in common with the late novels, especially *Daniel Deronda*

(1876). Whichever works are included, the distinction has tended to rest not so much on the stories that were told or the issues that were dealt with in the fiction, as on the world that was depicted within them – the environment of the novels. In the early works, George Eliot described "the quiet English country life" (*CH*, 469) of a former age, drawing on her childhood memories and knowledge of local customs and folklore. The fact that this was a way of life that, by the 1880s, was considered to have been lost was crucial to this evaluation: for many, George Eliot's achievement was that of a historian who had placed on public record memories of a disappearing way of life. "Its last traces are vanishing so rapidly amidst the change of modern revolution," wrote Stephens, "that its picture could hardly be drawn again" (*CH*, 469). But their impact was stronger than merely that of an archive. In the changing world of imperial Britain of the late nineteenth century, George Eliot's early novels stood as a corrective to the contemporary experience of migration, urbanization, and technological change; her visions of organic, village life, in Shepperton, Hayslope, or Raveloe, where, as one critic put it, the characters were joined to their environment by "vital threads that will not bear disruption" (*CH*, 187), presented an idealized social order and way of life, and, at the same time, a memorial to a unified national past.

By contrast, the later novels, which dealt with the 1832 Reform Bill, the "Woman Question," and the Jewish question, analyzed the ways in which communities were divided by competing claims of classes and professions, of genders and races, and admitted greater complexity and diversity of interest even within English society. This judgment was endorsed by the publication in 1885 of John Cross's *George Eliot's Life*. Cross emphasized George Eliot's early life in the Midlands, her attachment to particular rural localities, and her strong Christian faith as a girl. Despite the fact that she did not begin to write fiction until she was firmly ensconced in her life as an urban intellectual, living with a married man and cut off from her family, the early works were felt to reflect this earlier, more respectable and socially conventional period of her life. The late works, on the other hand, were considered tarnished by an overly intellectual approach and the ambience of moral decline in which they were composed. The late works had replaced feeling with philosophy, emotion with abstraction. Most of all, they told stories of complex, changing societies, and seemed to have abandoned the earlier attempt to summon rural idylls from the past.

This late-Victorian assessment responded to a nostalgic spirit that is certainly evident in the early novels. Despite George Eliot's avowed intent to document country life without any romanticization – as she puts it in her famous narratorial intervention in chapter 17 of *Adam Bede*, "to give no more than a faithful account of men and things as they have mirrored themselves in my mind" (17:175) – nevertheless the scenes she describes are frequently green and sun-drenched. Daily life is represented against the backdrop of picturesque landscapes, and is organized around communal celebrations, festivals and parties: take, for example, the harvest supper at the end of *Adam Bede*, peopled by an array of bucolic characters – the shepherd, the thresher, the waggoner – who hitherto had been nothing but shady background figures; or the evening sessions at the Rainbow inn in *Silas Marner*, or the New Year's party at the Squire's house, where the entertainment is provided by a band of local musicians, playing traditional songs on traditional instruments – fiddles and bassoons. These tunes, we are told pointedly, hold memories especially for the older members of the group: the Squire's "fav'rite" is "The flaxen-headed ploughboy," and Mr. Lammeter's is "Over the hills and far away." Lammeter comments, "My father used to say to me, whenever we heard that tune, 'Ah, lad, I come from over the hills and far away'"(11:99), showing, in passing, how migrants of the past have been incorporated into the community by folk memory; just as Silas, a more recent arrival from "far away," will be incorporated too.

The emphasis is always on local traditions and customary knowledge, passed on from generation to generation. Contemporary responses to *Adam Bede*, for instance, strikingly select for special appreciation the character of Mrs. Poyser, who plays little part in the main action of the novel. Her colorful brand of homespun wisdom and proverbial wit was felt to capture a mode of thinking representative of the rural past – practical common sense, as opposed to abstract or theoretical modern thinking. As Raymond Williams has pointed out, this folk wisdom is voiced by the rural people, not as individuals, but usually as a collective voice – "what middle-class critics still foolishly call a kind of chorus, a 'ballad-element'"[1] – which denies them the possibility of articulating ideas and developing a "higher consciousness." This is in sharp distinction to the central protagonists, like Adam and Dinah, or Maggie and Tom, who not only have individual personalities, but who grow and develop psychologically, and also advance economically. As Williams observes, the difference is often made evident in the speech patterns of the characters. The rural characters are given strong local dialects in which they voice simply constructed thoughts; on the other hand, even when they belong to the same communities, the main protagonists increasingly slip into standard English, in which they articulate complex ideas and distinctive individual opinions. As we shall see, the early novels tend to produce a split between this bucolic background of local and customary knowledge and habit, and, on the other hand, a world in which individuals have psychological complexity and are capable of economic and social progression. This division or fissure is an important feature of the early novels, but it is one that tends to be concealed under the heavy pastoral surfaces of the texts.

This brings us to a useful distinction between the early and late works. Unlike the late works, which are noted for their complexity and coherence as intellectual inquiries, the early works tend to have a much less highly-wrought and finished quality to them. Indeed, in terms of their presentation of ideas, the early works often appear to be contradictory and incoherent, divided in ways that we have noted above. Moreover, while in the late novels, the philosophical or theoretical aspects of the work are always rendered in part through strikingly intricate patterns of imagery, in the early works, imagery is used in a much more random and provisional way. Edith Simcox brilliantly captured the effect of reading *Middlemarch* as being like the uncanny experience of a child encountering a "live automaton toy," so complete and integrated is the world therein (*CH*, 324). By contrast, the early novels – flawed, incoherent, partial in their rendering of abstract ideas – seem less machine-like, more "human." In this light, Richard Simpson's observation back in 1863 seems particularly insightful. But while for Simpson and others, this lack of system within the early novels contributes to their pleasant sense of intimacy, for others, it has been the cause of suspicion and the focus of critique. Critics on the left, such as Raymond Williams and Terry Eagleton in particular, have found the early novels, much more than the late works, to be guilty of a kind of ideological subterfuge: that is, they present a vision of rural England as natural and harmonious, but which in reality disguises all manner of class conflicts and interests.[2] Paradoxically, it is the early novels' failure to present abstract ideas in a systematic or coherent way that, in this account, constitutes their ideological work; that is, the way in which Eliot's beliefs about society – her politics – masquerade as the operations of nature.

One place in which this "subterfuge" can be observed is in the varied ways in which time is represented. On the one hand, as has been noted, the novels present a strong sense of nostalgia for a romanticized past. The pastoral world is always framed by a retrospective narrative voice, and this endorses the sense of nostalgia to which Victorian critics responded so favorably. The act of remembering is dramatized in the narrative, and so too is an inevitable process of comparison between past and present. The early novels are deliberately located before events of national significance, which are frequently identified as pieces of legislation that are held to have shaped modern society. "Amos Barton" is set before the New Poor Law of 1834, for instance, legislation that crucially altered modes of charitable giving and reformulated relations between rich and poor. The main events of *Adam Bede* are set precisely between 1799 and 1801, prior to the repeal of the notoriously harsh 1624 Act to Prevent the Murder of Infant Bastards in 1803, one of the pieces of statute law that the penal reformers of the late eighteenth and early nineteenth centuries held up as symbolic of the cruel and inefficient legal system of the past. Less precisely, *Silas Marner* is set in Raveloe, before the advent of "public opinion" (ch.1, p.5). "Public opinion" invokes a distinctively modern form of public life, that had been shaped by the views and attitudes of a middle-class, professional public, disseminated through a national press and other forms of publishing. From the eighteenth century onward, this idea of "public opinion" was held up as the characteristic mark of modern society, in sharp contrast with traditional society, characterized by its adherence to local and customary knowledge. By situating the events in this way, the narratives give the impression that they tell stories of the world before it took on its specifically modern characteristics. They imply a chronology not of gradual change, staged over time, but one in which there is a distinct break between an old and permanent world, and a new and changing one. The distinction between the past and a modern society is often evident in the way in which time itself is conceptualized. In *Adam Bede*, for instance, we enter a world in which time is regulated by the natural cycles of the day and the seasons – even of the body. Adam complains at the beginning of the novel that his coworkers are clock-watchers, who throw down their tools "the minute the clock begins to strike," as opposed to himself, whose work is "pleasure," unregulated by time or money (1:11). In another way, the narrative appears driven by what we might think of as natural or bodily time. The second part of the novel covertly maps the period of Hetty's pregnancy alongside the changes in climate and vegetation of the seasons: her mounting distress, and her eventual flight from Hayslope, as the months proceed from Arthur's birthday party in July, to August, when Arthur leaves, through the autumn and winter, and into early spring, when the baby is born. When she decides to leave Hayslope it is a bright February day, when "the slight hoar-frost that had whitened the hedges in the early morning had disappeared as the sun mounted the cloudless sky" (35:363). Decisive moments in the text are always recounted against a background of naturalistic detail. George Eliot went to great lengths to ensure an accurate record of the natural world in *Adam Bede*: she assiduously researched the minutiae of the weather and local flora and fauna through reading the *Gentleman's Magazine* for the period covered by the novel, and furthermore, as Jill Matus has reminded us, her account of Hetty's pregnancy was considered at the time of publication so full of biological details that it constituted an affront to public decency.[3] This attention to detail gives solidity to her representation of the past: it is rooted in nature, regulated by its very physical forms. The world of the past is thus represented as though it belongs to a different order of time: natural or mythic time, shaped before the onset of chronological, regulated, and commodified time: the time of modernity.

But this is only part of the story. Against this sense that the old world is separated from the modern world by an unbridgeable division, a crucial part of the project of the early novels is in fact to chart a shift from the old to the new, but also to show how modern society can, ideally, be infused with the values of the old. The shift from old to new is usually presented as a progression, and tends to be underwritten by ideas of gradual change, growth, or evolution. In *Adam Bede* the sense of the steady progression of time, and thus of continuity, is inescapable: chapters often begin with references to the date and time: chapter 1 begins in the afternoon of "the eighteenth of June, in the year of our Lord 1799" (5); by chapter 2, it is "[a]bout a quarter to seven"(14); by chapter 3, "less than an hour" later (33); chapter 5 begins "[b]efore twelve o'clock" (54) the following morning, and so on. The clock ticks throughout like a time bomb: tension mounts, a crisis looms. The crisis, of course, is Hetty's murder of her child, but tragic though that event is, it nevertheless precipitates the formation of a new society represented by the marriage of Dinah and Adam. This new society has the characteristics of modern, bourgeois society: Adam has progressed from wage-earning carpenter to self-employed businessman, and Dinah too has changed her role, from Methodist preacher to wife and mother, a version of "the angel in the house," that much-discussed ideal of Victorian womanhood and stalwart feature of domestic ideology. In the course of the novel, the landed gentry has, in a sense, withered away: Arthur's grandfather and his child significantly die within a chapter of each other. Arthur's seduction of Hetty, a typical story of interclass exploitation, is offset by a relationship of social (and moral) equals in Adam and Dinah. The end of the novel presents a world in which individual endeavor has been rewarded economically; social positions are shown to be open to change; moral authority has been severed from social class; and relationships between classes, although they continue to be deferential, are nevertheless not subservient.

The difference between the two societies is strikingly presented in terms of a distinction between animal and human forms of life, underlying which is a vague, evolutionist idea that a shift from species to species might take place. A whole menagerie of animals is invoked to describe the behavior of uneducated characters of low social class, morally degraded characters, or those in an impassioned, irrational state. Some of the animals are quite exotic: for instance, Mr. Poyser and his sons are compared with a family of elephants (18:186); Mr. Craig, the ridiculed gardener, speaks to others as "we" might speak to "Brazilian monkeys" (18:203); and Adam and Arthur fight like panthers (27:301). Others are more domestic: Hetty is endlessly described as a cat or a kitten, and Bartle Massey's dog provides a model of maternal affection that casts a dramatic shadow over the story: his dog, Vixen, with her puppies, is like "women with babbies . . . she's got no conscience – no conscience – it's all run to milk" (21:246). For the relentlessly misogynistic Massey, the difference between women and animals is so indeterminate that his "family" is literally a family of dogs, and his "bitch" is called "Vixen," as though to emphasize her bestial nature. Most tellingly, the workmen at Massey's night school are described as if they were "three rough animals . . . making humble efforts to learn how they might become human" (21:235). The last reference is important because it underlines a desired progression of human behavior and organization that is implicit in the novel: from animal to human, from barbarian to civilized man, from illiterate laborer to literate entrepreneur. Or from child murderer (like Hetty) to mother (like Dinah). Hetty cannot proceed beyond her animal-like existence, but Dinah, by contrast, is usually compared with a plant rather than a beast, and Adam is only animal-like when he succumbs to his passions. "Civilized" characters, like the Reverend Irvine, on the other hand, are never described in terms of animals. In the end, to be bourgeois is to be human, that is, not like an animal. The rebarbative social view that working people are like animals, who struggle to accede to higher forms of consciousness and take their place in "human" society, is one that is often found in George Eliot's work. This is despite the fact that her protagonists and heroes are often working men, like Adam, or later, Felix Holt, or, in a different mould, Silas Marner. Those particular characters are marked out from the generality by their superior physical strength, their moral virtues, their intelligence, or, in Marner's case, tragic experience.

LIBRARY, UNIVERSITY OF CHESTER

Over the course of the novel, then, a definite change is recorded, from an old, premodern, animal-like state, to a society that bears the characteristics of modernity and humanity. But the novel equivocates between representing this as a definite break between two distinct and incommensurable entities, as we have seen, and, alternatively, a gradual and natural progression. On the one hand, for instance, the courtroom in which Hetty is tried for the murder of her child, we are told, is "now [in the writing time of the novel] destroyed by fire" (43:430), a piece of detail that has no purpose except to emphasize the pastness of the events, that they took place in a world violently superseded. But on the other hand, the novel suggests that the two states can be traversed by individual endeavor and education, which is represented as a natural progression. Thus, in the very final scene of the novel, the epilogue, the sense of a natural growth or evolution is emphasized. It takes place "near the end of June, in 1807" ("Epilogue," 537) – almost eight years to the day since the novel began, as Adam and Dinah await the return of Arthur after a long absence. A quasi-Darwinian scenario is presented, in which individuals have struggled for survival, the strong flourishing as the physically weak decline. Arthur is a sick man, the feeble remnant of the old order. His deterioration after "the fever" (his "colour's changed, and he looks sadly" [538]) is starkly contrasted with the robust bodies of Adam and his family, whose ebullience and vigor is emphasized in every sentence: the "sturdy two-year old," Addy, rides on Seth's shoulders and "drum[s] his heels with promising force against uncle Seth's chest"; the little girl, Lisbeth, "clasp[s] her father's leg"; Dinah is "plumper, as thee'dst a right to be after seven year" (538–9). These strong, vital bodies are the people of the future; their ability to adapt has made them victors in the changing world. But the scene also exaggerates a sense of continuity between past and present: the children are named after Adam, their father, and Lisbeth, their grandmother; Dinah watches for Adam in the same way that Lisbeth had done at the beginning of the novel ("Thee't like poor mother used to be," says Seth); and Arthur "smiles . . . as he did when he was a lad" – he has "alter'd and yet not alter'd" (538). The new society, we may be confident, will maintain the best characteristics of the old while having shed the worst. And to signal this amalgamation of values, Dinah consults a watch that had been a gift from Arthur: in the new society, natural time of the body and the seasons is drawn together with clock time of modern, regulated society.

The representation of time in *Adam Bede* is complex and confusing, partly because these alternative notions of time are presented in a contradictory series of relationships with each other: they are at once mutually exclusive and part of a process, an evolution. While some readers feel that the epilogue, with its figures of amalgamation of the past and the future, presents a satisfactory resolution to this contradiction, others hold this to be nothing more than an attempt to paper over a lacuna that cannot be ignored. For the latter, the figures of amalgamation are seen as unsuccessful attempts to persuade us that the bourgeois subject (in this case, Adam), whose development has been charted in the novel, remains rooted in his traditional society, his local community, when in reality the novel has insisted on his irretrievable separation. Which ever way one chooses to read the ending of the novel, one effect of the existence of these complex varieties of time is to give the world of the novel a dreamlike quality: in dreams, conflicting wishes and desires characteristically rest beside each other, just as they do in the early novels. This dreamlike quality, which is evident in all the early novels, helps to explain not only the appeal of these works, but also the kind of representation of the past that they deliver. Like a dream, they seem to represent a fantasy of the past – a wish or a desire. And the popularity of the works for contemporary readers suggests that the fantasies were widely shared. Rather than an objective record of the historical past, therefore, the early novels are best understood as a fabric of desires, a distilling of contemporary dreams of the past and for the present.

This sense that we are entering a dreamworld is presented most strongly in *The Mill on the Floss*. In the opening chapter the narrator quite literally introduces the action of the novel as though the events were remembered in a dream. This device gives a special, almost supernatural, quality to the events of the plot. The dominating image is of the river, "the broadening Floss [which] hurries on between its green banks to the sea, and the loving tide, rushing to meet it, checks its passage with an impetuous embrace" (1:7). As in a dream, the river takes on a personality; later in the novel it is associated with a destructive pagan god, but here its character seems to be of a more domestic kind, and to function as an analogue for the central characters that we have yet to meet – Maggie's impetuous affection, always in conflict with her brother Tom, and her family. This anthropomorphizing process is intensified. Later in the same paragraph, we are introduced to a tributary of the river, the Ripple, also like Maggie, "with its dark, changing wavelets! It seems to me like a living companion while I wander along the bank and listen to its low placid voice, as to the voice of one who is deaf and loving". In a process of doubling, natural features are seen to behave like people, and people, by extension, like nature. This doubling is crucial to the way in which the events of the novel are explained. As in a dream, human agency is lost to forces beyond its control. In this case, these forces are those of nature – the river. Throughout the novel, the river is not just a convenient backdrop to the action. In crucial ways, it is shown to be the determining impulse, subsuming historical forces into its all-encompassing domain. It shapes the landscape but also the community that has grown up around it; it is also integrated with the scientific and technological forces of progress that drive historical change (it is the irrigation scheme that ultimately will destroy Tulliver's business). The river also has the power to destroy that which it has allowed to develop – as we see in the final tragedy of the flood. The opening of *Felix Holt* makes a useful contrast with this. As in *The Mill on the Floss*, this later novel opens with an account of a landscape, recounted from a retrospective point of view. But while in *The Mill on the Floss* the impression is given of a world in which natural forces are always determining, aspects of the landscape exerting their ineluctable control over the form of human life, *Felix Holt* presents a landscape that itself is shaped by political, technological, and social forces. Following a coach journey across England, we pass "meadows with their long lines of bushy willows . . . golden cornricks . . . full-uddered cows," then the "dingy" windows of laborers' cottages, past "big, bold, gin-breathing Protestant tramps," and then into the manufacturing district: "land . . . blackened with coalpits, the rattle of handlooms to be heard in hamlets and villages . . . powerful men walking queerly with knees bent out from squatting in the mine . . . the pale eager faces of handloom-weavers" ("Introduction," 5–7). Here the very landscape and the people who inhabit it – nature itself – have been shaped by historical forces – agriculture, industry, technology, religion, the (unequal) distribution of wealth; not, as in *The Mill on the Floss*, a landscape that shapes those factors itself.

Another distinction that we could make between the early and late works, then, is that the early works assume a different relationship between societies and historical processes. Critics such as U. C. Knoepflmacher, in his influential monograph *George Eliot's Early Novels* (1968), have suggested that the early works are "pastoral" works, unconcerned with the "historical life of men."[4] In the early works , the social arena appears to slip further and further into a dissociated world of dreams, myth, and fantasy: take for example, the strange, fairy-tale quality in *Silas Marner*; and the distant, faraway world of fifteenth-century Florence in *Romola*. In the latter case, paradoxically George Eliot's work that most conforms to the genre of the historical novel, the general air of dissociation is typified by the dreamlike sequence, in which Romola drifts down the river on a boat, and comes upon a plague-infested colony of Jews, escaping the Spanish Inquisition. Despite George Eliot's punctilious attention to historical detail, there is a sense in which the early novels present a social world detached from the grand narratives of history. But this emphasis on the fairy-tale-like quality of the early novels – which in any case is equally evident in the later works, for example, in *Felix Holt* and *Daniel Deronda* – is at the expense of recognizing the precise form of historical engagement that is evident in all George Eliot's work.

The nature of this engagement is usefully illustrated by the following passage from the second of the *Scenes of Clerical Life*, "Mr. Gilfil's Love-Story." Chapter 3 opens with the following scene-setting observation:

> The last chapter has given the discerning reader sufficient insight into the state of things at Cheverel Manor in the summer of 1788. In that summer, we know, the great nation of France was agitated by conflicting thoughts and passions, which were but the beginning of sorrows. And in our Caterina's little breast, too, there were terrible struggles. The poor bird was beginning to flutter and vainly dash its soft breast against the hard iron bars of the inevitable, and we see too plainly the danger, if that anguish should go on heightening instead of being allayed, that the palpitating heart may be fatally bruised. (3:89)

The reference to the French Revolution locates the action in historical terms: "Mr. Gilfil's Love-Story" takes place in the context of the momentous events that are about to change for ever the political face of Europe. However, rather than plot the action alongside a historical narrative, the text serves to distance events of the story from those of world history. As soon as we hear that "little" Caterina, the diminutive Italian orphan, is like France on the brink of the revolution, we begin to suspect that there is irony at work. In fact the narrative oscillates between allowing a comparison between Caterina and the Revolution to rest, and undercutting it. This technique is typical of George Eliot's style, especially in the early works: she affects a precision that sometimes seems more like prevarication, or at least an attempt to have things both ways. For instance, we are told that Caterina's father had been a copier of music manuscripts, like Jean-Jacques Rousseau, the philosopher whose work was considered to have had a huge impact on the revolutionary impulses of the time. In fact the passage reads, "Those were the days . . . when many a man who resembled Jean-Jacques in nothing else, resembled him in getting a livelihood 'à copier la musique à tant la page'" (3:90). The association is planted, but then withdrawn. More substantially, the comparison between Caterina and the Revolution seems apt in that she has fallen in love with Captain Wybrow, the English gentleman who will inherit the estate from the couple who have adopted her: the expectation is that she will marry Wybrow, inherit the property of the family who intended merely to bring her up to some subservient position, and thus upset the established order. At this stage, we are encouraged to believe that a cataclysmic disruption of tradition will occur, something like the French Revolution, provoked by Caterina; and that the story of little Caterina will present an allegory of the kinds of historical change brought about by the Revolution. However, as it turns out, Caterina is less like a catalyst of revolution than a "poor bird . . . vainly dash[ing] its soft breast against the hard iron bars of the inevitable." Wybrow will not marry her: he reasons on the basis of tradition and inheritance that marriage to the orphan girl is ruled out by her low status – what he calls his "hard fate" (2:87). As an agent of historical change, Caterina is rendered powerless. At the climax of the story, she goes to stab her seducer to death, but in fact finds that she is too late, and that he has already died of a heart attack. (This is a motif to which Eliot returns, especially in the late works: in *Daniel Deronda*, for instance.) The high point of the story is thus neither tragic nor triumphant, but bathetic: it is not possible for Caterina to make her mark on history, because nature, in a sense, has trumped her. Caterina marries Gilfil, but dies shortly afterwards, still pining for her first love, Wybrow. In turn, Gilfil spends the rest of his life mourning her loss.

Thus Caterina, in the end, does not bring about a change of any kind, and in fact the story seems to depict a world that is purposefully detached from historical change. In this fictional world, events follow a "natural" course – people die of heart attacks, not murders, and by the same count, marriages will occur between people of the appropriate class, and the social order will not be disrupted. The story ends as it begins, with the parishioners of Shepperton mourning the loss of a kindly clergyman, whose long presence in the village marked a period of unusual calm and stability. The final image of Mr. Gilfil is as an oak tree, a "poor lopped oak," but one that had "been sketched out by nature as a noble tree. The heart of him was sound, the grain was of the finest, and in the grey-haired man . . . there was the main trunk of the same brave, faithful, tender nature that had poured out the finest, freshest forces of its life-current in a first and only love – the love of Tina" ("Epilogue," 166). This extended simile recalls Edmund Burke's influential work of conservative ideology, *Reflections on the Revolution in France*, published in 1790, a work shot through with similar kinds of imagery – oak trees and cattle, in particular – to represent the solidity of a system of hereditary power and influence in England, in comparison with the quixotic effects of revolution on the French political system. According to Burke, the French revolutionaries were like grasshoppers, chattering in a field, whose noise was deafening, but whose impact would be negligible. The implicit linking of Caterina to France in the passage cited above is thus doubly significant, for it underlines a Burkean narrative. Distinct from Caterina, the birdlike (or insect-like) European, and her vain attempts to avenge her lover and a social system that patronizes her, Mr. Gilfil comes to embody stability and the unchanging social and political order of England.

This semi-detachment from the historical process is important to a Burkean narrative that asserts the indelible rights of inherited power and wealth. To a degree, this narrative is evident in all the early fiction, lying behind the fantasies of pastoral England that they spin. However, its presence is never uncomplicated, making it difficult in the final count to reduce these texts to Burkean fables. As ever, the texts eschew reduction to a theory or an idea. In "Mr. Gilfil's Love-Story," the sense of detachment from historical change is internalized in the character of Mr. Gilfil. Mr. Gilfil is an oak tree, but he is a "poor lopped oak." His life is a tragedy, given over to mourning for a woman who did not love him, and who died when she was young. Burkean detachment from the world of historical change is figured as a physical dismemberment, which comes to represent emotional unfulfillment. This rather haunting sense of loss and loneliness is at the heart of the first of the *Scenes* too. In this case it is Amos Barton who is destined to a life of loneliness after the death of his wife – the sickly and insipid Milly. Barton's mourning is intensified by his realization that he has neglected her in life, distracted as he was by the competing attentions of a Polish countess, who, as it turns out, was neither Polish, nor exactly a countess (she had married a count, now deceased, who in fact had been a dancing master). The problems of the first two stories, however, are resolved by the third of the *Scenes*, "Janet's Repentance." This story is more typical of George Eliot's fiction, in that it enacts a process of social change, brought about through tolerance of differences in belief and background: the end of the story sees the successful constitution of a community, through the unlikely liaison between the evangelical minister, Tryan, and Janet Dempster, the alcoholic wife of a violent and bigoted lawyer. This is a story not only about Janet's repentance, but of Tryan's too. His life of ministry is an act of repentance for his seduction and ruin of a young girl in an earlier phase of his life. Janet and Tryan thus are drawn together in an economy of guilt and redemption, whereby one redeems the other through acts of mutual salvation. Unlike in the previous stories, Tryan's death is not tragic, but triumphant; Janet is not left to mourn, but, having been redeemed, able to constitute around her a new community. The final image of Janet is as a "noble-looking elderly woman" (in nobility, like Mr. Gilfil) surrounded by children: "Janet in her old age has children about her knees, and loving young arms round her neck" (28:301). But unlike Mr. Gilfil and Amos Barton, Milly and Caterina (who in any case, both end up dead), Janet is allowed the capacity to change the conditions of her existence – from childless victim to loving mother – to determine the course of her own life, and to nurture future generations.

This is the first of George Eliot's fictions in which she represents an ideal society through the idea of a consciously fabricated family, headed by a mother figure who is usually not a natural mother, but an adoptive or surrogate one like Janet or Romola, or even a man, like Silas Marner. (Even Adam Bede is attributed motherly qualities.) The ideal community is thus not exactly a family, but *like* a family. Many commentators have pointed out that this mirrored George Eliot's own experience. Although not a natural mother herself, she was nevertheless deeply invested in her role as stepmother to Lewes's sons, and "spiritual mother" to her young women acolytes, like Edith Simcox and Elma Stewart.[5] While this may suggest that her representation of the family is to be taken more literally than I suggest, within the fictions, the family usually functions in this broader, socially representative way. The ideal family, like the ideal society, is constituted on the basis of bonds of mutual love, and, specifically not unquestioned, hereditary duty. An issue that becomes increasingly prominent in her work is how to balance a proper respect for hereditary or familial duty with the desire to be a free and self-determining individual. This fundamentally domestic formulation comes to be the form in which George Eliot articulates the dilemma explored in all her work: that is, how to reconcile tradition with innovation, stability with change? From *The Mill on the Floss* onwards, this question of broader social and cultural relevance tends to be posed specifically in terms of a family drama, or – to adopt Freud's term for the psychological investments in imagining our families – a family romance.

In *The Mill on the Floss* the conflict of tradition and innovation is played out in the character of Maggie, who seems to be split irresolvably between a devotion to the past, and a desire for a different kind of future. These opposing impulses are made evident in aspects of her characterization. On the one hand, she has a very strong sense of duty to her family, and her father in particular; but on the other hand, she is rebellious and impulsive, most touchingly in childhood, as her nonconformity runs the gamut of eccentric behavior, from stabbing her wooden doll with pins to a precocious love of books. Such conflict is also apparent in her appearance: her physical appearance – wild, black hair (her "phiz" [I:5:33]), and her dark skin and eyes – marks both her family inheritance (her resemblance to relatives, especially Aunt Moss), but also her failure to conform. Her hair is notoriously uncontrollable, and her darkness makes her look like someone of a different race: her mother says she is like a "mulatter" (I:2:13) and her resemblance to gypsies is continually emphasized. "She's more like a gypsy nor ever," says Aunt Pullet; "it's very bad luck, sister, as the gell should be so brown . . . I doubt it'll stand in her way i'life to be so brown" (I:7:68). One of her childhood acts of rebellion is to run away to the gypsies – ironically, to teach them how to be "civilised" by imparting to them her knowledge acquired from books: "I can tell you something about Geography too – that's about the world we live in – very useful and interesting," she offers; and "it's in my Catechism of Geography" (I:11:109). Even at this early stage in her development, one has a sense that tradition and conformity will out. For the adult Maggie, her impulsive spirit emerges in the form of her transgressive romantic liaisons, first with Philip Wakem, the crippled son of her father's hated enemy; and secondly with Stephen Guest, her cousin's fiancé. In these cases, the conflict of tradition and innovation is transposed into a conflict of duty versus feeling or compassion, or in relation to Stephen, more strongly, duty versus passion. During her fated boat trip with Stephen, when both fall asleep and unwittingly spend a night together, Maggie rationalizes her dilemma in precisely these terms. As an argument as to why she cannot follow her own desire and marry Stephen, she poses, "if the past is not to bind us, where can duty lie?" (VII:4:475). In the end, she chooses "duty" over passion, her brother and family over her lover, the past over the future. Her renunciation, however, is rewarded only by death: she and Tom drown together on another boat journey, sucked back into the past to which she has pledged herself: "living through again in one supreme moment the days when they had clasped their little hands in love, and roamed the daisied fields together" (VII:4:521).

The Mill on the Floss appears to be a deeply pessimistic novel, intransigently opposed to the possibility of change and innovation. All hope of a liberalization of her family's draconian expectation of loyalty and conformity fades in the final regressive, womb-like image of the two children in an amniotic flood. While *Adam Bede* offered an amalgamation of tradition and innovation, *The Mill on the Floss* offers no such compromise. Maggie chooses family and tradition, and for this she dies. However, the novel's message is more complicated and less clear than this, for when we read closely it seems that tradition, things hereditary, and innovation are never exactly opposed to each other; rather Maggie inherits her innovative spirit from the very paternal source that is so unyielding to her own desires. Her resemblance to her father is clearest in her willfulness and cleverness, which he, too, is held (by family tradition, or customary knowledge) to have inherited from an ancestor: "Mr. Tulliver's grandfather had been heard to say that he was descended from one Ralph Tulliver, a wonderfully clever fellow, who had ruined himself" (IV:1:274). In a paradoxical way, it is suggested that for the Tullivers, innovation constitutes tradition, although of course this does not square with Mr. Tulliver's stubborn conservatism, his refusal to comply with new technologies that threaten his mill, his litigiousness, which for George Eliot is always a sign of atavism.[6] Similarly, Maggie's impulsive rebellions are often her most conforming and consoling acts – like the episode with the gypsies, when she becomes a kind of missionary herself. Or when she cuts off her hair in childish rage, fulfilling Tulliver's "rash" paternal command, made earlier to her mother to "Cut it off – cut it off short" (I:2:13). The novel cannot be read as opting for tradition over innovation, because the two are imbricated within each other.

Many critics have noted that Maggie's dilemma bears a strong resemblance to that of Antigone, Sophocles' heroine who so fascinated George Eliot. In her essay, "The Antigone and its Moral" (1856), she explains that the basis of Antigone's tragedy is the "dramatic collision" of principles of *equal* validity; not the triumph of one set of principles over the other. Thus Antigone, who persists in carrying out funeral rites on her dead brother, despite Creon's edict, acts on "the impulse of sisterly piety which allies itself with reverence for the Gods," and this "clashes with the duties of citizenship; two principles, both having their validity, are at war with each other" (Pinney, p. 244). Clearly Maggie shares Antigone's strong-minded, rebellious spirit, and her "sisterly piety," and she too is torn by opposing principles "at war with each other." But when we consider Maggie's case, she seems to be divided by principles of a very different kind to those exerting their contrary influence on Antigone. For opposing Maggie's version of "sisterly piety" and "reverence for the Gods" – which for her is a "reverence" for family, ancestry, and paternal law – are not the "duties of citizenship" as for Antigone, but rather other forms of feeling, or in George Eliot's vocabulary, varieties of sympathy: her compassion for Philip Wakem, and her passion for Stephen Guest. Although in the context of St. Ogg's, these are socially radical forms of feeling, nevertheless, this is a very different principle to the "duties of citizenship," as in Antigone's case. Indeed, Maggie's dilemma appears to be reducible to a conflict not of laws or duties, but of feelings, and, indeed, feelings for opposing men: the father and the brother, versus the friend and the lover. Moreover, despite her conspicuous intellectualism throughout, Maggie's choice is made not on the basis of reason and logic, but is led by feeling itself: she makes a decision of which "she was not conscious," and her separation from Stephen is described as "an automatic action that fulfils a forgotten intention" (VI:14:479). In the end the novel appears to dramatize an emotional conflict, which focuses attention on questions of individual human development, rather than the broader social questions that are raised not only by the tragedy of Antigone, but – even more centrally – George Eliot's other works of fiction.

The Mill on the Floss occupies the same imaginative terrain as the other works, that is, a world strained between opposing commitments to tradition and innovation. But the novel's focus on emotion and feeling puts a particular slant on the discussion. Not surprisingly, perhaps, *The Mill on the Floss* shows that the emotional attachment to the past is stronger than that to any imagined future. In contrast, the other novels, which are more interested in analyzing in a more dispassionate way the opposing forces of tradition and change on a society in transformation, display a stronger, although characteristically measured, commitment to innovation and progress. This has been seen in the conclusion to *Adam Bede*, but in subsequent works the idea of progress comes to be articulated through the idea of disinheritance: that is to say, the idea that an individual might choose *not* to inherit, to disavow the past. It is first used in *Silas Marner*, as Eppie chooses not to take up the life of privilege and wealth offered to her by her natural father, preferring instead to remain with her adoptive father, Silas, and the community to which she has grown accustomed; and is used again in *Felix Holt*, and in a different way, in *Middlemarch*, when Dorothea renounces her inheritance from Casaubon. The motif of disinheritance suggests that individuals are not passive recipients of tradition, but discerning participants in a process of reassessment and change. Specifically, it couches the idea of innovation in terms of a family romance, in a sense rewriting Maggie Tulliver's unfortunate history: unlike Maggie, Eppie and Esther are ostensibly able to renounce family duty and the ties of the past. But this of course is not the story that is presented. Eppie and Esther are tied to the bonds of family duty as much as Maggie. The difference is that in these texts, George Eliot has formulated an alternative notion of the family: the family formed on the basis of habitual love – the socially constructed family. This is in direct contrast to the idea of the natural family, the family based on ties of blood. Interestingly, the natural family is presented primarily as the means through which to convey material wealth: it is almost as though blood is equated with money. Thus when Eppie, and later Esther, choose to relinquish the fortunes offered to them by their blood families, they do so out of no less a commitment to duty to "past ties" than Maggie displayed. But for them, the alternative, surrogate family allows custom to be compatible with change, and fathers to be compatible with lovers. The blood family, in these works, is thrown up as the remnant of an ancient and intransigent order. In the late works, *The Spanish Gypsy* (1868) and *Daniel Deronda*, its potency will be reassessed, as blood comes to be associated with race, and is an important determining factor in a new episode of George Eliot's social investigations; but at this stage in her work, the ties of blood are posited as the ties of a crippling adhesion to the past.[7]

In a variety of ways, then, the early novels explore the transformation of traditional, pastoral societies into modern forms of social organization. While these are themes that preoccupy George Eliot throughout her writing career, the early novels tend to linger on the past in ways that make them seem more nostalgic and regretful of change than the later works. The early George Eliot has been praised as the custodian of old England, the treasurer of traditional, rural life. But not by everyone. Others have found that her commitment to the changing forms of society exerts an influence over the very substance of her fiction.

In the context of a series of essays published in the magazine, *Nineteenth Century*, between 1880 and 1881, John Ruskin picks out George Eliot for special criticism, as the "consumma[tion of] the English Cockney school," a writer of vulgar, popular fiction, a "common rail-road station novelist"(*CH*, 166–67). Ruskin's critique turns on a comparison between Scott and Eliot, the former representing for him the very best of English fiction. While Scott told stories of "lofty" characters in difficult circumstances, George Eliot instead presented "flawed" characters, whose "blotches, burrs and pimples" substitute for Scott's interest in plot. *The Mill on the Floss* is the "most striking instance extant of this study of cutaneous disease." According to Ruskin, George Eliot's characters are objectionable and self-absorbed (like Maggie), "clumsy and cruel" (like Tom), or else "the sweepings out of a Pentonville omnibus." The references to buses and trains in Ruskin's critique are telling.

Despite George Eliot's rural locations, for him, her fictional world is a modern one, characterized by the dislocated forms of social experience that are symbolized by new forms of public transportation, with their associations of social mixing and demographic uprootings. Among the generally approving voices on George Eliot at this time, then, Ruskin strikes an interestingly discordant note. He reminds us that her interest in changing societies had a necessary impact not only on the form of the novel, but on the shape of the characters that inhabit it. This is evident even in the early novels, and is an aspect of the work that continually disrupts their nostalgic spirit. Despite his negative assessment, then, Ruskin's account of George Eliot reveals a component of the early work that is often overlooked, but which needs to be taken into consideration in reaching an understanding both of her project, and its significance in the development of the novel in this period.

NOTES

1 Raymond Williams, "The Knowable Community in George Eliot's Novels," *Novel,* 2 (spring 1969). Reprinted in *George Eliot: Critical Assessments*, ed. Stuart Hutchinson, vol. II, *Twentieth-Century Perspectives, 1900–1970* (Mountfield, E. Sussex: Helm Information, 1996), pp. 292–306, at p. 295.

2 See, e.g., Terry Eagleton, *Criticism and Ideology* (London: Verso, 1976), and Raymond Williams, *The Country and the City* (Oxford and New York: Oxford University Press, 1973).

3 Jill L. Matus, *Unstable Bodies: Victorian Representations of Sexuality and Maternity* (Manchester: Manchester University Press, 1995), pp. 157–67.

4 See U. C. Knoepflmacher, *George Eliot's Early Novels: The Limits of Realism* (Berkeley: University of California Press, 1968).

5 For a compelling account of the ways in which George Eliot explored her own lived and imagined experiences of the family in her fiction, see Rosemarie Bodenheimer, "George Eliot's Stepsons," in *The Real Life of Mary Ann Evans* (Ithaca, N. Y.: Cornell University Press, 1994), pp. 189–233.

6 Cf. George Eliot, "The Natural History of German Life" (Pinney, pp. 266–99), in which she alludes to "the peasant's inveterate habit of litigation" (p.278).

7 In "The Lifted Veil," the blood transfusion at the end of the story associates blood with the revelation of a horrible truth – that the narrator's wife was killing him, thus dramatizing in a different way the crippling ties of blood.

4

ALEXANDER WELSH

The later novels

For twenty years from 1856 to 1876 George Eliot was actively engaged in writing novels. The last two, *Middlemarch* and *Daniel Deronda,* are generally acclaimed today as her greatest – they are certainly her longest. But is there a clear dividing line between the early and late work?

Rosemarie Bodenheimer has shown how habits of mind formed well before Mary Anne Evans became George Eliot persisted in her writings to the end; and David Carroll has argued persuasively that from start to last the novels were driven by practices of interpretation to which the young Marian Evans was exposed very early.[1] Telling changes in her life predated altogether her career as a novelist: her loss of formal religious belief, the death of her father, her move to London and work for the *Westminster Review*, the elopement with George Henry Lewes and return to live openly with him in England, even the turn to writing fiction itself. Characteristically she made her most daring decisions without consulting anyone – not because she was secretive by nature but because she was determined to have her way. Secrecy in fact made things worse when it came to explaining to family and friends who had not been consulted. But the *fait accompli* became means to her ends. After Lewes died and less than a year before her own death, she consulted no one about marrying Johnnie Cross.

In defending her commitment to Lewes, Marian scornfully declared, "Women who are satisfied with [light and easily broken] ties do *not* act as I have done – they obtain what they desire and are still invited to dinner" (*GEL*, II:214). The sexual *fait accompli* thus rendered her image superior to that of (some) other women. George Eliot's positioning of herself as a novelist was similarly defiant. Once the power of her writing had been acclaimed, the unseemly behavior of the author would become seemly – accepted in gratitude if not with grace. After *The Mill on the Floss*, during the writing of which her private identity became known, she had a still stronger motive to impress the public with each successive production. Not all novelists improve upon themselves as they proceed; but however these things come about, George Eliot is among those like Dickens and Dostoevsky, and notably Henry James, who continued to experiment and produce undeniably impressive later work.

No wonder the writing of *Romola* (1863) proved so daunting – and readers often have as difficult a time with the first hundred pages as the author had in getting started. According to another "secret" plan shared only with Lewes at first, the novel would be set in Florence in the late fifteenth century (*GEL*, III:306, 339). So alien or so ambitious was the task that the author found herself stopping to write the far better known *Silas Marner* first; yet as a novelist to be reckoned with she now also deserted her publisher, John Blackwood, for a lucrative contract with the new *Cornhill Magazine*, where *Romola* would be serialized in 1862. The book did not prove to be the success her new publishers had hoped for. That George Eliot returned to Blackwood for her last three novels in itself suggests the pivotal role of *Romola* in the development of her art.

The awkwardness of some pages should not be allowed to detract from the importance of this novel as transitional or from the acuteness of its portrayal of mind. Strangely, despite the bookish historicity that makes *Romola* differ from other novels that George Eliot attempted, it is still closer than any other to being a repeat performance of a previous work – namely, *The Mill on the Floss*. Both heroines, Maggie Tulliver and Romola Bardi, are conceived above all to be loyal – loyal almost to a fault, though that can never be admitted. "If the past is not to bind us, where can duty lie?" This rhetorical question was Maggie's principal argument against marriage to Stephen Guest, and the past that binds them consists of "feelings and expectations we have raised in other minds" (*MF*, VI:14:475; 11:449). Whatever the temptation – and episodes of drifting off to sea frame the endings of both novels – Maggie and Romola do not turn their backs for long on family and friends, most particularly not on fathers and equivalent male relations. But Romola is endowed with longer life, richer opportunities, and far more guilt than her sister heroine.

The invention of Tito Melema, the young man who comes to lighten the heroine's days as secretary to her blind father, and later makes off with the man's library, redoubles the psychological interest of *Romola*. Henry James, in a provocative essay for the *Atlantic Monthly* in 1866, held Tito to be "the leading figure" of the book, partly because he is the one haunted by secrets. Leslie Stephen, in his book on George Eliot for the English Men of Letters series, more nastily suggested that the success of the character was due to his being "thoroughly and to his fingers' ends a woman"; and a number of twentieth-century critics have pointed to ways in which Tito may conceivably stand in *for* Romola, as a kind of double. Tito, it seems, has even more of a past than she. Twenty-six chapters pass before the reader is afforded much of an inside look at Romola, while we hear far more about the dreamlike doings of Tito. He too has a father – or stepfather, an older man who rescued him "from blows" when he was only seven and "a bright lovely boy" (9:96) – and this man, Baldassare, was a scholar like Romola's Bardo. But Tito had deserted his father, left him behind in dire circumstances, and is terrified of being found out. Then in the second book of the novel the reader suddenly learns that Bardo *was*, that is, has died, somewhat to the relief of Romola – but Baldassare, the most dreamlike character of all, mysteriously *is*, and is murderously bent upon avenging his desertion by Tito.

George Eliot refuses to give much of an idea of what it is like for Romola to be married to Tito. The marriage, from the heroine's point of view, is the series of discoveries about this husband, who is even more terrified of being exposed for his desertion of Baldassare than he is of the man's dagger. In conjunction with Tito's, Romola's case is a very thorough study of psychological guilt: she, after all, has not deserted her father except in wistful longings kept to herself and barely hinted to the reader. Tito, on the other hand, is a creature of shame, precisely what Romola would despise and refuse to be. His death, indeed, ought to free her of the immoral temptation to break with the past. Thus, in a strange way, Baldassare is on her side. Though the plot of *Romola* is more fantastic than that of *The Mill on the Floss*, there is no rescuing flood and life loses "its perfection." Maggie may school herself to preserve the bonds of the past, but Romola experiences a "recurring conflict where the many-twisted conditions of life have *forbidden* the fulfillment of a bond" (69:528; my emphasis). Her marriage, shadowy as it seems, anticipates the mismatches of Dorothea Brooke in *Middlemarch* and Gwendolen Harleth in *Daniel Deronda*.

Romola and its heroine also engage with the past as history. In *The Mill on the Floss*, a Wordsworthian sense of place gives the countryside a felt pastness; the social history of St. Ogg's is presented with loving and sometimes mischievous detail. Above all, the childhood of Maggie and her brother Tom is described almost as if it were an aspect of natural history – which had become both a pastime and serious study for the author and Lewes. But in *Romola* George Eliot set out deliberately to write a historical novel in the manner of Scott, easily the most influential novelist of her youth. Her protagonist, like the male heroes of Scott, would not only live out her own story but serve as witness to the historical events of her era. Among the actual historical characters in the book, Romola is most drawn to and critical of the reformer of church and morals, Girolamo Savonarola.

By allowing the reader to share the heroine's point of view, the novelist can present Savonarola and others in a live perspective, as it were. In deciding to place the action in Renaissance Florence, which fostered many of the most famous artists and poets, doers and thinkers, of Western history, George Eliot would seem to have accepted a more ambitious undertaking than that of any single novel by Scott. Most certainly, as Carroll has argued, there came together in Florence the two great traditions, classical and Christian, from which so many codes of interpretation in the West have been drawn, a mixture that was still potent in Victorian reactions to the Enlightenment. According to Felicia Bonaparte, George Eliot was writing a kind of "prospectus for the future progress of Western civilization."[2]

One does not need to allegorize the novel, as Bonaparte tends to, to see that the historical aggrandizing and distancing performed by *Romola* was all important to the novels still to be written. *Felix Holt* (1866), the slightest of these, has seemed to some a welcome retreat to better-known scenes between the Avon and the Trent, but it is also more specifically historical than the early fiction. It is set in a manufacturing town at the time of the Reform Bill of 1832, and written during the run up to the second Reform Bill of 1867. *Felix Holt* is a work of realism that owes as much to Scott as *Romola* does – one minor indication of this is the adoption, in all three remaining novels, of the chapter epigraphs, which was also Scott's practice. The protagonist is male this time, and he stands fastidiously aside from the partisans of the day, only to be inadvertently drawn into the fray by his effort to curb mob violence. Holt is arrested for manslaughter, and Esther Lyon publicly testifies on his behalf, much as the heroine testified in Elizabeth Gaskell's Scott-inspired *Mary Barton* of 1848. Esther's role is less central than Maggie's or Romola's. The writing of *Romola* seems to have exorcised the need to project a heroine's wishes upon characters like Tito and Baldassare, or even the historical Savonarola. With *Felix Holt* there will begin to be less displacement, more representation of social conditions, for "there is no private life which has not been determined by a wider public life" (3:43).

Reform was an incremental means of political change. Victorians understood for the most part that continuing extension of the franchise was all but inevitable after the passage of the first Reform Bill, the one that Holt is resisting in the novel. But George Eliot and he resist in the very spirit of reform itself; they want better education to precede extensions of the franchise. They distrust raw democracy without an informed public opinion. Holt has an overweening faith in public opinion. He calls it "the greatest power under heaven . . . the ruling belief in society about what is right and what is wrong, what is honourable and what is shameful. That's the steam that is to work the engines" (30:248). But public opinion must first be somehow contained and directed. That George Eliot concurred is evident from her character's subsequent "Address to Working Men," which appeared in *Blackwood's Magazine* the following year. John Stuart Mill and other liberals essentially shared this view, though Mill had recently written in *On Liberty* of the dangers to individual freedom inherent in the sway of public opinion.

George Eliot's novel also showed that the force of opinion could be two-edged. Holt is not far off when he indicates that public opinion tends to equate "what is wrong" with "what is shameful": politicians and others can sometimes be shamed into doing what is right. But individuals can also be coerced, by threatened publicity, in matters that are private; or they may be dissuaded from thinking and doing the right thing if public opinion is against them (hence still another need for educating public opinion itself). George Eliot's last three novels begin to regard very seriously what she herself protested as "entire knowingness" in others after the secret of her pseudonym failed her (*GEL*, III:164). In *Felix Holt* one begins to feel sorry for those poor people who have secrets to conceal, when still inferior characters treat the secrets as if they ought to be in the public domain, because they see advantage in so treating them. In this novel George Eliot also begins to stress how chancy it is that this or that private matter may become known.

In certain respects *Felix Holt* served as a preliminary exercise for the writing of *Middlemarch* (1871–72), George Eliot's most accomplished and deservedly famous work. Both novels are set in the time of the first Reform Bill, and the themes of public opinion and chance discovery are played out in *Middlemarch* in still more intricate and thoughtful ways. George Eliot's confidence in the telling, and in the relation of the narrator to her characters and readers, would prove stunning. Her brief "Introduction" to *Felix Holt* gives some idea of what to expect in *Middlemarch* as well:

> For there is seldom any wrong-doing which does not carry along with it some downfall of blindly-climbing hopes, some hard entail of suffering, some quickly-satiated desire that survives, with the life in death of old paralytic vice, to see itself cursed by its woeful progeny – some tragic mark of kinship, in the one brief life to the far-stretching life that went before, and to the life that is to come after, such as has raised the pity and terror of men ever since they began to discern between will and destiny. But these things are often unknown to the world; for there is much pain that is quite noiseless; and vibrations that make human agonies are often a mere whisper in the roar of hurrying existence.
>
> (11)

To the extent that these reflections concern *Felix Holt*, they would seem to apply to a moving but nevertheless peripheral character, Mrs. Transome. But they apply more widely in *Middlemarch*, and are indeed echoed in the famous passage of authorial reflection suggesting that "if we had a keen vision and feeling of all ordinary human life, it would be like hearing the grass grow and the squirrel's heart beat, and we should die of that roar which lies on the other side of silence" (20:192). The coachman Sampson, who is featured as a guide in the same introduction, "could tell the names of sites and persons, and explain the meaning of groups, as well as the shade of Virgil in a more memorable journey" (9). The allusion is to Virgil as a guide in the first third of Dante's *Divine Comedy*, and the writer alludes to Dante and Virgil again at the end of the introduction. Dante's modern epic (modern to him, Christian as well as classical) was the most lasting gift that George Eliot carried away from Florence, and Dante's acute sense of past and present, of personal achievement and moral being, and of sensitivity to fame can be felt in *Middlemarch* and *Daniel Deronda* both. These epics of modern life cost her what Dante in the first canto of the *Inferno* called the double strife of the journey and the pity.

The historicism of *Middlemarch* is diffuse, neither forced nor narrowly focused. It provides perspective – forty years have passed since the first Reform Bill – but George Eliot, after all, was as Mary Anne Evans a girl very much alive herself at that time. The treatment of politics is far more relaxed than in *Felix Holt*. Perhaps because of the intervening passage of the second Reform Bill, the author no longer takes a fixed political position. The most deliberately involved politician, the sixty-year-old Mr. Brooke, is something of a caricature; Will Ladislaw's election to Parliament, referred to in the finale, occurs well after the novel's main actions are completed. Instead, political history has given way to the history of medicine represented by Tertius Lydgate's career, to glimpses of the pursuit of natural history by Camden Farebrother and of mythologies by Edward Casaubon, and above all to the social history of Middlemarch and the surrounding area. The novel is subtitled *A Study of Provincial Life*. *Middlemarch* itself is a generic term meaning the middle borderland, a representative place but by no means a center of civilization. There is more commitment to the incipient study of sociology, with which the author was well acquainted both in German and English, than to history as usually told in books.

Therefore *Middlemarch* is very appropriately a multiplot novel. It seems not to have been conceived as such: George Eliot began writing separate stories and then fused them together.[3] The first chapter drafted with something like the final design in mind falls well after Miss Brooke has become Mrs. Casaubon and left for Rome: a chapter in which Lydgate, still new to Middlemarch, attends a meeting of the directors of the Infirmary. The reader already knows a good deal about Lydgate, most notably his intelligence and ambition, his enlightened clinical practices and his promise as a scientist. The purpose of this meeting, however, is to appoint a chaplain for the infirmary, a position that will draw a stipend. Lydgate regards the appointment as none of his business, is partially aware of the petty politics of the matter, and cannot decide how he will vote, even though the candidate who has been performing the duties without pay – Farebrother – has become a casual friend. George Eliot prepares the scene carefully, detailing Lydgate's state of mind and holding back dialogue until she can introduce the character of each of the participants. The climax she then delivers in a few sentences of direct discourse. The newcomer Lydgate is taunted by one of the other physicians, a Farebrother supporter, into voting for Tyke, who is chairman Bulstrode's candidate. The chapter fixes itself in the reader's mind, just as the episode becomes "a sore point" for Lydgate thereafter. What could be more endemic to modern life than committees? Even before the meeting is under way, "Lydgate was feeling the hampering, threadlike pressures of small social conditions and their frustrating complexity" (18:178).

"*Threadlike* pressures" are an instance of George Eliot's favorite metaphor for connectedness in *Middlemarch*: a kind of network of circumstances, opinion, and individual motives over time. But she does not neglect character. Lydgate's impulsive decision to marry Rosamond Vincy comes about in much the same way that he finds himself voting for Tyke. He despises what others may think and ends up doing what they expect of him. He feels himself detached from these Middlemarchers and is suddenly attached. Connectedness, as in *Felix Holt*, is not continuous but greatly depends on chance. Arguably, if modern society were not generally disconnected, connectedness would not draw us up so short. Lydgate and the banker Bulstrode are the truly modern inhabitants of the novel: like George Eliot in real life, they come from elsewhere. Their mobility – lateral and thereby upward – is the ordinary commercial, professional, and intellectual case of modern times. Dorothea Brooke, by contrast, is very old-fashioned – fashioned by her quixotic yearnings to be noble rather than mobile. Mary Garth and her family (for theirs is still another story in the multiplot novel) are steady as they are, solid as they seem, honest even to themselves. But the two plots of modern social connectedness, soon woven into one, are Lydgate's and Bulstrode's. Lydgate comes to Middlemarch to practice medicine and stumbles into the hampering net of connections; Bulstrode has arrived earlier, made it his business to study the connections, and now manipulates them to his advantage. He and Lydgate come to need one another. And observe that they are not friends. Each rather dislikes the other. Theirs is an intertwining of alien modern beings.

In short, Lydgate and Bulstrode have careers to make or break them. Oddly, the character most like Mrs. Transome of *Felix Holt*, with a secret in her past, is Bulstrode. Once again a blackmailer threatens to reveal the secret. But it is important to remember that Raffles, disreputable as he is (a kind of personification of scandal), is threatening to reveal a true story about Bulstrode, and the hold he has on his victim is public opinion: if the banker did not have to care what people think, Raffles would diminish to the nobody he seems. As the narrator generalizes from Bulstrode's quandary, "Who can know how much of his most inward life is made up of the thoughts he believes other men to have about him, until that fabric of opinion is threatened with ruin?" (68:677). Note the "fabric" of opinion that clothes us round. In the following paragraph Bulstrode feels a "scorching" from his neighbors that would strip the clothes from his nakedness. Earlier we hear that Lydgate habitually "shrank, as from a burn, from the utterance of any word about his private affairs" (63:631). The younger man does not have a secret in his past that he is ashamed of or that will ruin him. (If anything, he is like Harold Transome in the earlier novel, stumbling into another's secret that will effectively end his own political ambitions.) But Lydgate's marriage to Rosamond has become like a black hole, vacuuming in his social life, his profession, and his science.

The fate of Casaubon is just as fearsomely tied to reputation as the fate of these two potentially more successful men. It is easy to satirize Casaubon, as Celia Brooke and Mrs. Cadwallader do in the novel, and then to feel aghast at Dorothea's marriage to him. His unfinished "Key to All Mythologies" and outmoded scholarship, to say nothing of his premature agedness, are such inviting targets that we forget the sentient man, as George Eliot is at pains to point out. But more than that and more broadly, Casaubon represents something close to his author's experience as a writer in the burgeoning print culture. Books are written for the public, written for readers unknown to the author (the more numerous they are, the less predictable) and some too well known (all too predictable reviewers). Once the writer commits herself to print, her relations to the public take on a life of their own. George Eliot was hypersensitive to the reception of her writing, and her Casaubon even more so. Casaubon lives – or tries to – so that his conduct "would be unimpeachable by any recognized opinion," but "the difficulty of making his 'Key to All Mythologies' unimpeachable weighed like lead upon his mind" (29:277).

This is the chapter of *Middlemarch* of which the first sentence breaks off – "but why always Dorothea?" With all three of her principal men in this novel – as with Tito Melema and others – the author has no more difficulty exploring male consciousness in depth than she has with female consciousness. Few other novelists – Richardson, Tolstoy, Flaubert, James certainly – have comparable power to thrust aside the ordinary gender barriers to understanding others. No single novel by any hand is so balanced in its examination of the needs, percepts, reason, fears, and follies of both sexes as is *Middlemarch*, and that achievement is partly its design.

Dorothea Brooke is justly famous as a heroine. It is not true, as some have claimed, that she is a close copy of her author (and even Maggie and Romola do not follow George Eliot's plot-line to anything like a career in London). The impression that she is a stand-in for the novelist grows rather from a certain favoring or indulgence of her in the narrative that would hardly be noticed in the protagonist of a more usual sort of novel, one not bent on recording so many different consciousnesses and points of view. From the beginning, I have suggested, Dorothea's difference from the others – and barely conscious superiority – is archaic: she will stand out from this study of modern life, provincial or otherwise. Thus she has "the impressiveness of a fine quotation from the Bible – or from one of our elder poets – in a paragraph of today's newspaper" (1:7). Quite evidently she is the later-born Saint Theresa of the prelude to *Middlemarch*, "helped by no coherent social faith and order which could perform the function of knowledge for the ardently willing soul" (3).

Just as much alone – and with faith only in herself – is Rosamond Vincy. Miss Vincy's superiority is attested to by general admiration of her face and manners; her isolation as Mrs. Lydgate is nearly complete. Ironically, because George Eliot writes of Dorothea with warmth and Rosamond with an edge of scorn, the former seems the invented character and the latter simply described, hence the real thing. Her narrow education is made explicit, and is perhaps what we expect from the limitations of provincial life – hence again more real to us, because expected. Her selfishness and devotion to her own person contrast with Dorothea's generosity, and a different kind of knowledge is missing here, almost the knowledge of other people's existence. As Rosamond's marriage to Lydgate plays out, an egotism akin to stupidity stuns both husband and the novel's readers: it is not just that Rosamond takes her own way but that she does so even when the simplest calculation would tell her that she will be found out, and thus defeated without as well as within her marriage. Her true opposite in the novel, I judge, is Mary Garth, who knows both herself and the man she is pledged to – Rosamond's brother Fred – too well. Though finely drawn, theirs is the most conventional love story of *Middlemarch*: steadfast heroine, unsteady hero, numerous obstacles to their happiness, with a one-time marriage saved to the end. Mary's character recalls that of some of Shakespeare's heroines in the comedies, a woman of wit and pluck, sure of what she wants and of the means to get it.

It is not conventional for English novels, so dedicated to the time of courtship, to study young marriages close up. Students of the novel like to say that

Middlemarch begins where other novels leave off. Both the Casaubons' and the Lydgates' stories unforgettably show that marriage, of itself, cannot be equated with close confidence, common purpose, shared intimacy, or even the rearing of children. Instead of the shelter that marriage affords at the end of Dickens's exposures of modern society, say, these marriages allow that threadlike pressures may swell to the strangulation point in the closeness of two persons living together. Casaubon is not worried that Dorothea might cuckold him because Ladislaw is lazing about; he is frightened that she will betray him in another sense. He had not realized that a bride eager to assist with his writing would be privy to his haltering research – and indeed Ladislaw's main criticism is that Casaubon does not read German. Dorothea is like one of those dreaded reviewers arrived in Casaubon's own study, from which he immediately wants to exclude her instead of welcoming her help. Lydgate, who hoped both to improve patient care in Middlemarch and to engage in basic science, confronts the opposite problem at home – "the circumstance called Rosamond" (36:341). Once his wife has concluded that medical practice is not "a nice profession, dear" (45:452), he stands more in danger than Casaubon of being cuckolded by Ladislaw.

When Fielding, Austen, or Dickens describes an existing marriage – as opposed to the true marriage in the making between a hero and heroine – they tend to exploit older couples for comedy. But in *Middlemarch* George Eliot bravely sketches the older Garths' marriage and the Bulstrodes' also as true. When Bulstrode's reputation implodes, his wife almost ritually joins him. "Look up, Nicholas," she begins. Those highly moving paragraphs conclude: "They could not yet speak to each other of the shame which she was bearing with him or of the acts which had brought it down on them. His confession was silent, and her promise of faithfulness was silent . . . She could not say, 'How much is only slander and false suspicion?' And he did not say, 'I am innocent'" (74:740). Here again local opinion has pierced a marriage. The interests of man and wife are not finally identical, yet this relation is supportive rather than destructive. The author patently dislikes Bulstrode, and she has portrayed Harriet Bulstrode as distinctly less prepossessing than her brother, Mr. Vincy; but the perspective she opens out on the marriage compels the reader's sympathy.

As several of the essays in this volume point out, feminists especially have been disappointed that George Eliot never portrayed in fiction a woman with a career like hers: no woman with a career uniquely her own, much less a woman prepared to define her own relation to a man outside marriage. There are a number of professional singers, nevertheless, and singers will be prominent in *Daniel Deronda*. Before that novel, the only heroine who performs publicly is Dinah Morris in *Adam Bede*, and she duly gives over her preaching before the end. During the years spent writing her later novels, George Eliot had a number of notable feminist friends, including Barbara Bodichon and Bessie Rayner Parks. Strict Victorian manners dictated that less emancipated women, married or unmarried, could not be her friends. But the novelist was more conservative than these feminists and balked at advocating any cause – be it the suffrage or rewarding work for women – in her fiction. Nor was it realistic to invent independent opportunities for women in a society like that studied in *Middlemarch*. George Eliot felt strongly that novel-writing was ultimately justified by a determinate moral influence upon readers: this influence would emanate from motives, circumstances, and consequences that were true to life. There are indeed implicit lessons about the position of women in *Middlemarch*. Both Dorothea and Rosamond are expected to marry; there is no alternative for young women. But the results are not pretty, and in their different ways both wives protest. As Gillian Beer sums up this matter, George Eliot was not a radical feminist: "what is demonstrable is that she was intimately familiar with the current writing and actions of the women's movement and that in *Middlemarch* particularly, she brooded on the curtailment of women's lives in terms drawn from that movement and in sympathy with it.[4]

The brief "Prelude" seems to promise a more feminist novel. By claiming that in the sixteenth century "social faith and order" might supply the place of "knowledge," the prelude indirectly implies that *with* wider knowledge – with an education and then some – heroines like Dorothea might find a place in the modern world. This supposition becomes lost, however, in the telling of the heroine's disastrous marriage and of her possible, and later assured, recovery of a role as wife to Ladislaw. Beer makes the point that Ladislaw at least is not a prisoner of masculinity and is "kin to women, not polarized against them" – a liberated spirit for Dorothea to bond with (Beer, *George Eliot*, 171–74). Yet propriety and realism prevail: Ladislaw may have a more vital career than Casaubon's amateur scholarship, but it seems that Dorothea will continue to play no more than a supporting role. George Eliot gives a nod in the finale to those who think it "a pity that so substantive and rare a creature should have been absorbed into the life of another and be only known in a certain circle as a wife and mother"; but no one, she notes, has come up with an alternative (819). The finale's answer to the prelude's challenge has come to be called meliorism, a faith in diffuse and incremental contributions to "the growing good of the world."

The frame of *Middlemarch*, notwithstanding its appeal to Saint Theresa and the many Theresas of yesterday and today, ought not to be read as a strictly gendered set of observations. One of George Eliot's quietly feminist moves is to generalize about modern conditions without primary reference to men. The prelude and finale do insist on women's share in history, since their subject is epic action and traditionally Western epic creates few heroic scenes for women (as the recourse to a saint's life silently acknowledges). The broader question George Eliot poses is what great actions can be narratable under modern conditions. Since Adam and Eve, she replies to her question in the finale, marriage "is still the beginning of the home epic – the gradual conquest or irremediable loss of that complete union" (815). These remarks are a defense of the several actions of *Middlemarch* and also an indirect tribute to the English novel's repeated concern with how to contract lasting unions and how not to.

Within *Middlemarch*, the model for the novel as epic that George Eliot engages is that of Fielding: "A great historian," she intones, and need hardly name the author of *The History of Tom Jones*. That earlier comic epic in prose provided a rich precedent for this narrator's direct addresses to the reader. Mischievously, at the same time that she pays homage to Fielding by beginning this chapter much the way he might, George Eliot admits that such "belated historians" as she will sound "thin and eager" in comparison, then finishes by implying that her own interventions will be more purposeful or directed: "I at least have so much to do in unravelling certain human lots and seeing how they are woven and interwoven that all the light I can command must be concentrated on this particular web, and not dispersed over that tempting range of relevancies called the universe" (15:139). This narrator's voice picks up a large burden of the moralizing of *Middlemarch*; characteristically it urges the reader to be open-minded – that is, to keep this character in mind but then to review all the data that the narrative provides together with wise advice on how to interpret it. The overview will exceed the represented action, for the range of relevancies will still be large. From Fielding the narrator has learned how pleasing it is for writer and reader to share a certain distance from the characters, a distance that need not preclude taking sides – though once you have done so, George Eliot may insist that you change sides for a bit. An affinity with Fielding can be sensed in the humor and generous irony of *Middlemarch*, the good temper that pervades even distressing moments of the telling. Given George Eliot's persistent habit of recounting both sides of social and domestic differences, the sheer confidence of the telling breathes forgiveness.

One way George Eliot's commentary differs from Fielding's is in the reach of her metaphors (though the latter's mock heroics are a version of the same thing). Often her metaphors are a bit outrageous, and the simplest comparisons to facts of science or natural history invoke a range of relevancies wholly unexpected. Or sentiments that might seem portentous if delivered straight are defused and brought home by analogy to some experience so ordinary that the point seems undeniable. I instance just one example because it focuses on the still living personal past, the theme so important for George Eliot as for Dante:

> Into this second life Bulstrode's past had now risen, only the pleasures of it seeming to have lost their quality. Night and day, without interruption save of brief sleep which only wove retrospect and fear into a fantastic present, he felt the scenes of his earlier life coming between him and everything else, as obstinately as when we look through the window from a lighted room, the objects we turn our backs on are still before us, instead of the grass and the trees. The successive events inward and outward were there in one view: though each might be dwelt on in turn, the rest still kept their hold in the consciousness.
>
> (61:606)

The condition of living in lighted rooms with glass windows is of course modern, taken for granted, yet the clause beginning "as when" belongs to a tradition of refining epic similes that goes back to Homer. In its unaffected quiet the simile is more like some of Homer's than many poets' attempts; it clarifies Bulstrode's experience and hints that it may be commonplace.

Though Dorothea Brooke may be "foundress of nothing" – the language of the prelude again – *Middlemarch* as a whole, in its range and completed actions, its relevancies just short of the universal, its history of the times and even its meliorism, succeeds as an epic of modern life. *Daniel Deronda* (1876), an equally ambitious work, may seem less satisfying because less complete. Its hero comes to a deliberate decision to be founder of something – nothing less, it would appear, than a Zionist state – but that intent looks very much to the future. *Daniel Deronda* is actually the only one of George Eliot's novels to be set in the present, the only one to have scenes in London, and – except for *Romola* – the only one with extensive departures to the Continent. Its "home epic," meanwhile, falls in the category of irremediable loss rather than conquest: the future of Gwendolen Grandcourt, née Harleth, is unclear. Gwendolen partly resembles a few other wives in George Eliot, from Caterina Sarti in "Mr. Gilfil's Love Story" to Rosamond Lydgate; but there are touches of Lydgate's desperation as well. Her marriage is not merely mistaken, but dangerous, as she longs to put an end to "her husband's empire of fear" (35:364).

Because there are three principal characters and two principal storylines, readers have often differed as to this novel's center of interest – whether for George Eliot or themselves. Henleigh Mallinger Grandcourt, the husband, is so repellent a character that few can regret his demise off the shore of Genoa, whether or not he drowns because his wife wishes him to so badly. Deronda's persistent puzzling about his identity, the coincidence of his rescue of the young singer Mirah Lapidoth with the gradual discovery of his own Jewish birthright, and his goal of carrying out her brother Mordecai's Zionist ideas are story elements far different in kind from the taut psychological combat of the other two principals. In a lively "Conversation" on the novel for the *Atlantic Monthly* in 1876, Henry James seemed to say that there was a qualitative difference between "the figures based upon observation and the figures based upon invention," the latter constituting "the Jewish burden" and "cold half of the book" (*CH*,421). Recent critics have usually insisted on connecting the two halves – Deronda, after all, is undeniably a sort of lay confessor for Gwendolen, among other things. But *Daniel Deronda* is not *Middlemarch*: its particular multiplot does not beckon toward an overview of society at a given historical time but has designs upon its readers and the future; in important respects it repudiates the liberal intellectual assumptions of the previous novel.

For George Eliot, Deronda is undoubtedly the closest to an affective center of the novel. He is the title character and the one who will dedicate himself to a movement of ideas – something that is more important to the author at this point than specifically Zionist ideas (never very precisely defined). Deronda can be thought of as her first intellectual hero, neither a specialist like Lydgate nor an old-fashioned scholar but a self-taught generalist like herself, prepared to think largely about the world and to pursue some matters closely in several languages. Bodenheimer has pointed out that, in his relation to Mrs. Grandcourt, Deronda also plays a role comparable to George Eliot's relation to a number of devotees of both sexes during the last decade of her life – most notably Edith Simcox, who worshipped the older woman with an evident erotic longing that was not returned (Bodenheimer, *Real Life*, 242–65). Gwendolen, on the other hand, though brilliantly conceived as someone who deserves our pity, is studied rather coolly by the novelist and is scarcely idealized. One has only to think of Dorothea or Romola or Maggie in the last chapters of her novel, or Dinah and Esther for that matter, to feel that Gwendolen will not be much rewarded or consoled in the end. Beer argues that Gwendolen's promise to Deronda that she will "try to live," and her repeating to her mother, "I mean to live. . . . I shall live" (69:692), bode well for her (Beer, *George Eliot*, 223–26). I tend to read these hysterical words as promises not to kill herself. She has in effect changed places with Mirah at the beginning of the novel.

Yet to appreciate George Eliot's achievement, one needs to sympathize with Gwendolen, poised as she is between Grandcourt and Deronda. Just so, when James adapted a similar action for *The Portrait of a Lady*, he would treat his heroine sympathetically: the reader could be startled, alarmed by his American girl, but she would not seem as hollowed out as Gwendolen, or so abandoned to her own resources. As in so many scenes in James's later novels, characters in *Daniel Deronda* watch other characters trying to penetrate the others' consciousness. The action begins *in medias res* with Deronda watching Gwendolen, whom he has never seen before. Grandcourt surreptitiously watches his wife, who seems designed for being watched. Gwendolen's whole idea of herself is that of performance; but that idea entails concealment as well, the more particularly so if there is cause to be ashamed. Grandcourt effectively controls her merely by informing her that he knows that she knew about his mistress and four children when they were married. The idealized heroine of the novel, if you like, is Mirah – who nevertheless first appears on the scene as suicidal and remains for the most part a voice, face, and figure to please others.

The novel exposes power rather than celebrates love. Gwendolen marries Grandcourt because she fancies she has power over him; but he has no interest in life other than power – power, that is, over weak creatures like women or, in one comparison, subject peoples of a "difficult colony" (48:507). Similarly, "Grandcourt kept so many dogs that he was reputed to love them," but in reality it is so that he can kick them when he pleases (12:104). Yet Deronda comes to have an equal, if opposite power over Gwendolen. Both men study and learn something of her secret weakness, even though one seeks to subdue her and the other to help. She begins to entertain a "superstitious dread" of Deronda because of "the coercion he had exercised over her thought" (29:278). Both have become her monitors – Deronda "the strongest of all monitors" – but "her husband had a ghostly army at his back" (36:384). The striking metaphor evokes the maneuvering in Grandcourt's jungle empire, but also Gwendolen's fear of ghosts. Her husband could not mass troops against her without the implicit threat of wider disfavor from others, should the ghost of her faulty decision to marry him appear.

George Eliot's long-standing concern with confession has become more trammeled. In an early story she could write of "the impulse to confession" as salutary when "the man to whom we have no tie but our common nature seems nearer to us than mother, brother, or friend" (JR, 16:252). But in *Daniel Deronda*, Gwendolen's confessor has become very much more than this. Far from having no tie to her, Deronda becomes a person "in the stead of God" to Gwendolen (64:653). He is sufficiently aware of the erotic tension between them that "imminent consequences were visible to him" and he prudently avoids these. As to Gwendolen, "it was not her thought, that he loved her and would cling to her," yet when they talk in London she blushes "for the first time since that terrible moment" of her husband's drowning (65:659). More therapist than confessor after all, Deronda achieves what psychoanalysis would call the transference of his patient's feelings. In her last two novels George Eliot writes increasingly of consciousness, as in the passage on the "second life [of] Bulstrode's past" cited above. In *Daniel Deronda* she writes also of thoughts coming into consciousness. Referring to this process, the narrator refrains from saying what lies underneath many of Gwendolen's or Deronda's thoughts (we cannot really know, after all); though she does not use the word as such, she stresses the significance of unconsciousness in the characters selected for analysis.[5]

Bodenheimer succinctly and a little ironically states the relation between this story and Deronda's other mission in life as follows: "armed with a transfigured, suprapersonal sympathy, Daniel Deronda sails out of psychological space and into the mythic-historical beyond" (Bodenheimer, *Real Life*, 265). In truth, Deronda's trajectory has its starting place not merely in his boyish misgivings about his parentage but in George Eliot's growing conviction that knowledge and ideas by themselves will never bring humanity to change anything. She has always believed in emotional engagement: without feeling, our moral percepts or precepts would be sterile. But having put her faith in representing differing points of view in her novels, she now wonders whether any large social change will come of this liberal display. "A too reflective and diffusive sympathy was in danger of paralyzing in [Deronda] that indignation against wrong and that selectness of fellowship which are the conditions of moral force" (32:308). In *Middlemarch,* "reflective and diffusive sympathy" could be said to offer the best hope for the gradual improvement of society; now, some stronger commitment or set of beliefs is needed. Similarly, at the end of his life Mill could write in his *Autobiography*, "I am now convinced that no great improvements in the lot of mankind are possible, until a great change takes place in the fundamental constitution of their modes of thought . . . until a renovation has been effected in the basis of their belief, leading to the evolution of some faith, whether religious or merely human."[6] George Eliot had read Mill's *Autobiography* in November 1873.

In the light of George Eliot's concern with hermeneutics, Carroll has suggested, *Middlemarch* might be thought of as a "retrenchment" in the progress of her fictions. *Daniel Deronda* is certainly more concerned again with "visionary experience"; and E. S. Shaffer has well described the European context of the novel's prophetic bent.[7] In her last novel George Eliot explores the nature of ideologies – "whether religious or merely human," in Mill's words – and the need for them in a modern polity. Mordecai himself is as much an ideologue as a religionist, and he and his companions in the Hand and Banner debate "the causes of social change." "I praise no superstition," Mordecai insists; "I praise the living foundations of enlarging belief" (42:456). Note that Deronda submits himself to this teacher: the two are not on a par as far as this vision of the future is concerned. "So potent in us is the infused action of another soul, before which we bow in complete love" (65:659): those happen to be the narrator's words about Gwendolen's worship of Deronda, but they might apply as well to Deronda's discipleship under Mordecai. To bow before someone in complete love, is to submit oneself to that other person. Paradoxically, because the novelist is moving beyond the meliorism of *Middlemarch* – the "incalculably diffusive" effect of goodness such as Dorothea's, as the finale of the novel puts it – this novel tries to place submission in a favorable light.

This eventual direction of George Eliot's fiction need not be accepted uncritically. Some objections immediately spring to mind. Mordecai is an attractive figure, but suppose one puts oneself to school to a false prophet, a charlatan, or worse – a Grandcourt, perhaps? What if the set of beliefs comprising the favored ideology is false or cruel? Deronda waves that objection aside when he exalts "faith even when mistaken" (40:429). His ancestor Daniel Charisi used to say, "'Better a wrong will than a wavering; better a steadfast enemy than an uncertain friend; better a false belief than no belief at all'" (60:619). But is any one of these sentiments generally true? Then there is the question of the point of view and future of all those who are not included in the "selectedness of fellowship" required for moral advance. In the modern world ideologies are like the nationalism that they frequently serve, selective and the possession of this group but not that. In the novels, Mordecai's vision is more nationalist than religious.

George Eliot is too good a novelist not to tell of some resistance to "Mordecai's ideas" and Deronda's determination "to try and carry them out" (67:671–72). The bewilderment of Gwendolen about the plan, one suspects, is shared by many readers even if they cannot like her very much. In any case, Gwendolen's naïve assumption before marriage that she could wield power and its brutal correction afford a lingering lesson in what it feels like to be powerless. The Alcharisi, the successful performer who proves to be Deronda's mother and is sometimes compared to Gwendolen, fiercely resisted Jewishness and was able to defy the men who would impose it. Her son's attraction to Jewishness she cynically puts down to his love for Mirah, and like him, Mirah "is attached to the Jewishness she knows nothing of." Moreover, this woman who has farmed out her son by her first marriage and is now the Princess Halm-Eberstein and the mother of more children, "was never willing subject of any man." In another sense, "men have been subject" to her (53:571). The princess grants only two brief interviews to her exiled son, but her voice still resonates for readers after the book is done.

The history invoked by this novel of contemporary times is both ancient and a little mysterious, or what Deronda summarizes as "the effect of brooding thoughts in many ancestors" and associates most immediately with his grandfather Charisi (63:642). To his mother he has answered that Jewishness is "stronger, with deeper, farther-spreading roots" than her mere will, and George Eliot capitalizes "that stronger Something" for him, to give it more weight (53:568). History has become the race, and this emphasis has replaced the insistence on loyalty to fathers for heroines like Maggie and Romola. A trope of Mordecai's makes the point clear: "the past has become my parent, and the future stretches towards me the appealing arms of children" (42:451). But Mordecai is not a father, and his father is a rascally thief, pimp, gambler, and worse. One cannot help but notice the absence of other fathers. Gwendolen too has none: there is no other Harleth extant, and her stepfather Davilow long ago ran off with her mother's jewels, as if setting the precedent for the awkward return of Mordecai and Mirah's father, who runs off at the end with Deronda's "memorable ring," the symbol of his connection to those many ancestors (68:677).

I do not believe George Eliot introduced these low matters according to a careful plan. They spring from a lively dramatic instinct that nags at the high aims of ideology – Mordecai's hopes in particular – and function like the low scenes in Shakespearean history plays. With one hand the novelist assists Deronda, Mordecai, and Mirah to jettison their immediate parents, and with the other she gives the parents their day. Mordecai asks for it when he construes his authority as "hidden bonds that bind and consecrate change as a dependent growth" (42:451). His loaded words point in too many directions: bands that both conceal and are effective, that both bind the group and change things. Deronda's advice to Gwendolen – "Turn your fear into a safeguard. Keep your dread fixed on the idea of increasing that remorse" (36:388) – seems as archaic as his new-found Jewishness. Induced guilt feelings do not seem to be the answer to the problems posed by the novel.

But such measures are called for, George Eliot in part believes, in a remorseless modern society. Earlier heroines were at least attached to a place; Gwendolen's lack of any home is frequently noted. *Daniel Deronda* is a fine cosmopolitan novel at its warmest, but its hero is headed off to found a specifically Jewish state in another clime. James was surely wrong about the relative temperatures of the two actions. Gwendolen's world is colder still, and she shivers outside the covers of her little bed. This novel is no love story, and power chills the represented lives of more than one character.

NOTES

1 Rosemarie Bodenheimer, *The Real Life of Mary Ann Evans: George Eliot, Her Letters and Fiction* (Ithaca, N. Y.: Cornell University Press, 1994); David Carroll, *George Eliot and the Conflict of Interpretations: A Reading of the Novels* (Cambridge University Press, 1992).

2 Felicia Bonaparte, *The Triptych and the Cross: The Central Myths of George Eliot's Poetic Imagination* (New York: New York University Press, 1979). See pp. 13, 21, 28–29.
3 See Jerome Beaty, Middlemarch *from Notebook to Novel: A Study in George Eliot's Creative Method* (Urbana: University of Illinois Press, 1961).
4 Gillian Beer, *George Eliot* (Brighton: Harvester Wheatsheaf, 1986), p. 180.
5 Alexander Welsh, *George Eliot and Blackmail* (Cambridge, Mass.: Harvard University Press, 1985), pp. 337–45.
6 John Stuart Mill, *Collected Works,* ed. John M. Robson (Toronto: University of Toronto Press, 1963–), I:45–47.
7 Carroll, *George Eliot*, 233; E. S. Shaffer, *Kubla Khan and The Fall of Jerusalem* (Cambridge: Cambridge University Press, 1975), pp. 225–91.

5

SUZY ANGER

George Eliot and philosophy

James Sully, founder of the first English philosophical journal *Mind*, wrote a study of "George Eliot's Art" for an early number of the journal. This piece stands out, in a periodical devoted to academic and professional philosophy, as the single article in the journal's history (published since 1876) to treat a novelist or poet. But this fact is not surprising, given how seriously Eliot's contemporaries took her status as a philosopher and a moral teacher. Sully observes of George Eliot that people "are apt to think and speak of her as a discoverer and enforcer of moral truth rather than an artist," while George Cooke, in his 1884 study of her work writes, "she was an ethical prophet."[1] Such comments were standard among George Eliot's Victorian readers. Henry James, in fact, saw her work as too philosophical and intellectual, complaining that "the philosophical door is always open on her stage, and we are aware that the somewhat cooling draught of ethical purpose draws across."[2]

These commentators are right that George Eliot's extensive readings in and speculations on philosophy are crucial to her novels. This chapter examines prominent philosophical influences, the positions she develops on some key philosophical issues, and ways in which those positions are embodied in her fiction. George Eliot's thought ranged over problems of analytic philosophy: epistemology, ethics, philosophy of mind, metaphysics, philosophy of language, and aesthetics; and her fiction takes up such philosophical topics in a number of ways. Her characters and plots reflect the philosophical views that she finds compelling; her narrator often directly imparts George Eliot's beliefs; philosophical issues are often matters of discussion among her characters (for instance, in the "Philosopher's Club" scenes in *Daniel Deronda*); and the novels also become a ground for developing and questioning her professed philosophical views, often in ways of which she herself may not have been fully aware. Of course, George Eliot is finally a novelist and not a professional philosopher, so although many questions of long-standing philosophic debate inform her thought, she does not necessarily conform to conventionally philosophical arguments, or to a consistent set of positions on these matters. My analysis will focus on three main areas of philosophical concern in her work – morality, knowledge, and truth – although it is difficult fully to separate out these strands, given that they are tied together in Eliot's thought in what I will emphasize is essentially a hermeneutic view.

Early reading and translations

Before she ever began writing novels, Mary Ann (or Marian) Evans immersed herself in philosophical reflection. She studied philosophical texts, produced translations of philosophers, and wrote essays on philosophical topics. In these early years she read Hegel, Kant, Rousseau, and contemporary philosophers, in particular John Stuart Mill, who was at the time a strong proponent of Auguste Comte's positivism, which was to become a significant influence on her thought. In 1843, she records reading *A System of Logic* (1840), a study in which Mill opposes rationalism, the belief that reason gives access to truths about the world, to a method he prefers, radical empiricism (the doctrine that all knowledge is acquired via experience). Science, he argues, is not advanced by intuition, but is instead made up of generalizations derived from experience. When, early in life, Mary Ann Evans lost her religious faith, she turned to philosophy as a solace. In a letter of 1847, she comments on "the superiority of the consolations of philosophy to those of (so-called) religion" (*GEL*, I:240). Later in life, George Eliot was to return to Mill's epistemology in formulating her own theory of knowledge.

Charles Bray's *Philosophy of Necessity* (a now forgotten work), which she encountered when she became part of the Rosehill circle, also influenced George Eliot's thought in important ways.[3] Bray's work argues for causal determinism, the metaphysical doctrine that all events, including human choices, are necessitated by the conditions that precede them. Bray takes up what he regards as the invariable laws of nature and their effects on psychology and morality, in ways that resonate through Eliot's writing.

As editor of the *Westminster Review* (earlier edited by John Stuart Mill), a journal that published much work in philosophy, she found herself further immersed in contemporary philosophical debate. In those years with the review, she began her friendship with Herbert Spencer, whom she refers to as "a great philosophical writer" (*GEL*, II:165) – a view, one might add, that is not shared today but that was prevalent in the late nineteenth century. Spencer wrote voluminously, particularly on science, positivism (from which he wanted to dissociate himself despite the similarities of his thought), evolutionary theory, and ethics.

It was in the 1840s that Mary Ann Evans first became interested in the work of Auguste Comte (1798–1857), the founder of positivism and a figure of great importance in her thinking throughout her career. In his major work, the *Cours de philosophie positive* (1830–42), he argues that accurate and objective knowledge within the empirical sphere is entirely possible, both about the physical world and about human behavior, but that we can know nothing about metaphysical issues, those questions that cannot be answered with the evidence of the senses. Like Kant, that is, Comte believes that we cannot know things as they are in themselves. There has been a great deal of debate on the extent to which George Eliot agreed with Comte's ideas. While it seems clear that she was not a committed devotee of Comte's positivism – which came to take on the form of a religion, requiring bizarre daily rituals – she found key ideas in his thought compelling, particularly his consideration of the possibility of objective knowledge.

In these years, Eliot also translated the works of philosophers and critics of religion, such as Baruch Spinoza, David Strauss, and Ludwig Feuerbach. She began her translation of the seventeenth-century Dutch philosopher Baruch Spinoza's *Tractatus Theologico-Politicus* in 1843. In the *Tractatus*, Spinoza concentrates on, among other topics, the proper interpretation of Scripture, and his discussion would play a role in George Eliot's formulation of her own hermeneutics. Later (1854–56) she also translated Spinoza's *Ethics*. A rationalist, believing in the importance of the intuitive apprehension of truth, Spinoza asserts that there are three kinds of knowledge, the second and third of which – reason and intuition – are adequate forms of knowledge (intuition being the highest). The lowest form of knowledge, which includes perception, imagination and opinion, or what Spinoza refers to as "hearsay, or knowledge from mere signs," is inadequate. At times, George Eliot seems to adopt this view, for instance in her critique of gossip, particularly, in *Middlemarch*. The Middlemarchers' mistaken opinions are based on inadequate knowledge that they nonetheless act upon, for example in their condemnation of Lydgate, who, Eliot tells us, borrowing Spinoza's terms, is "known merely as a cluster of signs for his neighbors' false suppositions" (M, 15:140).

When she encountered Charles Hennell's work, and through him, the work of David Strauss, George Eliot found herself deeply involved in the writings of the "higher critics," students of Christianity who believed that the Bible was to be reread as a historical document that is essentially a collection of myths. Their views and methods were very important for her theory of knowledge. In the early 1840s she translated, with great difficulty and care and obvious spiritual strain, David Strauss's *Life of Jesus*. A decade later she translated the German philosopher and higher critic Ludwig

Feuerbach's *Essence of Christianity* (1853). Feuerbach, about whom she famously wrote, "with the ideas of Feuerbach I everywhere agree" (*GEL*, 2:153), naturalized the Bible also, claiming that Christianity projects the virtues of humanity on its God.

But George Eliot's most significant relationship with a philosopher was with her companion, her "husband," as she called him, George Henry Lewes. Although Lewes is not today considered to be an important philosopher, he was a prominent voice in philosophy, science, and psychology in his own day. His *Biographical History of Philosophy* (1845–46) was a relatively popular success, which brought the history of philosophy to its culmination in the work of Comte and the idea of positivism. He and George Eliot had read and were influenced by many of the same works even before they met. Lewes, for instance, was introduced by Mill in the 1840s to the work of Comte, and like Comte, Lewes saw in history a progressive development away from "Metaphysics," and toward "Positive Science" and "certain knowledge." He continued to write on philosophical subjects throughout the years he spent with George Eliot, who herself completed for publication after his death the final volume of his last work, *Problems of Life and Mind* (a work that was much discussed in *Mind* in the 1870s and 1880s).

Ethical views

As George Eliot's contemporaries recognized, her thought on morality is crucial to all her work, which repeatedly takes up questions about right action, responsibility, and how one should live one's life. When Dorothea, after her dark night, rises and asks herself "What should I do – how should I act now?"(M, 80:776). Eliot poses within the dramatic circumstances of an individual life a question she had asked many times through other characters and that had become the central question of modern ethics.

One of the dominant motifs of George Eliot's work, familiar to her at least since her reading of Bray's *Philosophy of Necessity*, is the idea that there is no escaping the consequences of one's actions and choices. "Our deeds are like children that are born to us; they live and act apart from our own will . . . they have an indestructible life both in and out of our consciousness" (*R*, 16:161). Eliot frequently chastises her weak characters for not taking sufficient responsibility for their actions, whereas in the case of an admirable character like Dorothea, "all the energy of [her] nature went on the side of responsibility – the fufillment of claims founded on our own deeds" (37:368). Yet Eliot is not a consequentialist in her views on ethics. Like Dickens, she criticizes the utilitarian ethics deriving from Jeremy Bentham, a moral view she describes as concerned with "arithmetical proportion," "'balance of happiness,'" and the "quantitative view of human anguish," a theory that regards "thirteen happy lives" as "a set-off against twelve miserable" ones. She denounces the tendency to turn individuals into abstractions, writing that "human pain . . . refuses to be settled by equations" (*SCL:JR*, 22:270; cf. *MF*, v:3:330).

Eliot's fundamental moral principle is that the capacity for sympathy is a necessary condition for a moral agent, since morality grows from the ability to imagine another's state of mind. Her presiding moral position is clearly expressed in an often-quoted passage from her letters: "My own experience and development deepen every day my conviction that our moral progress may be measured by the degree in which we sympathize with individual suffering and individual joy" (*GEL*, II:403). Morality grows from our ability to imagine and understand another's state of mind (hence the enormous importance of art and fiction), and the information needed to make correct moral judgments must come from sympathy, the only condition through which one can learn the effects of one's actions on others. The emphasis on "sympathy" is distinctly Feuerbachian, for Feuerbach argues that benevolence, sympathy, and love – qualities Christianity attributes to God – are innate qualities natural to humans.

Critics have ascribed a variety of meta-ethical views to her, yet it is clear that George Eliot is finally an objectivist in ethics. In her view, there are moral facts, which are not independent of humans, but objective all the same, and these can be known through intuition. Moral behavior requires what George Eliot regards as a kind of impartiality, an ability to maintain "that sense of others' claims" (*MF*, VI:13:466) against "clamorous selfish desires" (*SCL:JR*, 24:279). She worried about the justification for her moral principles, and may, in part, be seen as an ethical naturalist, that is, one who believes it possible to establish empirical means for deriving ethical truths. Both Lewes and Comte attempted to demonstrate that ethics is physiologically grounded, arguing that moral sentiments are inherited via a directed evolution, a process which moves humans from egoistic tendencies to altruistic ones (this project is obviously relevant to recent work in evolutionary ethics). Lewes's account of morality is close to Eliot's, for he argues that "Moral life is based on sympathy. It is feeling for others."[4] George Eliot was amenable to Lewes's and Spencer's goal of founding ethics on science, and egoism and altruism are key terms in her work, but Lewes, Comte, and George Eliot run into the same stumbling block: they begin by *assuming* that certain traits are inherently moral. In her thought, sympathy and altruism are unquestioned goods, but in the end, she is unable to provide any but intuitive grounds for accepting this view.

George Eliot's moral views are, in fact, hard to pin down within the categories of any standard philosophical view. She draws from various traditions, and comes up with a position that is neither systematic nor particularly consistent. Two general ideas are pervasive in her view: first, the stress on sympathy, and second, an emphasis on intuition as the method of making moral judgments. She is vehement in her assertion of the core idea of ethical intuitionism, that no general rules for how to act in every practical situation can be established:

> All people of broad, strong sense have an instinctive repugnance to the men of maxims; because such people early discern that the mysterious complexity of our life is not to be embraced by maxims and that to lace ourselves up in formulas of that sort is to repress all the divine promptings and inspirations that spring from growing insight and sympathy. And the man of maxims is the popular representative of the minds that are guided in their moral judgment solely by general rules, thinking that these will lead them to justice by ready-made patent method, without the trouble of exerting patience, discrimination, impartiality, without any care to assure themselves whether they have the insight that comes from a hardly-earned estimate of temptation or from a life vivid and intense enough to have created a wide fellow feeling with all that is human. (*MF*, VII:2:498)

Repeatedly, she insists that general laws cannot be all there is to morality, that any moral judgment must be made in light of the complex context of any event: "moral judgments must remain false and hollow, unless they are checked and enlightened by a perpetual reference to the special circumstances that mark the individual lot" (*MF*, VII:2:498). One must figure things out case by case, feeling the rich particularity of each situation. Further, sympathy, feeling with others, is the only sure guide to right judgment and action: "There is no general doctrine which is not capable of eating out our morality if unchecked by the deep-seated habit of direct fellow-feeling with individual fellow-men" (*M*, 61:610). Eliot's novels dramatize this view and attempt to provide models for such "deep-seated habit."

Her plots rely heavily on the moral struggle between altruism and egoism, between "self-interested desires" (*M*, 18:175), "the cloudy, damp despondency of uneasy egoism" (*M*, 21:208), and sympathy for and responsibility to others. *Middlemarch* plays out this ethical debate clearly. "We are all of us born in moral stupidity, taking the world as an udder to feed our supreme selves," says the narrator, but she also says "Dorothea had early begun to emerge from that stupidity" (21:208). Rosamond, on the other hand, "had been little used to imagining other people's states of mind except as material cut into shape by her own wishes" (78:765). She is, George Eliot writes, "entirely occupied not exactly with Tertius Lydgate as he was in himself; but with his relation to her" (16:164). But it is a struggle for even Dorothea to enter fully into Casaubon's point of view, to "conceive that he had an equivalent centre of self, whence the lights and shadows must always fall with a difference" (21:208), and much of the novel depicts her progress in the capacity for sympathy and altruism.

Because ethical judgments require sympathy and attention to context in all its particularity, in George Eliot's view only real-life situations (such as novels can depict) can teach us about ethics. Neither general rules nor rational arguments are sufficient. Hence, as George Levine discusses the point in his introduction to this volume, ethics and aesthetics are closely intertwined in her thought. A letter of July 5, 1859, often-quoted, makes the argument clear:

> If art does not enlarge men's sympathies, it does nothing morally. I have had heart-cutting experience that *opinions* are a poor cement between human souls; and the only effect I ardently long to produce by my writings is that those who read them should be better able to *imagine* and to *feel* the pains and joys of those who differ from themselves in everything but the broad fact of being struggling, erring, human creatures. (*GEL*, 3:111)

Repudiating "opinion," Spinoza's lowest form of knowledge, George Eliot hopes her novels will teach her readers the same sympathetic capacity that Dorothea develops and that is foundational both for her ethics and for her theory of knowledge.

Epistemology

Sympathy and feeling are crucial, in George Eliot's view, not only for moral judgment, but also for knowledge in general. As the narrator tells us of Dorothea after she has felt her way into Lydgate's situation, "all this vivid sympathetic experience returned to her now as power: it asserted itself as acquired knowledge asserts itself and will not let us see as we saw in the day of our ignorance" (80:775). Epistemology, or the theory of knowledge – questions about the nature of knowledge, the best means of acquiring adequate knowledge, its justification, and its limits – preoccupied George Eliot from her first writings to her last. All of her novels are centrally about the persistent problems of knowing the world and other minds. Part of Dorothea's progress in *Middlemarch* is towards more accurate – because less subjective – knowledge: "She was no longer struggling against the perception of facts, but adjusting herself to their clearest perception" (37:361). Yet, in George Eliot's view, it is not only through perception (on the model of natural science, in which knowledge was argued to be founded upon observation and experiment) that one gains knowledge, but feeling is also essential. Her ideal is expressed in *Middlemarch* in Ladislaw's sense of Dorothea: "a soul in which knowledge passes instantaneously into feeling, and feeling flashes back as a new organ of knowledge" (22:220).

Much recent criticism has treated George Eliot's focus on the difficulties of attaining knowledge and the problems caused by the limitations of perspective and subjectivity as prefiguring – whether intentionally or not – skeptical or poststructuralist views on knowledge. But making a connection between George Eliot and poststructural epistemology depends upon either ignoring a significant part of her professed views, or on reading her works as self-deconstructing. Although she is well aware of the difficulties in the way of such knowledge, she is not a skeptic, because "skepticism, as we know, can never be thoroughly applied, else life would come to a standstill" (*M*, 23:238). George Eliot assumes a roughly traditional view of truth and knowledge in which true beliefs are those that capture the facts as they really are and a person's knowledge consists of those of her beliefs that are supported by adequate grounds. Knowledge, in George Eliot's view, is something to be sought, rather than something to be unmasked and discredited, as much recent critical theory has assumed. Facts matter to her and she does believe in them. Although she was aware of and persuaded by Kant's views on the limits of knowledge and the impossibility of access to the world as it is independent of our experiences of it, she is not to be taken as a subjectivist. However rich and complex her views about the difficulties of interpretation and acquiring knowledge, they are very different from those of contemporary skeptics.

George Eliot's admiration for Feuerbach has sometimes been taken as evidence of her belief that certain knowledge is inaccessible, that all truth claims are illusory, constructed by humans, but this interpretation is based on a mistaken understanding of Feuerbach's views. Feuerbach's central claim in *The Essence of Christianity* is that God is a fictitious creation of the human mind, a projection of human predicates, and hence that Christianity is not literally true. Yet it is not valid to infer that Feuerbach denies that there is any such thing as truth. Feuerbach in fact sees his project as the uncovering of an established, but erroneous, belief system in the pursuit of "unveiled, naked truth."[5] He proclaims his aim to be "the triumph of truth and virtue" (*Essence of Christianity*, p. xxxiv). Things exist outside of human thought: "The object of the senses is in itself indifferent – independent of the disposition or of the judgment" (12), and certain knowledge is indeed possible through the senses. Feuerbach can be said to be a relativist only in a weak sense, in that he does not believe that we have access to a perfectly objective viewpoint, that is, a view outside of any human perspective. Nevertheless, he claims that truth is possible within this perspective: "It is true that I may have a merely subjective conception, i.e., one which does not arise out of the general constitution of my species; but if my conception is determined by the constitution of my species, the distinction between what an object is in itself, and what it is for me ceases; for this conception is itself an absolute one" (16). Feuerbach is committed to a version of perspectivism that does not entail that objectivity is impossible for humans. We need to see from others' perspectives in order to verify the truth of our own – thus the central importance of the I/thou relationship for Feuerbach. In attempting to see as another we attain objectivity. He writes: "Not to invent, but to discover; 'to unveil existence' has been my sole object; to see correctly, my sole endeavor" (xxxiv), and this might well stand as a statement of George Eliot's own aim. She also strives to establish certain knowledge within human constraints. Believing that grounds do indeed exist for adjudication among various interpretations of the world, she argues that knowledge is not limited to differing perspectives, each equally valid. Rather, some perspectives falsify and distort reality.

It has also been common to align George Eliot's views on knowledge with Lewes's professed relativism. Even if we suppose her to be in agreement with Lewes's epistemology (and there is no reason to assume they were in complete agreement on these issues), we cannot infer that George Eliot was a radical subjectivist. It is, in any case, a mistake to regard Lewes as holding a view that undercuts traditional understandings of objective knowledge and truth.[6] Lewes believes that we cannot attain a pure objectivity: "Consciousness can never transcend its own sphere, we cannot possibly have a test of Objective truth."[7] He continues by qualifying this view: "In one sense this is correct. We can never know more than states of consciousness, we cannot know objects except through these states. But to reach the Truth we have no need for deeper knowledge, since truth is simply *correspondence* between the internal and external orders" (*History of Philosphy*, I:lxv). Lewes makes apparent that he is committed to independent objects and the correspondence theory of truth, and to the possibility of knowledge. In *Problems of Life and Mind*, he discusses subjectivity and the difficulties of attaining an objective viewpoint. "How," he asks, "do we distinguish the Certitude of Truth" (note the Carlyle-like capitalization) from hallucination or false convictions? In the latter cases, he explains, "my conviction . . . turns out to be a subjective feeling without objective validity, – it is mine, and true for me; it is not true for others, therefore cannot be used as knowledge" (68). He then points to cases in which certainty is possible: "No such failure can exist when a conviction is objectively confirmed, and the equivalence of the sign and the thing signified is proved, by the ability to use the one in lieu of the other. The Certitude in that case is absolute" (69). Like Feuerbach, Lewes claims that we are limited to the human point of view, so our perspective is relative in this sense, but this counts as truth for us: "We arrive then at the conclusion that we can never know but *relative* truth, our only medium of knowledge being the senses, and this medium, with regard *to all without us*, being forever a false one; but being *true to us*, we may put confidence in its relativity."[8]

George Eliot, as her admiration for Comte's thought indicates, is always drawn toward empiricist accounts of knowledge. In an essay of 1856, "The Future of German Philosophy," she favorably reviews a book by a German positivist philosopher, Otto Gruppe, who dismisses the *a priori* (things that are knowable independently of experience), claiming that all knowledge is *a posteriori* (things that are knowable only through experience). She seems to agree with him that abstract concepts are formed from the generalization of particulars. Drawing on Kant's terms, she writes that "every analytic judgment has previously been synthetic," a view consonant with a radical empiricism (Pinney, p. 52).

Yet, George Eliot is not committed to science as the only route to knowledge and she never surrendered her view that feeling is a source of knowledge. Despite her empiricist leanings, she was influenced to some degree by idealist philosophy as it was developed through Carlyle and Coleridge; moreover, it is important to recall that for Spinoza, intuition is the highest form of knowledge. She writes in a late letter that "the most thorough experimentalists admit intuition – i.e. direct impressions/sensibility underlying all proof – as necessary starting points for thought" (*GEL*, VI:167). George Eliot, like Lewes and Comte, was concerned with the problem of how to reconcile objective and subjective viewpoints, and she believed that feeling played a central role in this reconciliation.

The realism and empiricism characteristic of her early fiction have encouraged critics to connect George Eliot with Comte. But Comte's work falls into two periods, the true empiricism of the *Cours de philosophie positive* (and it was to this early work that Lewes subscribed so enthusiastically), which was systematically committed to establishing a realist and objectivist account of knowledge, and the tempered positivism of the *System of Positive Polity*, which Lewes, among many others, found unpersuasive. In my view, Eliot is more drawn toward the later work in which Comte begins to dilute his empiricism.

In the *System*, Comte takes a more overt interest in moral questions than he does in his earlier work. Here he allows a larger place for feeling, placing the "affective" over the "intellectual," and concedes that it is possible to attain some knowledge through this more emotional, less rational means. Comte acknowledges that imagination often precedes more rational ways of understanding, and increases his emphasis on subjective states, though his aim remains that of presenting the "true universal point of view." He argues that we can accept a "subjective" theory for which we have no objective evidence if it is consistent with the facts we do know. George Eliot kept two notebooks (1875) in which she selected passages from the *System* which show Comte's attempts to combine objective and subjective methods.[9] Like Comte, she is drawn toward an objectivist view of knowledge, though for her this always means more than a purely empirical mode of investigation. What she found most compelling in Comte's epistemology were his efforts to connect a theory of knowledge to a theory of morality and his efforts to reconcile subjective and objective ways of knowing.

Ultimately, George Eliot's epistemology rests on the belief that morality is a necessary condition for full knowledge. Only a sympathetic disposition will allow one to escape subjective bias, to see from other viewpoints, and so attain a sort of impartiality. By overcoming one's own viewpoint and imaginatively entering into the perspectives of others, one can transcend the limitations of subjective experience. In a chapter epigram in *Daniel Deronda*, George Eliot identifies ignorance with false perspective. Ignorance is "like the falsity of eyesight which overlooks the gradations of distance, seeing that which is afar off as if it were within a step or a grasp." Knowledge, on the other hand, is "power reigned by scruple, having a conscience," the prerogative of those "having a practiced vision" (21:194). Knowledge is aligned with correct perspective and we see again the convergence of moral character and accurate interpretation.

Metaphysics

Two central topics in metaphysics are crucial to George Eliot's fiction. The first is the debate over realism and antirealism, which has also been at the center of recent literary theory, and the second is the question of determinism and its compatibility with free will.

In her final completed work, *Impressions of Theophrastus Such* (1878), George Eliot writes that "fine imagination is always based on a keen vision, a keen consciousness of what *is*, and carries the store of definite knowledge as material for the construction of its inward visions" (13:109). She asserts here that there is a truth about the way the world *is*, independently of our thinking about it. She acknowledges that our perceptions often do not correspond to the world as it really is, and the next step might be to claim that there is no such world. But George Eliot does not take that step. A number of recent critics, however, have seen her perspectivism as committing her to antirealism, the rejection of the belief that there are mind-independent facts that we can come to know. They have regarded her as moving from a Comtean-inspired realism and concomitant naïve theory of language in her early fiction to a more sophisticated antirealist position in her final works. I argue that George Eliot never holds either of these views.

Critics have gone astray in their interpretations of George Eliot by starting from an oversimplified understanding of Comte and therefore of her affinity with him, ascribing to him a simple reference theory of meaning and then connecting this view to her early views on language. Comte makes many statements that suggest that a word gains its meaning by directly hooking onto an object in the extralinguistic world. The value of signs, he argues, "depends entirely on their fixity, a thing which would be impossible, but for permanence in the system of nature."[10] Although he conceives of reference on such a model and connects this feature of language with its usefulness as a tool for the acquisition of objective knowledge of the external world, he attributes a second and more central purpose to language, that of language as a means of communication between humans: "We must steadily keep in view the social purpose, the special mark of Language, the communication from man to man of Feelings and thoughts" (203). He argues that clarity of understanding requires more than a perfect system of reference. In order for language to be most effective in its aim of allowing "mutual communication" (188), a certain ethical disposition is required of language users: "Its first function being to communicate emotions, Language, like Religion, has most natural affinity with the sympathetic instincts which alone are capable of complete transmission" (183). Comte speculates that language will function ideally only when the achievement of his social vision results in a certain ethical character. This perfection will occur when we have begun to practice "the habitual cultivation of the active instincts of Benevolence" (184). Commentators have overlooked this ethical aspect of Comte's thought on language, yet it is here that we find the significant connection between Eliot's views on language and Comte's.

Even before George Eliot begins to write fiction, she recognizes that language is not a scientific instrument – a clear medium that transmits thoughts perfectly and completely – and that understanding is always a potential problem. In an essay written in 1856 (the period during which she was most interested in the Comte of the *Cours*), George Eliot comments on the imperfections of language:

> It must be admitted that the language of cultivated nations is in anything but a rational state; the great sections of the civilized world are only approximately intelligible to each other; and even that, only at the cost of long study; one word stands for many things, and many words for one thing. The subtle shades of meaning, and still subtler echoes of association, make language an

> instrument which scarcely anything short of genius can wield with definiteness and certainty. (Pinney, 287)

It might be expected, given the premise that she subscribes to a naïve view of language at this time, that George Eliot would suggest that these deficiencies should be remedied through an improved system of reference. These putative improvements might include such measures as that all ambiguities be eliminated from language, that literal meaning be promoted, and emotive meaning excluded. She goes on, however, to propose that no perfect scientific system of language (such as was the aspiration of the twentieth-century positivists and the Wittgenstein of the *Tractatus*) will serve to improve communication:

> Suppose, then, that the effort which has been again and again made to construct a universal language on a rational basis has at length succeeded, and that you have a language which has no uncertainty, no whims of idiom, no cumbrous forms, no fitful shimmer of many-hued significance . . . – a patent deodorized and non resonant language, which effects the purpose of communication as perfectly and rapidly as algebraic signs. Your language may be a perfect medium of expression to science, but will never express *life*, which is a great deal more than science. With the anomalies and inconveniences of historical language, you will have parted with its music and its passion, with its vital qualities as an expression of individual character, with its subtle capabilities of wit, with everything that gives it power over the imagination.
> (Pinney, 288)

George Eliot clearly recognizes that it is the complicated, nonliteral features of language that allow language to do what we want it to do. While, as some recent critics have suggested, the inescapably metaphorical nature of language would seem inevitably to undermine her commitment to realism and successful understanding, George Eliot saw no such inevitability. Rather she saw metaphor as an important aid to understanding. Her solution to the problem of language is not, then, a simplification of the system of language. Instead, it is a matter of character and growth. Like Comte, she argues that successful communication will require a change in the humans who use language: "Language must be left to grow in precision, completeness, and unity, as minds grow in clearness, comprehensiveness, and sympathy" (Pinney, pp. 287–88).

Though Eliot does not hold to a naïve view of language, neither does she concede the antirealist position. In some recently published essays from the period during which it has been argued that her notion of language is radically revised, George Eliot discusses the development of language. She argues that there are limits to the ways that humans can develop and think and express themselves. She claims that “different groups of human beings, though in the very beginning of their existence sundered from each other, must inevitably fall upon the same devices for . . . communication and analogical representation.”[11] Eliot believes that language is not developed solely through cultural and social means, but that humans are constrained to think in certain ways:

> They might have in no single case the same name for the same thing, but . . . they would of necessity have much agreement in the metaphorical development of their speech: above & below, light & dark, fast & slow, warm & cold, sweet & sour, hard & soft, smooth & rough, heavy & light, noisy & still, cloudy & clear, wet & dry, far & near, & so on, would be the same qualities for each group, & the words expressing them would be transferred from the external to the internal, from the visible and palpable to the invisible and imaginary.
> (Collins, “Questions of Method,” 388)

The ways in which humans can conceive of the world, the range of possible conceptual schemes, then, are necessary and limited. They are neither chosen nor optional. Eliot argues that the world is inevitably to be carved up in certain ways, that language does not create these divisions, but instead reflects them:

> In short, their languages would be to a good extent translatable. They would be different media of ideas held in common. Their grammar must have corresponding elements, however differently rendered, since the main elements of grammar are simply indispensable facts of human existence; that I am not you, that He is neither of us, that the sky is still the sky though it may be either bright & sunny or dark & starry, that my hand is still my hand though it may be hot or cold. (Collins, “Questions of Method,” 388)

Rather than supporting a radical subjectivism, George Eliot insists on the constraints on human thought and so argues indirectly against the notion that language and thought create reality.

A second metaphysical issue crucial to George Eliot’s thought is the problem of free will. Her fiction often seems to imply a deterministic view of the world. Yet, if a strict scientific determinism holds, and all human choices are necessitated by the conditions that preceded them, it would seem that individuals have no control over what happens. If everything is a strict causal outcome of earlier events, then what room is left for responsibility and choice, since one could not have chosen to do anything else? Yet George Eliot consistently emphasizes that people are morally responsible for their actions, as she does, for example, in her depictions of characters such as Fred Vincy or Bulstrode, both of whom are severely criticized for constructing a worldview in which someone or something else (providence, inheritance, gambling) is held responsible for their actions and decisions, and thus protects them from responsibility for their results. Bulstrode, for example, believes that "God would save him from the consequences of wrong-doing" (61:611). George Eliot, it follows, is a "compatibilist" on this issue, believing that determinism does not eliminate moral freedom and responsibility. As she writes in a letter of 1875: "I shall not be satisfied with your philosophy till you have conciliated necessitarianism – I hate the ugly word – with the practice of willing strongly, of willing to will strongly, and so on" (*GEL*, VI:166).

In her novels, universal natural laws become moralized. It is not only that "undeviating" laws objectively exist, but recognition of their existence and submission to them becomes an ethical issue. In this, perhaps, George Eliot is influenced by Spinoza as well as Bray. Spinoza believes that while the world is deterministic, a certain sort of freedom is compatible with this view. He contends that the more we recognize necessity, paradoxically, the freer we become, since we no longer assume an illusory freedom. George Eliot expresses a similar view when she writes, in connection with Maggie, of "the irreversible laws within and without her which governing the habits become morality" (*MF*, IV:3:288).

Hermeneutics

George Eliot's philosophical views are essentially in accord with nineteenth-century hermeneutics, or the theory of interpretation. Nineteenth-century German hermeneutics extended thought on interpretation from the attempt to determine acceptable interpretive procedures for particular disciplines, such as theology, to the establishment of the general conditions for all acts of linguistic understanding. Eliot takes interpretation to be a universal activity and understanding to be always in question: "Signs are small measurable things, but interpretations are illimitable" (*M*, 3:24–25). She is concerned with interpretation both as the means of achieving knowledge of the world in general and with the question of how to correctly understand the meaning of an utterance. Her narratives demonstrate how her morality yields a method of interpretation: a hermeneutics of sympathy. By achieving impartiality and imaginatively entering into the perspectives of others, one can correct one's own distorting perspective.

Marian Evans's early translations of Strauss, Spinoza, and Feuerbach provided her with a solid foundation in theological hermeneutics. In her view, theological exegesis has been mostly a series of misguided distortions, usually prompted by personal need and rationalized by claims of infallibility or divine inspiration, and she extends this point to apply to interpretive activity in general. From the higher critic Strauss, she received a systematic overview of biblical exegesis. Her translation of Spinoza's *Tractatus* further familiarized Eliot with historical approaches to interpretation. In the *Tractatus*, Spinoza sets forth "the true method of interpreting scripture."[12] Spinoza argues that interpreters have made the Bible conform to assumptions and biases that they have brought to it, rather than approaching it with impartiality. He warns against the imposition of extreme or distorting interpretations, writing: "We cannot wrest the meaning of texts to suit the dictates of our reason, or our preconceived opinions" (103). Here Spinoza makes a point that will be repeatedly echoed in Eliot's own comments on interpretation: a critical aim of hermeneutics is the prevention of biased readings.

In the years that followed these translations, before turning to fiction, Marian Evans writes several essays which show that she remains at the forefront of nineteenth-century theological speculation on interpretation. Among these are her review of Mackay's *Progress of the Intellect* (1851), another review essay, "Introduction to Genesis" (1856), and her critique of Dr. Cumming's interpretive stance in "Evangelical Teaching: Dr. Cumming" (1855). This schooling in theological exegesis is developed into a general hermeneutic as Eliot's widening investigations lead to her development of broader views on knowledge and virtue. These allow her to place her interpretive theory on a ground of philosophical reflection about epistemology and ethics.

Eliot's concern with interpretation has been commented on primarily by deconstructive critics, who see Eliot as a precursor of postmodern thought on interpretation. These critics ascribe to her a radical hermeneutics in which interpretation is an endless and unconstrained activity. They take her as a proto-deconstructionist, apprehending the metaphorical nature of all language and the completely perspectival quality of all knowledge, demonstrating, wittingly or not, a fundamental relativism and skepticism. On this view, signs refer only to other signs; there is no transcendental signifier to ground meaning, thus there is no such thing as correct interpretation.[13]

Admittedly, for George Eliot, too, textuality is an important model for our understanding of the world, but her views on interpretation are far from poststructuralist or Nietzschean; they are more akin to the romantic hermeneutics of Friedrich Schleiermacher, who, while acknowledging that "the task of hermeneutics is endless," nevertheless maintains that truth is the goal.[14]

Eliot's hermeneutic also acknowledges the difficulties of complete understanding: "To shift one's point of view beyond certain limits is impossible to the most liberal and expansive mind; we are none of us aware of the impression we produce on Brazilian monkeys of feeble understanding" (*AB*, 18:203). She does not, however, celebrate the proliferation of interpretations, but rather contends that most interpretations are inaccurate. She concedes that an interpreter's own situation is inextricably involved in the process of understanding. Yet her response is not to applaud subjectivism. She enacts interpretive conflicts in her novels not to demonstrate indeterminacy, but instead to reveal the conditions for correct interpretation. Repeatedly, she acknowledges that there are constraints on the project: "Even the bare discernment of facts, much more their arrangement with a view to inferences, must carry a bias: human impartiality, whether judicial or not, can hardly escape being more or less loaded" (*FH*, 46:375). Yet – and this is typical of nineteenth-century thought – the goal of impartiality and objectivity remains.

The novels as philosophy

In the light of our contemporary concerns with literature and ethics, George Eliot's novels are particularly interesting. The moralizing tendencies of Victorian literature were largely denigrated throughout the twentieth century. Friedrich Nietzsche's disparagement of "little moralistic females à la Eliot" anticipates the general reaction against Victorian didacticism in the following century. "In England," Nietzsche writes in his aphorism entitled "George Eliot," "one must rehabilitate oneself after every little emancipation from theology by showing in a veritably awe-inspiring manner what a moral fanatic one is."[15] But recently literature has again come to be seen as an important mode of ethical interrogation. The philosopher Martha Nussbaum argues that some ethical truths are presentable only in the form of narrative, which can illustrate the complexities, particularities, and nuances of life, in ways that abstract philosophical treatments of ethics are incapable of doing.[16]

George Eliot made similar claims herself, so it is not surprising that analyses of her works are prevalent in this area of criticism.[17] A good deal of theorizing of the novel took place in her time – attempts to define what it was, what its function should be – as it became the ascendant literary genre. Both she and Lewes made contributions to these debates, Lewes declaring, for instance, that a novel is "an exhortation . . . not a demonstration, but it does not the less appeal to our moral sense."[18]

George Eliot's novels do philosophical work and enrich ethical discussion, partially through the tensions and contradictions in her own thought as they are embodied in the narratives. She often represents moral dilemmas, situations in which a character seems to be morally obligated to do both of two actions, but cannot do both of them. Though the narratives always invoke duty, it is not easy to see what particular duty might override another. The extraordinary power of *Middlemarch*, for example, depends in part on its dramatization of many such dilemmas. There is Lydgate's difficult public vote for Tyke, so ensuring patronage for his much-needed hospital, over the more honorable and attractive Farebrother, or Mary's decision not to destroy Featherstone's will. Note that Mary does not in fact decide, but *feels*, or intuits what is right, and the moral conflict only emerges in retrospect. She acts, as George Eliot puts it in another context, from "the immediate promptings of innate power, and not from laboured obedience to a theory or rule" (Pinney, 379). Similarly, Romola finds herself "thrown back again on the conflict between the demands of an outward law, which she recognised as a widely-ramifying obligation, and the demands of inner moral facts which were becoming more and more peremptory" (56:468). In such moments, George Eliot dramatizes her view that there are no absolute moral principles that can be everywhere applied, that there are always complexities involved in moral action.

Despite this view, George Eliot's narrator (who is, of course, typically the spokesperson for these views) is often also the representative of a strict moral view. That view, reiterated through the novels, is that self-interest is not to be balanced against sympathy for others, but that personal desires for one's own welfare must invariably be conquered. *The Mill on the Floss* explicitly presents such a conflict in the section entitled "The Great Temptation" which depicts "the great problem of the shifting relation between passion and duty" (VII:2:497) in Maggie's near elopement with Stephen. The narrator tells us that there is "no master key that will fit all cases" (VII:2:497), and it is in this novel that George Eliot makes many of her best-known statements on the impossibility of absolute moral principles. Yet here and elsewhere her rhetoric and her representation of similar conflicts put her consistently on the side of self-sacrifice. Certainly, she asks her readers to sympathize with her characters' lives, but in her narrator's pronouncements there often is a punishing severity of viewpoint at odds with both her general moral views and her advocacy of a "deep-sighted sympathy which is wiser than all blame, more potent than all reproof" (*SCL:JR*, 15:247).

Maggie is confronted with perhaps the most famous of moral dilemmas in George Eliot's novels. She must choose between her love for Stephen and her responsibility to avoid hurting Lucy and Phillip. But the narrator's rhetoric does not present these events as a true dilemma: it is not a real moral conflict, but instead, with all the religious connotations the word carries, a "temptation." When Maggie imagines acting for herself, the narrator describes it as "cruel selfishness" (VI:13:458). Resisting her attraction to

Stephen, Maggie speaks in terms that accord with the narrator's perspective on the scene. She must not, she tells herself, "set out by maiming the faith and sympathy that were the best organ of her soul" (VI:13:458). But, the question that arises is: sympathy with whom? Certainly sympathy alone is not enough to decide the question, since sympathy for Stephen would prompt a different sort of action than would sympathy with Phillip or Lucy – or for that matter, with herself.

Yet George Eliot is unsparing in the narrator's and Maggie's judgment of the situation. The rhetoric consistently urges renunciation, self-denial, and duty to the other: "I must not, cannot, seek my own happiness by sacrificing others," says Maggie (VI:11:450). (All of this is reminiscent of Comte, who maintains that submission, the repression of personal desires, and obedience to law are essential for altruism's defeat of egoism.) Yet Maggie's arguments refuse the complications that Eliot has elsewhere insisted upon: "If the past is not to bind us, where can duty lie? We should have no laws but the inclination of the moment." (VI:14:475). Here Maggie invokes strict laws as opposed to feelings that are sensitive to the specifics of the situation, and by so doing seems to undermine George Eliot's intuitionist account, for Maggie claims that without such laws we would be subject to mere whim and to treating equal cases unequally. When Maggie does briefly give in, drifting away with Stephen on the boat, the narrative pronouncement is absolute; her act is unequivocally immoral and the consequences will be relentless: "The irrevocable wrong that must blot her life had been committed" (VI:14:470–71).

Yet, to put the issue in modern perspective, Phillip is only Maggie's high-school boyfriend, and few would imagine that such a connection ties her to him irrevocably. And there is no denying that Stephen's arguments are good (of course, George Eliot writes Stephen's dialogue as well as Maggie's, though the narrative overtly rejects his view). He argues that "we have been saved from a mistake," that "there are ties that can't be kept by mere resolution"(VI:14:475). "What," he asks, "is outward faithfulness? Would they have thanked us for anything so hollow as constancy without love?" (VI:14:475).

The narrative aligns itself with the severe reading of Maggie's actions to such an extent that occasionally, as it moves into free indirect discourse, it is difficult to distinguish between the narrator's and Maggie's thoughts. But a novel works not only through direct statement, but also through its descriptions, and in these scenes the powerful representation of the joy Maggie feels with Stephen, in what is otherwise presented as a fairly bleak life, indicates that George Eliot also resists that harsh reading. On the boat, she tells us, Maggie experiences "the tremulous delights of [Stephen's] presence with her that made existence an easy floating stream of joy, instead of a quiet resolved endurance and effort" (VI:14:480). The novel's intensity of mood, its depiction of the "rapture," the "overflowing of brim-full gladness," as the two drift away pleads for Maggie's happiness (VI:13:464), and makes it impossible not to feel along with her – to invoke George Eliot's terms – the sense that "there was, there *must* be, then, a life for mortals here below which was not hard and chill – in which affection would not be self sacrifice" (VI:13:469). Yet the novel condemns her to the latter, making this unmistakable in its tormentingly needless repetition of the scenes offering Maggie one more chance to accept happiness, and we are ultimately asked to admire her renunciation and to join with the censuring Tom, who knows "the difference between right and wrong" (VII:1:485).

It is easy enough to be swept up in the thoughts of George Eliot's very smart narrator, to side with the "wisdom of George Eliot" that so appealed to the Victorians. Nevertheless, she seems philosophically confused here. She makes claims about the impossibility of fixed moral principles, argues that the world is not neat and it is not always clear what counts as a duty or how to rank duties. Yet she returns inevitably to the same consideration in her narratives: duty defined as the sacrifice of one's desires. She leaves out of her view other things that do matter: most particularly, that one has an ethical duty to foster one's own good as well. Her characters often seem to fail to achieve the impartiality that is her putative aim, but, instead, to embrace a sort of self-negation.

Eliot was conscious of this problem and conflicted over the question of balancing concern for one's own welfare with that of others. She had herself observed in her first work of fiction that "the very deeds of self-sacrifice are sometimes only the rebound of a passionate egoism" (*SCL:JR*, 10:229). Commentators have noted that George Eliot vacillates in her presentation of selflessness, sometimes acknowledging the difficulties of negotiating claims between self and other. So, on the one hand, she can write, "I know no speck so troublesome as self" (*M*, 42:413). On the other hand, she reveals, as much as she may really want to condone the view, that Dorothea's selflessness ("I try not to have desires merely for myself, because they may not be good for others" [39:387]), is too extreme, and Dorothea is ultimately (innocently) freed from her "duty" to Casaubon and rewarded with Will.

The narratives stage, then, a conflict between the ideal of sympathetic divination and selflessness and the longing to maintain a desiring self. A moral education similar to Dorothea's is again enacted in *Daniel Deronda*. Gwendolen is unable to see beyond her "own little core of egoistic sensibility" (2:13). She rarely considers the lives or desires of others except as they impinge on her own desires, and she detests "that unmanageable world which was independent of her wishes" (23:214). Deronda, on the other hand, is the paradigm of the moral sensibility that George Eliot presents for our approval, the embodiment of the ethics of anti-egoism: "Daniel had the stamp of rarity in a subdued fervour of sympathy, an activity of imagination on behalf of others" (16:151). While Gwendolen is tortured for her egoism, as accords with the moral scheme of the novel, Daniel's mother, the artist who has refused to sacrifice desire and self, even for her child, articulates another view – though she too is made to pay a price. While typically the Princess's perspective is one that George Eliot rejects, the contradictions in the narrative logic suggest that George Eliot vacillates, sometimes embracing the notion of the sacrifice of desire and sometimes drawing back from it in agreement with the Princess.

The point is – and George Eliot knows this – that moral questions are less simple than she sometimes presents them to be in the dramas of her narratives. After all, she herself broke off an early engagement, and spent her life living with a legally married man, and she allows Maggie to go off with Stephen in any case, before turning back to what the novel literally depicts as death. But, finally, beyond the brilliance and the learning that reveal themselves in the novels, the inconsistencies in George Eliot's handling of her themes and in her narrative logic do most to make her novels an important mode of philosophical interrogation. By revealing how difficult it is to attain impartiality, to finally position oneself in moral conflicts, the novels give us perhaps their greatest insight into the philosophical and ethical problems that mark our lives and the lives of her protagonists.

NOTES

1 James Sully, "George Eliot's Art," *Mind*, 23 (July 1881): 378; George Willis Cooke, *George Eliot: A Critical Study of Her Life, Writings, and Philosophy* (Boston: Houghton Mifflin, 1883), p. 254. Twentieth-century treatments of George Eliot in relation to philosophy include Minoru Toyoda, *Studies in the Mental Development of George Eliot in Relation to the Science, Philosophy, and Theology of Her Day* (Tokyo: Kenkyusha, 1931); Peter Jones, *Philosophy and the Novel* (Oxford: Clarendon Press, 1975); Valerie A. Dodd, *George Eliot: An Intellectual Life* (New York: St. Martin's Press, 1990).

2 Henry James, "The Life of George Eliot," *Partial Portraits* (London: Macmillan, 1899), p. 51.

3 Charles Bray, *Philosophy of Necessity: or Natural Laws as Applicable to Moral, Mental, and Social Science*, 2nd edn (London: Longman, Green, Longman & Roberts, 1863).

4 G. H. Lewes, *Problems of Life and Mind: The Foundations of a Creed*, 1st series (Boston: Houghton, Osgood, 1875–80), p. 66.

5 Ludwig Feuerbach, *The Essence of Christianity*, trans. George Eliot (New York: Harper & Bro., 1957), p. xxxix. Further citations will occur in the text. For dis-

cussion of Feuerbach's philosophy, see Eugene Kamenka, *The Philosophy of Ludwig Feuerbach* (New York: Praeger, 1970), and A. Van Harvey, *Feuerbach and the Interpretation of Religion* (Cambridge and New York: Cambridge University Press, 1997).

6 For further discussion of Lewes's views see Alice R. Kaminsky, *George Henry Lewes as Literary Critic* (Syracuse, N. Y.: Syracuse University Press, 1968), Diana Postlethwaite, *Making it Whole: A Victorian Circle and the Shape of Their World* (Columbus: Ohio State University Press, 1984), Hock Guan Tjoa, *George Henry Lewes: A Victorian Mind* (Cambridge, Mass.: Harvard University Press, 1977), and Rosemary Ashton, *G. H. Lewes: A Life* (Oxford and New York: Oxford University Press, 1991).

7 G. H. Lewes, *The History of Philosophy from Thales to Comte*, 4th edn (London: Longman, Green & Co., 1871): lxv

8 G. H. Lewes, "Hints Towards an Essay on the Sufferings of Truth," *Monthly Repository*, 2 (1837): 314, quoted in Alice R. Kaminsky, ed. *The Literary Criticism of George Henry Lewes* (Lincoln: University of Nebraska Press, 1964), p. ix.

9 T. R. Wright's *The Religion of Humanity: The Impact of Comtean Positivism on Victorian England* (Cambridge: Cambridge University Press, 1986) is a good study of Comte and positivism.

10 Auguste Comte, *System of Positive Polity*, trans. Frederick Harrison (Paris: Carilian-Goery and Vor. Dalman, 1852), VII: 214. All further references will occur in the text.

11 George Eliot in K. K. Collins, "Questions of Method: Some Unpublished Late Essays," *Nineteenth-Century Fiction*, 35.3 (December 1980): 385–405.

12 Benedict de Spinoza, *Tractatus Theologico-Politicus,* trans. R. H. M. Elwes (London: George Routledge & Sons, 1895), p. 99. All further references will be made in the text.

13 See, for example, J. Hillis Miller, "Narrative and History," *ELH* 41 (1974): 455–73 and Daniel Cottom, *Social Figures: George Eliot, Social History, and Literary Representation* (Minneapolis: University of Minnesota Press, 1987).

14 Freidrich D. E. Schleiermacher, selections from *Hermeneutics: The Handwritten Manuscripts by F. D. E. Schleiermacher*, ed. Heinz Kimmerle, trans. James Duke and Jack Forstman (Missoula, Mont.: Scholars Press for the American Academy of Religion, 1977), p. 95.

15 Freidrich Nietzsche, *Twilight of the Idols*, "Skirmishes of an Untimely Man," in Walter Kaufmann, trans., *The Portable Nietzsche* (New York: Viking, 1980), p. 515.

16 Martha C. Nussbaum, *Love's Knowledge: Essays on Philosophy and Literature* (Oxford and New York: Oxford University Press, 1990).

17 See, for instance, M.C. Henberg, "George Eliot's Moral Realism," *Philosophy and Literature*, 3.1 (spring 1979): 20–39; David Parker, *Ethics, Theory and the Novel* (Cambridge, Cambridge University Press, 1994); and Lisabeth During, "The Concept of Dread: Sympathy and Ethics in *Daniel Deronda*," *Renegotiating Ethics in Literature, Philosophy, and Theory*, ed. Jane Adamson, Richard Freadman, and David Parker (Cambridge: Cambridge University Press, 1998).

18 George Henry Lewes, "Ruth and Villette," *Westminster and Foreign Quarterly Review*, n.s.3 (April 1853): 475.

6

DIANA POSTLETHWAITE

George Eliot and science

Does not science tell us that its highest striving is after the ascertainment of a unity which shall bind the smallest things with the greatest? In natural science, I have understood, there is nothing petty to the mind that has a large vision of relations, and to which every single object suggests a vast sum of conditions. It is surely the same with the observation of human life. *The Mill on the Floss* (IV:I:173)

Writing in 1876, Henry James captured his ambivalence towards *Daniel Deronda* in a spirited "conversation" among three fictitious readers of the novel. Is George Eliot "too scientific," judicious Constantius wonders? One might as well call her too *Victorian*, ardent fan Theodora bristles: "So long as she remains the great literary genius that she is, how can she be too scientific? She is simply permeated with the highest culture of the age." Disgruntled Pulcheria begs to differ: "She talks too much about the 'dynamic quality' of people's eyes. When she uses such a phrase as that in the first sentence in her book . . . she shows a want of tact." Theodora parries: "it shows a very low level of culture . . . to be agitated by a term perfectly familiar to all decently-educated people." "I don't pretend to be decently educated," rejoins Pulcheria; "pray tell me what it means" (*CH*, 427).

While nineteenth-century Pulcherias stumbled over scientific neologisms in George Eliot's fiction, twentieth-century readers must excavate the historical meanings of her language. To begin at bedrock: according to the *Oxford English Dictionary*, the word *science* in medieval times was broadly and simply defined as "knowledge acquired by study." By the early eighteenth century, however, "science" had come to mean not so much a body of knowledge as an anatomy of knowing. According to this definition, "science" is "a branch of study which is concerned either with a connected body of demonstrated truths or with observed facts systemically classified and more or less colligated by being brought under general laws, and which includes trustworthy methods for the discovery of truth within its own domain."

The nineteenth century saw the further evolution of "science" in both practice and meaning. The British Association for the Advancement of Science was formed in 1831; William Whewell coined the word *scientist* in 1840. The quotation the *OED* offers to illustrate this new, Victorian, definition is dated surprisingly late – 1867: "We shall use the word 'Science' in the sense which Englishmen so commonly give to us; as expressing physical and experimental sciences, to the exclusion of theology or metaphysics" (W. G. Ward, *Dublin Review*).

On one hand, Victorian "science" was still a discipline-in-progress, not yet a subject to be studied at Oxford or Cambridge, often an enthusiasm pursued by the independent amateur. On the other, it was during the Victorian era that "science" began both to professionalize and to narrow itself to a study of the physical world. There was nothing narrow, however, about either the scope or the impact of scientific thought during George Eliot's lifetime. The thirty years before Charles Darwin's *Origin of Species* was published in 1859 saw the proliferation and dissemination of new scientific theories which anticipated those of Darwin. In dramatic contrast to the increasingly estranged "two cultures" of the twentieth century, most Victorian scientific discourse, except perhaps that which used mathematics or some of the advanced technical language of physics like that of Clerk Maxwell, was readily accessible to the nonscientist, and even the most technical developments were what we would now call "popularized" for fairly easy consumption by intelligent readers. Science, that is to say, was provocatively within reach of both the novelist and her readers.

In *Middlemarch*, set at the end of the 1820s, George Eliot portrays two typical – and dramatically contrasting – scientists of the early Victorian era, the Revd. Camden Farebrother and Dr. Tertius Lydgate. The third decade of the century is a "cheerful time for observers and theorisers alike," George Eliot writes, and the town has one of each (15:145). As befits a society on the cusp (or, as its name suggests, in the "middle") of old and new worlds, Middlemarch contains both the gentlemanly, old-fashioned "natural history" of a Farebrother and the theoretical, professionalized "natural science" of a Lydgate.

Old-style natural historian Camden Farebrother resides, appropriately, in a parsonage furnished by his father and grandfather. In defining "natural history," historian Lynn Merrill could just as well be describing George Eliot's affable cleric:

> relaxed, acquisitive, eclectic, natural history in the traditional mold appealed to the layperson. Anyone with a keen eye could ramble across the countryside, making field observations [and studying natural objects] . . . not systematically . . . but discursively, with pleasure and aesthetic appreciation . . . To the

> naturalist, natural objects, rather than being grist for scientific theories, were valuable in themselves, as distinct, beautiful, evocative "singularities."[1]

Like many an early nineteenth-century clergyman with butterfly net or excavating hammer in hand, Farebrother seems less interested in the Creator than in His creation: "I fancy I have made an exhaustive study of the entomology of this district. I am going on both with the fauna and flora; but I have at least done my insects well. We are singularly rich in orthoptera" (17:170).

By contrast, Middlemarch also contains arch-"theoriser" Tertius Lydgate, a small-town general practitioner with big ambitions both to discover the "primary webs or tissues" of which all organisms are composed, and "to contribute towards enlarging the scientific, rational basis of his profession" (15:145, 146). Predictably, laboratory scientist Dr. Lydgate is patronizingly dismissive of Revd. Farebrother's botanizing: "I have never had time to give myself much to natural history. I was early bitten with an interest in structure" (17:170). But the reader should not assume that George Eliot shares Lydgate's rather arrogant dismissal of "natural history." Is it coincidence that Farebrother's "subtle observation" (63:631) of his medical friend over the course of the novel leads him to compassionate moral insight of the sort Lydgate himself sorely – and ultimately disastrously – lacks?

In very many ways, George Eliot is a novelist who looks before and after; if we recognize Wordsworthian romantic raptures in her fiction, for example, we also find experiments with stream of consciousness that might be said to anticipate Virginia Woolf. It is thus consonant with George Eliot's intellectual temperament that there should be two, equally important, models for the "scientific" novelist: old-fashioned, observing "natural historian"; and modern, theorizing "natural scientist." On one hand, we find in all of George Eliot's fiction the keenly appreciative eye of the "natural historian," delineating the evocative particularities of a "singularly rich" array of human nature. On the other, those individualized characters are also richly contextualized within the reflective generalizations of an omniscient narrator "bitten with an interest in structure," a discriminating creator who identifies and delineates larger patterns of meaning.

Throughout her career as a novelist, George Eliot was to live and work alongside a man who was an observer and a theoriser rolled into one: George Henry Lewes who, while a scientific popularizer, wanted also to be known as a true scientist in his own right. But even before she met Lewes and became "George Eliot," Marian Evans was deeply engaged with contemporary scientific thought.

Before exploring some of the biographical contexts of George Eliot's lifelong interest in science, however, I want to return briefly to that cosmological, eighteenth-century definition of "science" quoted above. Like the fictional Lydgate, real-life nineteenth-century pioneers endeavored to "enlarge the scientific, rational basis" of a new, professionalized experimental science. But while doing so, they remained mindful of the earlier, epistemological definition of "science": "a connected body of demonstrated truths"; "observed facts systemically classified"; "trustworthy methods for the discovery of truth."

For George Eliot and many of her contemporaries, the word *science* was often prefaced by the adjective *positive*. In "The Progress of the Intellect" (1851), her premiere contribution to the *Westminster Review*, she makes the first of many admiring references in her essays and letters to the positivistic philosophy of Auguste Comte (whose six-volume *Cours de philosophie positive* was published between 1830 and 1842): "theological and metaphysical speculation have reached their limit, and . . . the only hope of extending man's sources of knowledge . . . is to be found in positive science" (Pinney, p. 28).

John Stuart Mill, an early mentor of George Henry Lewes and member of Lewes's and George Eliot's intellectual circle, shared this interest in positivism. Mill's definition of Comte's "positive science" epitomizes the quintessentially Victorian cosmology shared by George Eliot and the scientific thinkers who influenced her work: "What [Comte] really meant by making a science positive," Mill writes in 1865,

> is . . . giving it its final scientific constitution; in other words, discovering or proving, and pursuing to their consequences, those of its truths which are fit to form the connecting links among the rest: truths which are to it what the law of gravitation is to astronomy, what the elementary properties of the tissues are to physiology, and we will add . . . what the laws of association are to psychology. This is an operation which, when accomplished, puts an end to the empirical period, and enables the science to be conceived as a co-ordinated and coherent body of doctrine.[2]

Gravitation is to astronomy as tissues are to physiology as association is to psychology: the "general law" which articulates a "connected body" out of a myriad of particular and diverse empirical observations. As Lewes put it in the *Biographical History of Philosophy* (1845–46), the "highest condition" of the Positive Stage "would be to be able to represent all phenomena as the various particulars of one general view."[3] (Provocatively, Mill states that the "final constitution" of deductive science ["discovering or proving"] would "put an end to the empirical period." This claim is prophetic of both George Eliot's later novels and George Henry Lewes's culminating scientific and philosophic work, *Problems of Life and Mind*, wherein Lewes and

George Eliot question empiricism's traditional division of mind and matter; see below.)

Writing as he was six years after the publication of *The Origin of Species*, Mill could have added another, far more controversial, analogy to his list of "general laws," based upon what Victorians were calling the "development hypothesis." Charles Darwin concluded the *Origin* with a smooth rhetorical segue: "There is a grandeur in this view of life . . . that whilst this planet has gone cycling on according to the fixed law of gravity, from so simple a beginning endless forms most beautiful and most wonderful have been, and are being evolved."[4] By mentioning the "fixed law of gravity" in the same breath as the "grandeur" of the principle of natural selection, Darwin implies that these two "laws" stand on an equal footing. To read Darwin in terms of Mill's "positivistic" analogy: gravitation is to astronomy as natural selection is to biology – a single, elegant scientific principle operative across all creation (or, to borrow Lewes's words on Comte: natural selection "represent[s] all phenomena as the various particulars of one general view").

Between 1790 and 1840, geology's emergence as an independent science had enormous repercussions both for science and for religion. When Darwin set sail on *HMS Beagle* in the 1830s, he took along both John Milton's *Paradise Lost*[5] and Charles Lyell's *Principles of Geology* (1830–33). Darwin was to claim that his books came "half out of Sir Charles Lyell's brain."[6] Geology and evolutionary biology were conceptually linked: Lyell's uniformitarianism provided the vast span of time necessary for the evolution of new species and the descent of man. Uniformitarians held that there have been no divinely sponsored special creations, but rather that terrestrial forces, operating uniformly over eons, bring about gradual geological change.

For many Victorians, geology came into direct conflict with the biblical account of the earth's genesis which Milton had translated into such sublime poetry. But while readers of Lyell and Darwin (George Eliot among them) may have lost their faith in the God of Genesis, they did not necessarily lose their faith in the universe as (to reiterate Mill's words on Comte) a "coordinated and coherent" whole, what G. H. Lewes was to call in *Problems of Life and Mind* a "continuous cosmos."[7] The great Victorian treasure hunt for what Mill calls "general law" – or, to use George Eliot's famous phrase from *Middlemarch*, a "key to all mythologies" – can be seen *in itself* as a Victorian key to all mythologies, a foundational undergirding of the Victorian frame of mind.

As critics of *Middlemarch* have often pointed out, the novel overflows with failed monistic cosmologists, women and men seeking nonexistent or unattainable "keys to all mythologies." Casaubon, for example, cannot read the Germans, whose groundbreaking scholarship has scooped his academic enterprise; the "universal tissue" Lydgate is looking for is a misguided alternative to cell theory (which would not be discovered until 1838 by Germans Matthias Schleiden and Theodor Schwann). The "Prelude" to *Middlemarch* seems to announce that the doors to the continuous cosmos are locked for "later-born Theresas" of the doubt-full, change-full Victorian age, "helped by no coherent social faith and order which could perform the function of knowledge for the ardently willing soul"; "With dim lights and tangled circumstance they tried to shape their thought and deed in noble agreement."

But George Eliot follows this gloomy opening observation with a significant qualification: "after all, *to common eyes* their struggles *seemed* mere inconsistency and formlessness" (my emphasis). The inhabitants of Middlemarch – and of George Eliot's other fictional communities – will not be seen with "common eyes." They will be viewed by the microscopic eye of a "scientific" novelist "who . . . cares much to know the history of man, and how the mysterious mixture behaves under the varying experiments of Time" (I:1:3). In a letter to her publisher John Blackwood in 1876, George Eliot wrote, "my writing is simply a set of experiments in life." The words which follow that famous sentence are equally important: but I refuse, she continues, "to adopt any formula which does not get itself clothed for me in some human figure and individual experience" (*GEL*, VI:216–17).

Basil Willey made the oft-quoted pronouncement that "no English writer of the time . . . more fully epitomizes her century; [George Eliot's] development is a paradigm, her intellectual biography a graph, of its most decided trend."[8] George Eliot's biography can be read as a series of "experiments in life," in which the formulas of an era are tested on the pulse of a woman who could have been one of her own heroines.

No moment in young Marian Evans's life seems more paradigmatic of the Victorian frame of mind than the "loss of faith" she so melodramatically announced with her bold decision in 1842 to stop attending church. (This incident is discussed at length in chapter 2 above.) In the months leading up to that moment, Evans had been forming exciting new friendships with Charles Bray and his circle of provincial freethinkers, men and women steeped in the radical new theories of geological science, physiological psychology, and the "Higher Criticism" of the Bible. But Marian Evans's progress from fundamentalist faith to freethinking speculation was evolutionary rather than revolutionary. In the late 1830s and early 1840s, even as she was quoting Scripture she was also attending chemistry lectures, reading astronomy and geology. Her letters of the period overflow with metaphors that reflect the breadth of these scientific interests: "The poor girl's brain is fast losing its specific gravity and is flying off to Milton's limbo" (*GEL*,

1:108); "He is evidently a character made up of natural crystallization, instead of one turned out of a mould" (*GEL*, 1:98); "I take too much mental food to digest" (*GEL*, 1:47); "I have been in a sort of molluscous-animal state without voluntary motion" (*GEL*, 1:172); "I have been a horrid stagnant pool where you can hear nothing but croakings of miserable batrachian reptiles" (*GEL*, 1:244).

Eli Halevy points out that "the emotional piety of Evangelical religion and the hunger for experimental knowledge developed at the same time, with the same intensity, and in the same social milieu,"[9] the new industrial cities to the north of London, steeped in Nonconformity. One of the most elaborate and fully developed of George Eliot's early scientific metaphors can be found in an 1839 letter to her pious evangelical mentor, Maria Lewis:

> My mind, never of the most highly organized genus, is more than usually chaotic, or rather it is like a stratum of conglomerated fragments that shews here a jaw and rib of some ponderous quadruped, there a delicate alto-relievo of some fernlike plant, tiny shells . . . My mind presents just such an assemblage of disjointed specimens of history . . . scraps of poetry . . . Latin verbs, geometry entomology and chemistry . . . May I hope that some pure metallic veins have been interjected, that some spiritual desires have been sent up, and spiritual experience gained? (*GEL*, 1:29)

The vocabularies of geology and religion intermingle freely. In the same letter, she writes: "It was very kind of you to remember my requests about Phrenology . . . I will endeavour to tell you fully all I have been able to opine on the matter" (*GEL*, 1:30). It is no coincidence that Marian Evans so frequently uses metaphors drawn from natural science to describe mental states. Within three months of meeting the Brays, she writes to Maria Lewis that "having had my propensities sentiments and intellect gauged a second time, I am pronounced to possess a large organ of 'adhesiveness,' a still larger one of 'firmness,' and as large of conscientiousness" (*GEL*, 1:126). In the summer of 1844, Evans and Bray went to London so that she could have her head "cast" by phrenologist James Deville. Phrenology – a kind of "geology of the mind" – was a compelling scientific interest for Marian Evans during the decade of the 1840s.

Through the Brays, she became acquainted with George Combe, the leading English disciple of phrenology's founder Franz Joseph Gall (1758–1852). Phrenologists believed that (1) the brain is the organ of the mind (hardly a controversial claim today, though it was so in the nineteenth century), (2) that each region of the brain controlled a different aspect of personality, and (3) that character could thus be divined by the contour of the skull. To be sure, there was a wide-eyed faddist aura surrounding bump-reading prognostication ("crainioscopy," the phrenologists called it). As a result, phrenology has often been either ridiculed or overlooked by George Eliot's biographers and critics. But this new, would-be scientific psychology played an important role in the intellectual development of the future novelist.

George Combe's *The Constitution of Man* (1835) was the best-selling Bible of phrenology: "We are physical, organic, and moral beings, acting under general laws," Combe writes there.[10] Two decades before Darwin's *Origin of Species*, Marian Evans would embrace a scientific theory that viewed human beings as part of a biological continuum. Combe claimed that phrenology would do for the human sciences what Copernicus and Newton had done for the physical sciences. Phrenology, like positivism, is a perfect example of a would-be key to all mythologies, a hubristic Victorian synthesis on a par with the work of a "theoriser" like Tertius Lydgate (I note that Lydgate's "universal tissue" is no more scientifically correct – and no less theoretically ambitious – than phrenology's "crainioscopy").

But it should be emphasized that phrenology embraced the particular (Farebrother's "natural history") as well as the general (Lydgate's "theory"). Robert M. Young points out that Gall was "the first modern empirical psychologist of character and personality." Phrenology was the first psychology to focus on individual differences, drawing on the natural scientific skills of observation and classification. Young notes that phrenologists turned away from library and laboratory "toward common society, family life, schools, the jails and asylums, medical cases, the press, men of genius, and the biographies of great or notorious men."[11] If phrenology aspired to be natural science, it was also grounded in natural history.

Phrenology's empirical, individualistic vision of human nature spoke powerfully to the novelist-in-the-making. In July 1856, six months before beginning *Scenes of Clerical Life*, George Eliot published a lengthy review of Wilhelm Heinrich Riehl's *The Natural History of German Life* in the *Westminster Review*. In that essay, she writes scornfully of social scientists who believe that "the relations of men to their neighbours may be settled by algebraic equations," championing instead that "natural history" which bases itself upon "a real knowledge of the People, with a thorough study of their habits, their ideas, their motives" (Pinney, p. 272).

But in "The Natural History of German Life" George Eliot also reiterates the basic tenets of August Comte's positivism: "in the various branches of Social Science there is an advance from the . . . simple to the complex, analogous with that which is found in the series of the sciences, from Mathematics to Biology" (Pinney, p. 290). Comte's key to all mythologies commands both time and space. Human thought, he argues, has evolved historically through three successive "stages": from the "theological, or fictitious" to the "metaphysical, or abstract" to the "scientific, or positive."[12] Comte organizes the universe into a hierarchy of sciences, from mathematics and astronomy – the most abstract – up to biology and "social physics" – the most concrete (and note that Comte places the concrete "above" the abstract in his conceptual hierarchy). When the ultimate, positivistic stage is reached, the fundamental unity of all sciences will be clear, "all phenomena . . . particular aspects of a single general fact" (Comte, *Cours*, p. 72).

Once the "chasm between physics and physiology" has been bridged, the universality of causality and law established throughout the organic as well as the inorganic creation, the doors will be opened to a new, scientific, view of humanity. At first glance, this sounds suspiciously like the sort of abstract "algebraic equation" for human behavior that George Eliot preaches against in "The Natural History of German Life." But at the apex of Comte's hierarchy of sciences is a new science, "social science," which builds equally upon biology and psychology. (It should come as no surprise that in his *Cours de philosophie positive*, Comte spoke enthusiastically of phrenology as the embodiment of a new, "positive" psychology.[13]) "So social science," George Eliot writes in "The Natural History of German Life,"

> while it has departments which . . . correspond to mathematics and physics, namely, those grand and simple generalizations which trace out the inevitable march of the human race as a whole. . . has also . . . departments . . . which embrace the conditions of social life in all their complexity, what may be called its Biology, carrying us on to innumerable special phenomena which . . . belong to Natural History. (Pinney, p. 290)

George Eliot wrote "The Natural History of German Life" at the seaside town of Ilfracombe during the spring of 1856. She was there to stroll the beaches with George Henry Lewes, who was examining the local flora and fauna as field research for his articles on "Sea-Side Studies" for *Blackwood's* (reprinted in book form in 1858). "I felt delightfully at liberty and determined to pay some attention to sea-weeds," the apprentice natural historian writes in a marveling and marvelous journal entry:

> Indeed, every day I gleaned some little bit of naturalistic experience, either through G's calling on me to look through the microscope or from hunting on the rocks . . . There are tide-pools to be seen almost at every other step on the littoral zone at Ilfracombe . . . The Carallina officinalis was then in its greatest perfection, and with its purple pink fronds threw into relief the dark olive fronds of the Laminariae on one side and the vivid green of the Ulva and Enteromorpha on the other. After we had been there a few weeks the Corallina was faded and I noticed the Mesogloia vermicularis and the M. virescens,

which look very lovely in the water from the white cilia which make the most delicate fringe to their yellow-brown whip like fronds. (*GEL*, II:243–44)

Biological science was an interest shared by Marian Evans and Lewes from their earliest acquaintance in 1852. At the time they met, Lewes was in the midst of writing for the *Leader* on the controversial subject of the "development hypothesis" ("Lyell and Owen on Development," October 18, 1851; "Von Baer on the Development Hypothesis," June 25, 1853). Lewes and his good friend Herbert Spencer often dropped in to visit Marian Evans where she lived at 142 Strand, just around the corner from the *Leader*'s offices. Spencer himself – the object of George Eliot's affections before Lewes came on the scene – also published on "The Development Hypothesis" in the *Leader* of 20 March 1852. And Spencer's *Principles of Psychology* (1855) (a book, George Eliot enthusiastically wrote, that "gave a new impulse to psychology" [*GEL*, II:165]) would be the first to apply evolutionary theory to the human mind, arguing for the hereditary transmission of innate mental characteristics as the foundation of psychological study. (Familiar as she was with these earlier versions of evolutionary theory, Darwin's *Origin of Species* would come as little surprise to Marian Evans: "We have been reading Darwin's book on the 'Origin of Species' just now: it makes an epoch, as the expression of his thorough adhesion, after long years of study to the Doctrine of Development" [*GEL*, III:227].[14])

Marian Evans was to prove as bold sexually as she was intellectually. In 1854, she scandalized Victorian society by traveling with the married Lewes to Weimar while he worked on his biographical *Life of Goethe* (1855). The English writer was the first critic to discuss Goethe's scientific interests, in a chapter on "The Poet as a Man of Science": "Goethe was a poet in science; it is equally true that he was a scientific poet."[15] Both George Eliot and G. H. Lewes began new careers in the late 1850s, putting into practice the theories of the preceding decade. Lewes's *Physiology of Common Life*, begun in January 1858 as a series of highly popular articles for *Blackwood's*, was revised and expanded into book form in 1859–60. Working side by side with Lewes, George Eliot began *Adam Bede*, her first full-length novel, in 1857, publishing it in 1859. *The Mill on the Floss* appeared in 1860, within two months of the publication of the final volume of Lewes's *Physiology*.

After the apprentice work of Lewes's *Sea-Side Studies* and Eliot's *Scenes of Clerical Life* in 1856–57, he had proven himself a practicing scientist; she, a practicing novelist. There was a fundamental intellectual affinity between their endeavors: Lewes aspired to be a "poet in science"; Eliot, to be a "scientific poet." Reading George Eliot's fiction alongside George Henry Lewes's scientific writings reveals the complementary concerns of "poet" and "scientist." It also reveals an intellectual continuity across the two decades of their mature work – albeit a continuity characterized by what might be called an evolutionary development towards ever more complex explorations of theme and theory.

In *The Principles of Success in Literature* (1865), Lewes points out some affinities between science and literature. In both, he writes, "the relations of sequence among the phenomena must be seen . . . the experiments by which the problems may be solved have to be imagined . . . we must have distinctly *present* – in clear mental vision – the known qualities and relations of all the objects, and must *see* what will be the effect of introducing some new qualifying agent."[16] Scientist and novelist employ both observation (the "seen") *and* imagination (that creative energy which both devises the necessary "experiments" before the fact, and draws out their theoretical implications afterward). Both novelist and scientist delineate relationships, exploring ways in which those relationships alter when a "new qualifying agent" is introduced. Observation and imagination, order and change: these dynamic, interactive polarities animate all of George Eliot's fiction.

In the remaining pages of this chapter, I want to focus on three topics that characterize George Eliot the novelist as a woman of science (three "keys to all mythologies," if you will), and to offer examples of some of the ways these topics manifest themselves across the span of her fiction. The first two "keys" return us to that eighteenth-century definition of science with which this chapter began: I'll call them "observation" and "generalization." My third "key," by contrast, is distinctly nineteenth-century, a direct reflection of the new-found emphasis on physical and experimental sciences in the Victorian period. Using the terminology of George Eliot and her contemporaries, I will call this third scientific "key", "the organism and the medium."

As a fiction-writing, truth-telling "natural historian," George Eliot insisted on the importance of faithful and accurate observation as the foundation for the realism of all her fictions. Eliot was working her *Adam Bede* as Lewes penned his *Physiology of Common Life*, and the definition of "science" he offers there resonates with the central concerns of her first full-length novel. "Science," Lewes writes, "is the endeavour to make the order of our ideas correspond with the order of phenomena, to make our conceptions of things accord with the order of the things themselves; not to make out a scheme for Nature, which shall correspond with our ideas." (Echoing Lewes, Eliot was to write in her 1865 essay "The Influence of Rationalism" that "the great conception of universal regular sequence . . . could only grow out of that patient watching of external fact, and that silencing of preconceived notions, which are urged upon the mind by the problems of physical science" [Pinney, p. 413]).

Such "patient watching of external fact" is manifest in *Adam Bede* from the novel's opening paragraph. "With a single drop of ink for a mirror," the novelist recreates a carpenter's workshop in "the village of Hayslope, as it appeared on the eighteenth of June, in the year of our Lord 1799": "the afternoon sun," the "scent of pine-wood," a "rough grey shepherd-dog," and "the sound of plane and hammer" (1:5). Writing as a natural historian, George Eliot promises her readers the whole truth and nothing but, "a faithful account of men and things as they have mirrored themselves in my mind." "I feel as much bound," she says, "to tell you as precisely as I can what that reflection is, as if I were in the witness-box narrating my experience on oath" (17:175).

The novelist holds her characters to the same standards of accurate observation she sets for herself – and punishes them for failing to attain it. The two great tragedies of *Adam Bede*, Hetty Sorrel's moral downfall and Adam Bede's romantic disillusionment, stem from failures "to make our conceptions of things accord with the order of the things themselves." (This is true as well for Arthur Donnithorne's fall.) Adam looks at Hetty, Hetty looks at Arthur; each sees a subjective reflection of his own fantasies and desires. Hetty's "heart must be just as soft," Adam thinks, "her temper just as free from angles, her character just as pliant" as her beautiful body: "Every man under such circumstances is conscious of being a great physiognomist. Nature, he knows, has a language of her own, which she uses with strict veracity, and he considers himself an adept in the language" (15:152–53). In gazing at the objects of their affection, Adam and Hetty fail to see clearly because they elevate "preconceived notions" over "patient watching of external fact."

By contrast, George Eliot herself, confident that "Nature has her language, and she is not unveracious," aspires to read nature's text more accurately, succeeding where her characters fail. Although ostensibly humble ("we don't know all the intricacies of her syntax just yet") [15:153], she is ultimately confident that patient and thorough observation will reveal to both the novelist and her readers that the rough edges of reality are shaped by the underlying coherence of a "continuous cosmos": "as with every other anomaly, adequate knowledge will show it to be a natural sequence" (2:20).

To believe in "natural sequence" is also to believe in predicative ordering principles. For scientist and novelist alike, the necessary correlative of observed particulars must be universal truths. In the terms of the *OED*'s definition of science, "observed facts systematically classified" can be "brought under general laws." In *Adam Bede*, George Eliot devotes many pages to dissecting Hetty Sorrell's tangled psyche. In the light of George Eliot's thorough, accurate, and discriminating observation of her vain heroine, Hetty's ostensibly irrational actions (sleeping with Arthur, hiding her pregnancy, murdering her baby) take on both comprehensibility and a retrospective inevitability: "All the force of her nature had been concentrated on the one effort of concealment"; "necessity was pressing hard upon her" (35:365). If the realism of George Eliot's fiction is the correlative of scientific observation, then its determinism (what Eliot's early phrenological mentor Charles Bray called "the philosophy of necessity"[17]) presents itself as the counterpart to scientific generalization.

How can it be, Arthur Donnithorne frets to his friend and mentor the Revd. Irwine, that "after all one's reflections and quiet determinations, we should be ruled by moods that one can't calculate on before hand"? Not so, Irwine rejoins, clearly speaking for his author: "the moods lie in his nature . . . just as much as his reflections did, and more. A man can never do anything at variance with his own nature. He carries within him the germ of his most exceptional action" (16:172). From Hetty to Maggie to Dorothea to Gwendolen, George Eliot fills her novels with impulsive and seemingly unpredictable characters who are rationally dissected by their creator to reveal the "germ" of their "most exceptional actions."

There is a vital variable, however, which must be factored into this deterministic world of cause and effect. Arthur Donnithorne himself raises the point with the Revd. Irwine: is it not true, Arthur argues, that "one may be betrayed into doing things by a combination of circumstances" (16:172)? After all, human nature does not exist in a theoretical vacuum; a biological organism lives and grows within a complex and changeful "medium" or environment (geographical, cultural, social, historical).

The new physical, experimental natural sciences of the Victorian age thus played a major role in George Eliot's intellectual development: her early interest in phrenology (which anticipated Darwin by viewing human beings as part of a biological continuum), her botanizing expeditions with George Henry Lewes, her interest in the pre-Darwinian "development hypothesis" advocated by intellectual comrades Lewes and Herbert Spencer. In 1853, we find George Henry Lewes using a phrase in *Comte's Philosophy of the Sciences* that will appear many times in George Eliot's work: "So far from organic bodies being independent of external circumstances," he writes, "they become more and more dependent on them as their organization becomes higher, so that *organism* and *medium* are the two correlative ideas of life."[18]

In "The Natural History of German Life" George Eliot echoes Lewes, articulating a scientific principle which would have wide-ranging repercussions for her fiction over the next two decades: "The external conditions which society has inherited from the past are but the manifestation of inherited internal conditions in the human beings who compose it; the internal conditions and the external are related to each other as the organism and its medium" (Pinney, p. 287). Transposed from a scientific to a literary context, there are two, equally important, applications of the concept of "organism and medium." First: the novelist cannot study individual character (the "organism") apart from the social "medium," or environment, which surrounds and shapes it. Second: there is a vital connection, an organic link, among all "organisms" within a common "medium," each a living part of a larger whole. If *literary realism* is the correlative of scientific observation in George Eliot's fiction, and *necessitarianism* the product of scientific generalization, then *organic form* is the definitive attribute of that distinctively Victorian "medium" in which George Eliot's fictional organisms live and breathe and have their being.[19]

In an 1868 essay "Notes on Form in Art," George Eliot defines literary "form" as "wholes composed of parts more & more multiplied & highly differenced, yet more & more absolutely bound together by various conditions of dependence" (Pinney, p. 433). Any number of Lewes's scientific writings over the years could provide a source for this statement; in his book *Comte's Philosophy of the Sciences* (1853), for example, he defines the "social organism" in terms that are virtually identical to Eliot's definition of a fictional organism: "that regular and continuous convergence of an immensity of individuals, each endowed with an existence, distinct . . . and nevertheless all ceaselessly disposed . . . to concur by a multitude of various means in one general development."[20]

If Adam Bede and Hetty Sorrel are distinctively observed individuals, they are also members of an intricately interconnected community, "organisms" whose behavior is powerfully effected by both the biological and social "mediums" in which they live. Chapter 37 of *Adam Bede*, Hetty's "Journey in Despair," finds its heroine as much animal as she is human; wandering, both metaphorically and literally, in "the horror of . . . darkness and solitude. There were sheep in the next field . . . and the sound of their movement comforted her . . . Delicious sensation! She had found the shelter: she groped her way, touching the prickly gorse" (pp. 386–87). Hetty and Arthur's sexual transgressions have a profound effect on the entire community of Hayslope. "Men's lives," the Revd. Irwine reminds Adam, "are as thoroughly blended with each other as the air they breathe . . . I feel the terrible extent of suffering this sin of Arthur's has caused to others; but so does every sin cause suffering to others" (41:423). Listening to the townsfolk singing a ceremonial harvest song in chapter 53, *Adam Bede*'s narrator offers her "hypothesis" that the song's origin is collective, a compositional "unity" which "may rather have arisen from that consensus of many minds which was a condition of primitive thought" (519). The "Marriage Bells" of chapter 55 which unite Dinah and Adam are only a romantic afterthought to the novel's true resolution; the communal "harvest supper" where Hayslope reaffirms its organic unity.

It is a long way from the homely harvest supper in Hayslope that ends *Adam Bede* to the glittering gambling tables of Leubronn where *Daniel Deronda* begins; but the "scientific" concerns of George Eliot's fiction remain constant across the span of her career, even as they broaden and evolve. *Daniel Deronda* opens with the same keenly-observed naturalistic detail as *Adam Bede*: "It was near four o'clock on a September day, so that the atmosphere was well-brewed to a visible haze. There was a deep stillness, broken only by a light rattle, a light chink, a small sweeping sound, and an occasional monotone in French" (I:3). All of George Eliot's fictions dissect the dilemmas of determinism against a backdrop of meticulously surveyed social realism; all locate their heroes and heroines within a formative biological and social "medium." In each, organicism provides both a formal and a moral ordering principle.[21]

But the opening pages of *The Mill on the Floss* take us to another kind of landscape, markedly different from the opening of *Adam Bede*. We find ourselves not in a realistically realized carpenter's workshop, but inside the dreaming mind of the novel's narrator, where "black ships," "rich pastures," and "golden clusters of beehive ricks" (I:1:7) exist subjectively, in deeply colored childhood memory. The (literal) awakening of chapter 2 then jolts us, abruptly and self-consciously, into the "real" world of the Tulliver family and Dorlcote Mill: "'What I want, you know,' said Mr. Tulliver – 'what I want is to give Tom a good eddication'" (I:2:9). Rest assured, this "second opening" of the novel shows her readers, George Eliot is not abandoning her keen-eyed "natural history"; but the novel's opening chapter dramatically signals she will be expanding her definition of the concept.

The Mill on the Floss is replete with Darwinian explorations of the roles both heredity and environment play in shaping and determining the lives of Tom and Maggie Tulliver. Both the town of St. Ogg's and the people who inhabit it are thoroughly anatomized: George Eliot calculates the "law of life" by which Mr. Tulliver lives (III:1:197); Maggie is subject to "irreversible laws within and without her" (IV:3:288); her meeting with Stephen Guest takes place in a chapter "Illustrating the Laws of Attraction" (VI:6). But chapter 1 of *The Mill on the Floss* signals that George Eliot's fieldwork for the novel will reach farther and dig deeper than that for *Adam Bede*. "At present my mind works with the most freedom," she wrote to Barbara Bodichon during the summer of 1859; "in my remotest past, and there are many strata to be worked through before I can begin to use *artistically* any material I may gather in the present" (*GEL*, III:128–29). With *The Mill on the Floss*, George Eliot undertakes an ambitious and radical "experiment in life": autobiography as natural history, a geological expedition into the interior of the human psyche which stakes out new territory for empiricism.

Congruently, George Henry Lewes's scientific interests were turning more directly at this time to the science of psychology. In 1867 he would begin *Problems of Life and Mind* (the work he and George Eliot jokingly called his "key to all psychologies"), an ambitious, multivolumed synthesis of scientific and philosophical theory that remained unfinished at his death (George Eliot herself edited and published the final volume of the series). In many aspects, Lewes's remarkable *magnum opus* falls within the province of philosophy, but ultimately, any categorical distinction between "science" and "philosophy" in George Eliot's intellectual history must be artificially imposed.

In *The Physiology of Common Life* (two volumes, 1859–60), written during the same period as *The Mill on the Floss*, we find Lewes looking ahead to the psychological exploration which would consume him for the next eighteen years, culminating in *Problems of Life and Mind.* He does so in language which suggests that the man of science and the woman of letters, "poet scientist" and "scientific poet," were in mutually enriching communication as she wrote her novel, he his science. "The various streams of sensation which make up our general sense of existence," Lewes writes,

> separately escape notice until one of them becomes obstructed, or increases in impetuosity. When we are seated at a window, and look out at the trees and sky, we are so occupied with the aspects and the voices of external Nature, that no attention whatever is given to the fact of our own existence; yet all this while there has been a massive and diffusive sensation arising from the organic processes . . . Of two men looking from the same window, on the same landscape, one will be moved to unutterable sadness . . . the other will feel his soul suffused with serenity and content . . . The tone of each man's feelings is determined by the state of his general consciousness . . . Our philosophy . . . is little more than the expression of our personality.
>
> (*Physiology of Common Life*, II: 64–65)

Similarly, at the end of *The Mill on the Floss*, we find Maggie sitting "in her lonely room, with a window darkened by the cloud and the driving rain, thinking of [her] future" (VII:5: 513). At the climax of these meditations, "Maggie [feels] a startling sensation of sudden cold about her knees and feet: it was water flowing under her . . . She was not bewildered for an instant – she knew it was the flood!" (VII:5:515). "Dream-like," Maggie is "driven out upon the flood" (VII:5:517). To use Lewes's words: a powerful, "impetuous," "stream of sensation" impels Maggie to Dorlcote Mill and her brother

Tom. The adult passions drawing her towards future happiness are "obstructed" by childhood loves and loyalties, pulling her back into the past: "Huge fragments, clinging together in fatal fellowship, made one wide mass across the stream" (VII:5:521). River and flood are *both* literal and metaphoric, naturalistic scene and psychological symbol equally "real."

In this, *The Mill on the Floss* anticipates *Daniel Deronda*, another novel filled with watery collisions between inner and outer worlds, ideals made real. "I saw my wish outside me," Gwendolen Harleth confesses to Deronda, describing Grandcourt's drowning at sea (56:596); the same could be said of Morcedai, Mirah, and Deronda himself. For George Eliot and George Henry Lewes, natural scientist and metaphysician inhabit a continuous cosmos. "The ancient barrier between Matter and Mind," Lewes writes at the opening of *Problems of Life and Mind,* "so long regarded as impassable [has] vanished . . . Idealism is vindicated in all that it has of truth, and Realism is rescued. The Inner and Outer forms of Consciousness, the Subjective and Objective forms of Existence, are no longer antagonistic, but homogeneous and differentiated."[22] As science evolves into philosophy, another significant transposition takes place: "the primary law, which in Biology is expressed in the formula: Every vital phenomenon is the product of two factors, the Organism and its Medium; . . . in Psychology is expressed in the equivalent formula: Every psychical phenomenon is the product of two factors, the Subject and the Object" (*PLM*, I:101). *Daniel Deronda* explores the implications of this transformation in many fascinating ways.

I want to conclude my survey of George Eliot and science, however, with *Middlemarch*, that most "scientific" of Victorian novels. The titular subject of *Middlemarch* is overtly sociological: it is a "study of provincial life" – a title with a natural-science ring. Similarly, Lydgate is working on "The Physical Basis of Mind," the real-life subtitle of volume III of Lewes's *Problems of Life and Mind. Middlemarch* is thus a dissection of the social organism in carefully documented detail. The vocabulary of biology informs much of the novel. Eliot depicts the "myriad-headed . . . social body" of Middlemarch in metaphors which at times seem ominously literal: "Middlemarch, in fact, counted on swallowing Lydgate and assimilating him very comfortably" (15:152). In between biology and sociology in the Comteian hierarchy lies psychology: "Human psychology," Lewes writes, "has to seek its data in Biology and Sociology" (*PLM*, I:101); "if we desire to decipher Human Psychology we must study the Human Organism in its relations to the Social Medium" (*PLM*, I:140). Likewise in *Middlemarch*, biology and sociology provide the data for George Eliot's psychological investigations.

George Eliot has moved far beyond the simple empiricism of *Adam Bede*:

that "drop of ink for a mirror" with which she so confidently began *Adam Bede* is now the scratched pier-glass of *Middlemarch*, an inaccurate reflector whose surface organizes itself, pleasingly but deceptively, into "a fine series of concentric circles" around the "little sun" of the beholder's egotism (27:262). Eliot's goal in *Middlemarch* is a more complex kind of realism: "to conceive with that distinctness which is no longer reflection but feeling – an idea wrought back to the directness of sense, like the solidity of objects" (21:208). Simple reflection is both inadequate and inaccurate; the "solidity of objects" demands three dimensions, not two. It is the microscope, not the mirror, which provides the model for scientific "seeing" in *Middlemarch*.[23]

In chapter 16, George Eliot describes the scientific endeavors of her biologist-hero Lydgate. His research demands

> imagination that reveals subtle actions inaccessible by any sort of lens, but tracked in that outer darkness through long pathways of necessary sequence by the inward light which is the last refinement of Energy, capable of bathing even the ethereal atoms in its ideally illumined space . . . he was enamoured of that arduous invention which is the very eye of research, provisionally framing its object and correcting it to more and more exactness of relation; he wanted to pierce the obscurity of those minute processes which prepare human misery and joy, those invisible thoroughfares which are the first lurking-places of anguish, mania, and crime, that delicate poise and transition which determine the growth of happy or unhappy consciousness. (15:162–63)

Is Lydgate a biologist, examining specimens under a microscope, the "eye of research?" Or is he a psychologist, investigating the "minute processes" which "determine the growth of a happy consciousness?" Or is he an artist, creating order out of the "inward light" of imagination? Like his creator, Tertius Lydgate is something of all three; his research aspires to "the most perfect interchange between science and art" (15:143).

Lewes's definition of scientific research in *Problems of Life and Mind* meshes seamlessly with Lydgate's – and George Eliot's – ambitions for this novel:

> Science deals with conceptions, not with perceptions; with ideal and not real figures. Its laboratory is not the outer world of nature, but the inner sanctuary of the Mind. It draws indeed its material from Nature, but fashions this anew according to its own laws . . . having thus constructed a microcosm, half objective, half subjective . . . *Science everywhere aims at transforming isolated perceptions into connected conceptions.* (*PLM*, I:397; my emphasis)

George Eliot and George Henry Lewes have traveled a considerable distance from those definitions of "science" I discussed earlier in this chapter ("Science is the endeavour to make the order of our ideas correspond with the order of phenomena" [*Physiology of Common Life*]; science is a "patient watching of external fact, and . . . silencing of preconceived notions" ["The Influence of Rationalism"]). In *Middlemarch*, as in *Problems of Life and Mind,* science begins in "the outer world of nature" but ends in the "inner sanctuary of the Mind." Science discovers organic connections between part and whole, "transforming isolated perceptions into connected conceptions."

The microscope is both the perfect tool for scientific research and the perfect metaphor for the creative vision of a "scientific" novelist. Unlike the mirror, it illuminates objects three-dimensionally, both by the external light of the natural world and in the "ideally-illuminated" space of the imagination. The microscope "frames its object," displays it in the surrounding medium, "correcting it to more and more exactness of relation." Lydgate's researches are directed towards the discovery of "primary webs or tissues." His impulse is towards a grand Victorian synthesis, the discovery of a "common basis" for all biological structures: "he longed to demonstrate the more intimate relations of living structure" (15:147). But significantly (and very much in a Victorian frame of mind), Lydgate seeks this unity based on minute detail, careful dissection. What Lewes calls "the telescope of Imagination" must necessarily cooperate with "the microscope of Observation" (*PLM*, I:289). As Lydgate himself puts it, "a man's mind must be continually expanding and shrinking between the whole human horizon and the horizon of an object-glass" (63:630). Dissection and unification, observed particular and grand generalization, go hand in hand.

Illustratively, George Eliot intersperses her discussion of Lydgate's researches with her own dissection of his character, deftly practicing what she preaches. The novelist, like the scientist, relies on particular detail, fine distinctions ("who could appreciate all the possible thwartings and furtherings of circumstance, all the niceties of inward balance?"; "Where then lay the spots of commonness?") to support her generalizations ("all conceit is not the same conceit, but varies in correspondence with the minutiae of mental make in which one of us differs from another"; "Lydgate's spots of commonness lay in the complexion of his prejudices" [5:147–48]). The novelist employs both "telescope" and "microscope" in her efforts to "transform isolated perceptions into connected conceptions." Concrete particular and abstract generalization are as interconnected, as fundamentally interdependent, as organism and medium.

In *Middlemarch*, George Eliot imagines the novelistic "vortices" revealed by the microscopic vision of her omniscient narrator as a "web": "I at least have so much to do in unravelling certain human lots, and seeing how they were woven and interwoven, that all the light I can command must be concentrated on this particular web" (15:139). The central unifying element of

Middlemarch is the "medium" of Middlemarch itself, shared by the novel's many and varied human inhabitants, "moving with kindred natures in the same embroiled medium, the same troublous fitfully-illuminated life" (30:287).

"There is no creature whose inward being is so strong that it is not greatly determined by what lies outside it . . . the medium in which their ardent deeds took shape," George Eliot writes in the novel's finale (821–22). The medium in which George Eliot's ardent deeds took shape was the Victorian age, an era permeated by and fascinated with scientific thought. The luminous fictions of this "scientific" novelist shed light not only on the universal turmoil and truths of human nature, but on the particular intellectual concerns of that time and place in which they came to life.

NOTES

1 Lynn Merrill, "Natural History," in Sally Mitchell, ed., *Victorian Britain: An Encyclopedia* (New York: Garland, 1988), p. 530.
2 John Stuart Mill, *Auguste Comte and Positivism* (1865), rpt. in John M. Robson, ed., *Collected Works* (Toronto: University of Toronto Press), x: 290.
3 George Henry Lewes, *The Biographical History of Philosophy, From its Origins in Greece Down to the Present Day* (New York: Appleton, 1866), p. 789.
4 Charles Darwin, *The Origin of Species* (1859; rpt. W. W. Norton, 1979), p. 131.
5 See Gillian Beer, *Darwin's Plots: Evolutionary Narrative in Darwin, George Eliot and Nineteenth-Century Fiction* (New York: Routledge and Kegan Paul, 1983), pp. 34–37 for an illuminating discussion of the Darwinian and Miltonic cosmologies.
6 Charles Darwin, quoted in Michael Shortland, "Geology," in Mitchell, *Victorian Britain*, p. 328.
7 I am indebted to George Levine, "George Eliot's Hypothesis of Reality," *Nineteenth-Century Fiction*, 35 (1980):1–28 for pointing out this phrase; Levine's essay remains the best concise overview of George Eliot's scientific/philosophical ideas and their influence on her novels. See also Beer, *Darwin's Plots*. George Levine, *Darwin and the Novelists: Patterns of Science in Victorian Fiction* (Chicago: University of Chicago Press, 1991), while not directly focused on George Eliot, also illuminates "scientific" values and patterns in her fiction.
8 Basil Willey, *Nineteenth-Century Studies* (1949; rpt. New York: Harper & Row, 1966), p. 260.
9 Eli Halevy, *England in 1815*, trans. F. I. Watkin and D. A. Baker (1924; rpt. New York: Barnes & Noble, 1960), p. 559.
10 George Combe, *The Constitution of Man Considered in Relation to External Objects*, 6th American edn. from the 2nd English edn, corrected and enlarged (n.p., 1838), p. vii.
11 Robert M. Young, *Mind, Brain and Adaptation in the Nineteenth Century: Cerebral Localization and Its Biological Context from Gall to Ferrier* (Oxford and New York: Oxford University Press, 1970), pp. 18, 19.
12 Auguste Comte, *Cours de philosophie positive*, trans. Harriet Martineau, in

Gertrude Lenzer, ed., *Auguste Comte and Positivism* (New York: Harper Collins, 1975), p. 7.

13 Auguste Comte, *The Positive Philosophy of Auguste Comte*, trans. Harriet Martineau (London: Trubner, 1875), I: 388.

14 Lewes later championed Darwin's theories in a widely read series of essays for the *Fortnightly Review* on "Mr. Darwin's Hypothesis" (1868). Darwin himself enjoyed reading George Eliot's novels, though he much preferred *Silas Marner* to the more "Darwinian" *Mill on the Floss* (a fact George Levine amusingly attributes to Darwin's escapist aversion to a novel "committed to a strenuous and necessarily unpleasant moral exploration of the implications of a Darwinian world" [*Darwin and the Novelist*, p. 190]).

15 George Henry Lewes, *The Life of Goethe*, 2nd edn. (London: Smith, Elder, 1864), p. 278.

16 George Henry Lewes, *The Principles of Success in Literature* (1865; rpt. Berkeley: University of California Press, 1901), p. 66.

17 Charles Bray, *The Philosophy of Necessity; or, The Law of Consequences: As Applicable to Mental, Moral, and Social Science* (London: Longman, Green, Longman & Roberts, 1863).

18 This concept was also central to Herbert Spencer's *Principles of Psychology*, wherein Spencer put forth his "broadest and most complete definition of life" as "*the continuous adjustment of internal relations to external relations*" (Longman, 1855), p. 374.

19 George Eliot's "organicism" is the central focus of Sally Shuttleworth's *George Eliot and Nineteenth-Century Science: The Make-Believe of a Beginning* (Cambridge and New York: Cambridge University Press, 1984).

20 George Henry Lewes, *Comte's Philosophy of the Sciences* (London: Henry G. Bohn, 1853), p. 263.

21 Shuttleworth points out the rich interpenetration of theory, form and values in Eliot's fiction: e.g., in *Daniel Deronda,* where "it is impossible to divorce George Eliot's methodological reflections . . . from the narrative form of the novel or its social themes" (*GE and Nineteenth-Century Science*, p. 177).

22 George Henry Lewes, *Problems of Life and Mind: The Foundations of a Creed, 1st series: Houghton, Osgood* (Boston, 1875–80), I: 69. Hereafter cited in the text as *PLM.*

23 See Mark Wormold, "Microscopy and Semiotic in *Middlemarch*," *Nineteenth-Century Literature,* 50.4 (March 1996): 501–24 for an extended discussion of *Middlemarch* and microscopes.

7

BARRY QUALLS

George Eliot and religion

And so the poor child, with her soul's hunger and her illusions of self-flattery, began to nibble at this thick-rinded fruit of the tree of knowledge . . . For a week or two she went on resolutely enough, though with an occasional sinking of heart, as if she had set out towards the Promised Land alone, and found it a thirsty, trackless, uncertain journey. *The Mill on the Floss*, 1860

Pray, don't ever ask me again not to rob a man of his religious belief, as if you thought my mind tended to such robbery. I have too profound a conviction of the efficacy that lies in all sincere faith, and the spiritual blight that comes with No-faith, to have any negative propagandism in me. George Eliot, 1862

What is George Eliot's New Providence . . . ? Towards what in earth and heaven does she beckon us on? Robert Laing, *Quarterly Review*, 1873

"She is the first great *godless* writer of fiction that has appeared in England . . . the first legitimate fruit of our modern atheistic pietism," declared W. H. Mallock in 1879 as he reviewed *Impressions of Theophrastus Such* (*CH*, 453–54).[1] In a century of so many doubters, Mallock exaggerates; but he also sees George Eliot's crucial place – even more than Thomas Carlyle's – as (in Lord Acton's words about her) "the emblem of a generation distracted between the intense need of believing and the difficulty of belief" (*CH*, 463). Her Maggie Tulliver and Esther Lyon and Dorothea Brooke and Gwendolen Harleth are women in search of a vision, of a faith that might sustain and give their lives purpose. But the words that sustained the Bible's Hebrews and Bunyan's pilgrim, that mapped their journeys towards the Promised Land, offer no sure guides. Silas Marner finds his belief in the Bible's truth destroyed by a drawing of lots in the name of what Bunyan called that "book that cannot lie"; Maggie Tulliver, not even reading the Bible, finds no aid – and finally drowns because of it. Silas lives; the hand of a little child leads him "towards a calm and bright land" – in "merry England" (14:130; 1:5).

Tellingly, the author who represented to her generation what the novel could accomplish did not write, did not think, without the texts that she abandoned when she lost her faith, without the language of the Bible and the traditions that formed around it, without the histories of its texts that she transformed into contexts and structures for the lives of her characters. Her history of religious engagement is a history of Victorian England's engagement with God and the Bible. Yet perhaps no image better tells *all* of George Eliot's religious story than the one of her reading Tennyson's *In Memoriam* after the death of George Henry Lewes. Like Queen Victoria at the death of Prince Albert, she needed the poet's "sanctification of human love as a religion" (Pinney, p. 191). This sanctification was also the work of her novels.

George Eliot's Straussian scriptures

> It seems to me the soul of Christianity lies not at all in the facts of an individual life, but in the ideas of which that life was the meeting-point and the new starting-point. We can never have a satisfactory basis for the history of the man Jesus, but that negation does not affect the idea of the Christ either in its historical significance or in its great symbolic meanings.
>
> (*GEL*, 30 July 1863; IV:95)

George Eliot in this letter is discussing Renan's *Life of Jesus*. Her comments come out of a three-decade history of struggling with the meaning of the Bible and Christianity for the nineteenth-century mind. Her idea of social and moral development and her belief in the inexorable progress of history required that the Bible's texts be read historically as the products of human efforts to find language for ideas that were not human but incorporated human aspirations. Indeed, in her last published book, *Impressions of Theophrastus Such* (1878), she returned again to the Bible and Israel, and to the sources of much of her writing life. In "The Modern Hep! Hep! Hep!" she celebrated Israel and its scriptures as the source of that "divine gift of a memory which inspires the moments with a past, a present, and a future, and gives the sense of corporate existence that raises man above the otherwise more respectable and innocent brute" (*ITS*, 144). Focusing on the anti-Semitism of her world, she reminded her readers that "a people owning the triple name of Hebrew, Israelite, and Jew" created, and kept alive, religious traditions that constituted "the birthplace of common memories and habits of mind, existing like a parental hearth quitted but beloved" (156).

This statement of 1879 offers a final summation of George Eliot's central religious ideas, ideas that had been developing since she began questioning the Anglican faith of her father. Reading in 1841 Charles Hennell's *Inquiry Concerning the Origin of Christianity* (1838), she was impressed to find him considering "Christianity as a divine revelation" and "as the purest form yet existing of natural religion."[2] That "natural" is for her crucial; she understood Hennell to be arguing that "the true account of the life of Jesus Christ, and of the spread of his religion, would be found to contain no deviation from the known laws of nature, nor to require, for their explanation, more than the operation of human motives and feelings, acted upon by the peculiar circumstances of the age and country whence the religion originated." For Hennell, who had no acquaintance with the work of the German "higher critics" like David Friedrich Strauss, who set out to demythologize the scriptures through reading them as documents for anthropological investigation, the life of Christ was the work of human myth-makers who seized on the truth they apprehended in the historical Jesus and created grand fictions of belief.

In Hennell's work, George Eliot found what were to be the fundamental beliefs of her "religious" life. When in 1846 she published her translation of David Friedrich Strauss's *Leben Jesu* (1836) and in 1854 her translation of Ludwig Feuerbach's *Das Wesen des Christenhums* (1845), she was putting into circulation in England ideas more sophisticated and developed than those she had discovered in Hennell, that she would discuss often as a reviewer for the *Westminster Review*, and that she would represent more often in her fiction. Strauss wrote in his opening discussion:

> A main element in all religious records is sacred history; a history of events in which the divine enters, without intermediation, into the human; the ideal thus assuming immediate embodiment. But as the progress of mental culture mainly consists in the gradual recognition of a chain of causes and effects connecting natural phenomena with each other; so the mind in its development becomes ever increasingly conscious of those mediate links . . . and hence the discrepancy between the modern culture and ancient records, with regard to their historical portion, becomes so apparent, that the immediate intervention of the divine in human affairs loses its probability. *(Leben Jesu*, 39)[3]

Near the end, as he considers "the dogmatic import of the life of Jesus," he says: "The history [of Jesus] is not enough; it is not the whole truth; it must be transmuted from a past fact into a present one; from an event external to you, it must become your own intimate experience" (*LJ*, 784). These words, which for many in the nineteenth century summarized Strauss's work of destroying the historical basis of Jesus and thus of Christianity, are important, I think, for an understanding of George Eliot's lifelong need of the Bible, its language and typologies. Understanding how she read Strauss and Feuerbach allows us to see why at the end of her writing career she turned so definitively to Israel's history and the Jews in *Daniel Deronda* and *Theophrastus Such*. The novel is her last rewriting of that story she had told so often: the story of men and especially women seeking texts by which to live, sources in historical and cultural memory that would sustain the private life and allow one to be a part of a moral community. In the end she is still rendering characters who would discover in *human* history sources of the sacred, who would find in the historical past a vision of how to live. The assertions in *Theophrastus Such* that Israel has given the world a source of "common memories" and aspirations is, finally, a critic's evaluation of her methods in writing *Deronda*.

In the letters written during her work of translation in 1844–46, she spoke of her "soul-stupefying labour," and even interpreted her headaches as the "leanness" sent by Heaven into her soul "for reviling" the Gospel writers (*GEL*, I:182, 185). But she persisted. Strauss offered her ways of belief *then* that made faith – no matter what its foundations, or lack of them – possible even amidst what her contemporaries would call unbelief. Strauss, as Theodore Ziolkowski pointed out, basically rediscovered the ancient Christian way of reading scriptures figurally – the ways of scriptural reading that George Eliot's evangelical heritage had taught her. Ziolkowski notes that Strauss's "mythic interpretation of the life of Jesus is in effect nothing but figural interpretation applied in reverse."[4] For Strauss, the Gospel writers engaged in self-conscious typological reading of scriptures, consciously constructing the life of Jesus to fit the predictions and prophecies of the Hebrew scriptures. Strauss added irony to typology: where traditional readers, from the contemporaries of Jesus through the Church fathers, through Patrick Fairbairn in the nineteenth century (the foremost typologist of the period), through Mary Ann Evans, "read" Jesus' life as the fulfillment of the promises of Hebrew scripture, Strauss read him as a literary "construction," not a deception but certainly not a historically accurate fact. Strauss's remarks, above, establish his sense of the connection between inexorable historical and scientific progress and the resulting necessity of a mythical reading of the Bible. For George Eliot, such progress made fictions of all religions *unless* they could be cast free from history, from their dependence on "past fact," and become part of the "intimate experience," the spiritual and psychological life, of each individual. In the 1840s she found in Strauss both the typological structures familiar from her evangelical upbringing, and the irony about those structures that *for her* secured them as spiritual truths while disconnecting them from what was scientifically unacceptable.

She also found in Strauss a focus on the community of believers and a way of writing this community that would bedevil her representations of women throughout her writing. In Strauss the consciousness of the community has power, not Jesus, and certainly not the women who people *his* story. Seeking to represent the "unity of the divine and human natures" in "the whole race or mankind," seeking to overthrow the focus on Jesus as the realization of this idea and to place that focus on the human community, Strauss could not separate himself from the rhetoric of separate spheres that marks so much of nineteenth-century representations of women – and so much of the Victorian debate about the "Woman Question."

> Humanity is the union of the two natures – God becomes man, the infinite manifesting itself in the finite, and the finite spirit remembering its infinitude; it is the child of the visible Mother and the invisible Father, Nature and Spirit; it is the worker of miracles, in so far as in the course of human history the spirit more and more completely subjugates nature, both within and round man, until it lies before him as the inert matter on which he exercises his active power. (*LJ*, 780)

Strauss's book constitutes an impressive effort to make humanity the carrier of religious value, to make the story of Jesus the sacred text formed by the religious consciousness of Jesus' community. But another hierarchy prevails here even as Strauss would remove Jesus from his spiritual hierarchy and substitute the human beings who believed and wrote. That hierarchy is a hierarchy of nineteenth-century sexual distinctions: Mother/Nature, Father/ Spirit – this latter "subjugating" the former until it is "inert" before *his* "active power."

Feuerbach, whose *Essence of Christianity* George Eliot translated (signing for the only time in her life as Marian Evans) refuses this Straussian formula of male power. Indeed he reverses the subjugation and elevates woman in the Comtean positivist way: the Madonna is the community's angel. Yet these ideas provide no solution to the problems George Eliot was to have in developing plots for the women in her fictions who might live outside of loving. Feuerbach wrote of love and of Christ:

> the essential idea of the Incarnation, though enveloped in the night of the religious consciousness, is love. Love determined God to the renunciation of his divinity. . . . Love conquers God . . . Who then is our Saviour and Redeemer? God or Love? Love; for God as God has not saved us, but Love, which transcends the difference between the divine and human personality.
> (*Essence of Christianity*, 53)

> we have, if not *in concerto* and explicitly, yet *in abstracto* and implicitly, the feminine principle already in the Son. The Son is the mild, gentle, forgiving, conciliating being – the womanly sentiment of God. God, as the Father, is the generator, the active, the principle of masculine spontaneity; but the Son is begotten without himself begetting, *Deus genitus*, the passive, suffering, receptive being; he receives his existence from the Father . . . The Son is thus the feminine feeling of dependence in the Godhead; the Son implicitly urges upon us the need of a real feminine being . . . Where faith in the Mother of God sinks, there also sinks faith in the Son of God, and in God as the Father . . . Love is

> in and by itself essentially feminine in nature. The belief in the love of God is the belief in the feminine principle as divine. Love apart from living nature is an anomaly, a phantom. Behold in love the holy necessity and depth of Nature!
> (*Essence of Christianity*, 71–72)[5]

George Eliot would in her reviewing career echo both Strauss and Feuerbach. In her 1855 essay, "Evangelical Teaching: Dr. Cumming," she laments the absence in evangelical zealots like Cumming of any sense of "the life and death of Christ as a manifestation of love that constrains the soul, of sympathy with that yearning over the lost and erring which made Jesus weep over Jerusalem" (Pinney, p. 163).

> The idea of God is really moral in its influence – it really cherishes all that is best and loveliest in man – only when God is contemplated as sympathizing with the pure elements of human feeling, as possessing infinitely all those attributes which we recognize to be moral in humanity . . . The idea of a God who not only sympathizes with all we feel and endure for our fellow-men, but who will pour new life into our too languid love, and give firmness to our vacillating purpose, is an extension and multiplication of the effects produced by human sympathy.
> (Pinney, pp. 187–89)

George Eliot: the typologies of her realism

In her translations and reviews, as in her novels, we confront George Eliot's lifelong need for the Bible's language and typologies in order to ensure the representation, and comprehension, of the sacred in her realistic project. Her famous pronouncements on art – "If art does not enlarge men's sympathies, it does nothing morally" – derive from this sense of the necessity of faith in a human being's capacity for love and fellowship achieved through suffering; that is: for a human being's capacity to represent, typologically as it were, the incarnation. Her commitment to the "typical" in her novels was, she said, her way of securing her readers' lasting sympathies (*GEL*, II:86); the typical allowed her to build a community between her fictive characters and her readers. And more: her commitment to a realist aesthetic, which is after all part of the Straussian project[6] that began her writing career, involved a commitment to the representation of particulars that threatened always to obliterate the "typical," to sever characters from the very traditions of memory and human feeling that were to "bind" them and their actions into the human community.

To achieve these double representations, at once "real" and "typical," George Eliot, from *Scenes of Clerical Life* through *Daniel Deronda*, used the language and tropes of the Bible.[7] Indeed, in her early fiction she represents her concerns through characters and scenes placed among dissenting religious groups, particularly Methodist. Amos Barton and Edgar Tryan in *Scenes of Clerical Life* and Dinah Morris in *Adam Bede* are derived from the rich tradition of dissent that so shaped English social and cultural – as well as religious – life in the early decades of the nineteenth century. (Rufus Lyon in *Felix Holt* also comes from this tradition.) Yet the Reverend Irvine in *Adam Bede* joins Tryan before him and Farebrother in *Middlemarch* as voices of the Feuerbachian religion of love (the Anglican clergy in *Deronda* show none of this "ministry"). What George Eliot does to these ministers is significant: she "naturalizes" their faith, giving them a Feuerbachian typicality. Irving and Farebrother are Anglican; Tryan is Methodist. But all three take on the character of "natural supernaturalism" that Carlyle defined as the one path towards apprehending the sacred in the modern world.

George Eliot's art of naturalization of the sacred committed her to the use of traditional religious iconography, especially the emblem tradition (which originated in medieval Catholic Europe and achieved high popularity in the English Renaissance, especially in Francis Quarles's *Emblems Divine and Moral*). The revival of the emblem book in the nineteenth century, through the many editions of Francis Quarles and the new emblem books that appeared throughout the century, attests to the needs of readers and authors to find in pictorial representation a sense of "the dual character of all things."[8] The scene in *Adam Bede* where Hetty Sorrel sits admiring her image in the mirror while Dinah Morris sits before the window meditating is organized emblematically to remind readers of the moral significance of quotidian gestures (5). The numerous vanity mirrors that surround the solipsistic women characters are a traditional device of religious iconography. The burden on the backs of Silas Marner (1:3) and of the man Dorothea Brooke sees from her window (80:776) comes from the "Old Testament" prophecies of Isaiah by way of *Pilgrim's Progress*. These obvious emblems allowed George Eliot to battle against the implications of her realism. Their very *un*reality – the ways they call attention to their significance outside the "realistic" enterprise of the novels – urged readers to locate significance in the material world, to hear the parable in the particular. Her emblems function rather as do her book and chapter titles and those mottoes that she affixed to chapters in her last three novels: they proclaim, with Bunyan, "I have used similitudes." And if they do not make the heavens and earth and other human beings "emblems of his glory," as Quarles asserted was the function of his emblems, they were intended to "rouse the soul," to appeal to the inward world of readers – to become, in Strauss's words, part of their "intimate experience."

Yet the representations of memory and of women in these novels tell us about the problems George Eliot encounters in using the language of tradition to represent something very different. *Adam Bede* and *Silas Marner* are novels that carry epigraphs from Wordsworth, and repeatedly remind us that human beings find their spiritual resources in other human beings and in their sense of long-developed communion with people and place. The famous passage in which the narrator of Marner's history reminds us that "In the old days there were angels who came and took men by the hand and led them away from the city of destruction" (14:130) recalls not only Bunyan's pilgrim but the great stories of rescue that George Eliot always needs. The epigraph from Wordsworth replaces the angel with the child who, "more than all other gifts / That earth can offer to declining man, / Brings hope with it, and forward-looking thoughts." Past and present, Bunyan and Wordsworth, meet in George Eliot's language; the ways to the celestial city – to Raveloe – are surely through a Wordsworthian landscape. Her repeated evocations of Wordsworthian memory – of spots of time – work to establish in the individual consciousness a sense of connection with past and present, of the ways memory redeems the barrenness of existence. The narrator's invocation of memory in *The Mill on the Floss* is one of the most characteristic moments of George Eliot's Wordsworthian meditations in her early novels:

> . . . what grove of tropic palms, what strange ferns or splendid broad-petalled blossoms, could ever thrill such deep and delicate fibres within me as this home scene? These familiar flowers, these well-remembered bird-notes, this sky . . . such things as these are the mother tongue of our imagination, the language that is laden with all the subtle inextricable associations the fleeting hours of our childhood left behind them. Our delight in the sunshine on the deep bladed grass to-day, might be no more than the faint perception of wearied souls, if it were not for the sunshine and the grass in the far-off years, which still live in us and transform our perception into love. (I:5:41–42)

If "the loves and sanctities of our life had no deep immovable roots in memory" (II:1:152), the narrator wonders, how can life rise above its barrenness? It was a question George Eliot's critics also asked.

The memory that verses and hymns and communal traditions – and the image of the child and good woman – recall are repeatedly invoked in George Eliot's fictions. Janet Dempster (in *Scenes of Clerical Life*) is rescued by the ministrations of the Reverend Tryan; the "burthen" is removed from her, "the water-floods that had threatened to overwhelm her had rolled back again, and life once again spread its heaven-covered space before her" (25:289). Tryan is the "heaven-sent friend who had come to her like the angel in the prison, loosed her bonds, and led her by the hand till she could look back on the dreadful doors that had once closed her in" (27:299). The result: "Infinite Love was caring for her. She felt like a little child whose hand is firmly grasped by its father" (27:290). But though rescued, she cannot rescue her brutal husband; she feels "as if she were standing helpless on the shore, while he was sinking in the black storm waves" (24:282). He dies as the narrative tells us that their last look at each other "was almost like meeting him again on the resurrection morning, after the night of the grave" (24:282). The similes throughout, with their insistent reminding of the reader (through "like") that they are tropes (George Eliot does not have Charlotte Brontë's metaphorical certainties), show us the work the writer is doing.

And this work continues. Esther Lyon in *Felix Holt* finds that in knowing Felix she achieves the "first religious experience of her life . . . the first longing to acquire strength of great motives and obey the more strenuous rule" (27:225). Writes the narrator: "It is only in that freshness of our time that the choice is possible which gives unity to life, and makes the memory a temple where all relics and all votive offerings, all worship and all grateful joy, are an unbroken history sanctified by one religion" (44:359). In an earlier novel, Romola, betrayed and miserable, sits in the darkness:

> No radiant angel came across the gloom with a clear message for her. In those times, as now, there were human beings who never saw angels or heard perfectly clear messages. Such truth as came to them was brought confusedly in the voices and deeds of men not at all like the seraphs of unfailing wing and piercing vision . . . The helping hands stretched out to them were the hands of men who stumbled and often saw dimly, so that these beings unvisited by angels had no other choice than to grasp the stumbling guidance along the path of reliance and action which is the path of life, or else to pause in loneliness and disbelief, which is no path, but the arrest of inaction and death.
>
> (36:309–10)

We are not far from Dorothea Brooke of *Middlemarch*, whose "influence" produces in Lydgate a belief that she "has a heart large enough for the Virgin Mary" (76:757); and she indeed does rescue him – if only to a life of failed ambitions lived with Rosamond Vincy. No more than Dinah Morris' prison-cell rescue of Hetty Sorrel do these rescues have the magical effect that Silas Marner's golden-haired child has on him when she enters his cottage in place of the stolen gold. From the perspective of George Eliot's realism, the Marner story is indeed a parable, one to teach Eppie's father Godfrey Cass that his "promised land" (of family and children) is only a sentimental fiction because he refused rescue when he had the opportunities (15:131). Real visions of such lands do not come in George Eliot without self-sacrifice and an acceptance of sorrow. Love begins in the recognition that (Christ's) suffering connects us to our fellow human beings in communion.

All the biblical language and traditional iconography of rescue show the work George Eliot does – and her need of religion's signs – to create her fictions. But there is a problem here, and the story of Maggie Tulliver begins to define its nature. "If the past is not to bind us, where can duty lie?" she asks. "We should have no law but the inclination of the moment" (VI:14:475). This sense of connection of past to present, of individual to community, is an issue of faith in these novels, but it does not rescue Maggie, nor make her a figure of rescue (except to Philip Wakem); she does seek to rescue her brother but brings him down to drown in the effort. She can find no way to the "promised land," nor does she even know what that land might be. She chooses home over her passion for Stephen Guest; and the narrator comments: "Home – where her mother and brother were – Philip – Lucy – the scene of her very cares and trials – was the haven towards which her mind tended – the sanctuary where sacred relics lay – where she would be rescued from more falling" (VI:14:479). This language, like the language of passages about Esther Lyon and Romola, is religious in its effort to convert the home to a sanctuary, the natural world around us to a sacred space of love and rescue. Except: Maggie's home has never been this, neither in childhood nor later, and it cannot be. This woman who wishes for "a world outside of [loving]" (VI:7:413) never escapes that need of love, and of giving love, that is so crucial to establishing the iconic nature of George Eliot's heroines. The invocation of "deep immovable roots in memory," by the narrator and by Maggie, is a fiction; it will not, does not, rescue the heroine. No wonder the flood that ends the novel is so melodramatic; it cannot be read typologically because no biblical restoration or blessing on the good is possible in this "real" world.

Among George Eliot's women, only Romola is totally successful in turning herself into that emblem of divine love that so much marks Dickens's and his contemporaries' celebration of the angel in the house. (Even Dorothea's name – gift of god – does no work allegorically; Casaubon cannot be saved.) George Eliot wants, I think, to question these modern recastings of women as secular versions of Christ; she is suspicious of representing women as selfless angels of rescue – particularly because the men they rescue tend always to signify the power of patriarchy to silence a woman's will to act, her need to make a world for herself outside of loving. Thus George Eliot uses very ambiguously the emblem of rescue from shipwreck, so much a part of her imagination of rescue (and an emblem that had great power in the nineteenth-century imagination).[9] Her heroines often pray to submerge their wills, to find some way forward out of confusion. But only Romola, floating passively on a river, and wishing for death, brings rescuing life – and becomes a Madonna of the Italian rocks.

As George Eliot resists the sexual politics of these representations, her sense of the need for something to reverence and her commitment to the ideas of development from Strauss, Feuerbach, and Darwin push her towards women as the sacred care-givers, the bringers of light to the lives of community. "Love is in and by itself essentially feminine in nature" – in Feuerbach and in George Eliot. She may resist the implications of male power and control, but love for her remains feminine, and women and their "influence" its great source. Philip Wakem's sublime letter to Maggie Tulliver gives witness to this: "I believe in you," he begins, and then blesses her for "the new life into which I have entered in loving you": "The new life I have found in caring for your joy and sorrow more than for what is directly my own, has transformed the spirit of rebellious murmuring into that willing endurance which is the birth of strong sympathy" (VII:3:502–3). George Eliot needs types; she depends on typology to create the moral territory of her realism. Her "happiest women, like the happiest nations, have no history" (VI:3:385); they are subjugated by the spirit, the type becomes their spiritual overseer, and, as Deirdre David notes, they patrol the moral territories of their world.[10]

George Eliot's contemporary Richard Simpson, a Roman Catholic, saw this and wrote in 1863, before Romola and Dorothea Brooke appeared to confirm his assertions,

> It is no small victory to show that the godless humanitarianism of Strauss and Feuerbach can be made to appear the living centre of all popular religions . . . In the relation she gives to the sexes we see something of the old Teutonic veneration for women, and something of the worship of mother, wife, and daughter enjoined by Comte . . . Woman is put before us as the treasury of divine gift; and man has very little to give to her, but much to accept from her . . . Her women, perhaps, are so much alike, because her idea of woman is so one-sided and so simple . . . That which gives the religious charm to George Eliot's novels is the way in which she handles the doctrine of renunciation and self-sacrifice for the benefit of others. In this she speaks as a Christian, even as a Catholic . . . It is indeed a Christian anthropology, without the basis of Christian theology.
> (*CH*, 225, 240, 243, 245, 247)

George Eliot also understood this. For her, history and development made such anthropology a necessity. The ideological commitments she made to Strauss and Feuerbach ensured – even dictated – that she represent women like Dorothea as more than complex individuals, as gifts of God to their worlds. In her last novel she asserted these commitments more fiercely than ever – and also questioned them.

George Eliot and the promised land

When she turned to *Daniel Deronda*, George Eliot gave up those "roots in memory" that were defined by Wordsworthian nature. Readers have always noted *Daniel Deronda*'s difference from the other novels: it is a bolder enterprise than George Eliot's usual emblematic representations and plottings. Its titular hero is so much a character "type" (and the word is used constantly about him) that, for many, he scarcely seems "real" at all – at least not so real as Gwendolen Harleth. The plot that propels this new Moses towards Israel at the novel's end is scarcely what the plots of *Middlemarch* or *The Mill on the Floss* had been. George Eliot takes *Deronda*'s plot from the Bible, more specifically from the story of Israel's exile and its desire to secure the promised land. Her use of biblical tropes and emblems becomes an explicit method of representation; the coincidences that sometimes appeared flaws in her novels become here signs of a *religious* apprehension of reality that is more defined by her sense of Israel's history than by Strauss and Feuerbach. The novel begins in a gambling casino, in a contemporary harsh, decadent world, from which "Old England" has vanished. It ends with Manoa's elegy from the conclusion of *Samson Agonistes* – as if the Philistines who populate England and the casinos of the Continent had been destroyed and the children of light were triumphant in their cleansed promised land. There is no real closure here, especially for the woman whose "story" constitutes half the novel. This ending seems to make nonsense of the structures of realism through which George Eliot had hitherto constructed her world.

And yet this ending is not nonsense. In this final novel, George Eliot has come face to face with the implications of her need both for Strauss and his mythical reading of the scriptures (which had inaugurated in the 1840s her work of public writing) and for Feuerbach and his celebration of love as feminine. This bald plotting at the end of her writing career is George Eliot's own ironic return to Strauss, a return necessitated by her sense that her fictions, as "experiments in life," needed to be even bolder if they were "to keep hold of something more sure than shifting theory." The "past revelations and discipline" (*GEL*, VI:216–17) that she found sustaining at the end of her career required a return to Israel, to the Jews with what Mordecai calls their "divine principle" of "action, choice, resolved memory" (42:459). Yet this return to Strauss also questions the very work of realism to which he and George Eliot had committed their careers.

Daniel Deronda is organized typologically. Its formal construction insists that we recognize its epic historical foundation: a beginning *in medias res*, constant allusions to the Bible and to religious epics of Milton and Dante and Tasso, and a structure modeled on Tasso's *Gerusalemme liberata* (we remember that this is one of the "genteel romances" that Gwendolen has "by heart" [5:37]). George Eliot bases the novel's structure, *its two plots*, on an episode in Tasso's epic, and, very likely, on Handel's *Rinaldo*, which uses the same episode (the last song Mirah sings in the novel [61:623] is the aria "Lascia ci'io pianga" from Handel's opera). This episode involves a Christian knight, Rinaldo, in love with Almirena, the daughter of Godfrey, the Christian leader of the forces trying to liberate Jerusalem from the heathens; the opposition to the Christians – and to the heroine's love – is Armida, an enchantress who commands dragons and who loves Rinaldo. Her reward is conversion; his, Almirena; Godfrey's, Jerusalem. In Tasso, there is no Almirena as there is in the opera; there Armida takes both forms – helpless maiden in the water crying out for Rinaldo to rescue her and queen of the heathen forces.

Daniel Deronda's basis in Tasso is important because it indicates the kind of typological work George Eliot self-consciously undertook.[11] In the novel everything is reversed: George Eliot's Christians are the heathens, and they need the Jews for liberation. And this is the point. Facing, like Strauss, a world where miracles do not happen, and where religious language has become mere "nomenclature" (to judge by the book's English clergy), George Eliot decides to save her world "dogmatically" by once more resurrecting, and only sometimes ironically, the old stories, the old plot that had formed the substance of her evangelical upbringing and of her first public writing. This old plot offers readers an "accustomed pattern" (22: epigraph, 202) of representing faith and moral community. George Eliot places form so baldly on the surface of this novel because of religion's basic absence from the communities of power and material significance the novel represents, and because she wants to confront those communities with the historical meaning of Israel and its "resolved memory."

But there is a problem in this use of scriptural typology that George Eliot could not resolve, and that accounts, I think, for the dissatisfaction with the novel expressed by critics from the time of its publication. So powerfully have Gwendolen's needs been represented that readers long for something more for her than Daniel's words of wisdom before he goes off to seek a newer world. Gwendolen's failure to rescue Grandcourt from the water ("I did kill him in my thoughts," she says to Deronda) implicitly contrasts with the selfless Deronda's saving of Mirah as *he* floats passively along the river: a scene of action that prepares him to be recognized as Mordecai's long-sought "type" and to go off to rescue Palestine for his people. This man is reunited with his heritage, and with the powers of the typological imagination towards which he himself had been moving. Gwendolen is left alone, lost in a space larger than she ever imagined, "with the look of one athirst towards the sound of unseen waters" (65:658). As so often in this last novel, the image is a note from the Bible – and from George Eliot's long career of writing such characters. Yet there is a sense of absence here.

And it is not simply the absence of God, though it is that too. God and the idea of Israel shape Deronda's romance; Gwendolen lives in the "realism" of a deadened world. What happens here implies George Eliot's sense of the limitations of typological tradition – even Strauss's ironically conceived one – for representing women who would be more than mere rescuing vessels. Victorian commentators on types and typology rarely suggest any possibility of women as significant actors outside the territory of moral/ethical/spiritual issues. Anna Jameson, the art historian and a close friend of George Eliot, considered various types of women in painting. She pronounced the Hebrew matriarchs Rebekah "a type of the Church" and Rachael a type of the "contemplative or holy life." She denied Bathsheba, Uriah's adulterous wife whom David coveted, any place "among the types." Of Eve she says, tellingly: "in the temptation, the accepted characteristics of the sexes are reversed: Eve falls through ambition and the desire of knowledge; Adam falls through weakness, affection, or by persuasion."[12]

The women who refuse the typical in George Eliot are inevitably reversers of type, haters of the typical. Her ambitious women are almost always the guardians of an unemblematic realism, the despisers of tradition and its confinements, the enemies of the typologies of the patriarchs. Unlike her women whose typical work removes them from the actions of history (Dorothea Brooke is the sublime example), Daniel Deronda engages the world typologically, and thus historically. Typology of whatever kind rests on patriarchal traditions. The window that gave Dinah Morris a vision of Providence showed Dorothea Brooke that her role was one of rescue. It shows Gwendolen Harleth nothing; although she finally detaches herself from the vanity mirror, and from the need to be always a spectacle for the gazes and speculations of others ("Church was not markedly distinguished in her mind from the other forms of self-presentation"[48:516]), she remains in her labyrinth, waiting for Deronda or another to give her a "clue" about how to read her world and her place in it.

George Eliot sees that the typology so necessary to her realistic enterprise is a male tradition, and that it allows women no freedom to act *in* history. That seeing is represented, however ambiguously, in the appearance of the Princess Leonora Alcharisi, Deronda's mother, who tells him he is a Jew and thus reconnects him to the past and its traditions that he so desires and that she would have obliterated, for him and herself. She certainly has "no place among the types" because she has chosen against types; like Eve she reverses the type of the sexes. Not for her the patrolling of moral terrains: "Had I not a rightful claim to be something more than a mere daughter and mother? . . . acknowledge that I had a right to be an artist . . . you can never imagine what it is to have a man's force of genius in you, and yet to suffer the slavery of being a girl. To have a pattern cut out – 'this is the Jewish woman; this is what you must be; this is what you are wanted for'" (53:570–71, 51:541). As for love: "It is a talent to love – I lacked it . . . I know very well what love makes of men and women – it is subjection. It takes another for a larger self, enclosing this one" (53:571). The Judaism of her father patterned everything to bondage. The only act of love she is capable of is suppression of her son's heritage: "I delivered you from the pelting contempt that pursues Jewish separateness" (51:544). For Daniel, his meeting with this dreamed-of mother is a "disappointed pilgrimage to a shrine where there were no longer the symbols of sacredness. It seemed that all the woman lacking in her was present in him as he said . . . – 'Then are we to part, and I never be anything to you'" (53:566).

This is, for me, the signally illuminating scene in all of George Eliot's fiction, the point where she allows all that she values, all the ideas and beliefs embodied in her fictional worlds, to be questioned without qualification. The old language is here; pilgrimages to shrines in *Felix Holt* and *Romola* and *Middlemarch* allow rescue, love. But here, for this one woman, love is bondage, the appropriation of others for a "larger self." Declaring she is no "monster," she reminds her son that the roles of woman and mother mean nothing to her; she wants nothing to do with Daniel's vision of himself as a new Moses who will found a new Israel. Women have no roles in that vision except to serve. The Brontëan intensity of this woman defeats all of Deronda's words – and George Eliot's. She is not to be rescued into *their* world. The dangers of the very myths that animate Deronda and his creator are exposed by Alcharisi, for whom they have been binding chains on her nature. The "great current" the novel celebrates has been for her a drowning. And the paradox is not resolved by the "Judaism with a difference" that will be Deronda's messianic theme. It is the paradox involved in the very need of myths – and in the ways that women have never, whether in the Bible's or in Strauss's or Feuerbach's, occupied in them roles outside loving or disobedience.

And yet the princess sends for Deronda because of the power of those types and the patriarchal tradition that they serve. At the end, Strauss's Spirit and Nature battle once more, and Nature is subjugated. Judith Wilt calls this encounter of "The Mother and the Son" "the foundation of the novel's moral situation." Alcharisi's father, as Wilt notes, is a "God who created Eve, instead of Adam, by mistake, and then was forced to work through her, fashioning his typological man from her womb, not her rib." The princess herself, says Wilt, is "an Eve who awakened fully to herself immediately and who felt in herself the 'charter' to all Adam's heritage . . . the acting out of [the earth's] myriad possibilities."[13] We are surely not surprised when Alcharisi questions Deronda about the woman *he* loves:

> "Not ambitious?"
> "No, I think not."
> "Not one who must have a path of her own?"
> "I think her nature is not given to make great claims."
> . . .
> "Why, she is made for you, then." (53:569–70)

In this acid remark, as in the two chapters that are hers, the Princess Alcharisi counters the novel's typological energies with her own; she argues that typology shuts a woman out of history, closes off a woman's choices, denies her any possibilities but performing according to pattern.

And yet the Spirit – of her father, of the typological tradition that constitutes the novel's fundamental structuring principle – crushes her. Her last words in the novel tell all: "Good-bye, my son, good-bye. We shall hear no more of each other. Kiss me" (53:571). Her words have no power to create a world, for herself or for a son. For George Eliot, in rejecting her religious heritage, Alcharisi has rejected life. The rest is silence.

Bunyan asked "Whether we were of the Israelites, or no?" George Eliot asks this same question in her last novel. Alcharisi is, but only literally. Gwendolen is not; and yet this Englishwoman is an Israelite in the most urgent way imaginable: in her suffering. Daniel Deronda gives his name to the novel because the name emphasizes its parable: Daniel – "God is my judge." In George Eliot's last novel, God is "the heart of mankind," as Mordecai defines Israel, "the core of affection which binds a race and its families in dutiful love" (42:453). This understanding, this vision, requires one thing: "The sons of Judah have to choose that God may again choose them . . . The divine principle of our race is action, choice, resolved memory" (42:459). This idea of consciously *choosing* something beyond the self that lives in memory and that enlarges our lives and gives us the power to acknowledge and then to reconcile the ideal and the demonic within us must be recognized, accepted, if the world is not to become our imprisoning hell. As the novel's motto says, "Let thy chief terror be of thine own soul."

George Eliot's Straussian and Feuerbachian scriptures constitute one of the essentials of her art, and one of its signal stumbling blocks in representing women who would be more than figures of rescue, more than figures outside of history and without individuality. For Gillian Beer, the novel's conclusion marks Gwendolen Harleth's liberation: "She has come through plot and out of plot, into the indeterminacy of that which succeeds the text."[14] Perhaps. But early in the novel George Eliot had lamented that "the religious nomenclature belonging to this world was no more identified for [Gwendolen] with those uneasy impressions of awe than her uncle's surplices seen out of use at the rectory" (6:52). George Eliot is not easy in a world without some patterns and typologies; they recall our roots in sustaining memory. She wanted these typologies understood according to Strauss and Feuerbach; and perhaps she intended her readers to see Gwendolen's unclosed story as a sign that Daniel's words and the typologies they represent have been "transmuted from . . . an event external to [her]" and "become [her] own intimate experience," working spiritually and psychologically from the past into her undetermined future. Perhaps. But images of Romola instructing children before a portrait of Savonarola, of Dorothea without a history, of Maggie absorbed in the flood – all hover over this last ending. And Strauss's figure of the Spirit subjugating Nature, making her "inert" before the triumph of his "active power," shadows the close of *Daniel Deronda* because it summarizes the life of the Princess Alcharisi.

George Eliot understood this, and risked it. One of her most discerning critics, R. H. Hutton, who found in *Middlemarch* something "dark and cold," calls her work in *Daniel Deronda* "religious."

> no book of hers before this has breathed so distinctly religious a tone, so much faith in the power which overrules men's destinies for purposes infinitely raised above the motives which actually animate them, and which uses the rebellion, and the self-will, and the petty craft of human unworthiness, only to perfect the execution of His higher ends, and to hasten His day of deliverance. It is true that so far as this book conveys the author's religious creed, it is a purified Judaism, – in other words, a devout Theism, purged of Jewish narrowness, while retaining the intense patriotism which pervades Judaism . . . it would be as idle to say that there is no conception of Providence or of supernatural guidance involved in the story, as to say the same of the Oedipean trilogy of Sophocles. The art of this story is essentially religious . . . (*CH*, 366)

It *is* essentially religious because George Eliot, as she was also to do in "The Modern Hep! Hep! Hep!," placed in Israel the "deep immovable roots" of English spiritual memory. (A comparable movement happens in Matthew Arnold's religious writings.) She gave up her appeals to the Wordsworthian world of "the old days" represented in all her novels before *Deronda*; Deronda himself warns that "There's no disappointment in memory, and one's exaggerations are always on the good side" (35:362). Israel is real, the idea of Israel a matter of historical development and survival. George Eliot found in Israel the type of the "divine gift of memory" uniting past, present, and future that had history as its witness. She saw its role as "the birthplace of common memories and habits of mind" essential for modern man if the spirit of belief was to survive a mind-numbing materialism. Its literature, she noted, "has furnished all our devotional language" (*ITS*, 161); the Jews' "ways of thinking and . . . verbal forms are on our lips with every prayer which we end with an Amen." These are "the influences which have made us human" (*ITS*, 163). She turned boldly to Israel at the end of her writing life because she found there memories that could not lie; she found there a narrative of survival through history that suggested the power of a language and literature; she found in the "divine gift of memory" that Israel represented the source of a people's faith and of a fiction's power.

No wonder many of her readers found her books to be "second Bibles" (*GEL*, VI:340). The Bible's tropes and language *and* its religion recalled readers to their heritage of faith and its language and sounds, and to the developing history of that heritage. George Eliot intended this. For her, Israel's endlessly developing idea of God "pour[s] new life into our too languid love, and give[s] firmness to our vacillating purpose," as she said in the 1855 review of Dr. Cumming. Earlier, in a review of F. D. Maurice's sermons, she wrote: "The Jewish nation and the 'man Christ Jesus' are . . . types of the normal relations to God."[15] From the beginning she kept the Bible "by heart." Or else all was silence.

NOTES

1 All quotations from contemporary critics of George Eliot's work are found in *CH*.

2 All quotations from Basil Willey's consideration of Hennell in *Nineteenth Century Studies* (1949; New York: Harper & Row, 1966), pp. 210–16.

3 David Friedrich Strauss, *The Life of Jesus Critically Examined*, trans. George Eliot, ed. Peter C. Hodgson (Philadelphia: Fortress Press, 1972). Hereafter cited in the main text as *LJ*.

4 Thoedore Ziolkowski, *Fictional Transfigurations of Jesus* (Princeton: Princeton University Press, 1972), p. 52.

5 Ludwig Feuerbach, *The Essence of Christianity*, trans. George Eliot (New York: Harper & Bros., 1957). Feuerbach notes that "Protestantism has set aside the Mother of God; but this deposition of woman has been severely avenged" (72), an idea that deserves consideration alongside George Eliot's comment, in her 1856 review of von Riehl's *The Natural History of German Life*, that "Protestantism and commerce" have transformed English traditional life and severed the "roots intertwined with the past" that so much characterize the history of European men (Pinney, p. 288).

6 Hans Frei discusses the impact of Strauss in *The Eclipse of Biblical Narrative: A study in Eighteenth- and Nineteenth-Century Hermeneutics* (New Haven: Yale University Press, 1974). See also E. S. Shafer, *"Kubla Khan" and The Fall of Jerusalem: The Mythological School in Biblical Criticism and Secular Literature, 1770-1880* (Cambridge: Cambridge University Press,1975)

7 Both Elisabeth Jay, in *The Religion of the Heart: Anglican Evangelicalism and the Nineteenth-Century Novel* (Oxford: Clarendon Press, 1979), and Valentine Cunningham, in *Everywhere Spoken Against: Dissent in the Victorian Novel* (Oxford: Clarendon Press, 1975), trace the ways George Eliot's fiction found its sources in her Evangelical heritage, especially the Methodist tradition represented by her aunt, Elizabeth Evans (considered the model for Dinah Morris) and the Evangelical tradition she found during her years at Maria Lewis's school and in the journals and books she read. Jay (*Religion of the Heart*, ch. 4) stresses the crucial influence of the Evangelical background on the conception of realism that the novels offer. Cunningham (Everywhere Spoken Against, ch. 7) details how much in the novels, especially *Adam Bede* and *Felix Holt*, George Eliot took from her heritage – from Southey's *Life of Wesley*, from Methodist memoirs and hymns, etc. As Jay points out, George Eliot is "the one major novelist to portray Evangelicalism with detailed fidelity and imaginative sympathy" (209). Christopher Herbert provides a necessary perspective on this context of George Eliot's work in his discussion (in *Nineteenth-Century Fiction*) of the ways Dinah Morris and the Reverend Irvine offer the Methodist and established church responses to Nature and to human nature. U. C. Knoepflmacher, in *Religious Humanism and the Victorian Novel*, places George Eliot in a larger contemporary context, and gives particular attention to the late novels; his comment that for her "faith alone could be a substitute for faith" (p. 18) is important in considering the nature of "belief" in her work.

8 W. Harry Rogers, *Spiritual Conceits* (London: Griffith & Farran, 1852), n.p.

9 George Landow discusses this crucial image in his *Victorian Types and Shadows: Biblical Typology in Victorian Literature, Art, and Thought* (Boston: Routledge & Kegan Paul, 1980); he finds "a great, almost astonishing, revival of biblical typology" in the first two-thirds of the century (p. 3).

10 Deirdre David, *Intellectual Women and Victorian Patriarchy* (Ithaca, N.Y.: Cornell University Press, 1987), p. 223.

11 See my *The Secular Pilgrims* (Cambridge: Cambridge University Press, 1982), pp. 168–88, for an extended discussion of *Daniel Deronda* and typology.

12 Anna Jameson (continued and completed by Lady Eastlake), *The History of Our Lord, As Exemplified in Works of Art: with that of His Types, St. John the Baptist, and other Persons of the Old and New Testament* (London: Longman, Green, 1864), pp. 106, 146, 152–54.

13 Judith Wilt, "'He Would Come Back': The Fathers of Daughters in *Daniel Deronda*," *Nineteenth-Century Literature*, 42 (December, 1987): 320–21.

14 Gillian Beer, *Darwin's Plots: Evolutionary Narrative in Darwin, George Eliot, and Nineteenth-Century Fiction* (New York: Routledge & Kegan Paul, 1983), p. 218.

15 [George Eliot], *Westminster Review*, 59 (April 1853), 587.

8

NANCY HENRY

George Eliot and politics

"Confound their petty politics!" This is the curse of Tertius Lydgate in the days leading up to the fateful vote for the chaplaincy of the Middlemarch infirmary. He had hoped to remain above such trivial concerns and to concentrate on his medical research and practice. Yet, as in other affairs, Lydgate's character flaws are as much to blame for his unintentional entanglements as are the circumstances into which he is thrown. George Eliot's narrator describes Lydgate's state of mind before the vote by a metaphor that points outward to a greater political scene: "He could not help hearing within him the distinct declaration that Bulstrode was prime minister, and that the Tyke affair was a question of office or no office; and he could not help an equally pronounced dislike to giving up the prospect of office" (II:18:146). Lydgate's highly rationalized yet spontaneous vote for Tyke and against Farebrother wins him "office," but he eventually finds reason to regret his desire for this prize, so uncomfortably won by his public display of party loyalty.

For George Eliot, national and local politics reflect the same aspects of human psychology and may be explained in terms of each other. She did not need to elaborate and analyze a fictitious political cabinet, as Anthony Trollope would in his political novels, to show that temptations to power invite the placement of self-interest above both personal loyalties and the communal good. In *Romola*, the setting is Florence at the end of the fifteenth century. Here, in Savonarola's short-lived Florentine Republic, the treacherous local politics are state politics. In this volatile climate, the Greek Tito Melema, arguably her most political character, seems drawn to intrigue by his own fractured identity. His explicitly Machiavellian desire to advance himself by pleasing all parties entails a severing of fundamental bonds and a shifting personality that emerges through a series of calculations and performances. He betrays his wife Romola and denies his adopted father, fashioning himself by effacing his past.

George Eliot's next novel, *Felix Holt*, is traditionally viewed as her "political novel" because the social conditions leading up to England's Reform Bill of 1832 are its immediate subject and the machinations surrounding the election of the member from Treby Magna unify its plots. In contrast to Tito's denial of his origins, Felix Holt, as Catherine Gallagher has noted, "attempts to become one with his origins."[1] He rejects the values and material comforts of the social-climbing middle classes in order to recover his father's artisan-class origins. The rough and stubbornly unpleasing Felix lacks the complexity of the villainous Tito. His solidity of purpose and refusal to play political games make him the victim of a corrupt system which misinterprets honest motives.

Perhaps because George Eliot never experienced the first-hand disillusionment with English politics that Trollope did when he was defeated in his run as a Liberal candidate for Parliament in 1868, her narratives avoid cynicism as well as pointed social criticism. They punish egoism and reward virtue and therefore refuse to admit that calculating political players do sometimes win. Tito destroys himself politically and physically, dying a terrible and distinctly unrealistic death. Felix Holt is vindicated and left free to pursue his modest, unambitious personal life. Andrew Thompson observes that *Romola* suggests the limitations of the philosophy of Machiavelli, who appears as a character in the novel, in his "concentration on the game of politics to the exclusion of social, economic and religious factors except insofar as these impinge upon the political."[2] George Eliot viewed politics in the narrow sense as merely an integral part of the larger social tableau. The historical conditions in which Lydgate, Tito, and Felix move are drawn with such care to show us that politics, whether local or national, call forth and test moral character.

Women, however, are not similarly tested. Their moral character is measured by their responses to domestic situations. Romola obeys an ideal of marriage higher than any feelings for her faithless husband. Esther Lyon abandons her "fine lady" pretensions, renounces her inheritance, and thereby achieves happiness with Felix. Rosamond Lydgate fails absolutely as the wife who might have saved her husband. George Eliot's explorations of character and the historical settings of her narratives absolve her of the obligation to comment on contemporary politics. Her broadly social concerns make room for women as more than background characters, but her novels also suggest the futility of any woman's attempt to make a political contribution. Harold Transome tells his mother that it does not signify what women think because "they are not called upon to judge or act" (2:35). The words sting Mrs. Transome, but she is in the defeated position of old age, a silenced prisoner of her early mistakes. While the novel shows the bitterness with which she is forced to accept her son's wishes, there is nonetheless a truth in Harold's statement about English society in the early 1830s that still obtained in the mid-1860s when George Eliot wrote the novel.

George Eliot's life and fiction raise questions about whether women in mid-nineteenth-century England might be said to have a politics, and of whether their political views would be taken seriously by their contemporaries. Marian Lewes, like Mrs. Transome, felt the social disapprobation of an "adulteress," and was forced to live and work around the restrictions of this stigma. Her eventual moral authority as an author gave her no more political legitimacy than any other woman. Her women characters, for all their rebelliousness, never take part in politics. Their aspirations to effect social change, such as Dinah Morris's preaching or Dorothea Brooke's designs for workers' cottages, are subsumed in and extinguished by their responsibilities to men. Even those women characters who are surrounded by the world-historic events of past centuries, like Romola or *The Spanish Gypsy*'s Fedalma, understand their duties first and finally as wives and daughters. George Eliot seemed content to imagine them as better women, rather than as political agents. We have to wonder whether this apparent retreat from strong, political positions into the realm of psychology and domesticity might have followed from her recognition that women's political opinions did not yet signify. She even questioned whether they should signify before women were sufficiently educated to assume the responsibilities of participation in democratic government.

Some men took George Eliot's political opinions seriously. Her publisher John Blackwood came from a tradition of Scottish Toryism. The men in his family either entered the family business, which in addition to the publishing house of Blackwood and Sons included the nation's most influential conservative journal, *Blackwood's Edinburgh Magazine*, or they served in the Indian army, as did his brother, Major William Blackwood. Marian Evans's transfer of business in 1857 from John Chapman and the *Westminster Review* to *Blackwood's* represented a slide to the political right. It is in her correspondence with Blackwood that many of her opinions about contemporary politics emerge.

Blackwood was pleased with *Felix Holt*. On April 26, 1866 he wrote to his London agent, Joseph Munt Langford, that George Eliot's "politics are excellent." Referring to the debate surrounding new proposals for parliamentary reform, he added that her "sayings would be invaluable in the present debate" (*GEL*, IV:247). Later, he was inspired by Benjamin Disraeli's speech to the working men who would benefit from his proposed Conservative reforms. After the passing of the Second Reform Bill on August 15, 1867, Blackwood pursued his idea and entreated George Eliot to write an essay for *Blackwood's* applying some of Felix Holt's views about worker education and social responsibility to the political situation thirty-five years later.

The generically anomalous "Address to the Working Men by Felix Holt" (*Blackwood's*, January 1868) is the most directly political work that George Eliot ever published. It is an extension of her fiction, a footnote to the novel presented as an essay and carrying the name of a fictional author/character. During a period when journalistic articles were not signed, the author "Felix Holt" was familiar to readers who had read the novel by George Eliot. A few days after she began the "Address" (on November 22, 1866), Blackwood urged her on: "You have the knowledge of what the working men ought to do and the real feeling towards them which will give a force to your words which no ordinary address could possibly possess" (*GEL*, IV:402). An ordinary address presumably would be neither fictional nor written by a woman. Perhaps because he was dealing with a woman, whose authority to speak about a political process from which she was excluded was dubious, Blackwood emphasized feeling as the force behind her knowledge. When the "Address" was completed, Blackwood approved, musing that "[i]f the mass could appreciate rightly such words and feelings, what a grand nation we would become" (*GEL*, IV:411).

What were the sentiments expressed by Felix Holt, "the Radical," which Blackwood thought too fine for the fictional audience to which they were addressed? The conceit is that Felix Holt is addressing working men recently given the franchise. He looks back to the time of the First Reform Bill and refers to his own experiences with violence in Treby Magna in December 1832. The tone of the "Address," in keeping with Felix's character, is didactic and condescending while striving not to be. Felix explores variations on the organic metaphor – crops, the human body – to emphasize the great responsibilities that come with voting and the need to consider the good of all social classes within the nation when advocating reforms.

The organic metaphor had been a favorite with Marian Evans at least since the early 1840s: "I think the best and the only way of fulfilling our mission is to sow good seed in good i.e. prepared ground, and not to root up tares where we must inevitably gather all the wheat with them" (*GEL*, I:163). In his "Address," Felix Holt elaborates one organic metaphor which was central to the plot of *The Mill on the Floss*. The politics of water in that novel represent the confluence of social laws and the laws of nature. Mr. Tulliver makes the fateful decision to go to "law" over his "legitimate share of water-power" (II:2:154). He asserts that he will force Mr. Pivart, "with his dykes and erigations," not to redirect water away from the Floss and Dorlcote Mill, "if there's any law to be brought to bear o' the right side" (I:2:155). While the laws determining the flow of water are the indirect cause of Tom and Maggie's ruined lives, it is the water itself which obliterates the power of such laws by flooding and destroying human property and lives.

That the redirection of the Floss's tributary, the Ripple, for the purposes of irrigation might have broader political significance is suggested by Felix Holt's comments in the "Address": "Suppose certain men, discontented with the irrigation of a country which depended for all its prosperity on the right direction being given to the waters of a great river, had got the management of the irrigation before they were quite sure how exactly it could be altered for the better" (Pinney, p. 417). Such irrigating men, he claims, would be like working men voting before they were educated enough to know what to vote for, and the analogous consequences of natural disaster and political disaster show how serious George Eliot felt the question of worker education to be for English society and democracy.

Part of the need Blackwood imagined Felix Holt's words meeting was that of pacification. Agitation prior to the passing of the 1867 bill contributed to anxieties that the 500,000 newly enfranchised working men might overstep the boundaries of their legal rights and begin to demand further class-based reforms. Felix opposes class identification and agitation which, he argues, would divide the social body against itself, leading to "wretched calamities," "civil war," "bestiality," and insanity (Pinney, p. 423). He warns his fellow artisans and workers that if they descend into disorder and find themselves amongst the "brutal rabble," they will "see government in the shape of guns that will sweep us down in the ignoble martyrdom of fools" (Pinney, p. 424).

The "Address" argues in relatively simple language for a long-range view of national growth and change. Felix Holt offers few practical political suggestions and eschews the notion of an immediate amelioration of social injustice by political means. He asserts: "No political institution will alter the nature of Ignorance, or hinder it from producing vice and misery" (Pinney, 426). George Eliot's most political essay is in fact distinctly antipolitical.

Felix's views appear to be consistent with Marian Evans's thinking about politics in the years following the Reform Bill of 1832. The question, however, of whether Felix is merely, as Thomas Pinney writes, "a mouthpiece for his creator," is complicated by the pressure she felt to produce the essay (Pinney, p. 415). The role of political spokesman did not sit comfortably with Marian Lewes. Her journal suggests that she wrote the "Address" only at Blackwood's "repeated request" (*Journals*, 131). She felt under obligation to him for gracefully taking her back after her defection to George Smith for the publication of *Romola* in 1863. After she finished the piece, Blackwood thanked her for what he considered "a personal favour to myself" (*GEL*, IV:411). George Eliot never claimed that her characters spoke directly for her. Trollope wrote in *An Autobiography* that he used his characters "for the expression of my political and social convictions" because he was unable "to speak from the benches of the House of Commons, or to thunder from platforms."[3] The way George Eliot chose to present political ideas depended on her thorough absorption in the character she was creating and the readers she imagined as comprising both her fictional and her actual audience. There is as much characterization as politics in her political fiction. While Felix Holt's address is devoid of irony, her other most explicitly political writings, the chapters of *Impressions of Theophrastus Such*, also written under the double cover of the pseudonym and the voice of a male character, display a completely different tone.

When Theophrastus looks back on the issues of reform and radicalism recalling *Felix Holt* and *Middlemarch*, he describes the character of Spike, "A Political Molecule." Spike, a rising middle-class manufacturer, prides himself on being a liberal. In this "as well as in not giving benefactions and not making loans without interest, he showed unquestionable firmness" (7:65). Echoing the objections of Felix Holt to working-class interests, Theophrastus denounces similar class interests among the middle classes, but in contrast to Felix, his comments are ironic rather than didactic. Spike is ignorant and educated narrowly to understand only his own self-interest. "Radical" would be "an epithet which was a very unfair impeachment of Spike, who never went to the root of anything" (65). It is impossible to imagine a greater contrast among George Eliot's works than that between the insistent irony of Theophrastus and the solemnity of Felix Holt.

Even while daring to suggest, through the character of Felix Holt, what working men should do, George Eliot remained reluctant to support political causes of any kind. She declined the invitations to political advocacy from close women friends, such as Barbara Bodichon, to whom she wrote in March 1868 about women's education and women's work, that such points "do not come well from me, and I never like to be quoted in any way on this subject" (*GEL*, IV:425). Nor was she persuaded by the examples of other women, such as Harriet Martineau, Bessie Rayner Parkes, Clementia Taylor, and Edith Simcox. Unlike these women, she refused to donate time or (with rare exceptions) money to political causes. For example, she showed interest in aiding the Coventry workers in 1862 but gave only the token support of one pound to the cause (*GEL*, IV:72). She refused to give money to a fund for Italian patriot Giuseppe Mazzini because it might promote "conspiracy" (*GEL*, IV:199).

These reservations about embracing even the limited political action that was available to her have led to the general retrospective conclusion that she was "conservative." And she did not object to describe herself in these terms, telling Clifford Allbutt, for example, that "the bent of my mind is conservative rather than destructive" (*GEL*, IV:472). Consistently, she showed herself to be a social critic who believed in a gradual reform that would not destroy the traditions which provided continuity within the small communities about which she wrote. She believed in scientific and moral "progress," but she feared the too rapid imposition of progressive ideas that threatened the modest piety of religious belief. She lamented the effects of technologies, such as railroads, but was nonetheless happy to enjoy their convenience. Her concerns about the dangers of rapid change persisted from 1843, when she wrote that "with individuals, as with nations, the only safe revolution is one arising out of the wants which their *own progress* has generated" (*GEL*, I:162), through 1867, when Felix Holt warned that "the only safe way by which society can be steadily improved and our worst evils reduced, is not by any attempt to do away directly with the actually existing class distinctions and advantages" (Pinney, p. 421).

The grounding of individual identity in place and familial duty is central to all of George Eliot's novels. But it was in 1868, with *The Spanish Gypsy*, that her writing began to represent sacrifice and commitment to larger group identities. One of the ways to think about the difference between "early" and "late" George Eliot is in the matter of these political attitudes. In *Daniel Deronda* and *Impressions of Theophrastus Such* she resumed the themes of collective identity and nationalism. In the 1870s, her views were changing in response to personal experience and developments in international politics that transformed English society and culture. While continuing to distrust what she viewed as destructive change, she nonetheless became more critical of English society and English actions throughout the empire. By examining those aspects of her life and fiction which look outward to a world that was increasingly connected to England economically and culturally, the rest of this chapter will show the significance for Marian Evans and George Eliot of three interrelated and international categories of political events and movements that dominated the latter part of the nineteenth century: war, colonialism, and nationalism.

Like most of her novelist contemporaries, including Dickens, Trollope, and Charlotte Brontë, George Eliot never represented military conflict in her fiction. John Peck attributes this general paucity of war-related material in Victorian novels to a changing cultural climate in which "Britain appears to have re-constituted itself on an almost entirely non-military basis."[4] While not represented, war hovers on the margins of *Adam Bede*, George Eliot's only novel set during the period of English history when the Revolutionary and Napoleonic wars with France overshadowed English life, even in isolated towns like her fictional Hayslope. Yet Seth Bede does not enter the local militia because his brother Adam paid "his savings to free me from going for a soldier" (1:45). Arthur Donnithorne, a character reminiscent of Jane Austen's George Wickham in *Pride and Prejudice* (1813), is an officer in the militia. Donnithorne, who obtains his commission during a later stage of the Napoleonic Wars, is a duplicitous military figure. In *Adam Bede*, the virtuous avoid the military while the dishonorable find refuge in its ranks. Despite her respect for some of the military men she knew, such as Major William Blackwood and Major-General Edward Bruce Hamley, George Eliot never represented an admirable military man in her fiction.

Like her contemporaries, George Eliot feared spontaneous "mob" violence and her fiction suggested the threat to society that such outbreaks posed. "Janet's Repentance," *Felix Holt*, *Romola*, and *Middlemarch* all represent unruly crowds, which, fueled by drink and idled energy, erupt into aggressive or violent behavior. George Eliot's anxieties about such violence are traceable to the English legacy of fear about the French Revolution of 1789, and, within her own memory, to election day violence in Nuneaton in 1832, the Chartist demonstrations of the 1840s, and the European revolutions of 1848. Her attitudes about war, however, were ambivalent in the years before she began to write fiction. In her evangelical phase, she viewed war in an apocalyptic light as a scourge of divine wrath. On February 13, 1840, she wrote to Maria Lewis that she was "getting quite martial" and losing her hatred of war. She had come to believe that "such a purgation of the body politic is very likely essential to its health," adding that a "foreign war would soon put an end to our national humours that are growing to so alarming a head" (*GEL*, 1:37). Embedded in these general comments about war from King David to Louis XIV are allusions to contemporary social conditions.

Many of her early statements about the sociopolitical condition of England came in the context of reflections about literature. In 1840 she paraphrased Carlyle's *Chartism* (1839) on the subject of the artisans of Glasgow, who live in a world of "copperas-fumes, low cellars, hard wages, 'striking,' and gin" (*GEL*, 1:71). She reported to Rufa Hennell during a visit to Manchester that "the streets and houses where humans do actually live and breathe there are far worse than any book can tell." But she kept her distance and fled local injustices: "Horrid place! we were rather glad to leave it the next day" (*GEL*, 1:179). Novelists, such as Disraeli, Dickens, and Gaskell, would assume the task of representing this underworld life of the working classes, but the fervently Christian Mary Anne Evans was at this time intent on making the analogies between social poverty and the state of the soul: "After all is the moral chaos of the world more fearful or naturally unreducible to order than the heart of an individual sinner?" (*GEL*, 1:72).

Her perception that the moral and political conditions of the world could be represented and understood through the psychological and spiritual state of the individual person would distinguish her realism from that of other social protest novelists.

In her *History of the Peace*, which Marian Lewes read in 1857, Harriet Martineau describes the period 1839–40 as the "dark times."[5] Bad crops, expensive bread, typhus epidemics, and the perceived indifference of the landed classes and politicians were a prelude to the "hungry forties" and led to the unrest of Chartism among the working classes. The foreign war that Mary Anne Evans predicted would assuage if not put an end to bad "national humours" was the Opium War between Britain and China (1841–2). She and others hoped that this war of dubious morality would bring an alleviation of suffering to English workers through the enforced opening of trade with China. Elizabeth Gaskell referred to the English victory in *Ruth* (1853) as "some proud rejoicing of the nation, which filled every newspaper and gave food to every tongue."[6] But the Opium War was also condemned at the time by politicians such as William Gladstone and writers such as Martineau, who called it a national disgrace (Martineau, *History of the Peace*, p. 264) and lamented that "we are hated in China, not only as their conquerors, but for our forcing upon their society the contraband drug which they would have kept out of the reach of the intemperate of their people" (p. 277).

Martineau saw that the Opium War was brought on by English chauvinism and "our bigoted persistence" in dealing with the Chinese "according to our own customary methods and forms, and not theirs" (p. 265). In the 1870s, George Eliot came to a similar realization that this foreign war was not a healthy purgation of the body politic, but was rather the consequence of a national character flaw. She returned to the Opium War in *Impressions of Theophrastus Such*. In "The Modern Hep! Hep! Hep!" her narrator Theophrastus describes the British relationship to the Chinese as part of his defense of tolerance: "I am not bound to feel for a Chinaman as I feel for my fellow-countryman: I am bound not to demoralise him with opium, not to compel him to my will by destroying or plundering the fruits of his labour on the alleged ground that he is not cosmopolitan enough" (147). An amalgam of personal experience and a changing national political climate can account for the transformation from Mary Anne Evans's advocacy of war in 1840 to George Eliot's critical reflections on the same war in 1879. This development of her political thought paralleled her achievements in the art of fictional characterization.

On September 21, 1857 she wrote to Sara Hennell that she looked forward to a heaven "quite delivered from any necessity of giving a judgment on the Woman Question or of reading newspapers about Indian Mutinies" (*GEL*, II:383). The reading of newspapers brought depressing information that distracted her from her new vocation as a writer of fiction. During this same year, in which she published "The Sad Fortunes of the Reverend Amos Barton," she told Charles Bray that "our moral progress may be measured by the degree in which we sympathize with individual suffering and individual joy" (*GEL*, II:403). She preferred to encourage such sympathy through fiction, and her letters show minimal concern with how "our moral progress" was being measured in India.

Her early retreat from political realities, such as Manchester housing and the Indian Mutiny, changed as war came to affect her directly. By the time she wrote *Impressions*, George Eliot was able to create an English character who could criticize British foreign wars – conflicts which had seemed to her at the time of their occurrence to redress domestic problems and fulfill a divine plan. Theophrastus's impressions represent a revision of Marian Evans's attitudes to other national events. Theophrastus takes a moral position on the history of England's relations with the "Hindoos." Referring to the Indian Mutiny over twenty years after it occurred, he observes in "The Modern Hep! Hep! Hep!" that "though we are a small number of an alien race profiting by the territory and produce of these prejudiced people, they are unable to turn us out; at least, when they tried we showed them their mistake" (p. 146). George Eliot could publish such ironic observations only in the voice of a male character, who, while identified with her, was nonetheless not her. The experimental form of *Impressions* blurs the distinctions of author and character more thoroughly than had her novels. The book seems to look back not only on her life and writing but also on the history of English politics.

In 1848, striving to see an idealized order in an otherwise chaotic form of political discontent, she told John Sibree that she approved of Carlyle's assessment of the French Revolution of 1848. Joseph Butwin writes that George Eliot shared Carlyle's conservatism in interpreting these events in that she idealized the crowd "whose popular manifestations she is bound to resist."[7] The various democratic uprisings of 1848 in the German and Italian states were momentous for everyone in Britain and Europe. They also affected Charlotte Brontë, who wrote to Margaret Wooler on March 31, 1848 that she had lost her illusions about the "factious glitter" of war. Revolutions, she writes, "check civilisation, bring the dregs of society to its surface." Battles, she thinks, "are the acute diseases of nations," and "their tendency is to exhaust by their violence the vital energies of the countries where they occur."[8] George Eliot took up the theme of revolution, never addressed directly in her fiction, in "Debasing the Moral Currency." In this chapter, Theophrastus quotes Sainte-Beuve rather than Carlyle on the French "insurrectionary disturbance" of 1848. The French legacy of revolutionary violence provides a subtext to the general reflections on the ways in which "civilisation, considered as a splendid material fabric" (86), can be threatened and torn by burlesques and other forms of disrespectful and irresponsible cultural forms.

In principle, George Eliot distinguished between the uncontained disorder of revolution and the order of the military. As in the election day riot of *Felix Holt*, the military is called in to restore order – "government in the shape of guns" – as Felix ominously describes it in his "Address." But she became increasingly critical of the "barbarous" effects of war. After completing *Felix Holt*, she and Lewes traveled on the Continent and found themselves in the midst of the Austro-Prussian War (June – August 1866). They watched the "Prussian troops marching to take Eltville, which we had quitted ten minutes before" (*GEL*, IV:291). On the subject of this war, John Blackwood wrote to Lewes conveying his hope that "we are going to have at last a great united Germany, fit to cope with France" (*GEL*, IV:290). His position was determined by the traditional British policy of checking both French and Russian moves toward power. Yet he expressed sympathy for the Austrians, admitting that "nothing could have been more unscrupulous and unjust than Prussia's conduct, but only such make conquests" (*GEL*, IV:290). Marian Lewes responded in implied agreement with Blackwood and like him with mixed feelings about the war: "My heart goes to the losing side, even when it feels bound to fight with the winners." Sounding very much like a George Eliot narrator, she added: "Amid national calamities, it is the helpless and not the guilty who are the chief sufferers" (*GEL*, IV:292).

In addition to this brush with war, Marian Lewes was affected by the increasingly sophisticated and graphic coverage of European conflicts in the English press. In 1870, she followed the Franco-Prussian War (1870–71) in the *Times* and *Daily News* – "an excess in journal-reading that I was never drawn into before" (*GEL* V:117). In 1865 she had written in "A Word for the Germans" that "John Bull is open to instruction; slowly, by gentle degrees, he revises his opinions, his habits and his laws" (Pinney, p. 386). In this essay, she argued that the English needed to change their stereotypes about Germans. Accounts of the Franco-Prussian War, however, led her to transfer her own initially pro-German sympathies to the French. She lamented that the German nation and its government were not in a "higher moral condition" (*GEL*, V:118) and pitied the French, who suffered most in "this hellish war" (*GEL*, V:131). The extension of her sympathies to the victims of international warfare began to change the way she imagined the relationship between individuals and the momentous political events of her own recent memory.

The American Civil War and the Austro-Prussian War provide the historic context of *Daniel Deronda*. Their background presence intrudes upon the consciousness of both her readers and characters as the narrative unfolds. When Deronda travels to Genoa, where he will meet his mother for the first time and learn the secret of his Jewishness, the narrator observes that "the very air of Italy seemed to carry the consciousness that war had been declared against Austria, and every day was a hurrying march of crowded Time towards the world-changing battle of Sadowa" (VII:50:533). The Austro-Prussian War is a calamity in the present (1866), contending with the atrocities of the Jewish past for prominence in Deronda's thoughts. The narrator knows that this war will lead to the confederation of Germany, the formation of the Austro-Hungarian Empire, and the ceding of Venetia to Italy. She also knows that Deronda's meeting with his mother will be a crucial turning point in his rededication of his life to Jewish causes.

Through Deronda, Gwendolen Harleth Grandcourt is shaken out of her self-absorption and the tiny world of her own troubles. When Gwendolen learns of Deronda's plan to help further a revitalized Jewish nationalism, the narrator observes: "There comes a terrible moment to many souls when the great movements of the world, the larger destinies of mankind, which have lain aloof in newspapers and other neglected reading, enter like an earthquake into their own lives" (VIII:69:689). The lapping of the American Civil War and the Austro-Prussian War on the edges of her narrative in *Daniel Deronda*, as well as the novel's central theme of European-Jewish identity, reflect George Eliot's awakening to England's connection to the rest of the world.

Marian Lewes's harshest condemnation of warfare came after G. H. Lewes had died and after she had published her last book. Her comments about the Anglo-Zulu War (1879) have not been noted by critics as a significant development in her political thought. Yet the roots of her knowledge about South African politics stretch back to 1863, when Lewes's son, Thornton, emigrated to Natal. In 1865, Thornton fought with the Boers against the Basutos and wrote letters home to his father and "stepmother" explaining the complicated political entanglements of the Orange Free State, where he hoped to live in preference to British Natal. Her ongoing correspondence with Thornton and later with his brother Herbert, who emigrated in 1866, contributed to her knowledge of and interest in events in that part of the empire.

Initially, Thornton was urged to seek a career in the Indian Civil Service, but he failed to qualify for the desired position. Educated in Switzerland, Thornton was political in a romantic and fanciful way. Before emigrating to Natal, he had wanted to enlist himself on the side of the Poles, who were fighting for independence from the Russians. This decidedly unpragmatic ambition was vetoed by his father and stepmother, who were not sympathetic to nationalist ideals when it came to Thornton. Marian Evans wrote to Francois D'Albert-Durade of Thornton's "utter unfitness for military subordination" as one reason for persuading him to emigrate (*GEL*, IV:117). She did not anticipate that, rather than taking immediately to farming, he would participate in an apparently undisciplined form of colonial militia warfare.

The complex emotions Marian Lewes experienced as she took part in Thornton's career decisions are reflected in "Brother Jacob," her only fiction to address directly the issue of colonialism, which was so central to British culture and politics. While not an overtly political story, its uncharacteristically sarcastic narrative voice provides a critique of England's dependence on West Indian sugar and its policies of free trade. Her character, David Faux, trades legitimately in the products of his confectionery business. He trades dishonestly, under the assumed name of Edward Freely, in the exoticism of West Indian myths and stereotypes. As Susan De Sola Rodstein writes, the desire for David's sugar is created by "conventional imperial desires: the aristocrat's fantasy of a thriving, benevolent British plantocracy in the Indies and the middle class's desire for purchasable escapist orientalism."[9] One of the historical ironies of this indictment of David Faux's delusions about the potential of the "Indies" to bring out the superiority of a young person condemned to mediocrity at home, is its coincidence with the preparations of Thornton Lewes, who had not distinguished himself in his parents' eyes, for a colonial career.

George Eliot's narrator observes: "When a man is not adequately appreciated or comfortably placed in his own country, his thoughts naturally turn towards foreign climes."[10] David Faux's ignorance reflects a conventional English prejudice: he chooses Jamaica because "it appeared to him the most propitious destination for an emigrant who, to begin with, had the broad and easily recognisable merit of whiteness" (231). This critical attitude toward the English colonizing impulse would be echoed in *Impressions of Theophrastus Such*, in which Theophrastus notes that "we are at least equal to the races we call obtrusive in the disposition to settle wherever money is to be made and cheaply idle living to be found" (p. 160). Yet between the composition of "Brother Jacob" in 1860 and the publication of *Impressions* in 1879, Marian Lewes's daily domestic life was characterized by the exchange of letters and the export of money to the South African colonies.

The theme of the ungrateful and thieving son and brother was taken up by George Eliot (without the colonial motif) in her next novel, *Silas Marner*, but Eppie's love softens and redeems the theft of Silas's gold by the wayward

Dunstan Cass. There is no such redemption in the morally ambiguous "Brother Jacob." Kathryn Hughes muses about connections between "Brother Jacob" and all three Lewes boys, wondering if David's theft of his mother's guineas reflected how "Marian felt about the three careless young men who were spending her capital on their education."[11] Yet such biographical speculations should be tempered by the fact that after Thornton's emigration, George Eliot's fiction maintains a suppressed silence on the morality of colonialism. Despite the consistent theme of the feckless son – Dunstan Cass, Fred Vincy, Hans Meyrick – she never again introduced emigration as a solution to the conflicts of identity and profession experienced by young men. In *Daniel Deronda*, Rex Gascoigne, in a state of despondence over his unrequited love for his cousin Gwendolen, indulges with his sister Anna in a fantasy of emigration to Canada. Rex tells his father that he "shall never be up to the sort of work I must do to live in this part of the world" (I:8:72). George Eliot's gentle handling of this youthful scheme, authoritatively put down by Rex's father, the Reverend Henry Gascoigne, contrasts to her representation of emigration in "Brother Jacob." This episode suggests both her awareness of the place occupied by the colonies in British society and her refusal to offer the easy solution of emigration in her fiction.

It was only after the deaths of Thornton and Herbert Lewes in 1869 and 1875 respectively, that she addressed, in fiction and in her letters, the moral implications of colonialism. The emotional experience of losing these emigrant stepsons may have influenced her conviction to speak about British colonial history. Moving beyond *Daniel Deronda*, "The Modern Hep! Hep! Hep!" combines a critique of English prejudice and English colonialism. Theophrastus asserts that "we are a colonising people, and it is we who have punished others" (146). Rather than a call to reform, Theophrastus's comments are a call to national self-recognition: this is who we are; we are a colonizing people. In contrast to Felix Holt, Theophrastus speaks not in the voice of a realistic character, but as an authorial embodiment of national strengths and weaknesses.

In 1879, Eliza Lewes, the widow of Lewes's son Herbert, fled from South Africa to England in fear of the turmoil surrounding the Zulu War. This intrusion of the South African war into Marian Lewes's life prompted her to follow its progress in the newspapers. She conducted a detailed exchange with Blackwood about the causes of the war, writing: "I don't know what you think of Sir Bartle Frere's policy, but it seems to me that we cannot afford either morally or physically to reform semi-civilized people at every point of the compass with blood and iron" (*GEL*, VII:109). Blackwood responded that Sir Bartle Frere had not sufficiently "counted the cost of the war either in blood or treasure" (*GEL*, VII:112). The two agreed that the war was wrong. Later, she made a point of telling Harriet Beecher Stowe that the war in South Africa was "wicked on *our* part" (*GEL*, VII:132).

In the last years of her life, Marian Lewes saw colonial conflicts escalate and multiply, and just as she had done in her fiction, she understood these momentous political events in the personal terms of their effects on individuals. In January 1880 she wrote to Clementia Taylor of "the great public calamities" of the last year and spoke of a friend whose sons were fighting in the Second Afghan War (*GEL*, VII:24–42). Lewes's friend Edward Robert Bulwer Lytton (later Lord Lytton) had been Viceroy of India under Disraeli's administration since 1876, but his term ended as a consequence of the Afghan War. On April 24, 1880 she consoled his wife: "You have been very often in my thoughts, because I have associated you with public affairs, and have imagined sympathetically how they must have affected your private life. I am sure that this momentous experience in India has been a hard discipline both for you and for Lord Lytton" (*GEL*, VII:264).

Lewes had corresponded regularly with Lytton while the latter was in India, and the Lyttons were part of a familial and social circle that encompassed South Africa, India, Algiers, America, New Zealand, and of course Europe. George Eliot's attitude toward European and colonial wars throughout the 1860s and 1870s represented more than a generic pacifism or an unthinking English patriotism. The association of public and private affairs, as she mentions to Lady Lytton, was becoming more common. Her response to this "cosmopolitanism" was to assess its cultural and moral effects and to explore, through her fiction, the possibilities of nationalism – the historical and philosophical groundwork of what were becoming political movements.

In *Daniel Deronda* and *Impressions of Theophrastus Such*, George Eliot's characters express explicit political opinions about "the modern insistence on the idea of Nationalities" (*ITS*, 160). In "A Word for the Germans" she wrote that it was "the partition of mankind into races and nations, resulting in various national points of view or varieties of national genius, which has been the means of enriching and rendering more and more complete man's knowledge of the inner and outer world" (Pinney, p. 388). By 1865 her model of organic development was beginning to sound more constructed than natural; whether it is a human or divine act to "partition" mankind is ambiguous. In her 1856 review essay of Wilhelm Heinrich von Riehl's *Naturgeschichte des Volks*, "The Natural History of German Life," she had, paraphrasing Riehl, described the German peasants as a part of the German landscape, fauna and flora, observing that "many disintegrating forces have been at work on the peasant character, and degeneration is unhappily going on at a greater pace than development" (Pinney, p. 281). By the time she wrote *Deronda*, she saw the revitalization of national identities – Greek, Italian, German, and Jewish – as the product of individual as well as collective acts of will. Human intervention could redirect the course of national degeneration and development.

Deronda emerged from the combination of Marian Lewes's researches into Jewish history and her interpretation of contemporary nationalist politics, especially the unifications of Germany and Italy. The remarkable proto-Zionist vision of the novel represents an interpretation of the Jewish past and a projection of the world's future in light of reviving nationalist movements. As Marc E. Wohlfarth notes, "It is the intricate relation between the three temporal moments of past, present, and future that made nationalism into such a seductive form of politics to Eliot."[12] *Deronda* suggests that the Jews might be preparing for their identity to take the national form of their contemporaries in the late nineteenth century. The heroes of Italian unification, Garibaldi and Mazzini, were individual actors as well as manifestations of a collective will for political independence and cultural unity based on memories of a national past.

By imagining Jewish nationalism, George Eliot was able to maintain the ideals of continuity and change without rupture. "Revival" was a form of progress that was also a return to ancient traditions. The Jewish notion of a "return" to the Holy Land offered the perfect illustration of how a people's destiny could be altered, their "degeneration" resisted through a conscious effort to bring back a lost glory. Living among the complacent English aristocracy, Daniel Deronda has no conception of the passions of national revival until he meets Mordecai Ezra Cohen, a mystic and a zealot whose religious and national visions merge – a Savonarola without political power. Mordecai recognizes in Deronda a modern realization of his historically inspired dreams and works to make Deronda see and feel as he does.

In the "Hand and Banner" scene, Daniel Deronda himself is revived by the intensity of the discussion about national identities generally and the fate of European Jews in particular. He argues against the deterministic idea of "development" as applied to nations. The Scotsman Buchan has suggested that the laws of development are something inevitable, to be discovered. Deronda responds that "[t]here will still remain the degrees of inevitableness in relation to our own will and acts, and the degrees of wisdom in hastening or retarding; there will still remain the danger of mistaking a tendency which should be resisted for an inevitable law that we must adjust ourselves to" (VI:4:449). The tendency to assimilation, for example, is one the Jews have the choice to resist in a country which appeared to be "progressing" by removing the civil disabilities of its Jewish population.

Daniel Deronda frequently articulates principles with which George Eliot agreed. Yet the political perspective of the novel is not limited to his views, nor is it intended as a political platform. Amanda Anderson asserts that the novel "generates two distinct understandings of the project of Jewish nationalism, represented respectively by Deronda and Mordecai."[13] She defines these as "the universalist civic model" and the "collectivist romantic model," both of which reflect George Eliot's awareness of the contending political motivations and aspirations that characterized her society. If George Eliot's politics could be located, they would surely be found in a combination of these models; there is no evidence that any one character's beliefs represent her own. As in the case of Tito Melema or Felix Holt, her aim as an artist was to make a character's political opinions consistent with his psychology and behavior.

The Reverend Henry Gascoigne is perhaps George Eliot's most scathing portrait of the social-climbing clergyman, a man whose moral character has been compromised by his self-serving political maneuvers within English society. The details of his past are sketchy but indicting. His desire to rise entails a significant, though passingly noted, name change. What does it signify that the Reverend "had once been Captain Gaskin, having taken orders and a diphthong but shortly before his engagement to Miss Armyn" (1:3:23)? By this act, he falsifies his past, a blatant fabrication in contrast to the historical mutation of Mallingre to Mallinger and a direct parallel to the calculated change from Cohen to Lapidoth forced upon Mirah by her conniving father. The parallels between Gascoigne and Lapidoth are further suggested by the former's eagerness to marry his niece Gwendolen to Henleigh Mallinger Grandcourt, despite his knowledge that Grandcourt has several children by his mistress Lydia Glasher. This willingness to trade Gwendolen for the indirect benefits of income and status that such a match would bring to his family, is only a more genteel form of the barter that Lapidoth attempted when he arranged to give Mirah to a wealthy patron. Mirah escapes this shameful fate, but Gwendolen, through the pressures so carefully detailed in the novel, succumbs to the more subtle influence of her uncle and essentially prostitutes herself by marrying Grandcourt.

The idealistic vision of Jewish nationalism as imparted to Deronda by Mordecai appears as an antidote to opportunities for deceit made possible by dislocations in European culture as represented by both Gascoigne and Lapidoth. The women in the novel – Mirah, Gwendolen, and Daniel's mother – are the sometimes complicit victims in this corrupt system of exchange. In this way, George Eliot suggests that the promise of new beginnings inherent in nationalist movements might redress some of European culture's deepest corrosions. While the course that England might take to redirect itself and avert the cultural disasters of a negative "progress" is more obscure at the end of *Deronda* than the course some Jews see open to them,

Gwendolen's determination to live and become better is the type of moral redirection needed by the English generally. Deronda's decision to travel to the East is no more important or momentous than Gwendolen's resolution to live differently; it is merely more important-sounding in its "world-historic" implications.

Critics tend to forget that Deronda does not actually do anything political at the end of the novel. He merely expresses a wish to travel to the East "to become better acquainted with the condition of my race in various countries there." "At the least," he tells an uncomprehending Gwendolen, "I may awaken a movement in other minds, such as has been awakened in my own" (VIII:49:688). Yet the temptation to read *Deronda*, set in 1864–6 and published in 1876, with the retrospective knowledge of developments in the Middle East – the establishment of the state of Israel in 1948 and the Arab-Israeli wars and conflicts in the years since – has been too great for contemporary critics.

Edward Said initiated the explosive political question of the novel's collusion in late-twentieth-century Zionism. In an essay originally published in 1979, Said wrote that "Eliot cannot sustain her admiration of Zionism except by seeing it as a method for transforming the East into the West."[14] The Jews, Said argues, are "European prototypes so far as colonizing the East is concerned" (Said, *Dangerous Liaisons*, p. 22). Said, who insists, anachronistically, on speaking of George Eliot's "Zionism," has made her into an imperialist, first by defining the views expressed by Mordecai as hers and secondly by conflating Jewish nationalism and imperialism. His comments have been used by critics as an excuse for condemning George Eliot's "imperialist ideology" in an unquestioned equation of a Jewish national revival with British colonialism in other parts of the world.

When she explained her motivations in writing *Deronda*, George Eliot focused on the present social problems of English anti-Jewish prejudice and ignorance of Judaism, rather than on the future hope of a Jewish nation. She wrote to Harriet Beecher Stowe that she represented the Jews sympathetically to correct ignorance, adding that "towards all oriental peoples with whom we English come in contact, a spirit of arrogance and contemptuous dictatorialness is observable which has become a national disgrace to us" (*GEL*, VI:301). She was oddly silent in her letters about the project of reviving a Jewish homeland. For example, she made only a cursory acknowledgment of Blackwood's suggestion that she would be interested in Laurence Oliphant's expedition to Palestine (*GEL*, VII:108). Jewish nationalism, as a potential political movement, was important to her insofar as it seemed a positive current among the negative trends, the devaluing of standards in England that threatened what she felt was best about the nation.

Only in *Impressions of Theophrastus Such* did George Eliot take up the questions left hanging at the end of *Deronda*: what are the English to do about the loss of their distinctive national culture through immigration, emigration, and the general rootless cosmopolitanism she had represented among the upper classes in *Deronda*? Although Theophrastus argues that "The time is not come for cosmopolitanism to be highly virtuous, any more than for communism to suffice for social energy" (147), he is a cosmopolitan, who has "learned to care for foreign countries, for literatures foreign and ancient," and who belongs to the "Nation of London" (26). He checks his love of the foreign by locating himself in his rural English past. He sees the Jews as diminished culturally by their dislocation and would have them recover their remembered homeland. Cosmopolitanism, in the sense of belonging to all parts of the world rather than to one nation, was frequently a term of approbation when applied to nineteenth-century Jews. To George Eliot, cosmopolitanism was a condition from which Jews, along with many Englishmen, suffered. As Bernard Semmel writes, she believed that the "values of individualism and cosmopolitanism that prevailed in British liberal circles would impair both family affection and social cohesion."[15] Social cohesion, as *Deronda* and *Impressions* suggest, is predicated on a shared culture. Catherine Gallagher, in her discussion of the "politics of culture," argues that Felix Holt "is not opposed to change as long as it is accompanied by continuity." She adds that for George Eliot, "culture and continuity are one and the same thing" (Gallagher, *Industrial Reformation*, p. 257). Gallagher also notes that "Debasing the Moral Currency" shares its "politics of culture" with *Felix Holt*. In fact, the "politics of culture" as explored in *Impressions* goes beyond the "condition of England question" and includes the larger, interconnected issues of colonialism, nationalism, and cosmopolitanism.

Theophrastus, as an ancient Greek who has seen his own culture and empire rise, fall, and survive in its literature, offers the perspective of inevitable historical change. Yet he calls for the English to do what they can to control the increasingly rapid transformations of their language and literature. In the "Modern Hep! Hep! Hep!" he observes that

> An ancient Greek might not like to be resuscitated for the sake of hearing Homer read in our universities, still he would at least find more instructive marvels in other developments to be witnessed at those institutions; but a modern Englishman is invited from his after-dinner repose to hear Shakspere delivered under circumstances which offer no other novelty than some emphasis on prepositions, some new misconception of a familiar idiom. (159)

"Well!," he adds, "It is our inertness that is in fault, our carelessness of excellence, our willing ignorance of the treasures that lie in our national heritage" (159). We cannot arrest change, Theophrastus concludes, "all we can do is to moderate its course" (160). In George Eliot's last work, an ancient Greek is revived to scrutinize contemporary English politics, culture, and the "politics of culture" which were ultimately the politics about which George Eliot most cared and to which she attempted to contribute.

In 1862, Marian Evans wrote to an American doctor who had sent her a book about rattlesnakes and asked her about her political views. "I am by no means a politician myself" she wrote, but continued that she could not understand that men educated in the "processes of Science, trained therefore to be severe in their scrutiny of evidence, can be so ready to adopt profound conclusions on very complex subjects." On the evidence of unreliable newspaper reports, most English readers accepted "political facts of great importance and political interpretations of world-wide consequences" (*GEL*, IV:52–53). In other words, political views depended upon representations of the facts and to George Eliot, journalistic representations of political facts were no more reliable than the "silly novels by lady novelists" against which she formulated her views about realism. It is no wonder that George Eliot was hesitant to express, except under cover of a distinctive character, strong political views, nor that when she did so, these views were the mature product of considered thought and reflected the ambiguities of the specific political situation. It is no wonder, in short, that we understand George Eliot's relationship to politics through an examination of her fictional characters and of her own character as a novelist.

NOTES

1 Catherine Gallagher, *The Industrial Reformation of English Fiction: Social Discourse and Narrative Form, 1832–1867* (Chicago: University of Chicago Press, 1985), p. 259.
2 Andrew Thompson, *George Eliot and Italy: Literary, Cultural and Political Influences from Dante to the Risorgimento* (New York: St. Martin's Press, 1998), p. 79.
3 Anthony Trollope, *An Autobiography* [1883] (Harmondsworth: Penguin, 1996), p. 118.
4 John Peck, *War, the Army, and Victorian Literature* (New York: St. Martin's Press, 1998), p. 2.
5 Harriet Martineau, *History of the Peace: Being a History of England from 1816–1854*, vol. IV (Boston: Walker, Fuller & Co., 1866), p. 163.
6 Elizabeth Gaskell, *Ruth* [1853], ed. Alan Shelston (Oxford: Oxford University Press, 1985), p. 423.
7 Joseph Butwin, "The Pacification of the Crowd: From 'Janet's Repentance' to *Felix Holt*," *Nineteenth-Century Fiction*, 35 (December 1980): 354.

8 T. J. Wise and J. A. Symington ed., *The Brontës: Their Lives, Friendships and Correspondence*, vol. II (Oxford: Basil Blackwell, 1932), pp. 202–3.
9 Susan De Sola Rodstein, "Sweetness and Dark: George Eliot's 'Brother Jacob,'" *MLQ*, 52.3 (1991): 297.
10 George Eliot, *Silas Marner*, "The Lifted Veil," and "Brother Jacob," ed. Peter Mudford (London: Everyman, 1996), p. 231.
11 Kathryn Hughes, *George Eliot: The Last Victorian* (New York: Farrar, Strauss & Giroux, 1999), p. 239.
12 Marc E. Wohlfarth, "*Daniel Deronda* and the Politics of Nationalism," *Nineteenth-Century Literature*, 53.2 (September 1998): 196.
13 Amanda Anderson, "George Eliot and the Jewish Question," *Yale Journal of Criticism*, 10.1 (1997): 41.
14 Edward Said, "Zionism from the Standpoint of its Victims" [1979], *Dangerous Liaisons: Gender, Nation, and Postcolonial Perspectives*, ed. Anne McClintock, Aamir Mufti, and Ella Shohat (Minneapolis: University of Minnesota Press, 1997), p. 22.
15 Bernard Semmel, *George Eliot and the Politics of Inheritance* (Oxford: Oxford University Press, 1994), p. 6.

herself possessed extraordinary intellectual powers, who had a remarkably broad grasp of historical, philosophical, scientific, and literary issues, and whose relationship with George Lewes transgressed Victorian convention, be so apparently conventional in many of her views? In particular, why do many of her views concerning women, and the choices faced by women in her writings, seem to lack the boldness that might be expected – even desired – of her?

The poet and critic Mathilde Blind, writing a biography of George Eliot for W. H. Allen's "Eminent Women Series" in 1883, pondered this issue, wondering why her subject should place such an emphasis on the virtue of resignation, "should inculcate an almost slavish adherence to whatever surroundings, beliefs, and family ties a human being may be born to."[1] The list of examples which can be produced as instances of George Eliot's conservatism on gender issues is a long one, both outside and inside her fiction. They stretch from Patty, Amos Barton's daughter in the first of the *Scenes of Clerical Life*, who is given no existence beyond the role of being a pallid shadow of her mother, a support to her father in his old age, through Dinah Morris, the woman preacher in *Adam Bede*, who, having given up her vocation as a preacher settles into happy married life with Adam, to Armgart, George Eliot's rare portrayal of a gifted creative woman, who, losing the exquisite timbre of her singing voice after a long illness, retreats to the provinces where she will teach music and singing. She abandons public performance, as does Mirah, Daniel Deronda's eventual companion, and yet another character whose anxieties about displaying her artistic talent overlap with her knowledge that her own father regarded her voice, and indeed herself, as a commodity to be bought and sold. Public display is ultimately seen as degrading, in these latter cases, and it is unsurprising that various critics have sought to tie in these representations with George Eliot's own anxieties about performance, profession, visibility, and fame. These instances, like comments scattered through George Eliot's letters and prose, lie behind what Sandra Gilbert and Susan Gubar call her "feminine antifeminism."[2] This is a mode of writing which, although it emphasizes women's emotions, needs, and frustrations, also contains such disconcerting generalizations as one finds in *Romola*: "Romola was labouring, as a loving woman must, to subdue her nature to her husband's" (27:235); it is a mode that celebrates what she termed, in relation to Geraldine Jewsbury's *Constance Herbert*, "the beauty and heroism of renunciation," and which refuses, in plot terms, to provide strong, successful women striking out on their own (Pinney, 135). Florence Nightingale, reviewing *Middlemarch* for *Fraser's Magazine* in 1873, was the first of many to complain that George Eliot did not find a better outlet for a heroine with social ideals than marriage to an "ardent public man" ("Finale":782). Nightingale pointed out that "close at hand, in actual life, was a woman . . . and if we mistake not, a connection of the author's, who has managed to make her ideal very real indeed" (*Fraser's Magazine* 1873:567). This woman was Octavia Hill, whose work with settlements in London's East End was well known to George Eliot: her sister had married Lewes's eldest son. "Could not the heroine, the 'sweet sad enthusiast,' have been set to some such work as this?" asked Nightingale (567). The American Harriet Peirce, finishing *The Spanish Gypsy*, wrote plaintively that "the poetry was so beautiful, but must noble women always fail? Is there no sumptuous flower of happiness for us?" (*GEL*, VIII:463).

There are a number of ways in which one might seek to understand George Eliot's reluctance, or inability, to deliver up unequivocally feminist messages. These start with her aversion to producing the kind of writing which, given the double standards of the greater part of the reviewing community in the mid-Victorian period, would ensure that she was judged *as* a woman in literary terms. It was the assumption that literature, especially fiction, was one of the very few arenas in which women and men could be treated equally which led her to conclude her 1856 essay, "Silly Novels by Lady Novelists": "No educational restrictions can shut women out from the materials of fiction, and there is no species of art which is so free from rigid requirements. Like Crystalline masses" – she drops in the scientific simile easily, as if to emphasize an authorial competence which stretches across disciplines – "it may take any form, and yet be beautiful; we have only to pour in the right elements – genuine observation, humour, and passion" (Pinney, p. 324). Such attributes were not specifically gendered, in her eyes, and nor were the wider principles which she sought to put across in her writing, outlined by Blind, still preoccupied by trying to explain Eliot's philosophical commitment to the ideal of resignation, as the "doctrine that the individual is bound absolutely to subordinate his personal happiness to the social good, that he has no rights save the right of fulfilling his obligations to his age, his country, and his family" (Blind, *George Eliot*, p. 169). This is the conviction that is in many ways responsible for Maggie, in *The Mill on the Floss*, turning down Stephen Guest's offer of marriage; that leads Fedalma, in *The Spanish Gypsy*, to declare that she "will not take a heaven/Haunted by shrieks of far-off misery" (1901: 161). More than this, George Eliot was deeply mistrustful of creating idealistic exceptions. In a note on the historical imagination, she commented that "Utopian pictures help the reception of ideas as to constructive results, but hardly so much as a vivid presentation of how results have been actually brought about, especially in religious and social change" (Pinney, pp. 446–7). And, despite women's yearnings to be someone, or to do something which reaches beyond the circumstances in which they find themselves, she is continually aware that her responsibility is to portray them – and men – in the "imperfect social state" (*M*, "Finale":784) in which they actually lived. Thus Virginia Woolf writes, sympathetically, that George Eliot's women "do not find what they seek, and we cannot wonder." What they look for is "perhaps incompatible with the facts of human existence. George Eliot had far too strong an intelligence to tamper with those facts . . . Save for the supreme courage of their endeavour, the struggle ends, for her heroines, in tragedy, or in a compromise that is even more melancholy."[3]

In George Eliot's writing, alertness to these social conditions, and the acute consciousness of injustice to which they give rise, necessarily chafe against the doctrine of submitting to a sense of broader social duty. This duality shows itself well in her correspondence dealing with women's issues. In 1869 she wrote privately that she was very inclined to learn about the "Women Question," but that she felt "too deeply the difficult complications that beset every measure likely to affect the position of women and also I feel too imperfect a sympathy with many women who have put themselves forward in connection with such measure, to give any practical adhesion to them" (*GEL*, v:58). She did not sign John Stuart Mill's petition that women be granted suffrage on equal terms with men, and wrote to Mill's supporter, John Morley, in 1867 that "as a fact of mere zoological evolution, woman seems to me to have the worse share in existence . . . And in the thorough recognition of that worse share, I think there is a basis for a sublimer resignation in woman and a more regenerating tenderness in man" (*GEL*, VIII: 402–3). Yet she was explaining to another correspondent a fortnight later that she wishes women and men equally to be "secured as far as possible along with every other breathing creature from suffering the exercise of any unrighteous power," and expressing her hope that much good will come from the serious presentation of women's claims before Parliament (*GEL*, IV: 366–67). The only identifiable feminist issue on which she seemed to take a clear – and even then not a very outspoken – stand was that of education. This is apparent throughout her novels, whether in the low-key, but sustained critique of the fact that Tom Tulliver was forced to submit to classical works which would have stimulated his sister's imagination, or in the hunger of Dorothea Brooke, in *Middlemarch*, for learning. Dorothea's sheltered existence produces simultaneous fervor and myopia. She falls for the sexually and emotionally unsuitable Casaubon in large part because of his scholarly attributes, wishing to know Latin and Greek, since "Those provinces of masculine knowledge seemed to her a standing-ground from which all truth could be seen more truly" (7). Nonetheless, when writing to Emily

Davies, founder of Girton College, Cambridge, in 1868, George Eliot acknowledges that she finds "just that kernel of truth in the vulgar alarm of men lest women should be 'unsexed,'" arguing that we cannot "afford to part with that exquisite type of gentleness, tenderness, possible maternity suffusing a woman's being with affectionateness, which makes what we mean by the feminine character" (*GEL*, IV:467–68). Yet, as we shall see, she does not exclusively bestow these characteristics, or the potential to manifest these characteristics, on women: it is the releasing of what might be called "gentleness, tenderness, possible maternity" towards Eppie from within Silas Marner that acts as a regenerative force upon his suppressed feelings.

What all these examples attest to is that it may well be misguided, in addition to being often disappointing, to assess George Eliot by late twentieth-century – or, indeed, by nineteenth century – feminist standards. Her resolute even-handedness on very many issues, coupled with her determination to subordinate the claims of an individual to wider social demands, means that any such attempt continually comes up against contradictions. But what is undeniable is George Eliot's continual interest in the formation of gender characteristics by community, by expectations, and by ideological pressures. She is alive to the shifting connections of gender and power, as they manifest themselves in both familial and broader contexts; and making her readers think about the connections between power, authority, and gender relations is an inseparable part of her literary and critical enterprise. "Gender relations," the feminist theorist Jane Flax has written, "is a category meant to capture a complex set of social relations, to refer to a changing set of historically variable social processes. Gender, both as an analytical category and a social process, is relational. That is, gender relations are complex and unstable processes . . . constituted by and through interrelated parts. These parts are interdependent, that is, each part can have no meaning or existence without the others."[4] Such a definition, appropriately close in its organicist assumptions to George Eliot's own description of social structures in "Notes on Form in Art," offers a very useful place from which to start an exploration of Eliot's treatment of gender.

In *Middlemarch*, George Eliot is scathing about the education, or rather, the showy accomplishments which Rosamond Vincy has acquired: she is "that combination of correct sentiments, music, dancing, drawing, elegant note-writing, private album for extracted verse, and perfect blond loveliness, which made the irresistible woman for the doomed man of the date" (27:252). The reader is here brought face to face with the fact that interpreting and behaving according to dominant social conventions is a two-way process, in which both women and men play their parts, and assess the world through sexual stereotypes. Sometimes this stereotyping appears to have scientific authority behind it. In the prelude to the novel, George Eliot satirically complains against those who attempt to lay down, on sociomedical or other grounds, prescriptive roles for women: "if there were one level of feminine incompetence as strict as the ability to count three and no more, the social lot of women might be treated with scientific certitude" ("Prelude":3–4). Her careful reading of the *Lancet* as she developed the character and career of Lydgate, as well as her other connections, ensured that she was alert to contemporary medical debates about women's functions. But far more insidious, she shows, are those assumptions about gender roles which are so ingrained as to form part of individuals' automatic mental reflexes. Casaubon's choice of Dorothea, for example, is born of convention. Having reached that phase of life when he believed that he should defer the experience of matrimony no longer, "he had reflected that in taking a wife, a man of good position should expect and carefully choose a blooming young lady – the younger the better, because more educable and submissive – of a rank equal to his own, of religious principles, virtuous disposition, and good understanding" (29:261). Lydgate, on first meeting Dorothea, has no difficulty in distinguishing the point at which "Miss Brooke would be found wanting, notwithstanding her undeniable beauty. She did not look at things from the proper feminine angle" (11:88). Eventually, Lydgate swings round to an entirely less stern and governessy image of Dorothea, seeing her as a young creature with "a heart large enough for the Virgin Mary" (76:723). But despite Eliot's love for the pure, noble, desexed Madonna figure, one may still end up regarding this as a hint that his judgments about "furniture, or women" (15:141) – in that telling order – are invariably going to be ruled by his tendency to judge generically, rather than in terms of individuality, letting scientific categorization spill into social typing. The catastrophe of Lydgate and Rosamond's marriage lies in the propensity of each to adhere to the developing doctrine of separate spheres: "Each lives in a world of which the other knew nothing" (16:155). Rosamond may be selfish and shallow: George Eliot's compassionate charity withers in the face of a "silly" woman, novelist or not, who, with each sinuous movement of her swanlike neck, reinforces the sexual conventions which help structure, and retard, society. Yet Lydgate is also presented as to blame, never sharing his work or financial difficulties with her, keeping public and private spheres damagingly apart on the one hand, yet allowing the methodology of one to infiltrate the other in an inappropriate fashion.

By contrast, separation of interests, or of emotional power relations, do not divide Dorothea and Will. Although there is an embarrassed coyness in the narrator's tone when they first kiss, neither is credited with making the first move: "It was never known which lips were the first to move towards the other lips" (83:761). It was Dorothea whose principles, whose values of duty, of action rather than poseuring, lead Will into a purposeful life: by way of complementarity, it is Will who releases her into sexual awareness, and also, through marrying her, gives her a social role in which her "full nature" can, invisibly but importantly, find channels through which to diffuse itself: she gives him "wifely help"; she finds an outlet for her emotion in both loving marriage and in motherhood. The narrator anticipates the objections of both contemporary and modern critics in commenting that "many who knew her, thought it a pity that so substantive and rare a creature should have been absorbed into the life of another, and be only known in a certain circle as a wife and mother," which may also suggest a touch of unease on George Eliot's own part ("Finale":783). But crucially, as she sees it, Dorothea's role is bound up in the gradual social amelioration which will come through cooperation, and within which women may have an important intercessionary part to play. As the narrator remarks in relation to the power of sisterly affection to soften the antagonism between brothers in law: "Where women love each other, men learn to smother their mutual dislike" ("Finale":784).

The figure of the mother is a key one in George Eliot's writing, partly because of the emotional resonance that it held for her, and partly because it provides an ideal site on which to examine the nexus of ideas concerning the social and the natural that lie at the heart of her treatment of gender. She invested the role of motherhood with sacredness, representing the highest form of duty of which most women were capable. Once again, however, this must be placed in the context of her firmly held belief that members of both sexes must work to identify those social functions which will best suit their innate, individual capacities. If we return to the subject of George Eliot and education, we find that whilst she held a strong conviction that women and men alike should have "each the same store of fundamental knowledge" supplied them by their education (*GEL*, v:58), she also expressed grave doubts about brain-work being valued over other types of labor. This was not a gender specific anxiety: "No good," she wrote, "can come to women, more than to any class of male mortals, while each aims at doing the highest kind of work, which ought rather to be held in sanctity as what only the few can do well. I believe – and I want it to be well shown – that a more thorough education will tend to do away with the odious vulgarity of our notions about functions and employment, and to propagate the true gospel that the deepest disgrace is to insist on doing work for which we are unfit – to do work of any sort badly" (*GEL*, iv:425). Nonetheless, it would seem that for

George Eliot such unglamorous, sacred work for a woman will, for many, take place within her role as wife, mother, and earthly Madonna. She sympathetically responds to the painful, even morbid self-questioning to which the childless Nancy Cass subjects herself at the end of *Silas Marner*, which she sees as "inevitable to a mind of much moral sensibility when shut out from its due share of outward activity and of practical claims on its affections – inevitable to a noble-hearted, childless woman, when her lot is narrow" (17:49).

The importance which George Eliot accorded maternity – or rather, the qualities which at best it calls out of the individual – may be judged by the parallels she quietly drew between it and her own sphere of productivity: writing. In "Silly Novels by Lady Novelists," she remarked that the greatest deficiencies of "feminine literature" are "due hardly more to the want of intellectual power than to the want of those moral attributes that contribute to literary excellence – patient diligence, a sense of the responsibility involved in publication, and an appreciation of the sacredness of the writer's art" (Pinney, p. 323). These virtues – patience, diligence, and the faithful execution of a sacred role – correspond to the traditional attributes of mothering. Without doubt, George Eliot's attitudes toward motherhood were inflected by the fact that she was never a biological mother herself. But for her, parenting was not a strictly physiological role. She referred to her fictional characters as her "spiritual children," and to *The Mill on the Floss* as her youngest child (*GEL*, III:117, 335); Lewes explained to Blackwood, her publisher, that she regarded "the idea of the MS being taken away from her as if it were her baby." To the young women who, in her later years, identified themselves with her ideas and her well-being, she would on occasion sign herself "Mother." It would be a crude reading that saw these expressions of maternity as barely concealed sublimations of her own desires. Excusing her own effusiveness towards Emilia Pattison, she explained her position in a way that combines self-knowledge with a tacit recognition that circumstances determine what may be seen as best for an individual: "in proportion as I profoundly rejoice that I never brought a child into the world, I am conscious of having an unused stock of motherly tenderness, which sometimes overflows" (*GEL*, V:52).

In many respects, George Eliot can be seen to be playing into the ideological importance which mothering was widely accorded by far more conventional commentators in Victorian England, building on the kind of comment made by Sarah Lewis in *Woman's Mission* (1839) – a book which the young Mary Ann Evans enthusiastically recommended to her friend Maria Lewis (*GEL*, I:23). "Maternal love [is] the only purely unselfish feeling that exists on this earth; the only affection which (as far as it appears) flows from the loving to the beloved object in one continual stream," Sarah Lewis maintained (*Woman's Mission*, p. 129). Conceived of in these terms, it appears as the purest form of George Eliot's often-commended virtue of sympathy. But importantly, George Eliot also freely acknowledges not just that maternal propensities may find other outlets, but that not all biological mothers feel this commitment to their offspring. This is apparent in her earlier novels through developments in their plots: Godfrey Cass's first wife slips into opium-fueled oblivion in the snow without giving any consideration to Eppie's welfare; Hetty Sorrel abandons her crying new born baby in a hole under a tree. In a chapter on neonatal infanticide in her study of female aggression, *When She Was Bad*, Patricia Pearson comments that one major reason for such maternal murderers tending to be treated leniently, with compassion, or as suffering from temporary insanity, can be found in society's desire – despite the evidence – to regard maternal feeling as something intrinsic, natural. Indeed, she says, "the maternal ideal lies at the very heart of feminist resistance to the possibility of female aggression."[5] In *Adam Bede*, however, George Eliot implicitly cautions against this logic, not just through Hetty's actions, but through her very treatment of nature itself. She shows it to be something not necessarily conducive to inherent harmony, but beset by internal divisions and contradictions: cruel and remorseless as well as benevolent. The complex understanding of what constitutes the "natural" in relation to gender is something that George Eliot had already addressed in her 1855 piece on Margaret Fuller and Mary Wollstonecraft, where she commends the former for writing about the "folly of absolute definitions of woman's nature and absolute demarcations of woman's mission." "Nature," she says, "seems to delight in varying the arrangements, as if to show that she will be fettered by no rule; and we must admit the same varieties that she admits" (Pinney, p. 203).

Increasingly, in the later fiction, the fact that maternity is not the be all and end all of a woman's existence is made plain. In part, this is a further demonstration of natural variety, voiced at its most forceful by the Princess Alchirisi, Daniel's mother in *Daniel Deronda*: "Every woman is supposed to have the same set of motives, or else to be a monster. I am not a monster, but I have not felt exactly what other women feel – or say they feel, for fear of being thought unlike others. When you reproach me in your heart for sending you away from me, you mean that I ought to say I felt about you as other women say they feel about their children. I did *not* feel that. I was glad to be freed from you." Quite apart from the Princess's openness, what comes across here is George Eliot's recognition of the ideological pressure on women to conform; the expectation, which many women either internalize or profess, that maternity is somehow sufficient in its own right. This is explored in *Felix Holt* through Mrs. Transome's feelings towards Harold: "It is a fact perhaps kept a little too much in the background," comments the narrator, "that mothers have a self larger than their maternity, and that when their sons have come to be taller than themselves, and are gone from college or into the world, there are wide spaces of time which are not filled with praying for their boys, reading old letters, and envying yet blessing those who are attending to their shirt buttons. Mrs. Transome was certainly not one of those bland, adoring, and gently tearful women" (8:94). Her predicament, as George Eliot constructs it, is that the internalized valorization of maternity as such can leave a woman damaged, unable to locate a wider calling for herself, or any outlet for her capacity for loving engagement with others.

Indeed, Mrs. Transome's powerful maternal feelings become not the grounds on which to build a widening set of social relations, but instruments of emotional bondage, which, metaphorically speaking, inscribe their torture onto the individual: "The finest threads, such as no eye sees, if bound cunningly about the sensitive flesh, so that the movement to break them would bring torture, may make a worse bond than any fetters" (8:94). A mother may love her offspring, but there is no automatic guarantee that she will be loved back. Maternal feeling, in other words, although it may encompass George Eliot's most cherished social values – sympathetic involvement, recognition of the demands of alterity, patient adherence to duty – is not a freestanding attribute, but must always be seen in its intersections with broader social relations and pressures. Harold's callous indifference towards his mother's emotional needs is a central example of a larger theme which George Eliot explores in *Felix Holt* as elsewhere: the danger of women acquiescing to male power and influence. The novel is shot through with references to apparently essentialist assumptions that women readily assume a passive role. Even in Mrs. Transome, with all her enjoyment of power: "through all her life there had vibrated the maiden need to have her hand kissed and be the object of chivalry" (9:97). This willingness to adopt a subordinate position can work to woman's long-term advantage, as in the way Esther is worked on by Felix, unequivocally presented as a "stronger" power, providing a personal form of education: "The first religious experience of her life – the first self-questioning, the first voluntary subjection, the first longing to acquire the strength of greater motives and obey the more strenuous rule – had come to her through Felix Holt" (27:225). Here, it is easy to read a parallel between Esther's position and George Eliot's view that the working classes will only become deserving of the vote when they have been sufficiently educated.

Moreover, the narrator builds on the idea that women naturally put themselves in a receptive, rather than an active mode when it comes to personal affections: "Esther, like a woman as she was – a woman waiting for love, never able to ask for it" (32:260), or, again, "the best part of a woman's love is worship" (37:299). One of the real problems with this novel is that in order to work out her parallel between the private and the public spheres, George Eliot seems to have played up the inexperienced woman's subservience (notably, when revising the text for the Cabinet edition, she deleted some of the most suspect passages in this respect from chapter 46), and to have felt obliged to idealize Felix's essential nobility and strength of character – as well as his physical attractiveness. Rather like Adam Bede, an even more obvious masculine and national ideal archetype – Adam: the first man; Bede: the first English historian – Felix is asked to bear so much moral weight that he runs the risk of seeming incredible.

This is complicated yet further by the fact that prominent among his virtues is his holding of a much more radical view of woman, and woman's potential, than that of the other major male figures in the novel. For it is Felix who, above all, questions whether woman's capacity is in fact "natural," or whether it is, at least in substantial part, culturally produced. This neatly maps on to the whole issue of heredity and determinism which underpins the novel, and through which George Eliot implicitly asks whether women may be more determined by their conditions, be more socially circumscribed, have less freedom of choice than men: something which is not a fact of their sex, but of society. This disequilibrium of power between women and men is shown to be something that impacts on all kinds of choices, and, indeed, on the capacity to believe that one can make choices at all. "After all," Esther muses to herself in chapter 43, as she walks on Harold's arm: "she was a woman, and could not make her lot. As she had once said to Felix, 'A woman must choose meaner things, because meaner things are offered to her.' Her lot is made for her by the love she accepts. And Esther" – here the narrative voice starts splitting itself off from Esther's consciousness – "And Esther began to think that her lot was being made for her by the love that was surrounding her with the influence of a garden on a summer morning" (43:341). But there is love and love: the meaning of the word in this novel is, indeed, determined by the context in which it is found. As ever in George Eliot's writing, ease and the passivity it here induces is a sure pointer to the fact that the "love" between Esther and Harold rests on shaky foundations. The novel shows how dangerous it is in romance, as in the case of maternity, to allow oneself to be hemmed in, unquestioningly, by societal norms. It takes Esther a long time to learn the lesson that Felix tries to impart to her as early as chapter 10: "If a woman really believes herself to be a lower kind of being, she should place herself in subjection: she should be ruled by the thoughts of her father or husband. If not, let her show the power of choosing something better" (10:104). Felix's idea of change may be a gradual one, but it extends to women as much as to the working classes: his is the direct expression of an idea which George Eliot first articulated, with heavy irony, in her piece on Fuller and Wollstonecraft: "Anything," she wrote in 1855, "is more endurable than to change our established formulae about women, or to run the risk of looking up to our wives instead of looking down on them" (Pinney, p. 205).

Subordination in love is perceived, in *Felix Holt* as elsewhere, as a form of particularly undesirable bondage. "A woman's love," Mrs. Transome laments, "is always freezing into fear; she wants everything, she is secure of nothing . . . What is the use of a woman's will? if she tries, she doesn't get it, and she ceases to be loved" (39:313). But that is hardly the woman's fault: it is the man's. One of the truly radical aspects of this novel lies in the way in which the gender-specific hardness, cruelty, short-sightedness, or obsolescence of certain types of men is heightened. The dim Sir Maximus belongs to a species which is on the way out in explicit evolutionary terms, incapable of exercising effective self-scrutiny, "like those antediluvian animals whom the system of things condemned to carry such a huge bulk that they really could not inspect their bodily appurtenance" (7:82): a rapid dismissal, on George Eliot's part, of the power once wielded by the aristocracy. One may hope by inference that his patronizing attitudes towards women may likewise have had their day.

But more notable is the greater emphasis that George Eliot has come to place on masculine coercion and psychological bullying, something which will return with even greater force in the figure of Grandcourt in *Daniel Deronda*. Earlier male reprobates, like Arthur Donnithorne and Tito Melema, even Amos Barton, offended above all through weakness, through doing what was easy, rather than what their conscience told them was right: it is by making this weakness understandable, a trait of our own, that George Eliot attempts to stimulate some kind of didactically intentioned sympathy for them. But Harold is far more harshly treated. He believes dogmatically in separate spheres; telling his mother not to give him her opinions about politics, "matters, which properly belong to men" (2:35); and he announces that "women, very properly, don't change their views, but keep to the notions in which they have been brought up. It doesn't signify what they think – they are not called upon to judge or to act" (2:35). Harold is set up as Felix's antithesis in large part through his attitudes towards what constitutes the desirable and the correct at the level of gender relations. This is a man who ensured that there would be no problems about power relationships in his first marriage by marrying a slave: "Western women were not to his taste: they showed a transition from the feeble animal to the thinking being, which was simply troublesome." The novel is shot through with references to male shortcomings, culminating in the rage of Mrs. Transome towards the close of the novel: "Men are selfish. They are selfish and cruel. What they care for is their own pleasure and their own pride." "'Not all,' said Esther, on whom these words fell with a painful jar" (50:392). The precise nature of this jar is left for the reader to interpret, but the next day she leaves Transome Court for good.

Esther has to learn to think for herself, and to learn to distrust cultural expectations. When staying at Transome Hall, she "found it impossible to read in these days; her life was a book which she seemed herself to be constructing – trying to make character clear before her, and looking into the ways of destiny" (40:320). From her early article on "Silly Novels" onward, George Eliot frequently reminds her readers how foolish it is to live in one's imagination and to write one's future on the basis of preexistent, fanciful plots, particularly those which center on romance. A number of her characters discover that the scripts in which they believe themselves to be living are in fact inadequate or inaccurate. Thus in *Adam Bede*, Adam indulges in a fond contemplation of Hetty Sorrel's features, mistakenly equating outer with inward beauty, misguidedly prophesying "How she will dote on her children!" (15:153).

This is very much in accordance with George Eliot's suspicion about the artistic deception incurred "by substituting vague forms, bred by imagination on the mists of feeling, in place of definite, substantial reality" (*SEPW*, 368). The reader, in turn, should be suspicious of such moments as that in *Adam Bede*, when the male narrator temporarily colludes with Arthur in his description of the wood in which he meets Hetty: "just the sort of wood most haunted by the nymphs; you see their white sun-lit limbs gleaming athwart the boughs, or peeping from behind the smooth-sweeping outline of a tall lime" (12:130). This exercise of whimsy, coupled with hackneyed mythology, is devalued as a rhetorical form by its implicit close linkage with undisciplined sexual desire. The male narrator may at times display an uneasy combination of patronizing superiority and sexual attraction in his delineation of Hetty herself, but he never allows the reader to conspire in Hetty's fantasies concerning Arthur Donnithorne's selfish and irresponsible interest in her, reminding us sternly that "she is a woman, with a woman's destiny before her – a woman spinning in young ignorance a light web of folly and vain hopes which may one day close round her and press upon her, a rancorous poisoned garment, changing all at once her fluttering trivial butterfly sensations into a life of deep human anguish" (22:251).

How, however, might one conceive of "a woman's destiny?" In this instance, the reader can with some confidence anticipate the plot that Hetty does not recognize: indeed Blackwood, reading the manuscript, wrote to George Eliot that he hoped that Arthur's meetings with Hetty "will not come to the usual sad catastrophe!" (*GEL*, II:446). But in later novels, endings are far more chary of fictional convention. This does not mean that they avoid conservatism. *Romola*, again, is disappointing in this respect. At first glance, it certainly evades the standard romance plot, praising Romola first as an earthly Madonna, ministering to the poor in a time of plague, and then presenting Romola as living with Tessa, the mistress of her dead husband, a surrogate parent to her children. This is a community of women reminiscent of the ending of Elizabeth Barrett Browning's poem *Aurora Leigh*, but without the marriage with which the latter actually ends. But we are left wondering whether Romola's earlier internalization of duty ultimately finds her continuing to support patriarchy and its inheritance. Her first appearance in the novel is in her father's study, reading to him; at the close, she is teaching her husband's son, Lillo, who in turn has been reading Petrarch, the source of one of her father's most misogynist quotations. Romola, given Tessa's submissive, thankful feebleness, may be said, in this family grouping, to take on something of a male position: certainly her position as a facilitator for the transmission of texts from one generation of men to another has not changed.

However, most of George Eliot's endings may be read in a far more defiant light, as deliberately avoiding those preexistent fictional patterns which proved such a delusory lure for some of her characters. Indeed, her artistic growth follows the ability to let go of narrative paradigms. Even that uneasiness expressed both within the text, and by critics Victorian and modern, about the suitability of Ladislaw as a husband for Dorothea, testifies to George Eliot's refusal to provide an orthodox romantic closure in *Middlemarch*, despite her narrative's valorization of her heroine's fate. In *The Mill on the Floss* we see her avoiding other, more muted conventional endings. Whilst marriage to neither Stephen nor Philip would have fulfilled romantic criteria, and would, moreover, have meant destroying bonds of loyalty rooted in Maggie's family past, from which both her conscious and instinctive choices emanate, George Eliot refuses yet more self-sacrificial options. Dinah Mulock, reviewing the novel for *Macmillan's Magazine*, was anxious that it might not "influence for the good any other real lives . . . What – we cannot help asking – what is to become of the hundreds of clever girls, born of uncongenial parents, hemmed in with unsympathising kindred of the Dodson sort . . . ?" (*CH*, 157). But George Eliot is not going to provide any kind of answer that ennobled the spinster through the kind of sentiments fictionalized at the end of Charlotte M. Yonge's *The Daisy Chain* (1857), where self-fulfillment is found in the short term as an unmarried relative and in doing church works, and where hope and happiness lies in the life everlasting. Nancy Miller offers a useful way of thinking through the ending. As she shows, many nineteenth-century commentators, and the vast majority of novelists, assumed that women wished for romantic fulfillment above all: a socially based assumption prefiguring – and doubtless feeding into – Freud's observation in "The Relation of the Poet to Daydreaming" that male fantasies concentrate on dreams of ambition, female fantasies on erotic themes, in which they figure themselves as objects of desire. Yet, as Miller asks, since Freud allows a small space in male egocentric fantasy for erotic wishes, may not egocentric, ambitious desires exist within women's fantasy? She finds evidence for such desires not in specific forms of social achievement recorded in realist fiction, but in the way in which a female character manages to negotiate a plot with a self-exalting dignity, proving to be better than her victimizers. Miller claims that the "repressed content" which one might trace in a woman's text "would be, not erotic impulses, but an impulse to power: a fantasy of power that would revise the social grammar in which women are never defined as subjects; a fantasy of power that disdains a sexual exchange in which women can participate only as objects of circulation."[6] In these terms, Maggie's demise may be read not only as a capitulation, but also as an act of resistance: an act of resistance on George Eliot's part to letting Maggie's story take its place among any preestablished family grouping in fiction. It is rather, a kind of anti-*Bildungsroman*, that is, a novel that, instead of taking its young male protagonist to maturity, sophistication, and adequate worldly compromise, leads Maggie to an uncompromising moral triumph and death.

George Eliot's final novel, *Daniel Deronda*, is the most eloquent, and radical, of all her treatments of gender. This is manifested, once again, in her manipulation of the ending, which refuses to bring the two strands of the plot together by providing a romantic reunion between hero and heroine – despite the fact that we are teased from the opening by the possibility of a liaison between Gwendolen and Deronda. This promise is reinforced by the fact that this plot outcome is predicted by some of the fictional characters. Yet to believe this, to buy into this assumption, would be to reveal our own conventionality, aligning ourselves with Sir Hugo, to whom a marriage between Daniel and Gwendolen would be "as pretty a story as need be." There is a good deal of evidence that contemporary readers expected a happy ending, as revealed by the existence of an unauthorized American sequel by Anna Clay Beecher, *Gwendolen: or Reclaimed*. Beecher maintained that she had been motivated by the "almost universal disappointment at the unanticipated conclusion of the story – a conclusion which many readers have resented as though it were a personal affront."[7] On the last page, after a series of misunderstandings, Gwendolen faints into Daniel's arms as his declaration of love rescues her from a fatal illness.

> What a reclamation! Those only who, like them, have stood upon the brink of despair, who, like them, have been restored – unexpectedly restored – to life, to hope, and to happiness, can judge their emotions and sentiments at this time. And when, at last, Deronda confessed his undying devotion and love, she sank beneath gratitude and joy, into the expanded arms of her adored lover, – RECLAIMED. (311–12)

But such a wishful reading as this must necessarily read across the grain of pointers within the text which caution one against reading according to the expectations of romantic fiction.

And yet, *Daniel Deronda* is a novel that recognizes that fictional plots, even if they are to be subverted, are also the vehicles for a range of highly understandable emotions: the conventional plots that are brought off in fictions are the imaginary workings out of the patterns which we would wish to govern our lives. The characters in this novel are employed to suggest the limitations of fictional pragmatics. Gwendolen herself muses: "I wonder how girls manage to fall in love. It is easy to make them do it in books. But men [in real life] are too ridiculous." The desires at stake are not necessarily affective ones. This novel shows how, in practice, marriage is still a question of economics. Gwendolen's uncle remarks: "the point is to get her well married" (7:64); as the eldest and most beautiful of five sisters without a fortune, expectations fall on her to make a "good match" in order to resolve the family's financial crisis. This socioeconomic point is firmly brought home by the verse-drama epigraph, written by Eliot, which heads chapter 10, spoken by the 1st Gent., an apparently representative masculine voice:

> What women should be? Sir, consult the taste
> Of marriageable men. This planet's store
> In iron, cotton, wood, or chemicals –
> All matter rendered to our plastic skill,
> Is wrought in shapes responsible to demand:
> The market's pulse makes index high or low,
> By rule sublime. Our daughters must be wives,
> And to be wives must be what men will choose:
> Man's taste is woman's test. You mark the phrase?
> 'Tis good, I think? – the sense well winged and poised
> With t's and s's. (10:83)

This is the genteel counterpart of the marketing sentiments voiced by Mr. Tulliver in *The Mill on the Floss*, when he remarks that "an over 'cute woman's no better nor a long-tailed sheep – she'll fetch none the bigger price for that." Through the emphasis on woman as an object of exchange in a male-centered economy, Gwendolen is implicitly linked to Mirah, who, in a quite different social context, hears someone speculating about her father: "I wonder what market he means the daughter for" (20:183); and whose father exploits her gifts: "his wishing me to sing the greatest music and parts in grand operas was only wishing for what would fetch the highest price" (20:184). The logic of events in *Daniel Deronda* leaves Gwendolen with little choice about marriage: Klesmer (rightly) dashes her hopes of an independent musical career; she determines to be a governess, but at that point a note from Grandcourt arrives. This is, however, no romantic gesture. Fundamentally, Grandcourt is marrying Gwendolen in order to "master" her, to revel in his gloating knowledge: "She had been brought to accept him in spite of everything – brought to kneel down like a horse"; "You have married *me*, and must be guided by my opinion" (48:507). He had, comments the narrator, "the courage and confidence that belong to domination, and he was at that moment feeling perfectly satisfied that he held his wife with bit and bridle . . . His words had the power of thumbscrew and the cold touch of the rack" (54:582). Through such language, we have a revelation not of the desires, but of the anxieties of masculinity, above all, the violence of Grandcourt's desire to maintain a clear difference and hierarchy in relations between women and men. As I shall show below, the novel sets out to question and undermine the viability of such a polarity.

The unhappy marriage of Grandcourt and Gwendolen serves as an indictment of the power structures of Victorian society, not just in the psychological sadism which is practiced by Grandcourt in this destructive relationship, but in the way Grandcourt treats the figure of Lydia Glasher, his former mistress. She is not the dangerous fallen woman of earlier Victorian fiction who, by some means or another, must be transported and/or killed off, like Hetty Sorrel, or Elizabeth Gaskell's Ruth, or Dickens's Em'ly, in *David Copperfield*: rather she remains within the text, a deliberate agent of disruption, whether intervening in person or sending Gwendolen her jewels. Against such calculated moves, even the more *risqué* fiction of the 1860s – by, for example, Wilkie Collins or Mary Braddon – could not offer much by way of helpful models: "Gwendolen's uncontrolled reading, though consisting chiefly in what are called pictures of life, had somehow not prepared her for this encounter with reality" (14:130–31). George Eliot's commentary on marital relations is also suggested by the way the narrative organization is used to reinforce the emotional dynamics of the plot. Gwendolen and her consciousness disappear from the text for whole stretches of time after she marries Grandcourt. The Deronda plot becomes increasingly dominant. This *may* be seen as a possibly ironic authorial complicity with Gwendolen's "mastering": certainly, it is a device which shows up her diminished post-marriage selfhood. Nor do we see her being *released* into widowhood, as Dorothea, despite – or even because of – her husband's spiteful will and codicil, might be said to be. Rather, she is precipitated into guilt and remorse, for having married Grandcourt at all; for having had murderous thoughts about him, and for the fact that she made little active effort to save him after he went overboard.

It is not just female stereotyping which this novel revises. Daniel, from the start, appears an unconventional male type, with his marked capacity for sympathy and his lack of aggression. These characteristics have led to some slightly extravagant claims being made on his behalf – Jennifer Uglow, for example, says that in this novel, George Eliot makes "her 'good' feminine character a man – Daniel Deronda himself. His feminine receptivity is contrasted to the 'bad' feminine character of Gwendolen, warped by her education and by the ideology of women which it enshrines."[8] His characterization is indeed signed by a confusion, even a collapse of gender norms at times (even though his *actions* may be far more determined by standard masculine plotting devices: the quest for origins and hence identity, the chivalric rescue of a woman in distress, and so on). But the attributes assigned to him are stated rather tentatively: "an affectionateness such as we are apt to call feminine" is juxtaposed with a capacity for judgment, and mental independence, "held to be rightfully masculine" (28:271). This is in turn juxtaposed with an ability to feel for others with "perhaps more than a women's acuteness of compassion" (55:585). To some extent, how we gender Deronda depends on how we gender George Eliot's narrative voice itself in her later novels. His attributes, as described in chapter 16 – a "subdued fervour of sympathy, an activity of imagination on behalf of others" (16:151) – are once again those characteristics, as I have already indicated, which although they are frequently gendered feminine within society, may be possessed in equal measure by either sex. And yet, something new occurs in *Daniel Deronda*. The idea that sympathy can actually have its limitations is addressed, and it is linked to the question of gender. Daniel tries to empathize with his mother's situation as a young girl facing her father's opposition to her art: "Though my own experience has been quite different . . . I can imagine the hardship of an enforced renunciation." The princess replies: "No . . . you are not a woman. You may try – but you can never imagine what it is to have a man's force of genius in you, and yet to suffer the slavery of being a girl" (51:141). Moral and emotional transvestism, however valuable as a tool of imaginative understanding, can ultimately be no substitute for experience itself. Moreover, the sympathy which Daniel wishes to display clashes with his inability to draw back from his internalization of the social myth of motherhood, and to approach any understanding of why his mother fails to love him.

Daniel's plot, despite the problems of negotiating a satisfactory rapport with his mother, follows the model of a romantic quest, both to know his origins and to take up a goal set in the future. Within this trajectory, he, unlike Gwendolen, is also granted the happiness of a fulfilled love story, which follows the traditional romance formula – man rescues woman – about which one presumes Gwendolen reads, but which so resolutely refuses to unfold within her own life. This may, of course, be a means – for once – of employing convention in order to soften the potentially alienating (for a Victorian readership) Jewish element within the text, using it as a foil to the more informative and didactic sections. But the gap between the two strands of the plot is also the product of gender possibilities. Gwendolen, quite early in her courtship, remarks that "We women can't go in search of adventures . . . We must stay where we grow" (13:113). The ambiguity in that word "grow" suggests that Gwendolen is claiming more rootedness to an individual spot than has actually been her lot, and, equally misleadingly, suggesting that her consciousness actively admits of the possibility of personal growth. Her story is one of imprisonment within social forms: she has to realize, at the end, her own worth, without relying on a mentor to give her direction and self-valuation – but there is no real indication she can do this. She feels "reduced to a mere speck" in Deronda's "wide-stretching purposes." For the narrator, this is, of course, a sign of the potential for a reassessment of perspective: "she was for the first time being dislodged from her supremacy in her own world, and getting a sense that her horizon was but a dipping onward" (68:689). The earlier example of Rosamond in *Middlemarch* should make one cautious about this apparent optimism, however. A similar expansion of emotional horizons seemed to open up to her, and they closed down again. Gwendolen herself recedes at the end of *Daniel Deronda*. Her final presence is distanced through the medium of correspondence, as she wistfully writes to Deronda: "I have remembered your words – that I may live to be one of the best of women, who makes others glad that they were born. I do not yet see how that can be, but you know better than I" (70:694–95). This apparent expansiveness is double-edged: Gwendolen, still very far from standing on her own feet, looks to a departing Daniel for guidance rather than looking into herself: he is cast into the role of prophet by her, and hence perhaps the reader is also invited to adopt this trusting attitude, but the plot does not begin to suggest where she might begin. She is, ıck in a materialistically oriented and racially arrogant England .. George Eliot expressed a growing social pessimism.

By contrast to Gwendolen, Daniel's future is one of freely chosen exclusion from society. But his ending also has affinities with the position in which Gwendolen is left. Joseph Boone has summed this up well: "For, although the *structural* movement of Daniel's story reaches a point of stabilization in his simultaneous discoveries of identity, love, and vocation, the *thematic* implications do not: to Eliot's Victorian reader the mission on which Daniel embarks can only remain uncertain, incomplete, given the historical reality that there was no Jewish homeland in the 1870s."[9] Any "solution," in his case, as in Gwendolen's, for the Jewish people as for the English woman, must lie outside the bounds of current realist fiction. They must lie in a social future for her fictional characters of which, for once, Eliot can expect her readers to know nothing. Women, in particular, are going to find no guidance in the plotted lives which they encounter in their habitual reading; nor, it would seem, in the current condition of England, or indeed in its colonies. Rather than searching for a preexistent script, the plots of the future remain to be written.

Jane Flax, in writing about the relationship between feminist theory and gender studies, goes further than to claim – as George Eliot herself implicitly claims throughout her writings – that gender is a "social relation, rather than . . . an opposition of inherently different beings." She pertinently reminds us that "since within contemporary Western societies gender relations have been ones of domination, feminist theories should have a compensatory as well as a critical aspect": in other words, they should seek to bring out and explore aspects of social relations that have been suppressed or unarticulated; to recover and write histories of women in relation to the stories that cultures tell about themselves. They will need to ask how women's "activities are affected but also how they effect, or enable, or compensate for the consequences of men's activities" ("Gender Relations," p. 641). At the same time, she recognizes that no woman is going to be able to write or think from outside her own position and participation in social relations, including the relations of domination.

George Eliot recognized the power of a confident, analytical, culturally authoritative voice. This was the voice which she had, after all, developed herself, influenced by her intellectual companionship with men, and through participating in an almost entirely male-dominated London literary scene. Her choice of an unequivocally male pseudonym for her fiction was also testimony to this, as well as an attempt to dissociate her literary production from her relative personal notoriety in living with Lewes. As Lewes himself wrote to Barbara Bodichon: "the object of anonymity was to get the book judged on its own merits, and not prejudged as the work of a woman, or of a particular woman" (*GEL*, III:79). Although George Eliot acknowledged the variety and fallibility of masculine utterances – witness the anxiously self-preoccupied Latimer in "The Lifted Veil," or the rather ponderous fussiness of the earlier essays in *Impressions of Theophrastus Such*, or the unsympathetic fulminations which she finds in the writings of the evangelical Dr. Cumming. But she would never have dreamed of relinquishing the tones which her contemporaries identified as masculine ones, in favor of "the frothy, the prosy, the pious, or the pedantic," or any other stylistic traits which could be identified with "feminine fatuity" (Pinney, p. 301). To do so would have been to limit the breadth of sympathetic, rational and wide-reaching angles of vision and understanding for which she stood, and, necessarily, to diminish her own implicit claim to speak from a dominant position.

Yet it is this very breadth and even-handedness of vision which in fact constitutes her appeal for feminist readers, and as – whatever she would have thought of the appellation – a feminist. It allows her to see the part which conventions, both literary and social, have played in constructing the stories which cultures have been narrating about themselves, and to show how such stories are increasingly insufficient to carry the weight both of social injustices and of the stultifying effects, on both women and men, of gender-based expectations. Compensatory as well as critical, George Eliot's portrayal of gender relations demonstrates what must change and be thought afresh if new plots, in both life and literature, are to be written. Dorothea's son may inherit the Tipton estate, hence suggesting a continuity in English life, but what of her other child – a daughter? The narrative is silent. George Eliot's plots contain little by way of solutions, and a great deal that looks like expediency and compromise: hers is no utopian radicalism. Solutions were, in any case, the most difficult part of a work's composition for her, since they meant an artificial, arbitrary severance from the process of history. Here, however, lies her importance: in the recognition that questions of woman's power, status, psychology, and, indeed, maternal role were not freestanding, isolated issues. Rather, she shows that they must be regarded as part of a wider, organically conceived, and hence frequently contradictory whole.

NOTES

1 Mathilde Blind, *George Eliot* [1883] (London: W. H. Allen, 1888), p. 88.
2 Sandra M.Gilbert and Susan Gubar, *The Madwoman in the Attic. The Woman Writer and the Nineteenth-Century Literary Imagination* (New Haven and London: Yale University Press, 1979), p. 466.

10

DONALD GRAY

George Eliot and her publishers

George Eliot conducted her prosperous career as a novelist during a fortunate moment in the history of literary publishing in Britain. In the 1840s a generation of novelists somewhat older than Eliot – Charles Dickens, William Makepeace Thackeray, Edward Bulwer Lytton, Charlotte Brontë – had found and enlarged an audience of readers to whom fiction became a principal form, even a habit, of entertainment. By midcentury a group of well-managed and solidly capitalized publishing firms had emerged whose proprietors could pay high prices for novels they thought would be popular and who had the resources, if they guessed right, to keep novels in print, and their authors' names before the public, through successively cheaper editions. Magazines like the weeklies *Household Words* and *All the Year Round* (edited by Dickens) and the monthly *Cornhill Magazine* (edited by Thackeray), many of them founded in the middle of the century, used serialized fiction as a principal attraction in their competition for readers. Fiction was also a mainstay of subscription or lending libraries, at the height of their popularity in the 1850s and 1860s, from which by payment of an annual fee readers borrowed books, magazines, and the separately published installments of novels. Mudie's Select Library added almost a million volumes between 1853 and 1862, about half of them fiction,[1] and the purchases by Mudie's and other libraries of hundreds and sometimes a thousand or more copies of three-volume editions of novels assured publishers of a profit on their first printings and made fiction accessible to the many readers unable or unwilling to buy these expensive (31 shillings and 6 pence) books.[2]

These conditions of literary publishing put constraints on writers as well as offering openings to increasingly large numbers of readers. The three-volume form and serialization imposed formal requirements: how to fill three volumes and keep a story moving through seven or eight hundred pages, when and how to break it into parts. Editors of magazines and directors of lending libraries were uneasy about themes and events in fiction that might trouble readers of conventional moral and political views or disappoint their expectations of who should be in a novel and how it should end. Perhaps most important, writers customarily sold the copyrights to their novels to publishers for a lump sum, either outright or for a fixed number of years. To make a living in their profession, therefore, novelists had to produce a book every couple of years, until they created a body of writing that enabled them to sustain their reputations and their households by negotiating new payments for cheap reprints or parcels of collected works.

George Eliot adapted to, profited from, and helped to change all these conditions of the commerce of mid-Victorian literary publishing. The story of her participation in its enterprise is in many ways exemplary of how successful and esteemed Victorian novelists practiced their profession. There are three principal characters in this story. One is the novelist, poet, and essayist herself. Another is George Henry Lewes, who shortly after they began to live together in 1854 suggested to Marian Evans, not yet George Eliot, that she try her hand at fiction, and who became her literary agent and manager while he maintained his own productive career as a journalist, editor, and consulting editor of prominent magazines, and author of books on natural history and philosophy. The third is John Blackwood, directing partner of the publishing firm that bore his family's name, son of its founder, and editor of *Blackwood's Magazine*, known in the house and trade as "Maga," a well-established monthly that at midcentury published fiction to get itself talked about and to keep up and increase sales.[3]

One reading of the relationship of these three principals is that George Eliot stayed at home and turned out the product that two shrewd and inventive men brought to market. Unquestionably, Eliot wanted to appear to maintain a distance from the commerce of her vocation. She wrote anonymously or behind a pseudonym, preferred not to read reviews, and often negotiated with her publisher not only through Lewes but sometimes as Lewes, as in, "Mr. Lewes observes that the cheap edition of the Spanish Gypsy is only advertised in the list below Pollock's Course of Time, where it would hardly strike any one who is not in search of it."[4] But that reading is incomplete. Eliot resisted Blackwood's early attempts to make the tone and matter of her fiction more congenial to the readers of his magazine, and she often prodded him in her own name to attend to details of the production and promotion of her books. She participated so fully in Lewes's management of her career that after his death she continued its scrupulously attentive practices without missing an entry into her accounts or a chance to consider carefully how best to maintain the remarkable cultural and commercial enterprise she and her partners had made of her writing.

Marian Evans brought a useful sum of pertinent experience to the beginning of her career as a novelist. Her first book, her translation of Strauss's *Life of Jesus* (1846), was published by John Chapman, a London bookseller and publisher of secularist and politically liberal views and chronically uncertain financial means. She was not party to the negotiations concerning its subsidy and publication, but she attended nonetheless to such details as the type chosen for the book and the wording of its subtitle (*GEL*, I: 199, 216). Although she knew that she would not earn anything from her second book, a translation of Feuerbach's *Essence of Christianity*, beyond the £30 she had been paid for the translation, she lectured Chapman sternly about the cost to his reputation if he failed to publish the book, once he had advertised it (*GEL*, II:130–31). After its publication in 1854 with Marian Evans's name on the title page, she prudently cut her losses and did not write a second book advertised by Chapman ("for which I am to have 'half profits' = 0/0!" [*GEL*, II:128]). Similarly, she later abandoned the prospect of publishing her translation of Spinoza's *Ethics* when Lewes, perhaps less prudently, twice broke off correspondence with publishers who would not meet even his quite modest price.

Chapman also opened the way to her decisively important experience as editor and contributor to journals of marked intellectual and political standing and influence. In 1850 he asked her to review in the *Westminster Review* a rationalist and materialist study of Greek and Hebrew religion he had just published. A year later Chapman bought the *Westminster*, a quarterly journal which had been founded in 1824 by James Mill and other followers of Jeremy Bentham as a radical counter to the conservative or liberal politics of established quarterlies. He immediately enlisted her help, first in drafting a prospectus setting out his ambition to revive the *Westminster* as "the organ of the ablest and most liberal thinkers of the time" (*GEL*, I:351), and then in the editing of the journal.

Marian Evans came up to London to stay, lived in Chapman's house, and effectively became the editor of *Westminster*, unnamed and unpaid. She suggested and solicited topics and writers ("We are trying Mazzini to write on Freedom v. Despotism" [*GEL*, II:5]), cut and smoothed other people's prose ("There is a great, dreary article on the Colonies by my side asking for reading and abridgement" [*GEL*, II:54]), and read proof. She kept a close watch on the competition ("I have noticed the advertisement of the British Q[uarterly] this morning. Its list of subjects is excellent" [*GEL*, II:48]). She usually used the first person plural when she wrote of the journal to her friends, and she took its fortunes quite personally, for better ("I begin to hope that our next number will be the best yet" [*GEL*, II:33–34]) and for worse ("I am a miserable Editor" [*GEL*, II: 93]). Early in her work on the *Westminster* she complained to Chapman that "I feel that I am a wretched helpmate to you, almost out of the world and incog. so far as I am in it" (*GEL*, II:48). But through her association with him and the *Westminster* she moved in one of the strong currents of intellectual and literary culture in London, meeting or corresponding with many writers and thinkers and sitting in on events like the meeting chaired by Dickens in Chapman's house to protest against the price-fixing practices of a group of publishers. Her account of her presence during this evening is prophetic. "I sat *at* the door for a short time," she wrote to a friend, "but soon got a chair within it" (*GEL*, II:23).

She did indeed move herself into the room. When in 1853 she left Chapman's house to live at her own address, and especially after she and Lewes left together for Germany in mid-1854, she began the regimen of a professional literary journalist. She began to contribute to the *Leader*, a weekly newspaper of liberal opinion cofounded and coedited by Lewes. Already "a practised hand at journalism," in the words of Gordon Haight, whose work on Eliot is the foundation of all commentary on her life, she even wrote some of Lewes's articles for him when he was sick.[5] She also wrote for the *Saturday Review*, a new weekly magazine of politics and literature, and for *Fraser's*, a solidly respectable old-line monthly. Before she left for Germany she resigned "any connection with the editorship of the Westminster" (*GEL*, II:127). But she continued to write for it, in Germany and after she and Lewes returned to London in mid-1855. Some of her most important essays appeared in the *Westminster*, including her analyses of the vacuities of certain kinds of pious discourse and of the vapidities of "Silly Novels by Lady Novelists" (1856).

In 1855 Marian Evans earned a little less than £120 for her literary journalism, mostly from writing in the *Westminster*. The next year she earned over £250, including £52 and 10 shillings for the first part of "The Sad Fortunes of Amos Barton," the first of the *Scenes of Clerical Life* (*GEL*, VII:358–59). That sum is given meaning by the professional incomes in these years of the people with whom she associated. When she met Chapman he estimated a profit of £375 a year from his business and paid one of his assistants £120 a year.[6] When she met Herbert Spencer in 1850 he was earning £105 a year as subeditor of a periodical and living in rooms above its office (Haight, *George Eliot*, p. 111). In the mid-1850s, fifteen years into a career in which he had worked as an editor and written plays, a couple of novels, a four-volume biographical history of philosophy, biographies of Robespierre and Goethe, books on Spanish drama and Comte, and dozens of reviews and articles in newspapers and magazines, Lewes earned on average about £430 a year (*GEL*, VII:372–75). At the beginning of her identity as George Eliot, Marian Evans had worked herself by her writing into the lower realms of her profession.

Yet when she completed "Amos Barton" at the end of 1856, she asked, or allowed, Lewes to offer it for publication to John Blackwood. Lewes was then contributing a series of essays on the natural history of the seashore to *Blackwood's*, and he certainly knew more than she about the practices of literary publishing. But Lewes did not simply pass on the manuscript as a helpful and knowledgeable consort. He disguised her identity by referring to its author as a man, and by hinting (Blackwood took the hint) that he was a member of the clergy. Marian Evans was not shy of recognition as a journalist. Two months after Lewes's letter to Blackwood, she wrote to a friend that he "needn't observe any secrecy about *articles* of mine," which according to custom had been published anonymously. "It is an advantage (pecuniarily) to me that I should be known as the writer of the articles in the Westminster" (*GEL*, II:287). Perhaps in allowing Lewes to act as agent for her fiction she thought to protect the name she was making for herself as a journalist from the possible failure of her fiction. Perhaps she and Lewes thought that Blackwood would hesitate to publish a scene of clerical life if he knew that its author was making her reputation as a critic of religious orthodoxies, or that he would not read it with proper seriousness if he took it to be another silly fiction by a lady novelist. For any and all of these reasons, Eliot's address to Blackwood through Lewes can be read not as a feminine withdrawal from the arena of business, but rather as a professional tactic that was both careful and canny.

In his replies to Lewes's letters, and later to the writer he addressed as "George Eliot" (and then, for the rest of his life, as "My dear Madam" or "My dear Mrs. Lewes"), Blackwood introduced two themes that he was to restate and elaborate all through the first passage of their long relationship. The first theme expressed Blackwood's sporadic discomfort with the tone and tendency of Eliot's fiction. He took "The Sad Fortunes of Amos Barton" for *Blackwood's* within a week after Lewes sent it to him, and he agreed to publish it as part of a series without reading the stories to follow. "If the author is a new writer," he wrote to Lewes, "I beg to congratulate him on being worthy of the honours of print and pay" (*GEL*, II:272). But in the same letter he remarked on a minuteness of description that sometimes damped the feeling and slowed the movement of the story, on the "want of some softening touch" in "the amusing reminiscences of childhood in church," and on the fact that "his clergymen with one exception are not very attractive specimens of the body." When he read the next story in the *Scenes of Clerical Life*, "Mr. Gilfil's Love Story," the misery of Caterina moved him. But he wanted to take the dagger out of her hand when she went to meet the man who had trifled with her affections; it would be better, he thought, if she only felt or dreamed "as if she could stab the cur to the heart" (*GEL*,

II:308). He was glad to learn from its author that "his next story was to be on a brighter theme" (*GEL*, II:322). But the next story was "Janet's Repentance," and he found its opening scene "rather a staggerer," with its congregation of mean-spirited villagers, a brutish husband, and a wife whose sufferings "have driven her to so unsentimental a resource as beer." "I feel certain that I am right," he wrote to Eliot, "in advising you to *soften* your picture as much as you can" (*GEL*, II:344).

Eliot made a few changes in response to Blackwood's remarks, but she refused or ignored all his suggestions for substantial revision. "I am unable to alter anything in relation to the delineation or development of character," she wrote (*GEL*, II:299); and again, "as an artist I should be utterly powerless if I departed from my own conceptions of life and character" (*GEL*, II:348). "I undertake to exhibit nothing as it should be; I only try to exhibit some things as they have been or are, seen through such a medium as my own nature gives me" (*GEL*, II:362). Annoyed by Blackwood's criticism of "Janet's Repentance" (*GEL*, II:409), she decided to close the series with that story and offered to withdraw it from the magazine and publish it only in a book. "I shall accept that plan," she wrote to Blackwood, "with no other feeling than that you have been to me the most liberal and agreeable of editors and are the man of all others I would choose for a publisher" (*GEL*, II:348).

At this juncture the second theme of their correspondence becomes prominent. "I do not fall in with George Eliots every day," Blackwood replied to her, "and the idea of stopping the Series as you suggested in your letter gave me 'quite a turn' to use one of Thackeray's favourite phrases." He concluded his letter: "In continuing to write for the Magazine I beg of all things that you will not consider yourself hampered in any way" (*GEL*, II:352). Eliot had won her point about the necessity of her style, and an unusual latitude for a new writer. But Blackwood showed himself to be as confident of his judgment as she was of her talent. He often used the word "fresh" to describe her writing, an important quality to an editor and publisher who needed something distinctive to take to a market flooded with fiction. His experience told him how the reputation and sales of her writing would grow. "The public is a very curious animal," he wrote to her after the first part of "Amos Barton" had appeared in *Blackwood's*, "and those who are most accustomed to feel its pulse know best how difficult it is to tell what will hit the bull's eye, but I shall be much astonished if the death of Milly does not go to the hearts of all readers" (*GEL*, II:290). He probably knew he was exaggerating in order to reassure his sensitive author, but he himself was reassured by the favorable opinions of the book he heard from friends and other writers. After the no better than satisfactory sale of the two-volume edition of *Scenes of Clerical Life*, in a first printing of 1,500 copies, he counseled its author to be patient. "Unless in exceptional cases, a very long time often elapses between these two stages of reputation – the literary and the public" (*GEL*, II:433). "I am satisfied the great point is gained," he wrote to Lewes, "viz., that degree of reputation which ensures a market and readers for the author's next work. The book is talked of everywhere" (*GEL*, II:457).

Perhaps more quickly than Blackwood expected, the sales and reputation of George Eliot's fiction grew markedly with the publication of her next book, *Adam Bede*, in 1859. As her audience enlarged, relations between Eliot and the man who of all others she wanted as her publisher became increasingly strained. She was now absolutely secure in the purposes and practice of the realism she advocated in chapter 17 of *Adam Bede*, which has been read as her definitive answer to Blackwood.[7] But he continued to ballast praise and encouragement with uneasiness about the likely trajectory of "The Captain's unfortunate attachment to Hetty" in *Adam Bede* (*GEL*, II:446) and a wish that in *Silas Marner* the "picture had been a more cheery one and had embraced higher specimens of humanity" (*GEL*, III:379). It is likely that Eliot wrote at least the early chapters of *Adam Bede* in the expectation that they would be serialized.[8] But Blackwood, heir to his father's policy of keeping out of the magazine anything "approaching to grossness or profanity" that would "make it a closed book to many families" (Oliphant, *Annals*, I:402), hesitated along the way to his eventual decision to publish the novel first as a serial. Perhaps worried that her editor had not yet graduated from the uneasiness that had decided her to end the series of *Scenes of Clerical Life*, Eliot finally told him that she wanted the novel to appear first in three volumes. He replied to Lewes, "Give my best regards to George Eliot and tell him that he will find me quite ready to meet his wishes by the publication of Adam Bede as a separate work at once" (*GEL*, VIII:203).

The Mill on the Floss was also published without first being serialized, and for a similar reason that added to the strain between author and publisher. Eliot believed that the success of *Adam Bede* had given her "so large and eager a public" that the publication of the novel first as a serial "would sweep away perhaps 20,000 – nay, 40,000 – readers who would otherwise demand copies of the complete work from the libraries" (*GEL*, III:151). John Blackwood, however, wanted the novel for the magazine, and Lewes was considering a plan to publish it in 1-shilling monthly parts. Then the problem of the identity of George Eliot complicated these divergent schemes. By the end of 1857 John Blackwood and his brother and partner William knew that their popular contributor was, to use one of the several names she gave herself, Mrs. Lewes. For a while all parties wanted to keep the secret, Eliot and Lewes because they thought the mystery helped sales and revelation might hurt them, and the Blackwoods because they feared that the character of their magazine might be injured by rumor or general knowledge that one of its popular contributors was a woman of heterodox views who lived with a man to whom she was not married. But Eliot's irritation when another publisher announced the appearance of *Adam Bede Jr.*, an imitation of her novel, and her anger at the claims of one Liggins to be the author of her books, persuaded her and Lewes in 1860 no longer to maintain the secret of her authorship. William Blackwood declared that knowledge of the identity of its author prohibited the serialization of *The Mill on the Floss* in *Blackwood's*: "I would not have it now for Maga . . . The dropping of the incognito is the most serious part of the business and will, I feel satisfied, affect the circulation in families of any future work" (*GEL*, III:221). His brother tried to compose the difference by falling back on the magazine's policy of not displaying the names of authors, and he deployed all his abundant capacity for praise to reassure Eliot that "my opinion of your genius and confidence in the truly good, honest, religious, and moral tone of all you have written or will write is such that I think you will overcome any possible detriment from the withdrawal of the mystery" (*GEL*, III:217). But his insistence on anonymous publication hurt Eliot. "Your proposition . . . to publish the story without the name of George Eliot seemed to me . . . part of a depreciatory view that ran through your whole letter" (*GEL*, III:218). In the end she got her way. *The Mill on the Floss* appeared first in three volumes in 1860, and Eliot's next fiction, *Silas Marner*, was published by Blackwood in 1861 in one volume also without being serialized in the magazine.

Fundamentally, however, it was not even this painful difference that pulled apart Eliot and her publisher. It was rather the very success that John Blackwood had predicted. Eliot earned £443 for the serialization and first edition of *Scenes of Clerical Life*, of which she retained the copyright. In 1858 Blackwood paid £800 for the copyright of *Adam Bede* for four years. In the first six months of 1859 more than 3,000 copies of the three-volume edition had been sold, including 1,500 copies to Mudie's library: "In the circulating libraries the subscribers are all yelling for it," William Blackwood wrote to Lewes (*GEL*, III:31). By the end of the year the novel had sold 10,000 copies in its first printings and in a less expensive two-volume edition Blackwood published at midyear. Because he and his brother thought it right to "give you a further pecuniary share in the triumph" of the novel, John Blackwood wrote to Eliot in October that he planned to send her another £800 at the beginning of 1860 (*GEL*, III:190).

That gesture came out of the past of literary publishing, when publishers bought books as one would buy or rent land, to be worked solely for their own profit. The Blackwoods thought of the extra payment as a gift, a rather lordly act of generosity, something like the pug dog with which they presented Eliot in 1859. Eliot and Lewes, on the other hand, accepted the extra payment as money the book had earned, and Eliot's "*cool* note" of acknowledgment gave John Blackwood "a fit of disgust" (*GEL*, III:192).

Eliot had good reason to think herself underpaid even after her publisher doubled the price he paid for *Adam Bede*. In the fall of 1859 Lewes received a proposal from Dickens that Eliot write a weekly serial in his magazine, *All the Year Round*, of which she would retain the copyright for subsequent publication as a book. The American magazine *The Century* offered £1,200 for the right to serialize a one-volume novel. Bradbury and Evans, publishers of the magazine *Once a Week*, made an offer for the serialization not only of a novel by Eliot but also of one by Lewes. Lewes wrote in his journal, "she felt bound to give Blackwood the refusal; but they assured me that *whatever* Blackwood offered they would give more" (*GEL*, III:204). "G. E. has sold herself to the highest bidder," one of Blackwood's managers wrote at the end of 1859, slipping into a very interesting confusion of gender that makes sharp dealing masculine. "I said very early that he was an avaricious soul" (*GEL*, III: 204–5).

Eliot used the success of *Adam Bede* not just to raise the price of her fiction, but also to change the terms of the bidding. When she and Blackwood finally came to agreement on the publication of *The Mill on the Floss*, she won for herself the payment of royalties, then so unusual that the trade had not yet settled on a word for the practice. (Blackwood called it a "lordship.") Blackwood paid £2,000 for an edition of 4,000 copies in three volumes (that is, a payment to Eliot of 10 shillings per copy, a royalty of about 30 percent of the list price), payment at the same rate for the sale of additional copies, and similarly scaled royalties on the sales of cheaper editions. Two weeks after closing that agreement, Blackwood returned the copyright of *Adam Bede* (which he owned for three more years) to Eliot and put payment for future sales of that novel on the same schedule as payments for sales of *The Mill on the Floss*. When *Silas Marner* was ready in 1861, Blackwood again paid Eliot on a royalty scale. Blackwood then offered her £3,000 for the copyrights of her first four books (*GEL*, III:458). She declined ("In consequence of a letter from Bradbury and Evans," she wrote in her journal[9]) and accepted instead a 20 percent royalty of £60 per 1,000 on a 6-shilling edition of her fiction (*GEL*, III:464). Lewes also kept to himself the negotiations of payments for translations and American and European reprints. Additional rewards for a success like that of *Adam Bede* would not depend on the gallantry of the publisher. Eliot and Lewes had made them part of the contract.[10]

When Eliot and Lewes did sell one of her novels to a very high bidder, they gave back some of the ground they had won in their dealings with Blackwood. In 1862 the publisher George Smith called on Lewes to put before him "the most magnificent offer ever yet made for a novel," £10,000 for the serialization and six-year copyright of Eliot's next work of fiction (*GEL*, IV:17–18). Smith, like the Blackwoods, inherited the proprietorship of a major publishing firm, the house of Smith, Elder, cofounded by his father. He published Ruskin's *Modern Painters* and Darwin's *Voyage of the Beagle*, as well as novels by Charlotte Brontë, William Makepeace Thackeray, Elizabeth Gaskell, and, in the 1840s, George Henry Lewes. He tended to large schemes, and his new enterprise was the *Cornhill*, a 1-shilling monthly magazine whose first number in 1859 sold over 100,000 copies.[11] (In the 1860s *Blackwood's,* priced at an old-fashioned 2 shillings and 6 pence, sold between 7,500 and 10,000 copies a month.) Smith needed the novel in April or May as a serial for his magazine, and he wanted entire ownership of its copyright. Eliot was willing to return to magazine publication – she had not yet published a novel in serial form – but not as quickly as Smith required, and she thought that the novel would be injured if it were divided into the sixteen parts that Smith wanted so that he could spread his investment over almost a year and a half of the costs of producing the magazine. After some discussion of such unusual forms as a 6-penny serial and publication in a single volume at 6 shillings, Eliot agreed that for a payment of £7,000 Smith would receive the right to serialize the novel in twelve parts, copyright for six years, and the right at the end of six years to publish the novel in one form of his choice until 1905.[12] Eliot and Lewes did not consult Blackwood during these conversations.

"I fear this letter will seem rather abrupt to you," Eliot began when she wrote to John Blackwood to inform him of her agreement with Smith (*GEL*, IV:34). "I am glad to hear that you have made so satisfactory an arrangement," he replied; "it would destroy my pleasure in business if I knew any friend was publishing with me when he thought he could do better for himself by going elsewhere" (*GEL*, IV:35–36). Privately, he was less gracious, regretting "their extortionate views" and attributing the defection, perhaps unfairly, solely to "the voracity of Lewes" (*GEL*, IV:4:38). In the event, *Romola* appeared in fourteen rather than twelve numbers of the *Cornhill*, each installment with illustrations by Frederick Leighton, and then in a three-volume edition in 1863. The presence of the novel "did not increase the sales of the magazine," Smith wrote, and, "As a separate publication it had not, I think, the success it deserved" (Smith, "Birth and Parentage," p. 10). It took two years to sell 2,288 copies of the three-volume edition, and then nearly four more years to work off the 1,500 copies of a one-volume 6-shilling edition (*GEL*, IV:102; Glynn, *Prince of Publishers*, p. 140). Now it was the affluent Eliot's turn for a gesture Smith described as "princely" (*GEL*, VIII:318). She made him a gift of her short story, "Brother Jacob," for which he had once offered £262, for publication in *Cornhill*. In 1866 she offered her next novel, *Felix Holt*, to Smith for £5,000. After reading the novel in manuscript to his wife, he declined the chance to publish it (Glynn, *Prince of Publishers*, p. 141).

During her tenure on the list of Smith's firm, Blackwood had continued as the publisher of cheap editions of Eliot's first four books. "I hope G. E. is thinking of something new," he wrote to Lewes at the end of 1863, in a letter reporting the recently disappointing sales of the 6-shilling edition of her fiction (*GEL*, IV:113). In the spring of 1866 Eliot offered the nearly completed *Felix Holt* to Blackwood, apparently without telling him of Smith's refusal, for he was "much pleased that she should think in the first instance of her old friend as the publisher" (*GEL*, IV:240). He liked the novel, especially its cautiously reformist politics, and he thought her return to his firm "a great publishing triumph" (*GEL*, IV:247). "It quite takes me back to the days when Adam Bede won the Derby," he wrote to George Eliot (*GEL*, IV:244). In fact, in their agreement for the novel Blackwood, Lewes, and George Eliot did return to the old days. Instead of paying a royalty, Blackwood bought a five years' use of the copyright of the novel for £5,000, left the American rights to Lewes's negotiation, and published *Felix Holt* without serialization in three volumes at 31 shillings and 6 pence for sale at a discount mostly to subscription libraries. Most of the 5,250 copies printed of the three-volume edition were sold in 1866, but 2,000 copies of a cheaper two-volume edition sold very slowly (*GEL*, IV:307, 352). Blackwood realized that the old days were sliding away. "The next time we take the field together," he wrote to Eliot, "I think we must experiment in a new form" (*GEL*, VI:307).

Lewes suggested the new mode in which Eliot's final two novels were published, although Bulwer Lytton and Blackwood had considered the idea twenty years earlier.[13] *Middlemarch* (1871–72) and *Daniel Deronda* (1876) appeared first in eight parts, each containing half a volume and selling at 5 shillings, and then bound in four volumes to be sold at 42 shillings. The parts of *Middlemarch* were sold every other month, except for the final two parts, which came out a month apart. *Daniel Deronda* was sold in monthly parts. The scheme was intended, as Lewes put it, to make "the public *buy* instead of borrowing" from subscription libraries, although he foresaw that the libraries would buy and circulate the parts to readers who had entirely lost the custom of buying books (*GEL*, V:146). For each novel Lewes asked – all these details of publication were put before Blackwood in letters from Lewes

– either £6,000 for a four-year copyright or a royalty of 40 percent on sale of the parts, and equivalent royalties on the sales of other editions. Blackwood, probably hesitant to lay out a large investment because of the failure of *Romola* and the disappointment of *Felix Holt*, agreed to the royalty (*GEL*, IV:179–180, 182–183).

Lewes's other ideas for making money from *Middlemarch* and *Daniel Deronda* exemplify the energy and ingenuity with which he went to market. Despite the skepticism of Blackwood's London manager ("advertisers only understand numbers" [*GEL*, V:186]), Lewes profitably revived the practice of selling advertising in the bimonthly or monthly parts of both novels. At his suggestion Blackwood published the last two parts of *Middlemarch* a month rather than two months apart in order to have the whole book ready for the newly emergent Christmas book-buying season. He wanted to advertise *Daniel Deronda* by hiring men to walk around London wearing sandwich boards bearing the name of the book. Most interestingly, he broke new ground in his negotiations with American publishers.

Blackwood did not think American rights worth much. In the absence of international copyright agreements, American publishers could and did bring out pirated printings of British novels as soon as they got their hands on copies. An American publisher could purchase a few weeks head start by paying for "early sheets," copies of the books sent off shortly before their publishing dates in Britain. Blackwood's London manager sold the American rights to *Adam Bede*, asking for £50 in order to get £30 from the firm of Harper in New York (*GEL*, II:507). Lewes then took over, getting £100 from Harper for *Silas Marner*, £300 for *The Mill on the Floss*, "on condition of the work not being *published* here until 10 days after delivery to them of the last sheet" (*GEL*, III:268), and the same amount for *Felix Holt*. In suggesting that Lewes conduct the negotiations for the latter novel, Blackwood wrote, "The transatlantic vultures may be drawn a speck nearer honesty by the desire to propitiate a great author" (*GEL*, IV:251). Certainly Eliot's transatlantic standing as an eminent author helped Lewes in his agreements for her last two novels. He devised a complicated arrangement, which made Blackwood quite anxious – "I wish you had consulted me before making it," he wrote to Lewes (*GEL*, V:199) – in which Harper bought the right to begin to serialize the novels in its magazines before the publication of the parts in Britain. *Middlemarch*, despite Eliot's reluctance to cut her stories into small pieces, appeared in *Harper's Weekly*, *Daniel Deronda* in *Harper's New Monthly Magazine*, in which *Romola* had also been serialized. For these rights Eliot received £1,200 for *Middlemarch*, and £1,700 for *Daniel Deronda*. Lewes also markedly increased her payment for rights to reprint her novels in English on the Continent, playing two firms against one another to move from the £30 she received for *Scenes of Clerical Life* to payments of £250 for *Daniel Deronda* and about £200 for *Middlemarch* (*GEL*, VII:362–64).

"The sale of Middlemarch is wonderful out of all whooping," Eliot wrote in response to one of Blackwood's reports (*GEL*, VI:75). One of Blackwood's managers reported of *Middlemarch* that "they are selling copies over the counter in George Street [Blackwood's Edinburgh office] to people who never think of buying an ordinary novel" (*GEL*, V:224). W. H. Smith bought 1,000 copies of Part I for his railway bookstalls, and, as Lewes predicted, Mudie bought 1,500 copies of Part I for his library (*GEL*, V:223). Each of the eight parts sold between 5 and 6,000 copies (*GEL*, VI:6:10), and *Daniel Deronda* did even better, each part selling nearly 8,000 copies (*GEL*, VI:279). As soon as its last part appeared, Blackwood published a four-volume edition of each novel at 42 shillings, followed by an edition at 21 shillings, and then a one-volume edition at 7 shillings and 6 pence. Eliot recorded in her accounts that at the end of 1879, eight years after the publication of its first part, *Middlemarch* had sold over 33,000 copies, and *Daniel Deronda* over 22,000 copies in the three years since it began publication. She had earned over £8,700 from the first novel and more than £9,200 from the second (*GEL*, VII:364). It is more difficult to calculate profits to the firm of Blackwood. In explanations and budgets Blackwood sent to Lewes and Eliot (for example, *GEL*, V:421 and VI:309), it appears that Eliot was receiving about two-thirds of the profits of the sales of her books.

Lewes's and Blackwood's innovation with *Middlemarch* and *Daniel Deronda* did not displace publication in three volumes or in magazines as the principal modes in which readers read fiction. That change did not happen until the 1890s, and then fiction moved the other way, not toward the spacious, patiently developed narratives Eliot wound through four volumes, but to one-volume novels sold at 6 shillings, as publishers reached for readers in an increasingly literate society who would buy as well as borrow books.[14] But the sales of Eliot's final two novels confirmed her stature as an esteemed writer, a "great author," in Blackwood's words, that had been growing since the mid-1860s. The last passage of Eliot's life of course contains many such testimonies to her eminence. For example, when in 1871 Alexander Main, an admirer whom Blackwood called (although not to Eliot) "The Gusher," proposed a collection of *Wise, Witty, and Tender Sayings* selected from the works of George Eliot, Blackwood hesitated. "I am disappointed at your not taking the same view of Main's proposal as we do," Lewes wrote (*GEL*, V:195). Within two weeks Blackwood agreed to publish the book, which went into a second edition in 1873 and had two more reprintings before the end of the decade. Main also organized quotations from her writing into a *George Eliot Birthday Book* (1878), and extracts from her writing, including her poems, began to appear in textbooks prepared for the schools the state began to support in the last third of the century.

One of the most remarkable signs of Eliot's eminence is that her name could sell poetry. Honored in nineteenth-century Britain as the most exalted of literary forms, poetry did not usually sell well; only a handful of professional writers made their livings as poets.[15] When Eliot began *The Spanish Gypsy* in 1867 she told George Smith that the book "is likely to be dead against the taste of that large public" courted by publishers, and "would be quite ineligible for publication in the 'Cornhill'" (*GEL*, IV:377). Blackwood, still edgy about keeping Eliot on his list (in the fall of 1867 he sent her grouse from Scotland; Smith sent her bonbons [*GEL*, IV:389,391]), responded with the praise he knew that she needed and plans for an edition of 2,000 copies to be published in 1868, for which she refused a payment of £300 and accepted a royalty. After the publication of *Scenes of Clerical Life* Eliot and Lewes had consulted a life of Charlotte Brontë, "to see how long it was before 'Jane Eyre' came into demand at the libraries" (six weeks, compared to three weeks "for *my* book" [*Journals*, 294]). They now noted that Elizabeth Barrett Browning's *Aurora Leigh* (1856) required nine months to sell 2,750 copies. "But we have sold 2,000 in a little more than 2 months" (*GEL*, IV:470). After a small printing of the second edition, Lewes thought it good advertising to call every printing of 1,000 a new edition (*GEL*, IV:495). By that arithmetic *The Spanish Gypsy* had sold over 4,000 copies by the time of its fifth edition in 1875. Eliot also, quite unusually, received a royalty on copies of an American edition published by Ticknor and Fields. The American edition had sold more than 8,300 copies by mid-1869. "Longfellow, Lowell and the Boston set know the lyrics by heart and are in a high state of enthusiasm," Lewes wrote to his son (*GEL*, V:37).

After the publication of her long poem, Eliot began to sell poems to magazines. Blackwood paid £50 for "How Lisa Loved the King," explaining, "I will never give a fancy price for anything to appear in the Magazine" (*GEL*, V:15). That policy was the reason that Eliot sold "The Legend of Jubal," "Armgart," and "A College Breakfast Party" to the magazine of one of Blackwood's competitors, Macmillan, for a total of £650. "I did not mention ["The Legend of Jubal"] to you," she wrote to Blackwood, "because I know that you do not care to have exceptional contributions to Maga" (*GEL*, V: 81). Lewes arranged the sale of "How Lisa Loved the King" to the American magazine *Atlantic*, but the deal fell through when Blackwood would not allow 250 copies of the magazine into England to compete with his own monthly. The publisher of the *Atlantic*, Fields, Osgood, published the poem in a 50-cent pamphlet, and later bought Eliot's other poems for their magazine.

At this stage in their relationship Eliot no longer asked Blackwood if he was interested in publishing one of her books. She simply told him when one was ready. In 1874 she sent him word that she was ready to collect her poems in a volume. She wanted it to look like the 1820 edition of Keats's poems, on good paper, 200 pages of 18 lines, "a darkish-green cover, with Roman lettering" (*GEL*, VI:26). "You must have been thinking if not writing Poetry all your life," Blackwood replied (*GEL*, VI:37), and after some fussing about the quality of the paper and the price of the book, *The Legend of Jubal and Other Poems, Old and New* was published in 1874 in an edition of 1,500 copies at 6 shillings. The edition sold out in about six months. Its cover was red and the book did not look like the 1820 Keats, but Eliot made her point. She thought of her books as moral and intellectual engines; she rejoiced, for example, that "the 'mass of Positivism,' in the shape of 'The Spanish Gypsy,' is . . . rapidly finding acceptance with the public" (*GEL*, IV:496). But she also imagined them as physical objects that found their proper company with the handsome relics of the masters of her calling against whose achievement she now measured herself.

From the beginning George Eliot knew, or said she knew, that "I have not the characteristics of the 'popular author'" (*GEL*, III:6). But she wanted the influence testified to by large sales and the wide distribution of her writing. In 1869 she authorized a cheap American edition of her fiction published by Fields, Osgood, even though Lewes thought that because Harper was also publishing inexpensive reprints of each of the novels in the United States the price would be too low to yield "much of a *pecuniary* benefit" (*GEL*, V:36). Blackwood had been publishing her fiction in inexpensive uniform volumes since she returned to his firm's list in 1866. Late in that year he paid her £1,000 for the British copyright for ten years for all her fiction through *Felix Holt* (except *Romola*, of whose copyright Smith had the use until 1869). George Eliot agreed to Blackwood's suggestion of an illustrated edition, to be published in thirty sixpenny parts and then bound in four volumes, each volume priced at 3 shillings and 6 pence. Six months later he wrote to George Eliot to tell her, "The sale in numbers is a failure, but in the volume of Adam we have sold about 3,000" (*GEL*, IV:372). By the time the agreement expired in 1876, the edition had sold a little over 73,000 volumes, enough to give the publisher a small profit but well below the estimates on which Blackwood had based his offer ten years earlier (*GEL*, VI:300). When Blackwood offered £4,000 for a renewal of the lease (George Eliot and Lewes chose a royalty instead), he briefly considered publication in penny parts (*GEL*, VI:297) and worked out calculations for volumes at 4 shillings and 6 pence and 3 shillings and 6 pence (*GEL*, VI:308). Finally he decided to keep the fiction through (whose copyright had reverted to George Eliot) in inexpensive editions and to put all her writing, including her poems, in a new collection that came to be named the Cabinet Edition.

In 1877 she imagined her collected works in "the fine octavo page" of an edition of Fielding which we possess . . . *eight* volumes of like size with fine type and paper" (*GEL*, VI:351). But then she saw in a bookshop a big and clumsy edition of Tennyson (she and Lewes needed a good-looking copy of his works because the Poet Laureate was coming to read to them in their house), and she fell in with Blackwood's suggestion of an edition of nineteen or twenty volumes like those of a set he had caused to be cut to uniform size and bound "to catch the eye of some of your worshippers here . . . I think it will look well in the library or drawing room in Town or country" (*GEL*, VI:366). Blackwood wrote to his nephew and eventual successor as head of the firm, William Blackwood, that he expected to "make but very little of this edition and the author not much but it will be a steady on-going thing, a capital leading franchise in the business . . . This edition must be the permanent one of these works and the publisher of it the natural successor to all the people's editions which surely will come" (*GEL*, VI:405).

Blackwood priced the twenty volumes of the Cabinet Edition at 5 shillings a volume, £5 for the set. (After Eliot's death the edition was enlarged to include a volume of her essays and the three volumes of John Walter Cross's *Life of George Eliot.*) George Smith, Eliot's only other publisher, also recognized that the readers who bought Eliot's books at least thought of themselves as reading or displaying the books in libraries and drawing rooms, in town and country. He had used his right to publish *Romola* in one edition of his choice after his copyright expired to bring out a cheap edition at 2 shillings and 6 pence. But in 1880, shortly before her death, Eliot informed Blackwood that she had agreed to allow Smith to bring out "an *édition de luxe* of Romola, corresponding with that of Thackeray's works" (*GEL*, VII:250). Smith's edition was limited to 1,000 numbered copies and advertised in the *Atheneum* and other magazines as for sale by subscription without citing a price ("The Publishers reserve to themselves the option of at any time increasing the subscription price" [25 September 1880, p. 416]). Like Smith's *édition de luxe*, the compact volumes and clean, generously spaced pages of the Cabinet Edition appropriately embody what her publishers, her partner, and the author herself had made of George Eliot. The volumes of the Cabinet Edition sold modestly well; the edition crowned the work of Blackwood and his firm as the publisher of the then most eminent living British novelist; and it put George Eliot in the library along with Fielding and Thackeray and other worthies whose peer she had become.

George Henry Lewes died in late November 1878. Ten days before his death he sent the manuscript of *Impressions of Theophrastus Such* to Blackwood, instructing him that "we wish the volume to be out before the opening of Parliament. A 10/6 handsome volume" (*GEL*, VII:78–79). After Lewes's death Eliot prepared the last volume of his *Problems of Life and Mind* for the press (Blackwood, disturbed by its secularism, was not the book's publisher), and corrected the proofs of *Impressions*. But she shrank from its publication, partly because she feared "to create a notion on the part of the public of my having been occupied in writing Theophrastus" during her mourning (*GEL*, VII:111), and partly because, missing Lewes's encouragement, she fell into self-doubt and feared the book might "injure my influence" (*GEL*, VII:126). Blackwood responded with the praise that had become habitual to him ("It brings us all in a kind of way to the Confessional": [*GEL*, VII:94]) and even risked speaking for Lewes: "Theophrastus most certainly had his full sanction and . . . he who knew you best felt that your works were above criticism and incapable of being made better by the assistance of any human being" (*GEL*, VII:125). He suggested the inclusion of a notice stating that the manuscript was in the publisher's office before Lewes's death, and he tried to steady her fears about her public: "no one will be brute enough to be otherwise than glad to see any publication from you which may possibly divert your thoughts" (*GEL*, VII:118). When late in the spring of 1879 Eliot finally agreed to publish, she asked Blackwood to manage the sale of the American rights. She also left in her publisher's hands negotiations for a continental reprint and translation rights, although she wrote several paragraphs of advice about the latter. "You see," she wrote to Blackwood, "I have been so used to have all trouble spared me that I am ready to cast it on any willing shoulders" (*GEL*, VII:126).

But even before she agreed to the publication of *Impressions of Theophrastus Such*, Eliot showed herself still to be, in the well-informed opinion of Margaret Oliphant, "keenly professional" and "an admirable woman of business" (Oliphant, *Annals*, II:446–47). She worried about the look of the page on which she read the proofs of *Impressions*: "The margin seems perilously and unbeautifully narrow" (*GEL*, VII:111). She had something to say about the title page and the color of the stamping on the cover. She asked why she was receiving only a 30 percent royalty when she had received 40 percent for her last two novels, and after the book began selling well she got Blackwood to agree to a modest increase ("the question of increasing your lordship had already occurred to us," he wrote [*GEL*, VII:197]). She wondered when the check from Harper would be sent to her:

"I like punctuality in business matters" (*GEL*, VII:171). She wanted to postpone the sale of the right to a continental reprint until the autumn so that British tourists could not buy it on their summer travels. When *Impressions of Theophrastus Such* sold over 6,000 copies of three printings by the end of the summer, she advised against the publication of a cheap edition so soon after so many readers had paid for a more expensive one – the commercially aggressive Lewes probably would have disagreed. When in the fall of 1879 William Blackwood proposed a supplemental volume of *Wise, Witty, and Tender Sayings* to include material from *Daniel Deronda* and *Impressions*, she suggested instead their inclusion in a new printing on thinner paper, like that, she wrote, ever mindful of the company she wanted to keep, "of Matthew Arnold's Selections from Wordsworth" (*GEL*, VII:221).

John Blackwood died in October 1879. "What a run it has been," he wrote in one of his last letters to George Eliot, celebrating the sales of *Impressions of Theophrastus Such*. "How *he* would have enjoyed it" (*GEL*, VII:181). It was characteristic of his tact that he included Lewes in the celebration. The collaboration among Lewes, Blackwood, and George Eliot was remarkable in its durability and in the complicated complementarity of its principals. Neither Blackwood nor George Eliot could summon and sustain the energy with which Lewes kicked up ideas for making money. Their temperaments instead grounded the relationship in its eventual stability, and gave what was a commercial venture the warmth of feeling and dignity of purpose that mark the action of a George Eliot novel.

Blackwood learned early from Lewes to curb editorial advice and authority to a self-doubting writer and to substitute praise and encouragement. These reassurances – "as good as a dose of quinine" to her, Lewes told him (*GEL*, VI:228) – very soon became not just tactical but also expressions of the natural tenor of his regard. He was an admirably responsive reader; he wanted to jump out of his chair "to go and save the poor creature" when he read of Hetty's night-journey in the fields (Oliphant/Porter, *Annals*, III:50), and the scene in which Lydgate proposes to Rosamond recalled an episode in his own young manhood "when if the tear had been there as well as the smile I would have been done for at a very early stage of life" (*GEL*, V:246). He sometimes enacted his praise in engagingly domestic anecdotes, telling Eliot that when he read *The Mill on the Floss* in manuscript he exclaimed to his brother, "By God she is a *wonderful* woman" (*GEL*, III:276), and writing to Lewes that while reading "Amos Barton" he "chuckled and laughed so much that Mrs. Blackwood took up the slips as I threw them down and entered into the story with keenest relish" (Martin, "Two Unpublished Letters," p.52). He brought his wife to call on Eliot, a graceful acknowledgment of her wish to be known as Mrs. Lewes, and during the middle and last years of their relationship he filled out the pages of his letters on business with stories about his private pleasures, usually those provided by golf and his children. (Lewes and Eliot often reciprocated with accounts of their illnesses.) Near the end of his life he wrote to his nephew that after looking over his old letters George Eliot had written to him to say "pretty much that she could not have gone on without me . . . It is the greatest compliment a man in my position could possibly receive, and that and the context about herself brought warm tears to my eyes" (*GEL*, VI:293).

George Eliot, for her part, learned her worth as a writer, not only from the encouragement of Lewes and Blackwood, and from the satisfactions of her steadily expanding craft, but also from the returns it brought her. She wrote to Blackwood when she began as a novelist, "I don't want the world to give me anything for my books except money enough to save me from the temptation to write *only* for money" (*GEL*, III:152). The world gave her a great deal of money, and her accounts told her literally to the penny – £45,343, 11 shillings, and 8 pence – how much she had earned by her writing by the time of her death in 1880 (*GEL*, VII:361–63). But of course she grew to want more from the world than money and the independence it purchased. She wanted the influence she was so concerned to husband when she hesitated about the publication of *Impressions of Theophrastus Such*. With and without Lewes, she diligently superintended the practical details of being a successful author because, among other rewards, her success provided the means and a measure of her moral influence.

There is a difference between the mission and the marketing of George Eliot's writing, a difference on which the aesthetic and ethical sensibilities of her time insisted. There is also a connection. George Eliot understood the connection. An astute recent commentator on her professional life remarks that the fuel of Eliot's recurrent complaints to Blackwood that railway bookstalls stocked trashy novels but not hers is her "desire to imagine a whole trainload of commuters reading the works of George Eliot."[16] She maintained a distance from the market – or, more accurately, the illusion of a distance – not from disdain for its practices or indifference to the power to be won there. On the contrary, an important part of her idea about herself is that she would elevate the market by energetically helping to promote her dignified presence in it. With Lewes and her publishers, George Eliot worked knowledgeably at the business of her fame in order to become, in the vocabulary of her ambition, one of the saving institutions of her culture.

NOTES

1 Guinevere L. Griest, *Mudie's Circulating Library and the Victorian Novel* (Bloomington: Indiana University Press, 1970), p. 21.

2 See Richard D. Altick, "The Book Trade, 1851–1900" and "Periodicals and Newspapers, 1851–1900," in *The English Common Reader: A Social History of the Mass Reading Public, 1800–1900* (Chicago: University of Chicago Press, 1957), pp. 294–317, 348–64; John Sutherland, "Part One: The Novel Publishing World, 1830–1870," in *Victorian Novelists and Publishers* (Chicago: University of Chicago Press, 1976), pp. 9–98; F. A. Mumby and Ian Norrie, "The Mid-Nineteenth Century," in *Publishing and Bookselling*, 5th edn. (London: Jonathan Cape and R. R. Bowker, 1974), pp. 204–32; John Feather, "Part Three: The First of the Mass Media, 1800–1900," in *A History of British Publishing* (London: Croom Helm, 1988), pp. 129–79; Nigel Cross, *The Common Writer: Life in Nineteenth-Century Grub Street* (Cambridge: Cambridge University Press, 1985); Simon Eliot, *Some Patterns and Trends in British Publishing, 1800–1919* (London Bibliographic Society, 1994), and "Some Trends in British Book Production, 1800–1919," in *Literature in the Marketplace: Nineteenth-Century British Publishing and Reading Practices*, ed. John Jordan and Robert L. Patten (Cambridge: Cambridge University Press, 1995), pp. 19–43; Robert L. Patten, "The Professional Artist," in *Charles Dickens and his Publishers* (Oxford: Clarendon Press, 1978), pp. 9–27; and Peter Shillingsburg, "Book Production" and "The Artist and the Marketplace," in *Pegasus in Harness: Victorian Publishing and W. M. Thackeray* (Charlottesville: University of Virginia Press, 1992), pp. 146–99, 200–20; J. Donn Vann, "Introduction," in *Victorian Novels in Serial* (New York: MLA, 1985), pp. 1–17; Linda Hughes and Michael Lund, "Introducing the Serial," in *The Victorian Serial* (Charlottesville: University of Virginia Press, 1991), pp. 1–14; Laurel Brake, "'The Trepidation of the Spheres': The Serial and the Book in the Nineteenth Century," and Bill Bell, "Fiction in the Marketplace: Towards a Study of the Victorian Serial," both in *Serials and their Readers 1620–1914*, ed. Robin Myers and Michael Harris (Winchester: St. Paul's Bibliographies, 1993), pp. 83–101, 125–44.

3 See Margaret Oliphant, *Annals of a Publishing House: William Blackwood and his sons, their Magazine and Friends*, 3 vols. (Edinburgh and London:William Blackwood & Sons, 1897–98). The third volume (1898) on the firm under the direction of John Blackwood is by his daughter, Mrs. Gerald Porter. See also Gordon S. Haight, "George Eliot and John Blackwood," *Blackwood's*, 306 (1969):385–400.

4 *GEL*, IV:492. See also Rosemary Ashton, "New George Eliot Letters at the Huntington," *Huntington Library Quarterly*, 54 (1991):111–26 for additional information about Marian Evans's close supervision of the editing of the *Westminster Review*.

5 Gordon S. Haight, *George Eliot: A Biography* (Oxford: Oxford University Press, 1968), p. 144.

6 Gordon S. Haight, *George Eliot & John Chapman, with Chapman's Diaries* (New Haven: Yale University Press, 1940), pp. 181, 203.

7 See Ronald F. Anderson, "George Eliot Provoked: John Blackwood and Chapter 17 of *Adam Bede*," *Modern Philology*, 71 (1973–74): 39–47.

8 See Carol A. Martin, *George Eliot's Serial Fiction* (Columbus: Ohio State University Press, 1994), pp. 94–99, and "Two Unpublished Letters from John Blackwood on the Serialization of *Scenes of Clerical Life* and *Adam Bede*," *Publishing History*, 37 (1995): 51–59.

9 *The Journals of George Eliot*, ed. Margaret Harris and Judith Johnston (Cambridge: Cambridge University Press, 1998), p. 103.

10 See Ronald F. Anderson, "Negotiating for *The Mill on the Floss*," *Publishing History* 2 (1977): 27–40. See also Gordon S. Haight, "George Eliot's Royalties," *Publisher's Weekly*, 7 August 1954, 522–23.

11 See Jennifer Glynn, *Prince of Publishers: A Biography of George Smith* (London and New York: Allison & Busby, 1986); George Smith, "Our Birth and Parentage," *Cornhill* Magazine, n.s. 10 (1901): 4–17; and Sydney Lee, "Memoir of George Smith," *Dictionary of National Biography* (Oxford and New York:Oxford University Press, 1937–38) I: xxi-lix. On the sales of the *Cornhill* and *Blackwood's*, see Alvar Ellegård, *The Readership of the Periodical Press in Mid-Victorian Britain* (Stockholm: Almqvist and Wiksell, 1957), pp. 32–33; Altick ,"Book Trade," p. 393; and Oliphant Annals, II:102.

12 Ronald F. Anderson, "'Things Wisely Ordered': John Blackwood, George Eliot, and the Publication of *Romola*," *Publishing History*, 11 (1982): 5–39.

13 John Sutherland, "Eliot, Lytton, and the Zelig Effect," in *Victorian Fiction: Writers, Publishers, Readers* (New York: Macmillan and St. Martin's Press, 1995) pp. 107–13. See also Sutherland's essay, "Lytton, John Blackwood, and the Serialization of *Middlemarch*," *Bibliotheck*, 7 (1978): 98–104. On the publication history and tactics of *Middlemarch* see N. N. Feltes, "One Round of a Long Ladder: Gender, Profession, and the Production of *Middlemarch*," in *Modes of Production of Victorian Novels* (Chicago: University of Chicago Press, 1986), pp. 36–56; and Sutherland's chapter, "Marketing *Middlemarch*," in *Victorian Novelists and Publishers*, pp. 188–205.

14 See Peter Keating, "Novelists and Readers," in *The Haunted Study: A Social History of the English Novel* (London:Secker & Warburg, 1989), pp. 9–87; Peter D. McDonald, "The Literary Field in the 1890s," in *British Literary Culture and Publishing Practice, 1880–1914* (Cambridge: Cambridge University Press, 1997), pp. 1–27; and N. N. Feltes, "Publishing as Capital," in *Literary Capital and the Late Victorian Novel* (Madison:University of Wisconsin Press, 1993), pp. 3–34.

15 See Lee Erickson, "The Poets' Corner: The Impact of Technological Changes in Printing on English Poetry," in *The Economy of Literary Form: The Industrialization of Publishing, 1800–1850* (Baltimore: Johns Hopkins University Press, 1996), pp. 19–48; and Donald Gray, "Macaulay's *Lays of Rome* and the Publication of Nineteenth-Century British Poetry," in *Victorian Literature and Society: Essays Presented to Richard D. Altick*, ed. James R. Kincaid and Albert J. Kuhn (Columbus: Ohio State University Press, 1984), pp. 74–93.

16 Rosemarie Bodenheimer, *The Real Life of Mary Ann Evans: George Eliot, her Letters and Fiction* (Cornell University Press, 1994), p. 176.

11

KATHLEEN BLAKE

George Eliot: the critical heritage

Appreciation and depreciation

There is something strange in the account of George Eliot's reputation and influence. For a writer so much appreciated, and, one would hardly doubt, of appreciating fame, it is striking to observe the limit points of appreciation, in both senses of the word. I had not thought to find so much depreciation. Given her own vaunted values of sympathy and connection over time, it is all the more noticeable when she is met short of half-way by readers, writers, and critics over the years.

George Eliot herself knew something about reception – reception from others and from the past – and about accrual and passing along. In the last chapter of Book IV of *The Mill on the Floss*, Maggie Tulliver takes up a little old-fashioned book by Thomas à Kempis and finds that it works miracles to this day. It has gained by its reading over the years, for its name precedes it in familiarity. The corners of pages turned down, the pen and ink annotations now browned by time, mark a way back to à Kempis himself, with his fashion of speech different from that of Maggie's day, but still the voice of a brother.

But, of course, George Eliot also knew how few things last and keep their value, let alone gain and pass value along. This is the burden of the reflections opening Book IV of *The Mill on the Floss*. Through the symbolism of flood, in a description of three rivers, the destructiveness of time is registered. There are beautiful and romantic ruins along the castled Rhine, while along the Rhone are only dreary remnants of an obscure vitality that even in its best days seems to have been destined for a deserved oblivion. The passage ponders how the life along the River Floss, treated in the novel itself – prosaic, worldly, often unlovely – can offer anything to be appreciated, and how its remains can do other than depressingly decay.

The ending of *Middlemarch* contemplates an influence of Dorothea Brooke that is like a virtually anonymous river broken in strength. Yet its force, spent in channels, is incalculably diffusive and contributes to the growing good of the world. George Eliot may be figured as a type of the nobly aspiring Dorothea, but also as Maggie's materially minded Aunt Glegg. Mrs. Glegg has aspirations, too, and is a force in her own way. She is a careful preserver of her best garments, but they only emerge from the strata of her damp clothes chest spotted with mold. By contrast, she does not hoard the money that she carefully keeps from Mr. Glegg as her own, but she puts it out at interest. She invests to profit monetarily, and she gains respect and gratitude from the younger generation whom she stakes in her lifetime and to whom she will leave her money after her death.

George Eliot was a figure who was hugely appreciated in her own day. We have many accounts of the admiring loving-care of her unofficial husband, George Henry Lewes, and of the devotees attending the famous receptions at the Priory after the Leweses settled there. Leslie Stephen paints the picture in his *George Eliot* (1902):

> [Lewes] looked up to her as in her own field an entirely superior being, in the front rank of contemporary genius. Their house became a temple of domestic worship, in which he was content to be the high priest of the presiding deity. He stood as much as possible between her and all the worries of the outside world. He transacted her business, wrote her letters, kept her from the knowledge of unpleasant criticism, read all her books with her as they were composed, made suggestions and occasional criticisms; but, above all, encouraged her by hearty and sincere praise during the fits of depression to which she was constitutionally liable. (p. 49)

This is the author whose admirers, among them young men and women with a propensity for mother worship, truly loved her, according to Rosemarie Bodenheimer in *The Real Life of Mary Ann Evans* (1994). Such love led Alexander Main to compile his *Wise, Witty, and Tender Sayings of George Eliot* (1872); it made Edith Simcox dedicate a book to her with "idolatrous love," at one point praying to her at night and suffering pains of jealousy when her idol discreetly sought to evade or cool the devotee's passion; such love made John Cross marry George Eliot after Lewes's death and, when she too died, led him to produce an authorized biography (1885) that was almost a hagiography. In an essay on "A Too Deferential Man" in her last work, *Impressions of Theophrastus Such*, George Eliot shows her skeptical awareness that praise can be shallow, "an attitudinizing deference which does not fatigue itself with the formation of real judgments" (55).

She is speaking here through the persona of Theophrastus Such, though his is the skepticism of a failed, not famous, author like his creator. But she also knew the pain of praise denied. That is why it was important to her own writing that Lewes acted as censor for reviews, especially protecting her from bad ones. She was hypersensitive to depreciation, and was gripped with doubt at the start of each book, fearing that her powers had declined. Lewes wrote to Blackwood in the business correspondence he undertook for her that the author had aims so high as to be frightened by the possibility of failure; he wanted the publisher to understand "the sort of shy, shrinking, ambitious nature you have to deal with" (Stephen, *George Eliot*, p. 54).

Her failure of confidence was most obvious in her work on *Romola*, for which her research on the Florentine setting and the history of Savonarola extended almost endlessly: she began to write, then began again the following year, always in a despairing state of mind. Theophrastus Such can again give us a glimpse of his author's sore spots. In the essay "Looking Inward," he remarks that as his one venture into print has failed he prefers to write for himself alone to avoid "your well-founded ridicule or your judicious strictures." He is very well aware of his own faults, but "I like to keep the scourge in my own discriminating hand. I never felt myself sufficiently meritorious to like being hated as a proof of my superiority." Therefore he will not write for influence and reputation, nor for legacy, since he does not publish. His is a comically self-defensive self-sufficiency. Still, he does not altogether abandon "the pleasing, inspiring illusion of being listened to," and he entertains the fond thought of leaving his manuscripts to a later judgment, while taking comfort in the fact that "I will not ask to hear it." We get a wryly astringent portrait of the author as a shy, shrinking, ambitious nature. "I find within me a permanent longing for approbation, sympathy, and love." Here is an "affectionate disposition, who has also the innocent vanity of desiring to be agreeable" (6–13). Theophrastus's confessions are offbeat echoes of George Eliot's, recalling her girlhood letter on her "besetting sin [of] ambition – a desire insatiable for the esteem of my fellow-creatures" (Stephen, *George Eliot*, p. 21).

Sympathy and fellowship, and both sustained so that the present draws on the past and gives to the future – these are major themes of George Eliot's work. For an early declaration of her aesthetic faith there is "The Natural History of German Life": "The greatest benefit we owe the artist, whether painter, poet, or novelist, is the extension of our sympathies . . . extending our contact with our fellow-men" (Pinney, pp. 270–71). Chapter 17 of *Adam Bede* likewise declares this aesthetic aim of rousing sympathy – even for an old woman bending over a flowerpot, even for old women scraping carrots. Such sympathy justifies the representation of commonness or homeliness, and it resists the depredations of time. These old women become its exemplary objects.

"Looking Backward" in *Theophrastus Such* offers a late expression of the theme of loving memory. A cherishing of the natural landscape remembered from childhood leads to a cherishing of the national life and language. Theophrastus admits the kind of "conservative prepossessions" (22–23) that we may discern elsewhere in George Eliot. *The Mill on the Floss* dramatize how the present draws on the past. In a Wordsworthian meditations at the end of chapter 5, the narrator talks of "the sunshine and the grass in the far-off years which still live in us" and which transform present perceptions into love. Love of landscape is an aspect of human love, and the novel's dramatic center is the test of the continuity of the love of brother and sister, of Tom and Maggie.

George Eliot develops her themes of sympathy and fellowship sustained over time against counterthemes of egoism and breaking with the past, and these latter are not always negative in their implications. Her novels notably explore poor fellowship, shyness and shrinking, misfits and dropouts, isolation, indifference, self-defensiveness, self-seeking, hostility, harsh judgments of others, intended or unintended hurtfulness, misplaced deference, and misplaced loyalty. *Theophrastus Such* talks of these things in an ironic, jaundiced, but oddly fetching manner.

All are handled with great richness and sophistication, and I am among those who feel the force of the exclamation of admiration that Quentin Anderson describes, the moment when one looks up from the page – of *Middlemarch* – and says, "How intelligent, how penetrating this woman is!" ("George Eliot in *Middlemarch*," p. 90). Raymond Williams pays tribute as if to a still powerfully present George Eliot, even as he criticizes her. He says he feels "I could make these points in her presence . . . since her particular intelligence, in a particular structure of feeling, persists and connects" (*The Country and the City*, p. 170). John Holloway describes her as a "Sage" (*The Victorian Sage*, 1953), F. R. Leavis as belonging to *The Great Tradition* (1948). If *Silas Marner* has had a long career as a secondary school text, *The Mill on the Floss* and, above all, *Middlemarch* are staples in the present college classroom, as I have reason to be aware from editing the 1990 Modern Language Association's *Approaches to Teaching George Eliot's* Middlemarch. In this collection, as in her 1987 *Reading* Middlemarch, *Reclaiming the Middle Distance*, Jeanie Thomas affirms the deeply personal meaning this novel has for her and her desire to pass it along to her students as a resource for their lives. The distinguished novelist A. S. Byatt introduces the 1994 Modern Library *Middlemarch* with "George Eliot: A Celebration." In that year the BBC serialized the novel. In the 1990s a new stream of important biographies appeared – Frederick Karl's *George Eliot: Voice of a Century* (1995), Rosemary Ashton's *George Eliot: A Life* (1996), and Kathryn Hughes's *George Eliot: The Last Victorian* (1998). George Eliot even has two scholarly journals devoted to her life and work:

George Eliot – George Henry Lewes Studies and the *George Eliot Review – Journal of the George Eliot Fellowship*. She also appears on the Victoria Web http://landow.stg.brown.edu/victorian/eliot/eliotov.html. In 1999 the modern Language Association's online bibliography for George Eliot shows 2,123 entries, and this goes back only to 1981.

And yet, among our canonical authors she has attracted more than her share of censure. Indeed, even her appreciators deprecate her. Throughout her posthumous career, her heirs have frequently taken upon themselves to be uncommonly sage at her expense. A passage from *Daniel Deronda* comes to mind: "In mendicant fashion, we make the goodness of others a reason for exorbitant demands on them" (IV:29:304–5).

Terms of appreciation and depreciation – Victorian and modern

Since Main's *Wise, Witty, and Tender Sayings* and Cross's biography, there have been many notable tributes. Henry James pays her compliments as a reviewer, with the larger compliment of emulating her in his own fiction. His *Portrait of a Lady* (1880–81) finds direct inspiration in *Daniel Deronda*. In his critical essay in dialogue form, "*Daniel Deronda*: A Conversation" (1876), two speakers, Constantius and Theodora, praise the pure comprehensiveness of the novel, with its span of ideas and "overflow of observation," profuse creation of characters by a "much peopled mind," and drama that is "multitudinous, like life," rendering a "complete world." All this shows "a large conception of what one may do in a novel." The large scale is filled out with intellectual substance. Each particular "is like everything in George Eliot. It will bear thinking of." Above all, James admires the characterization, the plumbing of psychological depths, and this even in characters who might seem limited, vain, light and flimsy, like Gwendolen Harleth. She begins without the conscience to sustain tragedy, but "the tragedy . . . makes her conscience" (pp. 165–76).

James acknowledges the challenge set by George Eliot in his preface to *Portrait of A Lady* for the New York edition (1908). This challenge was to make matter a character who might not seem to matter, to call for sympathy against all odds. In particular it was to make a slim, slight girl the center of interest in a way that popular nineteenth-century novelists like Scott, Dickens, or Stevenson had not attempted. But James was inspired by "the difficulty of making George Eliot's 'frail vessel,' if not the all-in-all for our attention, at least the clearest of the call" (p. 50).

As a step from James's to Virginia Woolf's classic terms of praise, I may note again her father's – Leslie Stephen's – book. It makes very clear that by the time of *Middlemarch* "George Eliot was now admittedly the first living novelist" (*George Eliot*, pp. 172–73), and, on balance, his study serves the cause of passing her on as such to the twentieth century. He admires the social panorama, the intellectual scope in treating the largest religious and philosophical problems, the creation of characters who are among the "immortals" (p. 78), the minuteness of psychological analysis, and George Eliot's ethical aim of rousing readers' sympathies for the noble qualities of life. Beginning with *Scenes of Clerical Life*, "the depths below the surface of trivial life . . . give an impression of dignity to the work" (p. 63). Above all, Stephen prizes the vein of retrospection and depiction of rural life, as the author renders personal memories of her Midlands girlhood. He loves the pungent regional and dialect humor of Mrs. Poyser in *Adam Bede*, and of the gatherers at the Rainbow Tavern in *Silas Marner*; he admires the beauty not only of individual characters but of "the whole quiet humdrum order of existence of the rustic population" of a time gone by (p. 82). By these standards he locates the culmination of George Eliot's power in the childhood section of *The Mill on the Floss*. He is charmed by the recreation of an old-fashioned world, by the "glamour" cast on commonplace things through the rendering of childish imagination, and by Maggie as an example of the feminine characterization at which George Eliot excels – she is the heroine one most falls in love with (pp. 88–89). There is personal warmth of feeling here, and towards the close of his book Stephen writes of the influence upon him of his "intimacy" with the personality of the novelist herself.

Virginia Woolf, in her essay in *The Common Reader* (1925), registers a sense of the person, too, though assuredly not noting charm. Rather she writes of George Eliot's "dogged determination," "deep-seated and noble ambition," energy and heat, suffering, daring, and achievement. "Triumphant was the issue for her" (pp. 169–76). Woolf praises the remarkable range of social relations that George Eliot encompasses and the "roominess and margin" of her novels; she praises too pure intellect – "everything to such a mind was gain" (pp. 172, 170). She admires also George Eliot's resources of personal memory and power to evoke "the romance of the past," her spirit of sympathy with everyday, imperfect lives, her creation of characters – "great originals" like the Poysers, and, most of all, her creation of heroines. "The ancient consciousness of woman, charged with suffering and sensibility, and for so many ages dumb, seems in them to have brimmed and overflowed and uttered a demand for something – they scarcely know what" (pp. 171–75). Woolf's is the first powerful voice to suggest a feminist interest in George Eliot's women characters, and her accolades have attracted attention since her time: "That greatness is here we can have no doubt"; *Middlemarch* is "the magnificent book which with all its imperfections is one of the few English novels written for grown-up people" (pp. 175, 172).

Modern admiration for George Eliot reemerges in F. R. Leavis's *The Great Tradition*. He asserts the greatness of the novel form itself and argues for a great British tradition beginning with Jane Austen and proceeding through George Eliot, Henry James, and Joseph Conrad to D. H. Lawrence. Leavis identifies George Eliot's moral intelligence, which he claims cannot be discounted as Victorian didacticism. The great novel does not preach but, through profound psychological analysis, enacts its moral significance. The probing to the depths of psyches seemingly too ignoble for tragedy moves Leavis, as it had moved James. He finds it, for example, in Mrs. Transome in *Felix Holt*. George Eliot's capacity compassionately to make tragedy out of "human mediocrity" asserts human dignity, and "to be able to assert human dignity in this way is greatness" (p. 60). Like Woolf, Leavis praises George Eliot's maturity. He likewise admires Eliot's comprehensive treatment of sociological, economic, political, and cultural detail. Indeed, he prefers her concreteness to James's somewhat "cobwebby" treatment in his late phase (p. 16) of the world that constrains and cultivates the individual lives of characters. Like Stephen, Leavis appreciates the mellow picturing of rustic life in *Adam Bede* and the fresh directness of a child's vision in *The Mill on the Floss*, both drawn from childhood memory. But he does not dwell so much on the reminiscent and the rustic. He disagrees with Stephen's view that after the early retrospective novels, George Eliot's work loses charm, and he spends much time on the last novel *Daniel Deronda*, which is contemporary in its setting. George Eliot's greatness, he believes, was not in the tradition of nostalgia, but in the tradition of the modern.

Yet George Eliot's greatness is questioned in these major Victorian and modern assessments by James, Stephen, Woolf, and Leavis. The form itself of James's essay on *Daniel Deronda* – cast as talk between divergent voices – is unusual but suits the purpose of a sharp shifting of evaluation. Some of the speakers are relentlessly unsympathetic. Pulcheria, especially, complains that the novel is "addicted to moralizing and philosophizing," "protracted, pretentious, pedantic." It is over-intellectual, with a display of "too scientific" language. The characters are "described and analyzed to death, but we don't see them or hear them or touch them" (pp. 163–71). Pulcheria comes across as shallow and captious, but even the more discerning Constantius judges George Eliot to have achieved "at the best but so many brilliant failures" (p.165). The character of Daniel exemplifies this to Constantius. In him the novelist sets herself the extremely difficult job of exploring a faultless human being or one who is prone only to the faults of his universal sympathy (according to Theodora). To Pulcheria Daniel is "a dreadful prig"(p. 168). This mixed review carries over from Daniel to the whole Jewish portion of the novel in which he figures. Heroine versus hero, the English scene and plot versus the Jewish scene and plot – James sets them against each other and prefers the former in each case. Satisfactoriness of form and ending come into question. Pulcheria complains of "no sense of form" (p. 172) and of something unreal and even ludicrous about the ending in which the author sends her hero off to the East by train.

This Jamesian response paves the way directly to Leavis, who believes that *Daniel Deronda* should be cut down to a novel called "Gwendolen Harleth." This rather churlish jettisoning of the "bad half" (p. 80) of a work that Leavis himself places in a "great tradition" marks a critical extreme of negative commentary on George Eliot.

Stephen had anticipated elements of Leavis's critique, for he thought the Zionist material smacks too much of the Victorian intellectual. He raises questions about form and proportion, endings, and the author's artistic control, and complains that the hero lacks interest compared to the heroine. For Stephen, the novels fall off as they become more philosophical, less spontaneous, more consciously worked. *Romola* marks the shift. While there are things to admire, Stephen is also sometimes out-and-out "repelled" (p. 126). Even some of the backward-looking rustic novels that he prefers have problems: *The Mill on the Floss*, for example, also has something of a good half and a bad half and lacks proportion in giving fuller and more satisfying development to the childhood section than to Maggie's grown-up story (although, to be fair, George Eliot herself recognized that she had given an epic breadth to the first part of the novel that was not sustained in the last third of it). Stephen also complains that the catastrophe "jars upon us" (p. 103). He is particularly harsh in his judgment of the heroes as against the heroines. Stephen Guest is a "hairdresser's block." "He is another instance of [the author's] incapacity for pourtrayng [*sic*] the opposite sex" (p. 104). She makes mistakes with Tom Tulliver, being "too thoroughly feminine to be quite at home in the psychology of the male animal," and she makes Daniel Deronda too much of a model, an ethereal being, an angel, feminine, a "schoolgirl's hero." When her men do convince it is because they are "substantially women in disguise" (97, 190, 204).

Another problem attends the trouble with heroes. The author who does not understand her men may fall in love with them. How could Maggie fall for a "hairdresser's block?" Because her creator was susceptible. At stake is authorial control, at risk again control of proportion and endings. Thus Maggie's seduction is unsatisfactorily sudden and unprepared, and the plot jumps to a less-than-inevitable conclusion. Stephen adds another stricture, against George Eliot's melancholy. Drawing a contrast between the earlier and the later novels, he is sorry to lose the warm humor of the former. "A touch of pedagogic severity saddens her view of the frivolous world"

(p. 198). Stephen's low tolerance for melancholy helps explain the negative turn of his concluding judgment of "the partial misdirection of her powers in the later period."

Compared to this, Woolf's is a great tribute to a great author, but she too has damaging things to say. She begins with a cruel caricature of the George Eliot of the Priory. We get a contemporary description of her massive features, rather grim in profile, "incongruously bordered by a hat." Woolf sketches George Eliot as "a deluded woman who held phantom sway over subjects even more deluded than herself" (pp. 166–67), with a personality in her writing still colossally lacking in "charm." She also sniffs out male resentment of this charmlessness that grows from conventional expectations about women (expectations which she might have detected in her father, Leslie Stephen).

Although she then attempts to restore the stature of her diminished subject, her reservations – by now familiar – continue: George Eliot is guilty of intellectual overloading, self-consciousness, didacticism; her heroes are wooden; she lacks artistic control. Thus "the uncertainty, the infirmity, and the fumbling which shook her hand when she had to conceive a fit mate for a heroine." George Eliot's over-identification with her female characters and her over-investment in her themes weakened her control. They produced "the vindictiveness of a grudge which we feel to be personal," "a novelist straying across the boundaries" into a kind of overcharged inconclusiveness of speech and narrative action, "verbosity," with heroines who talk too much, scenes that do not end when they should, and plotlines that seem the "incomplete version of the story of George Eliot herself" (pp. 174–76). Woolf emphasizes the sadness of female unfulfillment; she does not treat it as her father did, as simply too sad. Yet Woolf writes eagerly of George Eliot's own ambition and triumph in life and sounds let down by her creating heroines who did not live up to their creator. Woolf's resentment, unlike her father's, is a feminist resentment (foreshadowing the feminism to come) – she resents, that is, the lack of success of George Eliot's heroines who seek to live by something besides charm.

In *A Room of One's Own* (1929), Woolf gives George Eliot a place in the genealogy of "Mary Carmichael," her hypothetical woman novelist of the modern day. She shares this honor with Lady Winchelsea, the Duchess of Newcastle, Aphra Behn, Jane Austen, Emily and Charlotte Brontë. Woolf herself is a modern woman novelist in this line, as Alison Booth shows in her *Greatness Engendered; George Eliot and Virginia Woolf* (1992). There are comparison-and-influence studies for Eliot and women writers of the Victorian and modern periods, Harriet Beecher Stowe, Olive Schreiner, Edith Wharton, Kate Chopin, and others. However, Elaine Showalter's *A*

Literature of their Own (1977) places emphasis on awe rather than on close communication and emulation for sister-authors of George Eliot's own age, such as Mrs. Oliphant, Eliza Lynn Linton, Elizabeth Robins, and Alice James. Indeed, she cites James's unkind remark about an "impression . . . of mildew" (p. 108), as if George Eliot had worn no better than Mrs. Glegg's laid-by old clothes. According to Showalter, most nineteenth-century women novelists found her a troubling and demoralizing competitor. Showalter theorizes a gender-switched Oedipal struggle against the foremother, the Angel in the House. As she sees it, it was George Eliot rather than other female forebears who took the fall. Some of the late-Victorian sensation novelists who most interest Showalter – Mary Braddon, Rhoda Broughton, "Ouida" – "saw themselves as daughters of Charlotte Brontë rather than George Eliot" (p. 154).

Turning to Sandra Gilbert and Susan Gubar's study of developments in modernism, the first two volumes of *No Man's Land: The Place of the Woman Writer in the Twentieth Century* (1988, 1989), we find George Eliot scarcely mentioned. She comes up in discussion of Schreiner, Wharton, Woolf and Willa Cather, and, in a small but surprising comment on Gertrude Stein. But as Gilbert and Gubar theorize a move beyond Oedipal agon toward voluntary affiliation with foremothers of choice, one might have expected George Eliot to have been chosen more often.

Women writers can look to a fairly modest stream of influence in literary modernism. Whereas for modernist male writers like James and Leavis, George Eliot belongs among the great novelists, there are virtually no parallel feminine evaluations. Still, E. M. Forster gives a small nod in his *Aspects of the Novel* (1927). He remarks the "preacher" in George Eliot somewhat to her disadvantage. Byatt is of the opinion that her great modern heirs – in intellectual range – are not in England (or America) but abroad: Marcel Proust, Thomas Mann.

Value accruing – mid-century and since

Gordon Haight's publication of George Eliot's letters in nine volumes from 1954 to 1978 and Thomas Pinney's edition of her essays in 1963 gave a big boost to George Eliot studies. Just predating these, John Holloway's *Victorian Sage* (1953) ranks George Eliot among the major writers. Holloway admires George Eliot's intellectual and moral seriousness, and her learned, sagelike, oracular discourse. He places her in the company of sages like Thomas Carlyle, Benjamin Disraeli, John Newman, Matthew Arnold, and Thomas Hardy. Unlike Leavis, however, Holloway selects George Eliot for honors not in that she was headed towards modernism but in that she was a Victorian. And she is marked out as special in the group – as we can see by looking back at Holloway through Carol Christ's later analysis in a collection on *Victorian Sages and Cultural Discourse* – because she is the only woman in it. Christ points out the masculinity of this form of nonfiction prose, which features "The Hero As Man of Letters."

Other critics of the mid-century resemble Leavis and Holloway in focusing on George Eliot's moral intelligence. In the style of "new critical" close reading of the time, they push the issue of literary form into prominence, and praise the formal construction of the novels. George Eliot becomes less liable to the critique of having no sense of form, as James's Pulcheria and sometimes Stephen, Woolf, and Leavis would have it.

Barbara Hardy's *The Novels of George Eliot* (1959) announces that it is "chiefly concerned with her power of form, a striking but relatively disregarded aspect of her work as a novelist" (p. 1). Hardy treats the aesthetic quality, as well as the meaning of repetitions of phrasings and images, doublings and paralleling of characters, symmetries and antitheses in plot actions, construction by ironies of every sort. She has a sharp eye for relations between chapters – Mrs. Bulstrode going to her husband to give him support in one chapter, Rosamond Vincy not going to hers in the next. While Hardy admits that there are greater and lesser degrees of balance and integration amongst the novels, she rejects any notion of radical loss of artistic control, and she does not take it as the critic's task to pick and choose between good and bad parts of a work.

Hardy also views George Eliot as a moralist, and especially emphasizes the themes of egoism and sympathy. She sees, above all, "the tragic education of the egoist" in growth towards redemptive sympathy (p. 236). She keeps in view the line of interpretation that makes George Eliot a great creator of women characters, but the feminist implications that Woolf had identified all but drop from Hardy's sight, scarcely to reappear in mid-century criticism. Hardy emphasizes another line of criticism that leads to later developments, an appreciation of the narrative voice in the novels, the speaking style of the moral and philosophical commentator.

Wayne Booth is best known for making the voice of the novelist a center of critical attention – distinguishing the narrator as a figure not to be simply identified with the author herself. His *Rhetoric of Fiction* (1961) does not spend a great deal of time on George Eliot, but he defends a Victorian convention of narration that is important to her fiction. The reaction against that convention can be seen in James's Pulcheria's dislike of a "pedantic" excess of character description and analysis in *Daniel Deronda*, so that "we don't see them, or hear them, or touch them." Pulcheria thus articulates the common modernist line opposing "showing" to "telling," a line hardened beyond anything in James by Percy Lubbock in *The Craft of Fiction* (1921). Another focus for the formal analysis of this period is narrative endings. Frank Kermode's *The Sense of an Ending* (1966) is perhaps the most important study of that question. Like Booth, Kermode gives limited attention to George Eliot, but he cites her as an example of novelists' awareness of the way in which endings are imposed on narrative forms. George Eliot's endings have elicited much discussion since James, Stephen, Woolf, and Leavis. The ending of *Middlemarch* is often admired in its open-endedness; other endings are more controversial – notably those of *The Mill on the Floss* and *Daniel Deronda* – when judged for proportion, for inevitability, for authorial control, and for satisfying readers' expectations.

Kermode deems the power and the trouble of endings to be features of the realistic novel as a genre, which offers to do two opposite things at once: to mime the ongoing, unresolved contingency of real life, and to provide resolution of meaning by a stop-action in time. With something of an existentialist outlook, he conceives of a world absent of God in which resolutions are all human-made. For him, the closure that novels bring to what is open or unresolvable in reality offers consolation. But this consolation creates a tension in the form of the realistic novel, its closure jeopardizing its realism, its realism jeopardizing closure.

Critics in whom one can recognize something of Kermode are J. Hillis Miller and George Levine. Miller's ideas are premised on the absence of God, an absence that, in *The Disappearance of God* (1963), he traces back to a Victorian crisis of faith. George Eliot does not figure among his chapters in this study, but she does in his *The Form of Victorian Fiction* (1968), which gives an account of the ways Victorians – including George Eliot – tried to make sense of the world through art, through human and not religious means. "Each man is the center of his own world and makes his own subjective interpretation of it. Each man casts outward in the world patterns of value which have no existence except in his own mind" (pp. 115–16). This argument forecasts Miller's later existentialism-turned-deconstruction in "Optic and Semiotic in *Middlemarch*" (1975). Here Miller discusses the famous pier-glass passage of chapter 27 in which the candle illuminating a mirror randomly scratched by the rubbing of a housemaid creates an appearance of pattern relative only to the placement of the light by the person holding it.

For Levine, the Victorian realistic novel still posits or is on a quest to confirm the reality of an external world, but "it self-consciously examines its own fictionality" (*Realistic Imagination*, 1981, p. 21). Through such an examination, George Eliot's late novels come near to a collapse of faith, whether faith in the dominant reality of the empirically verifiable or in the human meaningfulness of the real. Levine thus belongs with Kermode and

Miller in seeing the novelist's sophistication of form as a means of pressing sophisticated philosophical questions of ontology and epistemology.

Much other criticism shows us George Eliot as thinker, pondering philosophic questions. There are studies of George Eliot and Spinoza, Ludwig Feuerbach and David Friedrich Strauss. David Carroll in *George Eliot and the Conflict of Interpretations* (1992) makes extended reference to the German hermeneutic tradition in philosophy. As critics have shown, George Eliot ponders other large questions characteristic of the Victorians, in, for example, religion, science, and social theory.

Barry Qualls (whose chapter in this volume pursues these issues) argues in *The Secular Pilgrim of Victorian Fiction* (1982) that her religious faith was not altogether lost but relocated in a Romantic quest theme still recognizably Judeo-Christian in meaning. Thomas Vargish also places her work in a religious frame in *The Providential Aesthetic in Victorian Fiction* (1985), though he sometimes comes close to confirming the reviewer W. H. Mallock's characterization of her as England's first great godless fiction writer. Thus in Vargish's view *The Mill on the Floss* shows characters to be mistaken in their expectations of finding a providential pattern to experience. At the same time, he is fascinated by the Jewish vision in *Daniel Deronda,* where providence is fulfilled in Daniel's finding his birthright and his mission as a Jew. Kathryn Bond Stockton makes claims for quite another kind of spirituality in *God Between their Lips: Desire Between Women in Irigaray, Brontë, and Eliot* (1994), finding in George Eliot the spirituality of ecstasy in the mode of St. Theresa. This spirituality exhibits the dynamics of autoeroticism and/or of erotically charged interchange between women. Quite unusually, Bond even has kind words to say about Rosamond as well, of course, about Dorothea, focusing on the climactic scene (ch. 81) in which each is engulfed by inwardness and by the Other.

George Eliot also takes on the big question of science. Bernard Paris turns to her scientific concerns in his *Experiments in Life* (1965), and both Levine and Carroll bring science to bear in their discussion of issues of knowing and interpretation. They associate the idea of scientific hypothesis with that of the literary imagination, seeing it as a means – through fiction – of coming to understand reality. Lewes took on "Mr. Darwin's Hypothesis," and so did George Eliot, says Gillian Beer in *Darwin's Plots: Evolutionary Narrative in Dickens, George Eliot, and Nineteenth-Century Fiction* (1983). This study traces broad affinities between George Eliot and Darwin, such as mutual fascination with origins and with systems of relations that are dynamic and produce ever-diversifying variations, and it compares *The Origin of Species* to *Middlemarch* for images of the web.

In *George Eliot and Nineteenth-Century Science* (1984) Sally Shuttleworth concerns herself with organic theory carried over from biology to social analysis. Shuttleworth raises the questions of whether Eliot conceives of organic social evolution as progress, and whether she sometimes expresses ambivalence towards the ethics of self-subordination, submitting the ego to the demands of the social organism by means of sympathy and duty. Like Shuttleworth, Suzanne Graver is interested in organic theory, shifting attention more fully from its scientific application to its application to social theory. *George Eliot and Community, A Study in Social Theory and Fictional Form* (1984) uses the categories of Ferdinand Tönnies, *Gemeinschaft* and *Gesellschaft*, or organic community and modern society, which is characterized by its acknowledgment of self interest, its individualism, and its tendencies toward isolation and dispersion. As in Shuttleworth's study, Graver finds some ambivalence in George Eliot's work about the degree to which ego must be sacrificed to community, particularly by women. On balance, Graver finds that Eliot holds to the Comtean idea of women's special sympathetic power and its importance as a corrective for loss of community in modern society. Nancy Paxton, in *George Eliot and Herbert Spencer: Feminism, Evolutionism, and the Reconstruction of Gender* (1991), discusses Spencer's individualism, and shows how Spencer's views of woman changed until he came to regard her as the exception to the rule of competitive self-interest because of her natural submissiveness. Paxton explores George Eliot's fascination with such thinking, and her partial resistance to Spencer on feminist grounds. If that opposition was not based entirely on the idea that the sexes could be differentiated through a division between egoism and sympathy, it was strongly based on the notion that the division is biologically determined.

However they place her with regard to philosophical, religious, scientific, and social ideas, all of these studies shift the balance away from the earlier depreciation of the "pedantic" George Eliot, toward high valuation of her knowledge and scholarship and appreciation of the great Victorian sage.

Turbulence and fluctuation – the seventies and since

It is not only George Eliot studies that have been in turbulent flux since the seventies, with ideologically or politically identified criticism on gender, race, and class. Recent criticism typically brings a "hermeneutics of suspicion" by means of deconstructive or psychoanalytic or Marxist or Foucauldian theory. Probing texts for their subtexts, it seeks to expose the "political unconscious," to clear away mystifications and expose the underside of overt intentions. Here again, George Eliot has provoked strong criticism and resentment. Feminist criticism, after the post-Virginia Woolf hiatus, has made a powerful return in seeking to expose George Eliot's social conservatism and resistance to feminist practice.

Ironically, her very failures as a feminist have made her fiction required reading for feminists and have brought new attention to such essays as those on Margaret Fuller and Mary Wollstonecraft and on "Silly Novels by Lady Novelists" (1856). They have prompted a modest revival of interest in her poetry (still hardly her claim to fame), notably "Armgart." But Lee Edwards declares that *Middlemarch* "can no longer be one of the books of my life" ("Women, Energy, and *Middlemarch*," 1972, p. 238), and Zelda Austen explains "Why Feminists are Angry with George Eliot" (1976). The issue has not gone away as women continue to read and rebel against Eliot's fiction, according to Laurie Langbauer's *Women and Romance: The Consolations of Gender in the English Novel* (1990, p. 191). At the heart of the problem is George Eliot's emphasis on woman's sympathy, a condition that seems to demand not only self-sacrifice but sacrifice of life itself. Elaine Showalter in *A Literature of their Own* influentially pronounces against "the pattern of self-sacrificing masochism in George Eliot" (p. 162). She discusses Jane Eyre and Maggie as archetypal Victorian heroines, and between the two prefers Jane the rebel and survivor to Maggie, who gives up her desires, is "perversely drawn to destroy all her opportunities for renewal" (p. 128), hurts others in the process, and ends up drowned. Indeed, *The Mill on the Floss* is a text of scandal and fascination to feminists. Some, like Elizabeth Ermarth, find it less an endorsement than a study of the pathology of female self-abnegation ("Maggie Tulliver's Long Suicide," 1974). Some, like Nina Auerbach, find something in it that is also violent and rebellious ("The Power of Hunger: Demonism and Maggie Tulliver," 1975). But Sandra Gilbert and Susan Gubar in their influential *The Madwoman in the Attic* (1979) again make Jane, not Maggie, the feminist heroine of choice. They are on the lookout for the angry, intransigent, transgressive in literature by nineteenth-century women. Thus it is not even Brontë's Jane herself but Bertha Mason, the madwoman in the attic, who gets the place of honor in their title. She is read as Jane's double, a figure for the repression of women, and, when she breaks out and goes on the rampage, as a figure for the return of the repressed. While Gilbert and Gubar search out subtexts of violence in Eliot, such as in plots which tend to leave a lot of the men dead, they imply a certain self-contradiction to the point of bad faith in her subordination of such material. They take a disparaging tone: George Eliot internalizes patriarchal culture's definition of woman but evades identification with the sex herself, making hers a "feminine anti-feminism." She "resorts . . . to pledges of deference and doctrines of feminine renunciation that are directly at odds with her own aggressively pursued career" (p. 466).

This assessment harks back – in harsher terms – to Woolf's observation that George Eliot's heroines always achieve less than did their creator. I discuss this strain of feminist disappointment in *Love and the Woman Question in Victorian Literature: The Art of Self-Postponement* (1983). The view belongs with a feminist phase of looking to literature for role models, while it also fits with a longer-term dissatisfaction with what often feels like the unduly depressing in George Eliot, a perspective established early by Leslie Stephen. Levine may also be considered on this point. He identifies a characteristic plotline of the nineteenth-century realistic novel such as George Eliot's as an account of the idealist's accommodation to nonideal realities. While it seems not to offend Levine, it is a line that can give offense to others.

Such offense makes George Eliot the most controversial figure for feminist literary criticism of the 1970s, according to Showalter, in "The Greening of Sister George" (1980), whose title suggests that some reconciliation may be in the offing. My own chapter on *Middlemarch* throws oil on the waters by declining to judge a novel's success by whether it offers a success story for its heroine, given the options and likelihoods for women in the Victorian period. This perspective entails using the standard of George Eliot's realism. I also examine the way accommodations to reality can nevertheless allow for assertions and satisfactions of self that may still be discerned in George Eliot's complex portrayals. Such a perspective entails rejecting the view that George Eliot's narratives are "too depressing," and reweighing the themes of egoism and sympathy. If feminists dislike too much of the latter, because it implies feminine self-abnegation for the sake of others, they can be glad to find some of the former. Auerbach also detects some sense of self, not just selflessness, as does Ermarth in "George Eliot's Conception of Sympathy" (1985). Gillian Beer's *George Eliot* (1986) expresses admiration for Gwendolen in *Daniel Deronda* as a new kind of heroine: "the single ego is intransigent: 'I mean to live'" (p. 223). If, indeed, it is sympathy that enables the author to understand and write about a character such as Gwendolen, this is sympathy of a self-assertive type, "a form of claim, a claim to knowledge . . . even while it is more apparently a form of self-abnegation" (p. 18). Beer lays out the checkered pattern of George Eliot's affiliation with the women's movement of her day to disagree, on balance, with any view that she was "no feminist" (p. 180).

Margaret Homans, Nancy K. Miller, Mary Jacobus, and later Susan Fraiman offer appreciation along other lines. They all recognize an element of risk-taking innovation in George Eliot's breaks from male forebears and patriarchal narrative conventions and genres. Homans, in "Eliot, Wordsworth, and the Scenes of the Sisters' Instruction" (1981), notes an odd swerve from Wordsworth in the very Wordsworthian *Mill on the Floss*. Miller and Jacobus argue that in that novel's ending George Eliot oddly departs from norms of novelistic plausibility ("Emphasis Added: Plots and Plausibilities in Women's Fiction," 1986, and "The Question of Language: Men of Maxims and *The Mill on the Floss*," 1981). In *Unbecoming Women: British Women Writers and the Novel of Development* (1993), Fraiman finds that the novel swerves from the traditional storyline of the *Bildungsroman*, the educational novel – which normally traces the development of a male protagonist to maturity and metropolitan sophistication. Such a narrative cannot lead to good for the female protagonist, or for the male protagonist either, for that matter, when his story is mixed up with that of his sister. These critics stress thematic and formal imponderables and impasses. Their critical strategies – deconstruction and narrative and genre theory – allow them to find merits in what have often before been seen as demerits: lack of authorial control, flawed coherence, disproportion, and forced endings.

However, if George Eliot enjoys somewhat more favor with feminists than she used to, she is hardly now a figure beyond controversy. In criticism that shifts grounds from feminist to other social and political issues, she is often rebuked. The question of her class affiliation and analysis is often raised in regard to the novels, and the debate has brought two of her essays forward for special interrogation, "The Natural History of German Life" (1856) and "Address to the Working Men, By Felix Holt" (1868). Stephen had loved her portraits of the rural working class. Williams, in *The Country and the City*, salutes her dedication of fiction in *Adam Bede* to the task of attending to the old women scraping carrots, to describing the Poysers, the Dodsons, the Gleggs. Williams believes she advances the novel a step from Austen towards Hardy and Lawrence in treating working-class subject matter. She does so with affection, but, he says, it is a generalized affection that does not fully individualize these characters and can slip into patronizing them. A Marxist critic whose perspective is shaped by his own rural working-class background, Williams writes respectfully but critically of George Eliot's attempts at representing the working class. Marxist criticism has played a particularly important role in studies of fiction and of George Eliot since Williams, and since Terry Eagleton's *Criticism and Ideology* (1978). It informs Judith Lowder Newton's *Women, Power, and Subversion: Social Strategies in British Fiction 1778–1860* (1981), which perceives a wavering between political conservatism and a critique of bourgeois patriarchy in *The Mill on the Floss*, and itself wavers between appreciating the picture of "the powerlessness and pain of Maggie's socialization to the middle-class woman's traditional, and increasingly powerless, role" (pp. 152–53) and regretting that positive alternatives do not appear except perhaps in a utopian fantasy of radical social change by flood at the end of the novel.

There is some Marxist orientation in other important approaches, in which narrative theory and deconstruction and cultural studies by way of Michel Foucault seem to mix. A prominent example is D. A. Miller's *Narrative and its Discontents: Problems of Closure in the Traditional Novel* (1981), in which a note of disillusionment is struck. Miller scrutinizes Dorothea's acclaimed epiphany of fellow-feeling at her darkest hour when she looks out of the window to see a woman with a baby and laborers in the fields, finding broad limits to her understanding of the working people she sees. Miller notes that Dorothea is looking down on them from within a social hierarchy, and stresses her oversights in a process by which he deconstructs epistemological grounds for knowing, possibilities for transcending egoism in sympathy for others, and possibilities for democratic, cross-class fellowship. Miller writes, as he says, "almost with regret" (p. 178).

In other criticism the note of disillusionment often deepens, loses its compunction, and becomes chiding. Though Deirdre David expresses a desire for even-handed judgment, she tips the scales in the often damaging terms of her commentary. Her *Intellectual Women and Victorian Patriarchy* (1987) presents an Eliot who succeeds as a sage because of allegiance to traditions that are patriarchal and also elitist in class terms, "a 'man's woman' intellectual" with a "residual desire . . . to affiliate herself with the land-owning classes in England rather than with the liberal, educated middle class which encouraged and eventually adored her" (pp. 172, 167). David calls George Eliot "complicit," "necessarily collaborative" (p. 168). For her, *Felix Holt* is the author's "most explicitly political and most politically conservative novel" (p. 197). It is "an explicitly political novel disdaining political action," projecting resolutions outside history or real-world initiatives (p. 205). This analysis has affinities with Daniel Cottom's *Social Figures: George Eliot, Social History, and Literary Representation*, with a foreword by Eagleton (1987). For Cottom, *Felix Holt* leaves its ostensible concern with questions of property and class relations in order to transform them into ahistorical, universal questions about the moral and affective relations between individuals. Again, George Eliot's morality of sympathy becomes a sticking point. Giving priority to the more general moral issue – the need for sympathy in order to triumph over egoism – George Eliot seems to leave no room for class interest. This critique seems a variant of the feminist suspicion that the emphasis on sympathy allows George Eliot to sell women short.

Both Cottom's and David's criticism are connected to Catherine Gallagher's *The Industrial Reformation of English Fiction: Social Discourse and Narrative Form 1832–1867* (1985), which interprets Felix Holt as an Arnoldian "best self," a man of culture out of the working class but free of class conditioning and class partisanship. The problem is that being above the fray, he leaves it to roil on unchanged, which, in Gallagher's opinion, makes George Eliot (in a complex way) a preserver of the status quo.

Nancy Armstrong's *Desire and Domestic Fiction, A Political History of the Novel* (1987) conjoins feminist and class analysis so as to locate in nineteenth-century novels such as Eliot's a collaboration of gender with class in maintaining social hierarchy. In this account, the status quo that novels work to conserve is less that of the landlord or gentry than of the bourgeoisie. The idea is that, constrained within a "separate sphere" by middle-class ideas of femininity, women also find within that constraint an opportunity to exercise class power.

Homans and Elizabeth Langland, in show cases for ideological testiness, take similar positions but focus more on George Eliot than does Armstrong. In "Dinah's Blush, Maggie's Arm: Class, Gender and Sexuality in George Eliot's Early Novels" (1993), Homans claims that George Eliot condescends to the working class and promotes middle-class hegemony. According to Homans, George Eliot masquerades middle-class values as natural: "Eliot's novel almost completely covers up its own contradictions about the relation of class to nature," employing "sleight of hand" (pp. 161, 169). "The narrative," Homans argues, "humiliatingly and sentimentally dwells on Dinah's obsession with housework" (p. 164) but actually requires Dinah's subordination in the separate sphere of domestic femininity. Then too, "when Maggie seeks to be queen of the gypsies, what she really wants is to teach them the value of imperialism (she offers them a lesson on Columbus) and to be served her tea" (p. 171). Maggie's desires, the argument goes, are mystified, cast as if they were not economically self-interested and thus George Eliot gives cover to the aggressively materialistic and status-hungry self-aggrandizement of the Victorian middle class.

Similarly, Langland, in *Nobody's Angels: Middle-Class Women and Domestic Ideology in Victorian Culture* (1995), charges Eliot with doing too much "to excuse genteel women from their participation in the class project and its oppressions" (p. 191). She complains that the real class relations between servants and mistress or master are erased in George Eliot's depiction of the household. How about that housemaid who rubbed those scratches onto the pier-glass? Langland complains that the novel also erases the mistress, whose social power, whether for better or worse, was greater than George Eliot acknowledges. What about that middle-class woman as manager, maker and breaker of reputations, controlling signifiers of social status? So Langland thinks it is not only Lydgate but his creator who discounts ordinary women, and considers them little better than furniture (p. 192). "Advocating the impotence of women even in the social world, exposing their apparent ignorance and inability to act effectively, the novel more seriously extends the power of the patriarchal realm it is seemingly criticizing" (p. 195). Langland's criticism restates earlier feminist complaints that George Eliot created heroines lesser than herself and "somehow neglected to explain how the society that thwarted Dorothea produced George Eliot" (p. 185). Thus, George Eliot not only "contributes to the ideologies that cement the status quo" (p. 199) but even further narrows the already constraining ideologies that she herself had encountered in nineteenth-century bourgeois patriarchy. George Eliot's status, in this kind of criticism, falls to its lowest point.

In addition to critiques of George Eliot's treatment of gender and class, there has been criticism addressing matters of race, nationalism, and imperialism. This interest has promoted new attention to the essay in *Theophrastus Such*, "The Modern Hep! Hep! Hep!," and to the Jewish story in *Daniel Deronda* that Leavis and James had so denigrated. Both of these works contemplate the conditions of the Jews as race and nation in a way that prompts contemplation of the British as race and nation and empire.

Here the questions raised by Shuttleworth and Graver about "community" and "organic community" extend into postcolonial questions about race and nationhood. In this context, once again, community and sympathy can appear less attractive. Such are the views of Bernard Semmel in *George Eliot and The Politics of National Inheritance* (1994), Carolyn Lesjak in "Labours of a Modern Storyteller: George Eliot and the Cultural Project of 'Nationhood' in *Daniel Deronda*" (1996), and Susan Meyer in *Imperialism at Home: Race and Victorian Women's Fiction* (1996). Instead of showing it to be a rightful choice of independent individualism to reject family inheritance, as in *Silas Marner* and *Felix Holt*, says Bernard Semmel in *George Eliot and The Politics of National Inheritance* (1994), *Theophrastus Such* comes to be "virtually a compendium of the nineteenth-century conservative politics of inheritance and tradition" (p. 134), as George Eliot places increasing value on "sympathetic association" (p. 12) by family (blood) and nation. George Eliot, Semmel claims, "ran the danger of succumbing to the ideology of nationalism" as she "fell captive" to an ideology of supposed transcendence of ideology (13, 11).

Carolyn Lesjak focuses yet more intensely on questions of race. She complains that *Daniel Deronda* contributes to nationalist discourse in a way that promotes racialist thinking: George Eliot is pro-Jew and pro-Zionist but also shows residual racial bias by Jewish stereotyping. And while the novel criticizes British imperialism, it also advances it by its sanction of Daniel's

Zionist project as he moves into the East (whose native population is left out of account) as a Jew who is at the same time a carrier of Englishness. Susan Meyer mounts a similar argument with much judgmental language on what is "disturbing," "disquieting," "problematic," and "sinister" in the novel. Furthermore, she claims, *Daniel Deronda* displaces the Woman Question onto the Jewish Question, leaving Gwendolen at home, desolate and powerless, and implying that Daniel with his Jewish disabilities could resolve her problems and his too (and rid Britain of both) by confirming his race and founding a nation in the East. So the novel "firmly advocates nationalism and racial separation, and in doing so it suggests the suppression of female rebellion" (*Imperialism at Home*, p. 190). (For a critique of this kind of view, see Nancy Henry's chapter in this volume.)

All of which is to say that George Eliot's insistence on the necessity for sympathy leads critics to be particularly unsympathetic. Ideologically and politically identified criticism since the seventies has found it very hard to appreciate George Eliot.

The account . . .

For their 1994 volume, *No Man's Land*, on woman authors of the postmodern period, Gilbert and Gubar give scant index entries (two) to indicate George Eliot's influence. Male novelists since the mid-century have not taken much from George Eliot, according to Showalter (in "The Greening of Sister George"). Showalter counts up more heirs among women writers: Simone de Beauvoir, Gail Godwin, Joyce Carol Oates, P. D. James, and Margaret Drabble. Booth, on the other hand, says that Woolf has outstripped George Eliot as an enabling progenitor for women writers of the last fifteen years. Still, foremother to Woolf, that makes her foregrandmother to the others.

In a study of what she calls the "neo-Victorian novel," Dana Shiller is not so much concerned with the *homage* that postmoderns may pay by particular allusions to George Eliot, as she is with the more comprehensive inheritance of attitude and approach. "The Redemptive Past in the Neo-Victorian Novel" treats postmodern works by novelists of both sexes, particularly Peter Ackroyd's *Chatterton* (1987) and Byatt's *Possession* (1990). *Middlemarch* shows what it is these fictions aim to recover: a sense of history that affirms the possibility that we in the present may gain knowledge of the past, and through that knowledge affirm human connection over time. Questions about knowing – whether one can know other people, other times – are important in these postmodern novels. That makes George Eliot, with her preoccupation with questions of knowledge, interpretation, and memory, very much a precursor (see, Kermode, J. Hillis Miller, Levine, D. A. Miller, Carroll, Anger). Shiller takes neo-Victorian fiction seriously, not as nostalgic pastiche, nor as belonging to the facile, faddish, and antihistorical postmodernism characterized by Fredric Jameson (*Postmodernism, or, The Cultural Logic of Late Capitalism*, 1991). Shiller believes her end-of-the-century novelists succeed in preserving and celebrating the Victorian past.

But it is Margaret Drabble, among latter twentieth-century authors, who stands out as a successor to George Eliot, as we learn from Nicole Suzanne Bokat and Keith Cushman. Each of these, like Showalter, in *A Literature of their Own*, highlights allusions and character and plot parallels between *The Waterfall* (1969) and *The Mill on the Floss*. Each identifies in Drabble a spirit of critique of her source. Thus the Jane (Maggie) figure ultimately goes off with her James (Stephen), faces catastrophe with him in the form of a car crash (rather than a flood). Both survive; Jane feels some guilt for the hurt she causes her cousin Lucy (Lucy), James's wife, and her own husband Malcolm (Philip). But she bears up and successfully perseveres in her own desires, and the love story reaches a very physical consummation. Jane meditates extensively on Maggie as an embodiment of renunciation; Jane herself thinks "better to lose than to endure the guilt of winning" (p. 149), but she rejects this idea, in part at least because she perceives in pondering Maggie's case that self-abnegation on behalf of others does not prevent her from damaging them all and herself as well. Drabble's heroine is remarkably cold, withdrawn, out of touch. She is a person who plans a route for a walk through London that will involve her in no human incident or contact. That a work so closely caught up with George Eliot should make its heroine so very humanly isolated, so much more self-serving than of service to others is particularly interesting. Yet George Eliot was of a "shy, shrinking, ambitious nature" and knew something about that, something for Drabble to pick up.

Drabble's implicit critique is not, however, out of sympathy with critics like Ermarth and Auerbach who, we have seen, interpret *The Mill on the Floss* as a critique of self-sacrifice for the sake of others, of family feeling, and of loyalty to past ties. And we might recall that Daniel Deronda himself tells Gwendolen that he is cruel in leaving her to pursue his own important goals.

In *Repression in Victorian Fiction* (1987) John Kucich finds an intensely inward individualism to be everywhere expressed by George Eliot. He outlines a psychic dynamic of repression by which the very impulse toward wider sympathy in her characters turns back to become an interior play of consciousness and acts "not to extend the self toward others, but to enlarge and confine it in isolation from them" (p. 120). Kucich sees something asocial in George Eliot's characters, for instance, an essential remoteness in

Dorothea that derives from self-involvement with her own inner conflicts. He sees the author herself as most defined by her personal experiences of separation (from church, father, brother, in hostile love triangles at John Chapman's, in social ostracism following her liaison with Lewes). Kucich might be describing Drabble's Jane when he writes, "What is missing in Eliot is not fulfilled desire or passion, but the truly social, interdependent vision she tried so hard to create" (p. 200). Except that Jane did not try very hard to create it, and Kucich can only presume to know that this was what George Eliot was trying so hard for in her novels. There is an edge of disapproval for individualist ideology in Kucich, and this tallies to some extent with other politically engaged criticism (e.g., D. A. Miller, David, Cottom, Armstrong, Homans, Langland). This ideological critique also implies that the novels betray a loss of artistic control (in a critical tradition that goes back to James, Stephen, Woolf, Leavis).

Kucich's analysis of complex psychological patterns in George Eliot's characters relates to other psychological readings. Marc Redfield, for example, describes her rendering of some of the problems of sympathy in relation to ego. Sympathy, he argues, can be presumptuous; it makes vulnerable one's sense of identity. His *Phantom Formations: Aesthetic Ideology and the Bildungsroman* (1996) highlights the Alcharisi's proud denial that Daniel can imagine what it is to be a woman like her. Redfield also suggests that "the subject is lost in an excessive immediacy of communication" (p. 166), and he considers such strange essays, in *Theophrastus Such*, as "The Wasp Credited with the Honeycomb" and "Shadows of the Coming Race." The former, he says, shades literary influence into intertextuality, plagiarism, and a sharing of ideas in the air that puts in doubt their point of origin in a single person. The latter is shown to forecast weirdly a sort of artificial intelligence, entities functioning as inorganic processors of the stuff of consciousness, but themselves unconscious.

Nancy Henry's 1994 edition of *Theophrastus Such* may indeed bring this not so sympathetic Eliot into fuller view. The work's narrator is a prickly comic caricature of a loner, so hypersensitive as to be in retreat from other people, unsure of his reception, yet garrulous and opinionated. He presents himself as wanting nothing so much as to be appreciated, but he is self-defensive for fear of the reverse. He has not yet attained a lofty peak of magnanimity and sustains a lingering belief in his own importance, although he is aware that this strikes others as abnormal. Cut off from his fellow-men, he yet claims, "Dear blunderers, I am one of you" (4). He dares not risk publication but reaches out to a vague, delightful illusion of an audience, and will leave his manuscripts for possible perusal and judgment after his death.

Theophrastus says, as George Eliot might have, "If the human race has a bad reputation, I perceive that I cannot escape being compromised" (5).

George Eliot's critical heritage shows her to have been "compromised." She was ambitious (a publishing author, unlike Theophrastus) and, while seeking fellowship by writing for the present and beyond, she was shy of counting on it and has had to take her chances on the evaluations of posterity. One of her own comments on women writers can serve as a final accounting in her favor:

> No sooner does a woman show that she has genius or effective talent, than she receives the tribute of being moderately praised and severely criticised. By a peculiar thermometric adjustment, when a woman's talent is at zero, journalistic approbation is at the boiling pitch; when she attains mediocrity, it is already at no more than summer heat; and if ever she reaches excellence, critical enthusiasm drops to the freezing point.
>
> ("Silly Novels by Lady Novelists," p. 322)

12

TANYA AGATHOCLEOUS

Works cited and further reading

Works cited

Altick, Richard D. "The Book Trade, 1851–1900" and "Periodicals and Newspapers, 1851–1900," in *The English Common Reader: A Social History of the Mass Reading Public 1800–1900*. Chicago: University of Chicago Press, 1957.

Anderson, Amanda. "George Eliot and the Jewish Question," *Yale Journal of Criticism* (1997).

Anderson, Quentin. "George Eliot in *Middlemarch*," in *Discussions of George Eliot*, ed. Richard Stang. London: Heath, 1960.

Anderson, Ronald F. "George Eliot Provoked: John Blackwood and Chapter 17 of *Adam Bede*," *Modern Philology*, 71 (1973–74).

"'Things Wisely Ordered': John Blackwood, George Eliot, and the Publication of *Romola*," *Publishing History*, 11 (1982), 5–39.

"Negotiating for *The Mill on the Floss*," *Publishing History*, 2 (1977).

Armstrong, Nancy. *Desire and Domestic Fiction: A Political History of the Novel*. Oxford and New York: Oxford University Press, 1987.

Ashton, Rosemary. *G. H. Lewes: A Life*. Oxford and New York: Oxford University Press, 1991.

"New George Eliot Letters at the Huntington," *Huntington Library Quarterly*, 54 (1991).

George Eliot: A Life. London: Hamish Hamilton, 1996.

Auerbach, Nina. "The Power of Hunger: Demonism and Maggie Tulliver." *Nineteenth-Century Fiction*, 30 (1975).

Austen, Zelda. "Why Feminists are Angry with George Eliot," *College English*, 37 (1976).

Baker, William. *George Eliot and Judaism*. Salzburg: Salzburg Studies in English Literature, 1975.

Beaty, Jerome. Middlemarch *from Notebook to Novel: A Study of George Eliot's Creative Method*. Urbana: University of Illinois Press, 1961.

Beecher, Anna Clay. *Gwendolen; or, Reclaimed*. Boston: W. F. Gill, 1878.

Beer, Gillian. *Darwin's Plots: Evolutionary Narrative in Darwin, George Eliot, and Nineteenth-Century Fiction*. New York: Routledge & Kegan Paul, 1983.

George Eliot. Brighton: Harvester Wheatsheaf, 1986.

Bell, Bill. "Fiction in the Marketplace: Towards a Study of the Victorian Serial," in Robin Myers and Michael Harris, ed., *Serials and their Readers, 1620–1914*. Winchester: St. Paul's Bibliographies, 1993.

Blake, Kathleen, ed. *Love and the Woman Question in Victorian Literature: The Art of Self-Postponement.* Brighton: Harvester Wheatsheaf, 1983.

Approaches to Teaching Eliot's Middlemarch. New York: MLA, 1990.

Blind, Mathilde. *George Eliot.* London: W. H. Allen, 1888 (first published 1883).

Bodenheimer, Rosemarie. *The Real Life of Mary Ann Evans: George Eliot, her Letters and Fiction.* Ithaca, N.Y.: Cornell University Press, 1994.

Bokat, Nicole Suzanne. *The Novels of Margaret Drabble: "This Freudian Family Nexus."* New York: Peter Lang, 1998.

Bonaparte, Felicia. *Will and Destiny.* New York: New York University Press, 1975.

The Tryptic and the Cross: The Central Myths of George Eliot's Poetic Imagination. New York: New York University Press, 1979.

Boone, Joseph Allen. *Tradition Counter Tradition: Love and the Form of Fiction,* Chicago: University of Chicago Press, 1987.

Booth, Alison. *Greatness Engendered: George Eliot and Virginia Woolf.* Ithaca, N.Y.: Cornell University Press, 1992.

Booth, Wayne. *The Rhetoric of Fiction.* Chicago: University of Chicago Press, 1961.

Brake, Laurel. "'The Trepidation of the Spheres': The Serial and the Book in the Nineteenth Century," in Robin Myers and Michael Harris, ed., *Serials and their Readers, 1620–1914,* Winchester: St. Paul's Bibliographies, 1993.

Bray, Charles. *Philosophy of Necessity: or Natural Laws as Applicable to Moral, Mental, and Social Science.* London: Longman, Green, Longman & Roberts, 1863 (first published 1841).

Butwin, Joseph. "The Pacification of the Crowd: From 'Janet's Repentance' to *Felix Holt,*" *Nineteenth-Century Fiction,* 35.3 (December 1980).

Byatt, A. S. "Introduction," *Middlemarch.* New York: Modern Library, 1994.

Byatt, A. S. and Nicholas Warren eds. *George Eliot: Selected Essays, Poems and Other Writings.* Harmondsworth: Penguin, 1990.

Carroll, David. *George Eliot and the Conflict of Interpretations: A Reading of the Novels.* Cambridge: Cambridge University Press, 1992.

Carroll, David, ed. *George Eliot: The Critical Heritage.* London and New York: Routledge & Kegan Paul, 1971.

Christ, Carol T. "'The Hero As Man of Letters': Masculinity and Victorian Nonfiction Prose," in Thais Morgan, ed., *Victorian Sages and Cultural Discourse.* New Brunswick, N.J: Rutgers University Press, 1990.

Cockshut, A. O. J. *The Unbelievers: English Agnostic Thought, 1840–1890.* London: Collins, 1964.

Collins, K. K. "G. H. Lewes Revised: George Eliot and the Moral Sense," *Victorian Studies,* 32 (1978).

"Questions of Method: Some Unpublished Late Essays," *Nineteenth-Century Fiction,* 35.3 (December 1980).

Combe, George. *The Constitution of Man Considered in Relation to External Objects,* 6th American edition from the 2nd English edition, corrected and enlarged. n.p., 1838.

Comte, Auguste. *System of Positive Polity,* trans. Frederick Harrison. Paris: Carilian-Goery and Vor. Dalman, 1852.

The Positive Philosophy of Auguste Comte, trans. Harriet Martineau. London: Trubner, 1875.

Cours de philosophie positive, trans. Harriet Martineau, in Gertrude Lenzer, ed., *Auguste Comte and Positivism*. New York: Harper Collins, 1975.
Cooke, George Willis. *George Eliot: A Critical Study of her Life, Writings, and Philosophy*. Boston: Houghton Mifflin, 1883.
Cottom, Daniel. *Social Figures: George Eliot, Social History, and Literary Representation*. Minneapolis: University of Minnesota Press, 1987.
Cross, J. W. *George Eliot's Life as Related in her Letters and Journals*. 3 vols. London: Harper & Bros, 1885.
Cross, Nigel. *The Common Writer: Life in Nineteenth-Century Grub Street*. Cambridge: Cambridge University Press, 1985.
Cunningham, Valentine. *Everywhere Spoken Against: Dissent in the Victorian Novel*. Oxford: Clarendon Press, 1975.
Cushman, Keith. "Drabbling in the Tradition: *The Waterfall* and *The Mill on the Floss*," in *The Modernists: Studies in a Literary Phenomenon*, ed. Lawrence B. Gamache and Ian S. MacNiven. Rutherford, N.J.: Fairleigh Dickinson University Press, 1987.
Dale, Peter Allen. *In Pursuit of a Scientific Culture: Science, Art, and Society in the Victorian Age*. Madison: University of Wisconsin Press, 1989.
Darwin, Charles. *The Origin of Species*. New York: W. W. Norton, 1979 (first published 1859).
David, Deirdre. *Fictions of Resolution in Three Victorian Novels*. New York: Columbia University Press, 1981.
Intellectual Women and Victorian Patriarchy: Harriet Martineau, Elizabeth Barrett Browning, George Eliot. Ithaca, N.Y.: Cornell University Press, 1987.
Desmond, Adrian and James Moore, *Darwin: The Life of a Tormented Evolutionist*. New York: Warner Books, 1991.
Dodd, Valerie A. *George Eliot: An Intellectual Life*. New York: St. Martin's, 1990.
Drabble, Margaret. *The Waterfall*. New York: Knopf, 1969.
During, Lisabeth. "The Concept of Dread: Sympathy and Ethics in *Daniel Deronda*," in *Renegotiating Ethics in Literature, Philosophy, and Theory*, ed. Jane Adamson, Richard Freadman, and David Parker. Cambridge: Cambridge University Press, 1998.
Eagleton, Terry. *Criticism and Ideology: A Study in Marxist Literary Theory*. New York: Verso, 1978.
"Power and Knowledge in 'The Lifted Veil,'" *Literature and History*, 9 (1983).
Edwards, Lee. "Women, Energy, and *Middlemarch*." *Massachusetts Review*, 13 (1972).
Eliot, George. *Westminster Review*, 59 (April 1853).
Westminster Review 65 (April 1856).
The Spanish Gypsy. The Legend of Jubal, etc. London: William Blackwood & Sons, 1901.
Eliot, Simon. *Some Patterns and Trends in British Publishing, 1800–1919*. London: Bibliographic Society, 1994.
"Some Trends in British Book Production, 1800–1919," in *Literature in the Marketplace: Nineteenth-Century British Publishing and Reading Practices*, ed. John Jordan and Robert L. Patten. Cambridge: Cambridge University Press, 1995.
Ellegård, Alvar. *The Readership of the Periodical Press in Mid-Victorian Britain*. Stockholm: Almqvist & Wiksell, 1957.

Erickson, Lee. "The Poets' Corner: The Impact of Technological Changes in Printing on English Poetry," in *The Economy of Literary Form: The Industrialization of Publishing, 1800–1850*. Baltimore: Johns Hopkins University Press, 1996.

Ermarth, Elizabeth. "Maggie Tulliver's Long Suicide." *Studies in English Literature,* 14 (1974): 587–601.

"George Eliot's Conception of Sympathy," *Nineteenth-Century Fiction,* 40 (1985): 23–42.

Feather, John. "Part Three: The First of the Mass Media, 1800–1900," in *A History of British Publishing*. London: Croom Helm, 1988.

Feltes, N. N. "One Round of a Long Ladder: Gender, Profession, and the Production of *Middlemarch*," in *Modes of Production of Victorian Novels*. Chicago: University of Chicago Press, 1980.

"Publishing as Capital," in *Literary Capital and the Late Victorian Novel.* Madison: University of Wisconsin Press, 1993.

Feuerbach, Ludwig. *The Essence of Christianity,* trans. George Eliot. New York: Harper & Bros. 1957.

Flax, Jane. "Postmodernism and Gender Relations in Feminist Theory," *Signs: Journal of Women in Culture and Society,* 12.4 (1987).

Forster, E. M. *Aspects of the Novel.* London: E. Arnold, 1927.

Fraiman, Susan. *Unbecoming Women: British Women Writers and the Novel of Development*. New York: Columbia University Press, 1993.

Frederick, Karl. *George Eliot: Voice of a Century*. New York: W. W. Norton, 1995.

Frei, Hans. *The Eclipse of Biblical Narrative: A Study in Eighteenth- and Nineteenth-Century Hermeneutics*. New Haven: Yale University Press, 1974.

Gallagher, Catherine. *The Industrial Reformation of English Fiction: Social Discourse and Narrative Form, 1832–1867*. Chicago: University of Chicago Press, 1985.

Gaskell, Elizabeth. *Ruth*, ed. Alan Shelston. Oxford and New York: Oxford University Press, 1985 (first published 1853).

Gilbert, Sandra M. and Susan Gubar. *The Madwoman in the Attic: The Woman Writer and the Nineteenth-Century Literary Imagination*. New Haven: Yale University Press, 1979.

No Man's Land: The Place of the Woman Writer in the Twentieth Century. 3 vols. New Haven: Yale University Press, 1988–1994.

Glynn, Jennifer. *Prince of Publishers: A Biography of George Smith*. London and New York: Allison & Busby, 1986.

Graver, Suzanne. *George Eliot and Community: A Study in Social Theory and Fictional Form*. Berkeley: University of California Press, 1984.

Gray, Donald. "Macaulay's *Lays of Rome* and the Publication of Nineteenth-Century British Poetry," in *Victorian Literature and Society: Essays Presented to Richard D. Altick*, ed. James R. Kincaid and Albert J. Kuhn. Columbus: Ohio State University Press, 1984.

Griest, Guinevere L. *Mudie's Circulating Library and the Victorian Novel.* Bloomington: Indiana University Press, 1970.

Haight, Gordon S. *George Eliot and John Chapman, with Chapman's Diaries*. New Haven: Yale University Press, 1940.

"George Eliot's Royalties," *Publishers Weekly,* 7 August 1954.

George Eliot: A Biography. Oxford and New York: Oxford University Press, 1968.

"George Eliot and John Blackwood," *Blackwood's*, 306 (1969).
Haight, Gordon. ed. *The George Eliot Letters*. 9 vols. New Haven: Yale University Press, 1954–78.
Halevy, Eli. *England in 1815*, trans. F. I. Watkin and D. A. Baker. New York: Barnes & Noble, 1960 (first published 1924).
Hardy, Barbara. *The Novels of George Eliot: A Study in Form*. London: Althone Press, 1959.
Harris, Margaret and Judith Johnston, eds. *The Journals of George Eliot*. Cambridge: Cambridge University Press, 1998.
Harvey, A. Van. *Feuerbach and the Interpretation of Religion*. Cambridge and New York: Cambridge University Press, 1997.
Henberg, M. C. "George Eliot's Moral Realism," *Philosophy and Literature* 3.1 (spring 1979).
Herbert, Christopher. "Preachers and the Schemes of Nature in *Adam Bede*," *Nineteenth-Century Fiction*, 29 (March 1975).
Holloway, John. *The Victorian Sage: Studies in Argument*. New York: St. Martin's Press, 1953.
Homans, Margaret. "Eliot, Wordsworth, and the Scenes of the Sisters' Instruction." *Critical Inquiry*, 8 (1981).
"Dinah's Blush, Maggie's Arm: Class, Gender, and Sexuality in George Eliot's Early Novels," *Victorian Studies*, 36 (1993).
Hughes, Kathryn. *George Eliot: The Last Victorian*. New York: Farrar, Straus & Giroux, 1999.
Hughes, Linda and Michael Lund, "Introducing the Serial" in *The Victorian Serial*. Charlottesville: University of Virginia Press, 1991.
Hutchinson, Stuart, ed. *George Eliot: Critical Assessments*. 4 vols. Mountfield, E. Sussex: Helm Information, 1996.
Huxley, Leonard, ed. *The Life and Letters of T. H. Huxley*. 2 vols. London: Macmillan, 1900.
Jacobus, Mary. "The Question of Language: Men of Maxims and *The Mill on the Floss*," *Critical Inquiry*, 8 (1981).
James, Henry. "The Life of George Eliot," *Partial Portraits*. London: Macmillan, 1899.
"Preface to *The Portrait of A Lady*," in *The Art of the Novel: Critical Prefaces by Henry James*. New York: Charles Scribner's Sons, 1962.
"*Daniel Deronda*: A Conversation," in *George Eliot: A Collection of Critical Essays*, ed. George R. Creeger. New York: Prentice-Hall, 1970.
Jameson, Anna (continued and completed by Lady Eastlake). *The History of Our Lord, as Exemplified in Works of Art: with that of his Types, St. John the Baptist, and other Persons of the Old and New Testament*. London: Longman, Green, 1864.
Jameson, Fredric. *Postmodernism, or, The Cultural Logic of Late Capitalism*. Durham, N.C.: Duke University Press, 1991.
Jay, Elisabeth. *The Religion of the Heart: Anglican Evangelicalism and the Nineteenth-Century Novel*. Oxford: Clarendon Press, 1979.
Jones, Peter. *Philosophy and the Novel*. Oxford: Clarendon Press, 1975.
Kamenka, Eugene. *The Philosophy of Ludwig Feuerbach*. New York: Praeger, 1970.
Kaminsky, Alice R., ed. *The Literary Criticism of George Henry Lewes*. Lincoln: University of Nebraska Press, 1964.

George Henry Lewes as Literary Critic. Syracuse, N.Y.: Syracuse University Press, 1968.
Keating, Peter. "Novelists and Readers," in *The Haunted Study: A Social History of the English Novel*. London: Secker & Warburg, 1989.
Kermode, Frank. *The Sense of an Ending: Studies in the Theory of Fiction*. Oxford and New York: Oxford University Press, 1966.
Kimmerle, Heinz, ed. *Hermeneutics: The Handwritten Manuscripts by F. D. E. Schleiermacher*, trans. James Duke and Jack Forstman. Missoula, Mont.: Scholars Press for the American Academy of Religion, 1977.
Knoepflmacher, U. C. *Religious Humanism and the Victorian Novel: George Eliot, Walter Pater, and Samuel Butler*. Princeton: Princeton University Press, 1965.
George Eliot's Early Novels: The Limits of Realism. Berkeley: University of California Press, 1968.
Kucich, John. *Repression in Victorian Fiction: Charlotte Brontë, George Eliot, and Charles Dickens*. Berkeley: University of California Press, 1987.
Landow, George. *Victorian Types and Shadows: Biblical Typology in Victorian Literature, Art, and Thought*. London: Routledge & Kegan Paul, 1980.
Langbauer, Laurie. *Women and Romance: The Consolations of Gender in the English Novel*. Ithaca, N.Y.: Cornell University Press, 1990.
Langland, Elizabeth. *Nobody's Angels: Middle-Class Women and Domestic Ideology in Victorian Culture*. Ithaca, N.Y.: Cornell University Press, 1995.
Leavis, F. R. *The Great Tradition: George Eliot, Henry James, Joseph Conrad*. New York: New York University Press, 1973 (first published 1948).
Lee, Sydney. "Memoir of George Smith," *Dictionary of National Biography*. New York and London: Oxford University Press, 1937–38.
Lesjak, Carolyn. 'Labours of a Modern Storyteller': George Eliot and the Cultural Project of 'Nationhood' in *Daniel Deronda*," in *Victorian Identities: Social and Cultural Formations in Nineteenth-Century Literature*, ed. Ruth Robbins and Julian Wolfreys. New York: Macmillan, 1996.
Levine, Caroline. "The Prophetic Fallacy: Realism, Foreshadowing and Narrative Knowledge in *Romola*," in Caroline Levine and Mark W. Turner, eds., *From Author to Text: Re-reading George Eliot's Romola*. Aldershot: Ashgate, 1998.
Levine, George. "Determinism and Responsibility in the Works of George Eliot," *PMLA* 77 (June 1962).
"George Eliot's Hypothesis of Reality." *Nineteenth-Century Fiction* 35 (1980): 1–28.
The Realistic Imagination: English Fiction from Frankenstein to Lady Chatterley. Chicago: University of Chicago Press, 1981.
Darwin and the Novelists: Patterns of Science in Victorian Fiction. Chicago: University of Chicago Press, 1991.
Lewes, G. H. "Hints Towards an Essay on the Sufferings of Truth," *Monthly Repository*, 2 (1837), 314.
"Ruth and Villette," *Westminster and Foreign Quarterly Review*, n.s. 3 (April 1853).
Comte's Philosophy of the Sciences. London: Henry G. Bohn, 1853.
The Life of Goethe, 2nd edn. London: Smith, Elder, 1864.
The Principles of Success in Literature. Berkeley: University of California Press, 1901 (originally published 1865).

The Biographical History of Philosophy, From its Origins in Greece Down to the Present Day. New York: Appleton, 1845–46.

The History of Philosophy from Thales to Comte, 4th edn., vol. I. London: Longman, Green, & Co., 1871.

Problems of Life and Mind: The Foundations of a Creed. 1st series Boston: Houghton, Osgood, 1875–80.

Lubbock, Percy. *The Craft of Fiction*. London: Jonathan Cape, 1921.

Main, Alexander. *Wise, Witty, and Tender Sayings in Prose and Verse, Selected from the Works of George Eliot*. London: Blackwood & Sons, 1886 (first published 1872).

Martin Carol. *George Eliot's Serial Fiction*. Columbus: Ohio State University Press, 1994.

"Two Unpublished Letters from John Blackwood on the Serialization of *Scenes of Clerical Life* and *Adam Bede*," *Publishing History*, 37 (1995).

Martineau, Harriet. *History of the Peace: being a History of England from 1816–1854*, Vol. IV. Boston: Walker, Fuller & Co., 1866.

Matus, Jill L. *Unstable Bodies: Victorian Representations of Sexuality and Maternity*. Manchester: Manchester University Press, 1995.

McDonald, Peter. "The Literary Field in the 1890s," in *British Literary Culture and Publishing Practice, 1880–1914*. Cambridge: Cambridge University Press, 1997.

Merrill, Lynn. "Natural History," in Sally Mitchell, ed., *Victorian Britain: An Encyclopedia*. New York: Garland, 1988.

Meyer, Susan. *Imperialism at Home: Race and Victorian Women's Fiction*. Ithaca, N.Y.: Cornell University Press, 1996.

Mill, John Stuart. *Collected Works*, ed. John M. Robson. Toronto: University of Toronto Press, 1963–1978.

Miller, D. A. *Narrative and its Discontents: Problems of Closure in the Traditional Novel*. Princeton: Princeton University Press, 1981.

The Novel and the Police. Berkeley: University of California Press, 1988.

Miller, J. Hillis. *The Form of Victorian Fiction*. Notre Dame, Ind.: University of Notre Dame Press, 1968.

"Narrative and History," *ELH*, 41 (1974).

"Optic and Semiotic in *Middlemarch*," in *The Worlds of Victorian Fiction*, ed. Jerome Buckley. Cambridge, Mass.: Harvard University Press, 1975.

Miller, Nancy K. "Emphasis Added: Plots and Plausibilities in Women's Fiction," in Elaine Showalter, ed., *The New Feminist Criticism. Essays on Women, Literature and Theory*. London: Virago Press, 1986.

Mulock, Dinah. "To Novelists – And a Novel," *Macmillan's Magazine*, 3 (1861).

Mumby, F. A. and Ian Norrie. "The Mid-Nineteenth Century," in *Publishing and Bookselling*, 5th edn. London: Jonathan Cape and R. R. Bowker, 1974.

Newton, Judith Lowder. *Women, Power, and Subversion: Social Strategies in British Fiction 1778–1860*. Athens: University of Georgia Press, 1981.

Newton, K. M. *George Eliot: Romantic Humanist*. New Jersey: Barnes & Noble, 1981.

Nietzsche, Friedrich. "Skirmishes of an Untimely Man," in Walter Kaufmann, trans., *The Portable Nietzsche*. New York: Viking, 1980.

Nightingale, Florence. "A 'Note' of Interrogation," *Fraser's Magazine*, n.s. 7 (1873).
Nussbaum, Martha C. *Love's Knowledge: Essays on Philosophy and Literature*. Oxford and New York: Oxford University Press, 1990.
Oliphant, Margaret. *Annals of a Publishing House: William Blackwood and his Sons, their Magazine and Friends*. 3 vols. Edinburgh and London: William Blackwood & Sons, 1897–98.
Paris, Bernard J. *Experiments in Life: George Eliot's Quest for Values*. Detroit: Wayne State University Press, 1965.
Parker, David. *Ethics, Theory and the Novel*. Cambridge: Cambridge University Press, 1994.
Patten, Robert L. "The Professional Artist," in *Charles Dickens and his Publishers*. Oxford and New York: Clarendon Press, 1978.
Paxton, Nancy L. *George Eliot and Herbert Spencer: Feminism, Evolutionism, and the Reconstruction of Gender*. Princeton: Princeton University Press, 1991.
Pearson, Patricia. *When She Was Bad: Violent Women and the Myth of Innocence*. New York: Viking, 1997.
Peck, John. *War, the Army, and Victorian Literature*. New York: St. Martin's, 1998.
Pinney, Thomas, ed. *Essays of George Eliot*. New York: Routledge & Kegan Paul, 1963.
Postlethwaite, Diana. *Making it Whole: A Victorian Circle and the Shape of their World*. Columbus: Ohio State University Press, 1984.
Qualls, Barry V. *The Secular Pilgrims of Victorian Fiction: The Novel as Book of Life*. Cambridge and New York: Cambridge University Press, 1982.
Redfield, Marc. *Phantom Formations: Aesthetic Ideology and the Bildungsroman*. Ithaca, N.Y.: Cornell University Press, 1996.
Rodstein, Susan De Sola. "Sweetness and Dark: George Eliot's 'Brother Jacob,'" *MLQ* (1991).
Rogers, W. Harry. *Spiritual Conceits*. London: Griffith & Farran, 1852, n.p.
Said, Edward. "Zionism from the Standpoint of its Victims'" in Anne McClintock, Aamir Mufti, and Ella Shohat, eds. *Dangerous Liaisons: Gender, Nation, and Postcolonial Perspectives*. Minneapolis: University of Minnesota Press, 1997 (first published 1979).
Schneidau, Herbert N. *Sacred Discontent: The Bible and Western Tradition*. Berkeley: University of California Press, 1976.
Semmel, Bernard. *George Eliot and the Politics of National Inheritance*. Oxford and New York: Oxford University Press, 1994.
Shaffer, E. S. "*Kubla Khan*" *and The Fall of Jerusalem: The Mythological School in Biblical Criticism and Secular Literature, 1770–1880*. Cambridge: Cambridge University Press, 1975.
Shiller, Dana. "The Redemptive Past in the Neo-Victorian Novel," *Studies in the Novel*, 29 (1997).
Shillingsburg, Peter. "Book Production" and "The Artist and the Marketplace," in *Pegasus in Harness: Victorian Publishing and W. M. Thackeray*. Charlottesville: University of Virginia Press, 1992.
Showalter, Elaine. *A Literature of their Own: British Women Novelists from Brontë to Lessing*. Princeton: Princeton University Press, 1977.
"The Greening of Sister George," *Nineteenth-Century Fiction*, 35 (1980).

Shuttleworth, Sally. *George Eliot and Nineteenth-Century Science: The Make-Believe of a Beginning*. Cambridge and New York: Cambridge University Press, 1984.
Simcox, Edith J. *Autobiography of a Shirtmaker*. New York and London: Garland Press, 1998.
Smith, George. "Our Birth and Parentage," *Cornhill Magazine,* n.s. 10 (1901).
Spencer, Herbert. *The Principles of Psychology* (London: Longman, 1855).
Spinoza, Benedict de. *Tractatus Theologico-Politicus,* trans. R. H. M. Elwes. London: George Routledge & Sons, 1895.
Stephen, Leslie. *George Eliot*. London: Macmillan, 1919 (first published 1902).
Stockton, Kathryn Bond. *God Between their Lips: Desire Between Women in Irigaray, Brontë, and Eliot*. Stanford: Stanford University Press, 1994.
Strauss, David Friedrich. *The Life of Jesus Critically Examined*, trans. George Eliot, ed. Peter C. Hodgson. Philadelphia: Fortress Press, 1972.
Sutherland, John. "Part One: The Novel Publishing World 1830–1870," in *Victorian Novelists and Publishers*. Chicago: University of Chicago Press, 1976.
"Lytton, John Blackwood, and the Serialization of *Middlemarch*," *Bibliotheck,* 7 (1978).
"George Eliot's Art," *Mind*, 23 (July 1981).
"Eliot, Lytton, and the Zelig Effect," in *Victorian Fiction: Writers, Publishers, Readers*. New York: Macmillan and St. Martin's Press, 1995.
Svaglic, Martin. "Religion in the Novels of George Eliot," *Journal of English and Germanic Philology*, 53 (1954).
Tambling, Jeremy. "*Middlemarch*, Realism and the Birth of the Clinic," *ELH* 57.4 (winter 1990).
Thomas, Jeanie. *Reading* Middlemarch*: Reclaiming the Middle Distance*. Michigan: UMI Research Press, 1987.
"A Novel 'Written for Grown-up People': *Middlemarch* in the Undergraduate Classroom," in *Approaches to Teaching Eliot's* Middlemarch, ed. Kathleen Blake. New York: MLA, 1990.
Thompson, Andrew. *George Eliot and Italy: Literary, Cultural and Political Influences from Dante to the Risorgimento*. New York: St. Martin's Press, 1998.
Tjoa, Hock Guan. *George Henry Lewes: A Victorian Mind*. Cambridge Mass.: Harvard University Press, 1977.
Toyoda, Minoru. *Studies in the Mental Development of George Eliot in Relation to the Science, Philosophy, and Theology of her Day*. Tokyo: Kenkyusha, 1931.
Trollope, Anthony. *An Autobiography*. Harmondsworth: Penguin, 1996 (first published 1883).
Uglow, Jennifer. *George Eliot*, London: Virago Press, 1987.
Vann, J. Donn. "Introduction," in *Victorian Novels in Serial*. New York: MLA, 1985.
Vargish, Thomas. *The Providential Aesthetic in Victorian Fiction*. Charlottesville: University of Virginia Press, 1985.
Voegler, Martha. "George Eliot and the Positivists," *Nineteenth-Century Fiction*, 35.3 (December 1980).
Welsh, Alexander. *George Eliot and Blackmail*. Cambridge, Mass.: Harvard University Press, 1985.
Willey, Basil. *Nineteenth-Century Studies*. New York: Harper & Row, 1966 (first published 1949).

Williams, Raymond. *The Country and the City*. Oxford and New York: Oxford University Press, 1973.
Wilson, A. N. *God's Funeral*. New York: W. W. Norton, 1999.
Wilt, Judith. "'He Would Come Back': The Fathers and Daughters in *Daniel Deronda*." *Nineteenth-Century Literature*, 42 (December 1987).
Wise, T. J. and J. A. Symington. *The Brontës: Their Lives, Friendships and Correspondence*, vol. II. Oxford: Basil Blackwell, 1932.
Wohlfarth, Marc E. "*Daniel Deronda* and the Politics of Nationalism," *Nineteenth-Century Literature*, 53.2 (September 1998).
Woolf, Virginia. *The Captain's Deathbed*. New York: Harcourt Brace & Janovich, 1950.
"George Eliot," in *The Common Reader*, 1st series. New York: Harcourt Brace & World, 1953.
A Room of One's Own. New York: Harcourt Brace & World, 1957 (first published 1929).
The Essays of Virginia Woolf, vol IV, (1925–1928), ed. Andrew McNeillie, London: Hogarth Press, 1994.
Wormold, Mark. "Microscopy and Semiotic in *Middlemarch*," *Nineteenth-Century Literature*, 50.4 (March 1996).
Wright, T. R. *The Religion of Humanity: The Impact of Comtean Positivism on Victorian England*. Cambridge: Cambridge University Press, 1986.
Young, Robert M. *Mind, Brain and Adaptation in the Nineteenth Century: Cerebral Localization and its Biological Context from Gall to Ferrier*. Oxford and New York: Oxford University Press, 1970.
Ziolkowski, Theodore. *Fictional Transfigurations of Jesus*. Princeton: Princeton University Press, 1972.

Further reading

Even though, as Kathleen Blake notes in her chapter on George Eliot's legacy, Eliot's popularity has waxed and waned in the years since her death, an immense body of George Eliot scholarship has amassed since the end of the nineteenth century. This section of the Companion, then, does not purport to serve as a comprehensive bibliography to this scholarship; instead, it is organized so as to distill the abundance of information into a usable set of directions to further study. While there will, of course, be some overlap with the list of works cited , the works here are organized according to the different kinds of material available and also into different periods of criticism, in order to highlight the shifting concerns that mark the past 100-plus years of its history. Though not comprehensive, and necessarily more selective than one might ideally want, the selections listed below are meant to be representative, offering a survey of some of the most influential, historically significant, and critically incisive writings on George Eliot. There is a great volume of excellent critical work in essays in scholarly publications, but any attempt to be comprehensive with this work would entail another book in itself. The selections below are, with the exception of some particularly representative essays, all books.

MAJOR WORKS BY GEORGE ELIOT

Fiction

The Oxford World's Classics editions that are cited throughout this text are given here when available, but the paperback Penguin editions that are available for most of the novels also offer good introductions and annotations. Norton Critical Editions, which provide a range of primary and secondary resource material as well as the novels themselves, exist for *The Mill on the Floss* and *Middlemarch*. In addition, several of the works listed below are available in full-length version on the Internet; these web editions can often be useful for locating and transposing quotations. The best edition of George Eliot's works remains the Cabinet Edition, first published in 1878 by Blackwood. Oxford University Press has for many years been producing in *The Clarendon Edition of the Novels of George Eliot* definitive editions of the novels. Those available will be listed below and marked "Clarendon."

Scenes of Clerical Life (Edinburgh and London: William Blackwood & Sons, 1858). Reprint, New York and Oxford: Oxford University Press, 1988; Clarendon: ed. Thomas A. Noble, 1985.

Adam Bede (Edinburgh and London: William Blackwood & Sons, 1859). Reprint, New York and Oxford: Oxford University Press, 1998.

"The Lifted Veil" (*Blackwood's Magazine*, 1859). Reprinted in *The Lifted Veil and Brother Jacob*, ed. Helen Small. New York and Oxford: Oxford University Press, 1999.

The Mill on the Floss (Edinburgh and London: William Blackwood & Sons, 1860). Reprint, New York and Oxford: Oxford University Press, 1998; Clarendon: ed. Gordon Haight, 1980.

Silas Marner (Edinburgh and London: William Blackwood & Sons, 1861). Reprint, New York and Oxford: Oxford University Press, 1998.

Romola (London: Smith, Elder & Co., 1863). Reprint, New York and Oxford: Oxford University Press, 1998. Clarendon: ed. Andrew Brown, 1993.

Brother Jacob (*Cornhill Magazine*, 1864). Reprinted in *The Lifted Veil and Brother Jacob*, ed. Helen Small. New York and Oxford: Oxford University Press, 1999.

Felix Holt, The Radical (Edinburgh and London: William Blackwood & Sons, 1866). Reprint, New York and Oxford: Oxford University Press, 1998; Clarendon: ed. Fred Thomson, 1980.

Middlemarch (Edinburgh and London: William Blackwood & Sons, 1872). Reprint, New York and Oxford: Oxford University Press, 1998; Clarendon: ed. David Carroll, 1986.

Daniel Deronda (Edinburgh and London: William Blackwood & Sons, 1876). Reprint, New York and Oxford: Oxford University Press, 1998; Clarendon: ed. Graham Handley, 1984.

Impressions of Theophrastus Such (Edinburgh and London: William Blackwood & Sons, 1879). Reprint, ed. Nancy Henry. Iowa City: University of Iowa Press, 1994.

Non-Fiction

While some of the works listed below are available in other editions, Gordon Haight's edition of George Eliot's letters is definitive. Thomas Pinney's selection of her essays remains the best collection although it is of course incomplete. In addition to the reprints noted here, both published and unpublished primary source material on Eliot is available for public use at the British Museum, the Pforzheimer Library, the Folger Shakespeare Library, the Princeton University Library, the Beinecke Rare Books Room at the Manuscripts Library at Yale University and the New York Public Library's Berg Collection.

Poetry

The Spanish Gypsy (Edinburgh and London: William Blackwood & Sons, 1868).
The Legend of Jubal and other poems (Edinburgh and London: William Blackwood & Sons, 1874).

Translations

The Life of Jesus Critically Examined (London: Chapman Brothers, 1846). Translation of D. F. Strauss's *Das Leben Jesu*. Reprint, Mifflintown, PA: Sigler Press, 1994.
The Essence of Christianity (London: Chapman, 1854). Translation of Ludwig Feuerbach's *Das Wesen des Christentums*. Reprint, Amherst, NY: Prometheus, 1989.

Essays, journals, and letters

Ashton, Rosemary, ed. *Selected Critical Writings*. New York: Oxford, 1992.
Byatt, A. S. and Nicholas Warren, ed. *George Eliot: Selected Essays, Poems and Other Writings*. Harmondsworth: Penguin, 1990.
Haight, Gordon S., ed. *The George Eliot Letters*. 9 vols. New Haven: Yale University Press, 1954–78.
Harris, Margaret and Judith Johnston, eds. *The Journals of George Eliot*. Cambridge: Cambridge University Press, 1998.
Irwin, Jane. *George Eliot's* Daniel Deronda *Notebooks*. Cambridge: Cambridge University Press, 1996.
Pinney, Thomas, ed. *Essays of George Eliot*. New York: Columbia University Press, 1963.
Pratt, John Clark and Victor A. Neufeldt, eds. *George Eliot's* Middlemarch *Notebooks: A Transcript*. Berkeley: University of California Press, 1979.

BIOGRAPHY

Though the first major biography of George Eliot was written by her husband, John Cross, it was, in the manner of many Victorian life-and-letters biographies, a purification of her life. The groundbreaking first major biography after Cross was Gordon Haight's, a factual and extremely detailed account based on his edition of her letters, and one to which all subsequent biographies refer. Redinger's biography, the first after Haight's to make a significant contribution to our understanding of George Eliot, concentrates on her early development as a writer. In the last ten years, several large-scale and important biographies have improved on Haight's work: the works by Ashton, Karl, Hughes, and Bodenheimer in particular. These works, and others included here, stand out from a long list of existing George Eliot biographies and serve as complements to each other – for example, Haight's factual and extremely detailed account of Eliot, based on her letters and journals, is far more thorough and somewhat less hagiographical than Cross's; Hughes pushes speculation about Eliot's psychology even further with a racy reinterpretation of the author's life through the prism of her sexuality. Bodenheimer's work, perhaps the most balanced of all the biographies, is an excellent close reading of Eliot's life in the context of both her fiction and nonfiction writing. Rosemary Ashton's is a thorough, balanced, and sympathetic account that is regarded by some critics as the best we now have.

Ashton, Rosemary. *George Eliot*. Oxford and New York: Oxford University Press, 1983.

G. H. Lewes: A Life. Oxford and New York: Oxford University Press, 1991.

George Eliot: A Life. Harmondsworth: Penguin Books, 1997.

Bodenheimer, Rosemarie. *The Real Life of Mary Ann Evans: George Eliot, Her Letters and Fiction*. Ithaca, N. Y.: Cornell University Press, 1994.

Cross, J.W., *George Eliot's Life as Related in her Letters and Journals*, 3 vols. Edinburgh and London: Blackwood, 1885.

Dodd, Valerie. *George Eliot: An Intellectual Life* (New York: St. Martins Press, 1990).

Haight, Gordon S. *George Eliot: A Biography*. Oxford and New York: Oxford University Press, 1968.

George Eliot and John Chapman. London: Methuen, 1986.

Hughes, Kathryn. *George Eliot: The Last Victorian*. New York: Farrar, Straus & Giroux, 1999.

Karl, Frederick R. *George Eliot: Voice of a Century*. New York: W. W. Norton, 1995.

Laski, Marghanita. *George Eliot and her World*. New York: Charles Scribner's Sons, 1973.

McKenzie, K. A., *Edith Simcox and George Eliot*. London: Oxford University Press, 1971.

Postlethwaite, Diana. *Making it Whole: A Victorian Circle and the Shape of their World*. Columbus: Ohio State University Press, 1984.

Redinger, Ruby. *George Eliot: The Emergent Self*. New York: Knopf, 1975.

Rose, Phyllis. *Parallel Lives: Five Victorian Marriages*. New York: Knopf, 1983.

Uglow, Jennifer. *George Eliot*. London: Virago Press, 1987.

BIBLIOGRAPHY

Used in conjunction with each other, the bibliographies here offer a thorough account of Eliot criticism and source material up to 1988. Fulmer offers a valuable listing of materials up through 1971. The work of Marshall and Higdon is an important compilation of the earlier criticism (until 1977); Pangallo's and Levine's focus on more recent materials. Pangallo offers factual annotations to entries, which are usefully organized both alphabetically and chronologically; Levine's are more detailed and analytical, giving critical evaluations of the works listed and organizing entries under pertinent topics such as "feminism" and "science."

Fulmer, Constance Marie. *George Eliot: A Reference Guide:* Boston: G. K. Hall, 1977.

Higdon, David Leon. "A Bibliography of George Eliot Criticism, 1971–1977," *Bulletin of Bibliography*, 37.2 (April–June 1980): 90–103.
Levine, George. *An Annotated Critical Bibliography of George Eliot*. Brighton: Harvester Wheatsheaf, 1988.
Marshall, William H. "A Selective Bibliography of Writings about George Eliot, to 1965," *Bulletin of Bibliography*, 25 (1967): 70–72, 88–94.
Pangallo, Karen. *George Eliot: A Reference Guide, 1972–1987*. Boston: G. K. Hall & Co., 1990.

GEORGE ELIOT CRITICISM

Collections of Criticism

Carroll's and Haight's texts – valuable earlier collections of criticism – both supply over fifty assessments of George Eliot's work; Haight's focusing on the responses of her contemporaries. Holstrom and Lerner's compilation is also valuable for a sense of Victorian responses to her major novels: *The Mill on the Floss*, *Middlemarch*, and *Daniel Deronda*. Stuart Hutchinson's more recent and truly massive four-volume compilation of Eliot criticism from her era to the present is an important new resource for Eliot scholars.

Carroll, David. *George Eliot: The Critical Heritage*. London and New York: Routledge & Kegan Paul, 1971.
Creeger, G. R., ed. *George Eliot: A Collection of Critical Essays*. New York: Prentice-Hall, 1970.
Haight, Gordon S. *A Century of George Eliot Criticism*. Boston: Houghton Mifflin, 1965.
Hardy, Barbara. *Critical Essays on George Eliot*. London: Routledge & Kegan Paul, 1970.
Holstrom, John and Laurence Lerner, eds. *George Eliot and her Readers: A Selection of Contemporary Reviews*. New York: Barnes & Noble, 1966.
Hutchinson, Stuart, ed. *George Eliot: Critical Assessments*. 4 vols. Mountfield: Helm Information, 1996.
Pangallo, Karen, ed. *The Critical Response to George Eliot*. Westport, CT.: Greenwood Press, 1994.

Early criticism (to 1925)

The following selections provide a sense of the range of reaction from Eliot's contemporaries and successors: often amongst the harshest of her critics. As well as the much-cited responses of James, Stephen, and Woolf to Eliot, the list includes works of topical interest to today's scholars, such as Cleveland's work on Eliot's poetry (still frequently overlooked by critics) and Kaufmann's work on Eliot and Judaism.

Brunetière, Ferdinand. *Le roman naturaliste*. Paris: Calmann-Lévy, 1896.
Cleveland, Rose Elizabeth. *George Eliot's Poetry and Other Studies*. New York: Funk & Wagnalls, 1885.
Cooke, G. W. *George Eliot: A Critical Study of Her Life, Writings and Philosophy*. Boston: Houghton Mifflin, 1883.
James, Henry. "The Novels of George Eliot," *Atlantic Monthly*, 18 (1866): 479–92.

"*Daniel Deronda*: A Conversation," in *George Eliot: A Collection of Critical Essays*, ed. George R. Creeger. New York: Prentice-Hall, 1970.
"Preface to *The Portrait of A Lady*," in *The Art of the Novel: Critical Prefaces by Henry James*. New York: Charles Scribner's Sons, 1962.
Kaufmann, D. *George Eliot and Judaism*. New York: Haskell House, 1970 (first published 1879).
Lubbock, Percy. *The Craft of Fiction*. London: Jonathan Cape, 1921.
Oliphant, James. *Victorian Novelists*. New York: Harper & Bros., 1901.
Stephen, Leslie. *George Eliot*. London: Macmillan, 1902.
Woolf, Virginia. "George Eliot," in *The Common Reader*. London: Harcourt, Brace & World, 1953 (first published 1925).

Criticism to 1970

Rescuing Eliot from the condemnation of the modernists, Leavis played a central role in her induction into "The Great Tradition" by focusing on her work in his 1948 book of that name. Consequently, in the second half of the twentieth century she was increasingly the subject of single-author works (some of the most influential of which are listed below) and a constant reference in important works on the novel as genre, such as those of Kermode, Miller, Van Ghent and Williams.

Beaty, Jerome. Middlemarch *from Notebook to Novel: A Study of George Eliot's Creative Method*. Urbana: University of Illinois Press, 1961.
Bennett, Joan. *George Eliot: her Mind and her Art*. Cambridge: Cambridge University Press, 1948.
Booth, Wayne. *The Rhetoric of Fiction*. Chicago: University of Chicago Press, 1967.
Cecil, Lord David. *Early Victorian Novelists: Essays in Revaluation*. London: Constable, 1934.
Couch, John Philip. *George Eliot in France: A French Appraisal of George Eliot's Writing, 1858–1960*. Chapel Hill: University of North Carolina Press, 1967.
Forster, E. M. *Aspects of the Novel*. London: E. Arnold, 1927.
Hardy, Barbara. *The Novels of George Eliot: A Study in Form*. London: Althone Press, 1959.
Harvey, W. J. *The Art of George Eliot*. London: Chatto & Windus, 1961.
Holloway, John. *The Victorian Sage: Studies in Argument*. New York: St. Martin's Press, 1953.
Kermode, Frank. *The Sense of an Ending: Studies in the Theory of Fiction*. Oxford and New York: Oxford University Press, 1966.
Knoepflmacher, U. C. *George Eliot's Early Novels: The Limits of Realism*. Berkeley: University of California Press, 1968.
Leavis, F. R. *The Great Tradition: George Eliot, Henry James, Joseph Conrad*. New York: New York University Press, 1973 (first published 1948).
Miller, J. Hillis. *The Form of Victorian Fiction*. Notre Dame, Ind.: University of Notre Dame Press, 1968.
Milner, Ian. *The Structure of Values in George Eliot's Art*. Praha: Universita Karlova. Acta Universitätis Carolinae Philogica Monographia, 1968.
Paris, Bernard J. *Experiments in Life: George Eliot's Quest for Values*. Detroit: Wayne State University Press, 1965.

Thale, Jerome. *The Novels of George Eliot.* New York: Columbia University Press, 1959.
Van Ghent, Dorothy. *The English Novel: Form and Function.* New York: Harper & Row, 1953.
Williams, Raymond. *The English Novel from Dickens to Lawrence.* Oxford and New York: Oxford University Press, 1970.

Criticism since 1970

Between the seventies and nineties, George Eliot and her novels were of special interest to influential feminist critics, such as Armstrong, David, Gilbert and Gubar, and Showalter (for a useful encapsulation of the earlier part of the feminist debates to which Eliot gave rise, see Austen's essay below). This list of works, then, gives not only a sense of the diverse historical and cultural contexts on to which George Eliot's texts opened, but also traces important critical trends in Victorian studies in this turbulent and exciting period: Sedgwick's queer reading of the nineteenth-century novel, Gallagher's Marxist interpretation of the industrial novel, and Levine's and Beer's studies of Victorian scientific discourse are key examples of these.

Armstrong, Nancy. *Desire and Domestic Fiction: A Political History of the Novel.* Oxford and New York: Oxford University Press, 1987.
Austen, Zelda. "Why Feminist Critics are Angry with George Eliot." *College English,* 37.6 (February 1976): 549–61.
Beer, Gillian. *George Eliot.* Brighton: Harvester Press, 1986.
Darwin's Plots: Evolutionary Narrative in Darwin, George Eliot and Nineteenth-Century Fiction. New York: Routledge & Kegan Paul, 1983.
George Eliot. Brighton: Harvester Wheatsheaf, 1986.
Bonaparte, Felicia. *The Triptych and the Cross: The Central Myths of George Eliot's Poetic Imagination.* New York: New York University Press, 1979.
Cottom, Daniel. *Social Figures: George Eliot, Social History, and Literary Representation.* Minneapolis: University of Minnesota Press, 1987.
David, Deirdre. *Intellectual Women and Victorian Patriarchy: Harriet Martineau, Elizabeth Barrett Browning, George Eliot.* Ithaca, N. Y.: Cornell University Press, 1987.
Ermarth, Elizabeth. *Realism and Consensus in the Victorian Novel.* Princeton: Princeton University Press, 1983.
"George Eliot's Conception of Sympathy," *Nineteenth-Century Fiction,* 40 (1985): 23–42.
Gallagher, Catherine. *The Industrial Reformation of English Fiction: Social Discourse and Narrative Form, 1832–1867.* Chicago: University of Chicago Press, 1985.
Gilbert, Sandra M. and Susan Gubar. *The Madwoman in the Attic: The Woman Writer and the Nineteenth-Century Literary Imagination.* New Haven: Yale University Press, 1979.
No Man's Land: The Place of the Woman Writer in the Twentieth Century. 3 vols. New Haven: Yale University Press, 1988–94.
Graver, Suzanne. *George Eliot and Community: A Study in Social Theory and Fictional Form.* Berkeley: University of California Press, 1984.

Hardy, Barbara. *Particularities: Readings in George Eliot.* Athens: Ohio University Press, 1982.
Forms of Feeling in Victorian Fiction. London: P. Owen, 1985.
Hunt, Linda. *A Woman's Portion: Ideology, Culture and the British Female Novel Tradition.* New York: Garland, 1988.
Kucich, John. *Repression in Victorian Fiction: Charlotte Brontë, George Eliot, and Charles Dickens.* Berkeley: University of California Press, 1987.
Levine, George. *The Realistic Imagination: English Fiction from Frankenstein to Lady Chatterley.* Chicago: University of Chicago Press, 1981.
Darwin and the Novelists: Patterns of Science in Victorian Fiction. Chicago: University of Chicago Press, 1988.
McDonagh, Josephine. *George Eliot.* Plymouth: Northcote House, 1997.
Miller, D. A. *Narrative and its Discontents: Problems of Closure in the Traditional Novel.* Princeton: Princeton University Press, 1981.
Mintz, Alan. *George Eliot and the Novel of Vocation.* Cambridge, Mass.: Harvard University Press, 1978).
Myers, William. *The Teachings of George Eliot.* Totowa, N.J.: Barnes & Noble, 1984.
Qualls, Barry V. *The Secular Pilgrims of Victorian Fiction.* Cambridge and New York: Cambridge University Press, 1982.
Sedgwick, Eve Kosofsky. *Between Men: English Literature and Male Homosocial Desire.* New York: Columbia University Press, 1985.
Showalter, Elaine. "The Greening of Sister George." *Nineteenth-Century Fiction,* 35 (1980): 292–311.
A Literature of their Own: British Women Novelists from Brontë to Lessing. Princeton: Princeton University Press, 1977.
Shuttleworth, Sally. *George Eliot and Nineteenth-Century Science: The Make-Believe of a Beginning.* Cambridge and New York: Cambridge University Press, 1984.
Vargish, Thomas. *The Providential Aesthetic in Victorian Fiction.* Charlottesville: University of Virginia Press, 1985.
Welsh, Alexander. *George Eliot and Blackmail.* Cambridge, Mass.: Harvard University Press, 1985.
Williams, Raymond. *The Country and the City.* Oxford and New York: Oxford University Press, 1973.
Witemeyer, Hugh. *George Eliot and the Visual Arts.* New Haven: Yale University Press, 1979.

Recent criticism (since 1990)

The subtitle of Handley's book, *A Guide Through the Critical Maze*, indicates the increasingly complex directions in which George Eliot criticism will tend in the twenty-first century. The selections below reflect the ways in which earlier feminist investigations into Victorian cultural identities have been supplemented and extended by considerations of race, nationalism, imperialism, and internationalism in the nineties (see, for example, Cheyette, Lesjak, Meyer, and Rignall); they also give a sense of how many underexamined aspects of George Eliot's life offer opportunities for further study in light of new literary-historical methodologies: her relationship with her contemporaries (as in Paxton's work on Spencer) and the material production of her works (as in Martin's study of serialization) are only two of the paths open to future writing on George Eliot.

Booth, Alison. *Greatness Engendered: George Eliot and Virginia Woolf.* Ithaca, N.Y.: Cornell University Press, 1992.

Carroll, David. *George Eliot and the Conflict of Interpretations: A Reading of the Novels.* Cambridge: Cambridge University Press, 1992.

Cheyette, Bryan. *Constructions of the Jew in English Literature and Society: Racial Representations 1875–1945.* Cambridge and New York: Cambridge University Press, 1996.

Handley, Graham. *George Eliot: A Guide Through the Critical Maze.* Bristol: Bristol Press, 1990.

George Eliot's Midlands: Passion in Exile. London: Allison & Busby, 1991.

Lesjak, Carolyn. "'Labours of a Modern Storyteller': George Eliot and the Cultural Project of 'Nationhood' in *Daniel Deronda*," in *Victorian Identities: Social and Cultural Formations in Nineteenth-Century Literature*, ed. Ruth Robbins and Julian Wolfreys. New York: Macmillan, 1996.

Martin, Carol A. *George Eliot's Serial Fiction.* Columbus: Ohio State University Press, 1994.

Meyer, Susan. *Imperialism at Home: Race and Victorian Women's Fiction.* Ithaca, N.Y.: Cornell University Press, 1996.

Paxton, Nancy L. *George Eliot and Herbert Spencer: Feminism, Evolutionism, and the Reconstruction of Gender.* Princeton: Princeton University Press, 1991.

Rignall, John, ed. *George Eliot and Europe.* Aldershot: Scolar Press, 1997.

Semmel, Bernard. *George Eliot and the Politics of National Inheritance.* Oxford and New York: Oxford University Press, 1994.

INDEX

LIBRARY, UNIVERSITY OF CHESTER